The Cambridge Companion to Chomsky

15/04/2014

- 9 JUL 2014

21/08/2014

11/09/14

The Cambridge Companion to Chomsky

Edited by

James McGilvray

McGill University

CAMBRIDGE
UNIVERSITY PRESS

PUBLISHED BY THE PRESS SYNDICATE OF THE UNIVERSITY OF CAMBRIDGE
The Pitt Building, Trumpington Street, Cambridge, United Kingdom

CAMBRIDGE UNIVERSITY PRESS
The Edinburgh Building, Cambridge, CB2 2RU, UK
40 West 20th Street, New York, NY 10011–4211, USA
477 Williamstown Road, Port Melbourne, VIC 3207, Australia
Ruiz de Alarcón 13, 28014 Madrid, Spain
Dock House, The Waterfront, Cape Town 8001, South Africa

http://www.cambridge.org

First published 2005
Reprinted 2005

Printed in the United Kingdom at the University Press, Cambridge

Typeface Times 10/12 pt.   *System* LATEX 2$_\varepsilon$ [TB]

A catalogue record for this book is available from the British Library

Library of Congress Cataloguing in Publication data
The Cambridge companion to Chomsky / edited by James McGilvray.
    p.   cm.
ISBN 0 521 78013 6 (hardback) – ISBN 0 521 78431 X (paperback)
1. Chomsky, Noam.   I. McGilvray, James A. (James Alasdair), 1942–
P85.C47C36   2005
410′.92 – dc22   2004051104

ISBN 0 521 78013 6 hardback
ISBN 0 521 78431 X paperback

the URLs for external
ress. However, the publisher
guarantee that a site will
iate.

Contents

The contributors

AKEEL BILGRAMI is Johnsonian Professor of Philosophy at Columbia University. He specializes in the philosophies of mind and language. His *Self-Knowledge and Intentionality* and *The Moral Psychology of Identity* are forthcoming.

JEAN BRICMONT is Professor of Theoretical Physics at the Catholic University of Louvain. He co-authored with Alan Sokal the volume *Fashionable Nonsense*. He often writes and speaks on political topics.

STEPHEN CRAIN is Professor of Linguistics at the University of Maryland, College Park. He is primarily interested in issues of child language development – especially, recently, in children's acquisition of semantic knowledge. He is co-author with Rozz Thornton of *Investigations in Universal Grammar*.

B. ELAN DRESHER is Professor of Linguistics at the University of Toronto. He has written many articles on phonology. Among his interests is the history of phonological theory.

CYNTHIA FISHER is an Associate Professor in the Department of Psychology and Beckman Institute, University of Illinois at Urbana-Champaign. Her research focuses on child language acquisition, both words and linguistic structures.

IRENE GENDZIER is Professor of Political Science at Boston University. She works on issues of political economy and international political development, comparative politics, and the politics of the Middle East. She is the author of *Notes From the Minefield: United States Intervention in Lebanon and the Middle East, 1945–1958* and *Development Against Democracy*.

LILA GLEITMAN is Steven and Marcia Roth Professor in the Department of Psychology and Professor in the Department of Linguistics at the University of Pennsylvania. She focuses on linguistic structure (morphological and syntactic) and the acquisition of language (sounds, structures, and words). She is the editor of *Invitation to Cognitive Science*, vol. I, *Language* and, with Barbara Landau, author of *Language and Experience: Evidence From the Blind Child*.

NORBERT HORNSTEIN is Professor of Linguistics at the University of Maryland. His research currently focuses on issues of Chomsky's minimalist approach to syntactic structure. He recently edited (with Louise Anthony) the volume *Chomsky and His Critics* and is the author of *Move! A Minimalist Theory of Construal*.

HOWARD LASNIK is Board of Trustees Distinguished Professor Emeritus, University of Connecticut, and Distinguished University Professor, University of Maryland. He has co-authored several works in linguistics with Noam Chomsky and is the sole author of several books, including the recent *Minimalist Investigations in Linguistic Theory*.

DAVID LIGHTFOOT is Professor of Linguistics and Dean of the Graduate School of Arts and Sciences at Georgetown University. His primary research interests are in language acquisition, language change, and syntactic theory; he is the author of eight books, including *Syntactic Effects of Morphological Change* and, with S. Anderson, *The Language Organ*.

JAMES McGILVRAY is Associate Professor of Philosophy at McGill University. He focuses on the natures of language and mind, with particular attention to Chomsky's contribution to these areas; he is the author of *Chomsky: Language, Mind, and Politics*.

LAURA-ANN PETITTO is Professor of Psychology and Chairman of the Department of Education at Dartmouth College. She is the author of many articles on language acquisition and development in children, especially bilinguals and users of sign.

PAUL PIETROSKI is Professor of Philosophy and Professor of Linguistics at the University of Maryland College Park. He is currently interested in the ways in which linguistic structure contributes to linguistic meanings. He is the author of *Causing Actions* and the forthcoming *Events and Semantic Architecture*.

MILAN RAI is a journalist and political activist who lives in East Sussex, UK. He is the author of *Chomsky's Politics* and, with Chomsky, of *War Plan Iraq: Ten Reasons Against War on Iraq*. He recently published *Regime Unchanged: Why the War in Iraq Changed Nothing*.

CAROL ROVANE is Director of Graduate Studies and Professor of Philosophy at Columbia University. She has a special interest in the history of philosophies of mind, focusing on Descartes, Kant, and the pragmatists. She is the author of *The Bounds of Agency: An Essay in Revisionary Metaphysics*.

NEIL SMITH is Professor and Head of Linguistics at University College London. He focuses on language acquisition and the general linguistic theory, but especially on the work of Noam Chomsky; he is the author of *Chomsky: Ideas and Ideals*, and, recently, *Language, Bananas, and Bonobos: Linguistic Problems, Puzzles, and Polemics*.

JAMES WILSON is James A. Thomas Distinguished Professor of Law, Cleveland-Marshall College, Cleveland State University. He does research on imperialism and the use of power, and on the political thought of Noam Chomsky. He is the author of *The Imperial Republic: A Structural History of American Constitutionalism From the Colonial Era to the Beginning of the Twentieth Century*.

Introduction

James McGilvray

At the time of writing, Noam Chomsky has produced over eighty books, hundreds of articles, and thousands of speeches. He has given thousands of interviews, written countless letters, and supervised scores of theses. He has made important, sometimes groundbreaking, contributions to three areas – linguistics, philosophy of mind and human nature, and politics. He set linguistics on a successful naturalistic, biologically oriented scientific course; his theoretical contributions continue to lead the field. Like Descartes, Galileo, and Hume, and unlike the eighteenth-century philosopher Kant and the great majority of philosophers thereafter, Chomsky is both scientist and philosopher, and his philosophical work is continuous with his scientific. His science of language and incipient science of mind offer a genuine prospect of coming to a biologically based grasp of human nature and of the way it allows for human understanding and action. His political work, like both Hobbes's and Rousseau's, seeks a foundation in a science of human nature, although with better prospects for developing such a theory – and for exploring its implications for political ideals and goals – than Hobbes's misguided attempt to construct a causal theory of human action or Rousseau's fanciful assays into a "state of nature." And unlike both of them – and far too many contemporary political "theorists" – there is no sign in Chomsky's political work that his views and critical analyses are driven by a wish for power.

One purpose of this volume is to offer to a general audience several people's perspectives on Chomsky's contributions in linguistics, philosophy of mind and human nature, and politics. The first chapter in each section provides an overview of Chomsky's views in these areas. Succeeding chapters develop major themes. I sketch some of those themes and how contributors develop them near the end of this introduction. A sketch suffices: the chapters and organization are self-explanatory.

Chomsky the scientist of language

Linguists in the Chomskyan tradition think of themselves as natural scientists – not social scientists, and not engineers. It is important to see what this implies.

Ordinary usage is little help. The term "science," like "language," has no unique use in everyday speech: people apply it to everything from physics to astrology. And – in part because being a scientist is associated with expertise, specialized knowledge, intelligence, etc. – the desire for social status and political authority leads to applying the label "scientist" to some questionable candidates. Given this, we cannot expect more than a few hints about what science for the Chomskyan is by looking to the practices that have been called scientific, or to the range of people who have been called (or call themselves) scientists.

A more reliable source is the history of science and the shapes of the sciences that are universally agreed to be successful – physics, chemistry, biology . . . Their subject matters and degrees of progress differ, as do their principles, experimental techniques, and outstanding problems. There are, however, enough similarities to draw a composite sketch, especially where the characteristics chosen agree with those from other reliable sources.

Another such source is what those who began the development of successful sciences said they were doing. Chomsky often mentions Galileo and Descartes in this regard (e.g. 2002b); he considers himself to be working in a tradition of philosopher-scientists that they began. These pioneers developed and applied recommendations for how to proceed in carrying out investigations of natural phenomena that led to what were for their times remarkable successes. Focusing on Descartes in his *Discourse* – a work that explains how Descartes came to his scientific principles, says what they are, and outlines what he accomplished by using them – it is striking that he divorces science from another kind of understanding of the world. No one uses scientific concepts in solving the myriad problems encountered in everyday life. Everyone, including the young child and the scientist, has and uses what Descartes called "bon sens" ("good sense"), a practical form of problem-solving capacity that Descartes considers innate – a gift from God. "Bon sens" is sometimes translated as "common sense," and I will adopt that term. It is a capacity to deal with the problems of politics and commerce, doing the laundry, consoling a grieving friend, and putting out the dog.

While everyone relies on common sense, it does not assume a single form for all times and all circumstances. This is a benefit. Practical problem-solving must accommodate differences in method and individual style, different environments, cultures, and social organizations, and so on. To do so, common sense must rely on rich and productive native (innate) resources and a flexible form of mental organization. That is how it can arise so early in children and be so remarkably adaptable. Where Descartes said that *bon sens* is a gift from God, we are likely to say that its rich resources are biologically based. It is only thus that we – even the very young – can so quickly conceive, anticipate, and adapt to different environments, adopt (even if only in play) different social roles, and quickly change to meet unanticipated contingencies.

The contrast to science is instructive. Science is an intellectual project that – where successful at all – uses formal (mathematical) theory-construction techniques to focus on specific domains; it is guided by a desire for simplicity and – as Galileo and Descartes's work shows – it places simplicity before "data"; it makes progress (often in jumps) over centuries through contributions from many people towards solutions to the theoretical problems it constantly confronts, revises, and refines; and it creates its own standards of intelligibility (Chomsky 2002b: 68) that are far from the practical concerns of common sense. Physics, for example, has taken centuries to develop, has advanced in spurts, uses mathematical techniques to describe a world populated by entities and processes beyond the ken of commonsense understanding; and while no doubt far from complete, it has obviously progressed well beyond Galileo's and Descartes's "mechanical philosophy." This punctuated but deliberate pace is probably necessary because science does not rely on the rich and productive native systems, flexibly organized, that common sense utilizes. While it can and obviously does rely on apparently innate senses of simplicity and what counts as a good explanation and description (Chomsky 1980), construction of the theories that solve the problems science confronts requires invention, favorable conditions, and cooperative activity. That is why – with the exception of parts of mathematics – only rudimentary forms of natural science developed before the end of the sixteenth century. Unsurprisingly, it also takes a considerable amount of time and training for individuals to acquire sophistication even in a specific science; the full range of the developed sciences is out of the reach of everyone. Fortunately, science's findings are not needed for survival, or even to thrive. No doubt doing laundry benefits from engineering applications of fundamental scientific principles – those that lead to variable-speed electric motors and front-loading washing machines. But for millennia people managed with technology that required only the engineering solutions offered by unaided common sense. They built bridges of various materials, annealed metals into Samurai swords, and constructed cathedrals. In sum, science brings the developed formal tools of highly focused inquiry to bear on theoretical problems; progress – relying as it does on invention – is usually slow. Using their common sense, people utilize native resources, perhaps in forms of practice that have led to practical success before, to deal with the immediate demands of everyday problems. We invent scientific tools to deal with bosons and genomes; we depend on native resources to critically assess the performance of an elected representative – or the intentions of an artist.

One of the characteristics of scientific practice that science's history reveals is seeking a particular kind of objectivity – one that is universalized, so that it is not tied to person, circumstance, culture, or history. That notion of objectivity cannot serve the tasks that common sense deals with; commonsense understanding's concepts are "designed" to serve matters of human interest – including those of perception and action. It should be no surprise, then, that science can lead to denials of the "obvious" claims of commonsense understanding. Sciences of the mind tell us that the colors we experience are products of our visual systems, not "on" things outside, and that languages – including their sounds and meanings – are native and in the head, not somehow outside the head, perhaps products and properties of communities and polities. Scientists often must ignore appearances (as in colors and words outside the head) and invent, using the tools that mathematics – much of which is invented too – provides. And they must measure progress not by how well a proposed change in a theory satisfies untutored opinion or "raw experience" but by improvements in description and explanation of the relevant phenomena and greater formal simplicity. Descartes – had he lived long enough – would have seen his contact mechanics refuted by Newton's gravitational principle. The "obvious" idea that action and effect require contact seems to have its origin in common sense; it fails in science. Physicists learned long ago that the apparently obvious is at best a starting point. That lesson has been hard to learn with language, as we will see.

Chomsky's science of language is a science in the Cartesian–Galilean tradition. It is a branch of the study of biology. It is a naturalistic science that provides an "abstract" description and explanation of a biological system found only in humans, the system that Chomsky calls "the language organ." The language organ revealed by Chomskyan science of linguistics is far from the common-sense idea of a language as a social phenomenon. To reveal this organ, the science of linguistics had to develop standards of intelligibility that were consonant with those of the natural sciences, not with what some philosophers call "granny's view" of language. The result, after several decades of work, is that the language organ appears to be remarkably simple in its "design." This is unusual in biology, a domain that usually reveals what Jacques Monod calls the "tinkering" of evolution. Apparently, extending naturalistic science to the study of a biological system of the mind yields a fascinating result: language confirms Galileo's and Descartes's vision of a well-designed, elegant nature.

Descartes's mechanics – even in its rather primitive form – conflicted with the "obvious" principles taught by church and universities. It conflicted with the teleological world of Aristotle, modified by the seventeenth century to suit Christian doctrine. That is why his and Galileo's novel mathematical–mechanical theories of natural phenomena faced opposition from philosophical and religious systems that, like many today, take their task to be that of defending ideas that have their origin in common sense with its practical, not theoretical orientation. Successful sciences since Galileo and Descartes have continued to use simple, elegant, formal mathematical tools and invented theories and concepts to provide descriptively and explanatorily adequate theories of their domains. Like Galileo's and Descartes's sciences, they continue to be opposed, although some of the opposition is muted by the obvious success of the theories.

Chomsky's naturalistic inquiry into language, like Descartes's into cosmology, physics, optics, and neurophysiology, also gets opposition from the experts. Opposition comes from several fronts, but most seem to proceed on the assumption that language is not a natural phenomenon. They see language in terms of its use – perhaps as a set of social practices, a bunch of "tools" we have made to communicate, etc. In each case, one finds a version of what Chomsky calls an E-language approach to theorizing about language (external approach). Among the majority of philosophers, it appears as insistence that one or another form of the "obvious" idea that language is an institution created by humans to communicate – a "practice," a product of history, a set of habits, an "interpretive medium," a mode of communicating a speaker's intentions. From psychologists, philosophers, and other cognitive scientists wedded to one version or another of what Steven Pinker (2002) calls the "blank slate" picture of the mind, it comes as the idea that it is a form of behavior that solves cognitive problems such as classifying, describing, etc. Any organism or device that displays the "same" behavior has a language, they believe, and they "get" it by whatever means (training, programming) the blank slate advocate employs. So getting an ape (on which see Petitto, this volume) or a machine to simulate the behavior "proves" that language is not a biological organ with which only humans are born.

Perhaps these experts succeed sometimes by some standards – it is not clear which – but not by those of naturalistic inquiry. Philosophers who think language is a social phenomenon that children learn from their community ignore the fact that languages are quickly acquired by very young children without training. The same is true of concepts of social role. If neither language nor concepts of social role (and much else) is taught, they must somehow be built into the child's mind at birth; that is where to focus naturalistic inquiry. And blank slate advocates need to learn the elemental lesson that it is unwise to focus attention on sameness of behavior or "output" and the means by which these are induced. Even if one succeeds at getting a machine or ape to "speak" – it has not happened, probably for reasons that Descartes (and Alan Turing) pointed to – that is no proof that the systems that make this behavior possible (which is where Chomsky focuses his work) are the same as the ape's or the machine's. Manufacturing an excavator to dig ditches hardly proves that human gravediggers moving shovels with their articulated arms have hydraulic systems in their arms activated by diesel-powered compressors.

Chomsky on biology and evolution

To avoid confusion that might arise from speaking of Chomsky's view that language is a biological organ, I need to mention the matter of evolution (for detail, see Jenkins 2000). Chomsky, like Richard Lewontin (1990), has little sympathy for current efforts (e.g. Pinker & Bloom 1990) to try to show that language – especially in the form of the basic computational system that links sounds and meaning to produce a discrete infinity of sentential expressions – is the product of some sort of natural selection that tracks increased reproductive advantages afforded to those who are (on the Pinker–Bloom story) better communicators. Chomsky does not doubt that language evolved, in some sense: it is biologically based and appeared in the human species. And he has no doubt that it has proven to be extremely useful to humans. But selection-for-communication, selection-for-some-function-or-another, and even selection, period, do not exhaust the field. *Pace* Pinker and Bloom, there are alternatives.

One problem with the attempt to show that language was selected by reproductive advantage is that humans as a species have been relatively stable for a long time – probably 100,000 to 200,000 years. So language in the form of the basic computational system that seems to be unique to us must have emerged somewhere between now and 100,000 to 200,000 years ago. (The best current guess is approximately 60,000 years when the migration from Africa began.) It is all but impossible to find *evidence* in observable phenomena for the selectional emergence of such a system. Perhaps we will someday identify the computational-system specific gene(s) that provides us our languages' syntax; perhaps too by investigating remains we could say when this gene was introduced. But nothing would tell us why and how it developed. Speculation about selection-for-*any*-function of language's computational system (its "syntax") seems to be empty.

But that is not all that needs to be said. For one thing, while looking for a historical record seems hopeless, we can compare. Hauser, Chomsky, and Fitch do just that in their article in *Science* (2002). Comparison offers no immediate help to the Pinker–Bloom selection-for-communication cause, however: language's basic computational system can produce a discrete infinity of sentences, and there is no current evidence that other species can "express" discrete infinities of elements of *any* sort. For example, no other species enumerates arbitrarily large numbers of elements in a set by counting them out. But perhaps we have not looked far enough. Most comparative studies focus on human and animal communication systems; perhaps the computational system is found elsewhere. In concluding their discussion, Chomsky and his co-authors suggest looking at other kinds of system: look, they suggest, for non-communicative systems that rely on a recursive computational procedure that provides for a discrete infinity. Perhaps they will be found in navigational systems, or those that "parse" social relationships. If there were such a system, it – or its homologue or analogue in the developing human species – might have been exapted (coopting a system adapted to serve another function) for language. Selection-for-communication would fail, but perhaps aspects of the selectional cause would be salvaged. It is a project worth trying.

In his own work, Chomsky suggests we look wider still. Darwin pointed out that selection is only one part of evolution. And there are other, non-selectional traditions of biological development and speciation. One such tradition is found in Stephen Jay Gould's and Richard Lewontin's suggestion (1979) concerning "spandrels" – structural consequences of other, perhaps selected, systems. Another tradition, perhaps related, goes back to Goethe and his discovery of an Urform for plant morphology (cp. Chomsky 2002a: 66). Goethe thought he had discovered a formula that predicted all (biologically) possible forms plants could take. If there is such a formula, it indicates that there lies in plant morphogenesis a physical factor that yields very different-appearing plant forms (and "species"), given slightly different "input" conditions. The formula and different physical conditions, not selection, would account for differences. That tradition was represented in the nineteenth century by several individuals in Europe and, in the twentieth century, versions of it appeared in mathematical form in the work of D'Arcy Thompson (1917) and Alan Turing (1952). Many have pursued their suggestions; there is a growing mathematical science of morphogenesis.

Chomsky sometimes suggests (2002b: 57) that the development of the language organ might be explained as a mathematical consequence of the kind of complex form of mental biology humans have. Even selection has to operate within the "channels" provided by basic physical processes, after all; and our language faculty appears to be too "perfect" a solution to linking sounds and meanings to be the result of selectional tinkering. Perhaps the computational system built into our languages is "anticipated" in those physical processes and structures and arises "by itself" when other systems are in place. This would allow that the computational system of language came about as a complete package, perhaps 60,000 years ago. Or perhaps language is a spandrel. Either way, we abandon the gradualist, "historical" form of development and biological differentiation (and the "tinkering") that the selectional picture relies upon. We might even be able to find evidence.

In sum, while there is no doubt that language has proven to be an extremely useful biological faculty that has given the human species extraordinary cognitive advantages, there is little reason now – and there may never be – to hold that the computational core of the language organ developed slowly over a long historical period by virtue of affording reproductive advantages to successive generations of communicators.

On the unity of Chomsky's thought

A person's intellectual work as a scientist need not be connected to his or her political views – there is no reason, for instance, that a biochemist's scientific work should have anything to do with her neoliberal views. But Chomsky's linguistics and his political views seem to be special cases, particularly when one takes into account his philosophical/scientific work on the human mind and human nature.

One reason to look for connections and perhaps even a degree of convergence in all three areas of Chomsky's work is that each has, in its own way, something to say about human beings. More narrowly, each focuses on distinctive features of human beings – on language, a biologically unique mental faculty; on our distinctive natures and minds with their limited but biologically unparalleled intellectual capacities for dealing with both practical and scientific problems; and on those apparently unique forms of social organization that we think of variously as polities, communities, societies, and/or cultures. No other organism creates for itself organized groups of non-kin individuals in ways that allow for cooperative, non-contact, coordinated ways to meet needs and solve problems.

Some non-Chomskyans think that there is a connection between language and culture or community. Philosophers as varied as Foucault and Putnam and psychologists as different as Piaget and connectionists share the assumption that language depends on the society, culture, community (etc.) in which one is raised. By "depends" I mean not just that children born into a group of Japanese speakers come to speak Japanese; everyone acknowledges that and tries to explain why it happens. Rather, they take language to be *constituted by* the society or community in which one is born. This idea often appears as the view that children are taught the language of their community by their elders: the elders know the "rules of correct usage/correct practice" (given relevant circumstances) and instruct by encouraging correct verbal responses and discouraging incorrect. People (as a group), over a long historical period, are believed to have invented the practices that define a specific community, culture, etc. and, while doing so (or perhaps in doing so), to have also invented language – another form of practice that happens to allow individuals to communicate, coordinate, etc. Individual creativity in the exercise of one's intellectual powers does not figure in this story; the focus is on community practices/habits/rules for applying words correctly, etc. If defenders of this idea speak of human nature at all, they make it a historically conditioned notion: as people's fundamental practices change, people's social/cultural "natures" change. Alternatively, they might say that human beings are plastic (people are intellectual/cultural blank slates), so that human social/cultural natures are – unlike those of any other biological species – molded by the societies, cultures, etc. in which they are born.

Chomsky's view of language and the mind reverses priorities. For him, human languages are not expressions of culture and society – in effect, human artifacts. They are, in a sense, expressions of our genes: all the existing and possible natural languages (not technical symbol systems, such as those found in the sciences) are biologically encompassed within what he calls "Universal Grammar." If there is any dependency between language so conceived and society, culture, etc., it cannot make culture the condition of language. If anything, culture (etc.) depends on language. Suggesting that culture depends on language in this sense is not making a causal or deductive claim. The language organ does not secrete cultures or social arrangements. Rather, language provides the rich, unlimited set of conceptual structures (Chomsky informally calls them "perspectives") and the opportunity to communicate them that humans need to conceive of alternative ways to solve the problem of how to live together to the benefit of all, to discuss and come to agreement on the options, and the like. In effect, language and our other cognitive resources, but especially language, make it possible to create cultures and much else. Adopting this point of view – that native conceptual tools, and especially language, must be in place before articulated conceptualization and understanding, much less discussion, can occur – another matter falls into place too. Individual creativity – a curiosity on the culture-first approach – can now be seen as benefiting from the infinite scope of linguistic output of which our systems are, in principle, capable.

To see why language should have a central role in making sense of how we come to create our diverse communities and cultures – and individual cognitive and expressive styles – it is important to keep in mind that humans are the sole species to have language. Many other species have communication systems. And some others also have the "performance" systems that are involved in human language: auditory perception and production (for speech), visual perception and aspects of articulatory shaping (for sign), plus aspects of those resources that Chomsky calls "conceptual and intentional" – those non-linguistic resources that can be brought to bear on circumstances to yield various forms of intelligent behavior. But no other species has the capacity to develop a potentially infinite, *discrete* set of mental "outputs" in the form of expressions or sentences that link perception-related configurations, whether sound or sign, with conceptual materials (Hauser, Chomsky & Fitch 2002). That is, no other species can produce – apparently at will – innumerable sets of sentences or expressions. Given the obviously central role of language in human thought and action, our distinctive mental capacities – found in both practical and theoretical problem-solving – may be due, in large measure, to language. And, with these capacities, we also can develop social organizations: we can plan, organize, decide to cooperate, and create institutions. It becomes quite plausible that culture and our various forms of social organization depend on language rather than the other way around. So we have one connection between the areas Chomsky works on: the science of language might well provide the key to what is distinctive to our minds and natures, to making sense of why we have the distinctive mental capacities we do and, in turn, making sense of how we can create our various forms of social organization.

Another kind of connection depends on the fact that views of human nature are always behind people's attempts to justify their moral and political principles. In the background of every political and moral "ism" (including those largely indistinguishable forms of corporation-dominated plutocracy–oligarchy called "neoliberalism" and "neoconservatism") one finds assumptions about human nature – about what human beings "are" and what they are or are not capable of. These views of human nature typically play a justificatory role. "That's a silly view of democracy," someone might say of the fully participatory form Chomsky favors, "people (of their natures) don't have enough interest, intelligence, knowledge, or time to participate fully. We must give an elite managerial class the power to make decisions and run the economy, government, courts . . ." Someone else might say: "People are naturally aggressive and acquisitive. A good form of government must have full authority to restrict their unchecked exercise (a Hobbesian state of nature); we need authoritarian government to provide a form of rescue."

While justification of this sort is common, few of those employing it bother to elaborate their view of human nature. And the connections between whatever degree of articulation one finds and the moral/political/religious . . . claims they are supposed to justify can be quite hazy. Moreover, there is little if any effort to show that one's view of human nature is itself justified by the standards of empirical inquiry. A biologically based science of human nature would avoid these problems. Appeals to gods and revelation, or to what seems to be obvious to some group or another, are almost always self-serving efforts which reveal a desire to place or maintain oneself or one's group in a position of power or authority. We need a detailed, objective view of human nature, and scientific inquiry can provide that. It alone can say what is distinctive about our natures – as opposed, say, to those of various other primate species.

A plausible way to focus such an inquiry would be to look for aspects of the human mind that are distinctive – for faculties or forms of mental organization that humans have that other primates lack. The faculty of language, clearly, is such. A science of language and of what language provides humans should thus have an important role in such a science. Not only does language seem to be unique to humans, but it also seems to contribute to a unique form of mental organization. The biological faculty/organ of language acts rather like a central cognitive system, allowing us to coordinate materials provided by other cognitive systems in ways that other creatures seem to be unable to manage. And, of course, it provides the conceptual tools to allow us to speak of anything, anytime. In these and other ways, it enables us to "solve problems" in a wide variety of manners. It is almost as if language allowed our minds to be "universal instruments," to use Descartes's *Discourse* terminology. So Chomsky's science of language, even in its incomplete state, represents a good beginning to a science of the human mind and, thus, of human nature.

While the science of human nature is in its earliest stages, we can use what we have now to begin to think about how to craft a good society. We cannot move directly from biology – specifically, the biology of the human mind and what it provides us (for these are what make us distinctive in ways that we so obviously care about) – to a picture of an ideal. We must start by deciding what an ideal society should accomplish – what its function(s) should be. For social organizations are institutions, made by human beings, and a good one should fulfill its function well. A plausible suggestion is that the function of a human society is to meet not just the needs of survival, but those that are characteristic of the kinds of creatures we are. Call these characteristic needs of humans "fundamental distinctively human needs." Now what the science of mind tells us about language and the rest of the mind, and about how people use these cognitive tools, can come into play. To be brief, because we have language and language seems to be the key to our extraordinary mental capacities, we alone seem virtually designed to be creative creatures. Our languages provide an unlimited range of "perspectives" (Chomsky 2000a: 150, 180), and these can be – and are – used to serve all sorts of purposes, including those of art and labor. Language's unlimited range comes to play a role in virtually all our affairs – not just our thoughts and efforts to understand others, but in our jobs and everyday tasks, even putting out the dog. An ideal form of social organization must, then, give individuals ample opportunity to exercise their creativity. This need not mean that we must all become craftsmen and painters or composers. It might mean that if we labor with others in a factory, we have sufficient freedom and opportunity to fully contribute to all decisions that concern us, to bring about change, and to otherwise control the conditions under which we work. Or it might mean that operating an excavator, we not only do the job well and with a concern for those who will use what we do, but with a form of artistry.

Another candidate for a fundamental need is that for community, friendship, love, and nurture. It is only if one thinks of this need as that of an animal that is also "bred" for freedom and creativity, though, that the need for community becomes distinctively human. Many other primates display in their behaviors a need for association for mutual benefit. But the range of options available to them and the forms of organization that they can conceive are very much more limited than ours. They do not seem to be able to conceive alternatives, choose, and plan. Their "institutions" are suited to specific environments, with specific forms of threat and opportunity. They do not seem to be "made." And there is little change in them.

The experiments of history lead to a similar conclusion about fundamental, distinctively human needs: people need to be free and create while integrating this with ways of associating with others. Where we find people willing to make considerable sacrifices for goals other than mere survival (sacrificing for the young and future generations, revolting against oppressive authority, rejecting slavery – Chomsky 1988b), we can plausibly assume that the goals of the sacrifice represent fundamental needs – trumping even those of survival. History also suggests which forms of organization best meet needs. It reveals people in various forms of social organization in various environments. Investigating, we find cases where people resist the forms of organization they find themselves in and aim to improve them. Equally important, we look in the directions that they seek improvement, and we note the success of the solutions they work out. And where there is progress in meeting these goals in the social organizations that develop, we note that. There are complicating factors – as always, where there is entrenched power. And the tools of power have become increasingly sophisticated, especially in the twentieth century: media control, the tools of advertising, and similar forms of information control have proven to be powerful forms of mind control. But history suggests that people need choice and autonomy, and to place their stamp on the work they do.

Chomsky suggests that an ideal form of social organization would be one or another form of what he calls "anarchosyndicalism" or "libertarian socialism." These are "isms" that one does not usually encounter, although they are suited to the idea that freedom and community can integrate. The anarchist/libertarian aspect would satisfy the need for freedom and creativity, and the syndicalist/socialist that for community (often found not just with family, but with those at work, in community projects, at play, and so on). Explanations of why Chomsky chooses this as an ideal form of organization (and insight into how this political ideal guides his criticism of current political "management" and suggestions concerning policy) are found in his political writings. I do not pursue the matter further here. My aim is to indicate that seeking justification for a moral/political ideal represents another kind of connection between a science of language and politics. Again, the empirical scientific study of mind (prominently, language) and human nature plays a central role.

Whether readers pursue the question of integration or not, I hope this volume will encourage all to look further into Chomsky's work and the work of those who have extended it – including those in this volume who, in discussing Chomsky, speak not just of his work, but of what they and others have been able to contribute to "Chomskyan thought." Their efforts illustrate how fruitful Chomsky's contributions have been to the intellectual study of language, of human mind and human nature, and of our conduct and goals as members of political communities.

The chapters

Linguistics

Chomsky's work in the science of language began in the late 1940s with an undergraduate thesis at the University of Pennsylvania, the basis of his MA thesis, *The Morphophonemics of Modern Hebrew*. After appointment as a Harvard Junior Fellow in the early 1950s, he began the monumental *The Logical Structure of Linguistic Theory*, a chapter of which was submitted as his

Ph.D. thesis at Pennsylvania. Completed in 1955 and revised for publication in 1956, it was not actually published until 1975, and then only in part. But, as Howard Lasnik mentions in his discussion of the computational "levels" built into Chomsky's various theories of the language organ, it set the stage for, and anticipated, much of Chomsky's work in the science of language, including aspects of his recent "minimalist" program.

Neil Smith nicely outlines the nature of Chomsky's project for a science of language. He also points to the connection between the science of language and biology. That connection becomes particularly evident in Chomsky's solution to what he calls "Plato's Problem" – the task of explaining how we can acquire so much knowledge of language (its structure, sounds, and meanings) in such a short time. David Lightfoot focuses on this. The solution Chomsky offers, Universal Grammar (UG), is a hypothesis about what children start with, the "initial position." Lightfoot looks primarily at what must be a biologically inbuilt, structural schema for language. Succeeding chapters discuss other aspects of UG. Elan Dresher focuses on Chomsky's work on linguistic sounds during the 1950s and 1960s, culminating in Chomsky's and Morris Halle's *Sound Pattern of English*. This work indicates that human linguistic sounds are systematic, "abstract," and, apparently, unique to language alone. Further developing a small but revealing segment of this theme, Laura Petitto discusses research that localizes tissue in a part of the brain homologous to that found in several primates, tissue that used to be thought of as devoted to sound recognition but that in the case of humans seems to be language-specific, innately "programmed" to recognize, respond to, and lead to production of linguistic syllabic structure – syllabic structure, remarkably, in *both* speech and sign. The last chapter of the linguistics section presents some of Lila Gleitman's and Cynthia Fisher's work on "word" (lexical) learning. They do not attempt to say where sounds and meanings (concepts) come from. Presumably, a full theory of UG speaks to that. Instead, they focus on the kinds of information children rely on in order to associate or map sounds and concepts in their mental dictionaries. That information is syntactic and language-specific, which presupposes that the child, who so obviously recognizes what is relevant (and when), has the conceptual tools and a schedule for their application built into the mind at birth. A theory of UG describes those tools and points in the direction of making sense of how they come to be applied.

Philosophy of mind

Like Descartes, Chomsky makes his philosophical work continuous with his scientific. The study of mind and language is an attempt to characterize and explore the consequences of a developing science of mind – one in which a science of language plays a prominent role. The consequences that can and should be explored include those that involve the realization that we – and our language – are biological structures. This suggests a different way to understand ourselves and human communities and, thus, consequences for action – including political action. Seen in this way, philosophy well practiced aims to offer the best – most rationally defensible, all things considered – picture of our biological minds and natures while exploring the consequences if the picture that is drawn is correct.

Chomsky's work in this area began in the 1950s when he read historical works in linguistics and philosophy. His reading led him to develop and elaborate a framework for understanding the human mind and language that he called a "rationalist" approach, which he contrasted with a rival "empiricist" approach (Hornstein, this volume). The labels and the ways Chomsky characterized the rationalist and empiricist pictures of the mind are apt: they suit the philosophical views of the mind that traditional rationalists (Descartes, Leibniz, Cudworth, etc.)[1] and empiricists (Locke, Hume, etc.) held, and they characterize important differences between views of the mind and the science of mind found today. The contrasting approaches are explored in detail, although not under these labels, in *Cartesian Linguistics* in 1966 and they have been elaborated since. Rationalists hold that the mind is both structured and provided with rich and extremely useful "content" at birth. Rationalists are "nativists." The rationalist recognizes, of course, that experience and "external" factors play a role in the mind's "choosing" which concepts to activate or develop. But the rationalist denies that external elements shape and constitute concepts via the operations of some sort of domain-general learning procedure such as hypothesis formation and testing. Circumstances serve to "occasion" or "trigger" the introduction of a concept; crucially, the mind's own machinery dictates what "patterns" in the data count as appropriate "occasions." The patterns are, in a sense, built into the mind all along. Empiricists, in contrast, think of the human mind as getting its language-specific (and much else) structure and virtually all of its "content" by "learning" it from environmental conditions – interaction with things (world) and others ("speakers" who "train" their young, according to some). Chomsky's empiricists are anti-nativist. Further, his rationalists think that the most fruitful way to study the mind and its elements and "contents" is to focus on its internal structure and operations ("internalism"). For them, a study of language's various contributions to cognition, including the concepts that language expresses and the terms it puts in "referring positions" in sentences, is a study of internally constituted "tools" that people can use for various purposes. The ways people use these word-tools to say what they intend, or to refer to various things, are matters of free human action. Trying to deal with free action in a naturalistic science is for the rationalist hopeless. In contrast, the empiricist when dealing with concepts or reference looks outside to the mind/person in its/his/her interaction with the environment ("externalism"). They might construe a concept as a functional role in some overall account of humans using language (Wittgenstein 1963; Sellars 1974). And they might think of reference as a conventional relationship between word and world, or perhaps even look for a "natural" relationship in a realist construal of information theory (Dretske 1981); in either case, they apparently ignore the fact that people use words (and they use them in many ways) to refer to many things.[2] In some much-admired work (Kripke 1972; Putnam 1975; Burge 1979), the idea that environment constitutes linguistically expressed concepts/meanings has taken the extraordinary form of holding that meanings are individuated by properties and things outside the head, perhaps completely unknown to speakers. I might be told that the word *platypus* means – at least in part – some specific set of features of the platypus genome; these are unknown to me and – I venture – to anyone else. Yet that genetic structure is part of what I express when I say "Doesn't Harriet have a pet platypus?"[3] Finally, Chomsky's rationalists attribute the remarkable flexibility and adaptability of humans and the creativity of the human mind to those internal, largely innate structures and contents of the mind that *enable* flexibility, adaptability, and creativity. His empiricists, committed by the nature of the empiricist program to trying to find system in the multiple ways in which language and other cognitive systems are used, have little to offer in explaining human creativity. They tend to gesture in the direction of similarity and analogy, and say that these extend already-learned structures and contents. Chomsky indicates the failures of this approach in many places (1966, 1975, 1986, 1988b, 2000a, *inter alia*).

Norbert Hornstein outlines Chomsky's rationalist/empiricist distinction in both its historical and contemporary forms. Paul Pietroski and Stephen Crain present – focusing on recent evidence – a discussion of the nativist/anti-nativist issue. They explain why Chomsky thinks there are "innate ideas." Akeel Bilgrami and Carol Rovane show why Chomsky thinks that the current philosophical – and dominantly empiricist – preoccupation with language–world relationships under the topic "reference" is misguided. They also outline some aspects of Chomsky's view that human understanding and knowledge – based on biologically native systems as he thinks it must be – is of its nature limited by the cognitive "equipment" with which biology has provided us. In the last chapter of this section, I outline some of the considerations that lead Chomsky and several other rationalists to the conclusion that much of our conceptual range is built into us at birth. Following Chomsky (1966, 2002a), this idea is then linked to human creativity. That in turn introduces an important theme of Chomsky's political views.

Politics

Where Chomsky's elementary school classmates might have turned their commonsense form of understanding to analyzing sport teams or to detailed analyses of who was friends with whom, he focused on politics. His first political publication, a February 1939 reflection on the fall of Barcelona, Czechoslovakia, and Austria and the ominous rise of fascism, appeared soon after his tenth birthday in the school paper he edited. It helped spark an interest in the Spanish Revolution, a topic he could pursue in his trips to New York, where he frequented anarchist offices and the secondhand bookstores on 4th Avenue run by refugees from fascism (see Barsky 1997 for an account of Chomsky's early life). The research he did in his teens – plus, no doubt, a continued intense interest in the creative and developmental opportunities afforded individuals by a rich native endowment, including the possibility of anarchist forms of social organization – allowed him, many years later, to write a sophisticated review of a scholar's book on the topic. Chomsky has a prodigious memory and intense powers of concentration; few others could recall or consolidate enough of what they had read to use it many years later. What needs emphasis, though, is that his classmates had the same tools – the concepts of common sense – needed to understand people as individuals and in groups that Chomsky had.

The obvious lesson is that political systems and political events are within the reach of everyone: "experts" and "managers" are not needed for political analysis, criticism, or decisions. Political study and criticism is not science; the label "expert," warranted where specialized concepts are in play, does not apply. Granted, some people are more sophisticated in political analysis and criticism than others, and anyone can improve in discernment – experience tempered with skepticism does matter. But sophistication and improved discernment require no specialized knowledge and arcane concepts, just interest and – connected with that, surely – some expectation that one's interest can make a difference. Given this, why is there often more interest in sport and the latest Elvis Presley sighting than in political analysis and criticism, even in contemporary democracies, where – presumably – one can make a difference? Part of the answer lies in the fact that contemporary democracies are largely in the control of private power – in effect, corporations. Contemporary democracies respect James Madison's principle that those who own the country should run it. Individual voters choose from a list of candidates, often representing a narrow political range. While representatives nominally have considerable power and are elected to serve the interests of their constituents, their decisions in fact serve the interests of private economic power. The mechanism is straightforward: corporations won for themselves at the end of the nineteenth century many of the rights of persons (including free speech), and they use these "rights" and their massive economic power to influence elections (by contributions and advertisement) and to determine legislation (by lobbying and threat). In this way, the important economic decisions – those that are so crucial to people's lives – are, in effect, made solely by boards of directors of corporations, institutions designed to maximize accumulation (profit) and domination (monopoly), not "serve the people."[4] Most of the electorate recognizes that the system accords them little control; that is why there is often little interest in the political process. These considerations are rarely mentioned and never emphasized in corporate-run mass media, which studiously overlook the obvious ways in which policy, both domestic and foreign, accords with the needs of corporate power. For example, one of the consequences of continued US hegemony in the Middle East is a considerable degree of control over the oil resources of that region. That hegemony has, in part, been maintained since the mid twentieth century by massive financial aid to Israel – particularly in the form of military equipment. Other "initiatives" included military support for Turkey, "friendship" with the Saudis (who invest heavily in US markets), aid to an Egypt willing to accommodate Israel and suppress popular local movements, and support for Saddam in Iraq during the 1980s – including support for chemical warfare against Iran and a blind eye to Saddam's efforts to slaughter Kurds. When Saddam became less useful and made the mistake of challenging US control, it led to Bush the first's invasion, followed a decade later by Bush the second's. The most prominent beneficiaries of these efforts have been not the citizens of Iraq or the US (who inevitably must pick up the tab), but corporations (e.g. Halliburton) and markets, which, assuming US hegemony, are assured of continued control and low energy costs. The pattern is the same in other cases – even Vietnam, which has joined the capitalist market fold. No US administration publicly admits the imperialist intentions of the project of "bringing freedom" (i.e. freedom for markets and corporations) (Chomsky 2003), and corporate-owned media seldom mention this or other unwelcome facts about the nature of the project (Chomsky 1989). Instead, both craft and foster what Chomsky calls the "necessary illusions" that portray the 2003 invasion of Iraq, for example, as motivated by an effort to bring democracy to the Iraqis, fight terrorism, corral the Butcher of Baghdad, etc. Chomsky deals with this phenomenon – and its motivations – under the topic "the manufacture of consent." Jean Bricmont explores this topic in the last chapter of the volume; the other authors in the political section also touch on it. Chomsky's work in this area – often in cooperation with Edward Herman – has to be counted as one of the most important – and increasingly influential – studies of political behavior in recent times.

Milan Rai provides an overview of Chomsky on politics by placing political views in an Enlightenment conception of morality. Chomsky has spoken to so many political topics and issues that it is impossible to offer a complete picture; but one can – and Rai does – bring many issues together by detailing Chomsky's moral motivations: why in all his political efforts he emphasizes freedom and reason. The three other contributors focus on central themes in Chomsky's political works. Jean Bricmont has been mentioned. James Wilson discusses Chomsky's views of the individual, the state, and corporation, and relations between them; this helps make sense of Chomsky's views of the United States' (and other corporate-run states') internal affairs. Irene Gendzier focuses on Chomsky's attempts to elucidate the motivations of US foreign policy: she concentrates on the North/South divide and US imperialism.

Part I

Chomsky on the human language

1   Chomsky's science of language

Neil Smith

Language makes us human.

Whatever we do, language is central to our lives, and the use of language underpins the study of every other discipline. Understanding language gives us insight into ourselves and a tool for the investigation of the rest of the universe. Martians and dolphins, bonobos and bees, may be just as intelligent, cute, adept at social organization, and morally worthwhile, but they don't share our language, they don't speak "human." One of Chomsky's achievements is to have demonstrated that, despite the easily observable richness of the world's languages, there is really only one human language: that the complex and bewildering array of different languages surrounding us are all variations on a single theme, most of whose properties are innately given.

The scientific study of language

Linguistics is conventionally defined as the "scientific study of language" – "language" in the singular. Although its domain is usually taken to include not just the wealth of the world's languages – Amharic, Berber, Chinese, Dutch, English, etc. – but also all possible languages, past, present, and future, for Chomsky the focus of linguistics is the study of knowledge of language, of "human." This chapter will attempt to justify and explain this emphasis, spell out its implications, and motivate the description of his linguistics as "scientific."

There are several strands to the claim that linguistics is a science. The first is that linguistics provides a general theory explaining *why* languages are the way they are: each language is a particular example of a universal faculty of mind, whose basic properties are innate. The second is that the theory should spawn testable hypotheses about those properties: like a physicist or a biologist, the linguist manipulates the environment experimentally to see what happens and, crucially, he or she may be wrong. The third is that the investigation of language should proceed no differently from the investigation of physical and chemical entities: there is no justification for placing requirements on linguistic theories beyond those placed on physical theories. In both domains, the theories are underdetermined by the data, but their respective hypotheses are comparable in that they aim to discover the truth about aspects of the natural world.[1]

It is important to note that characterizing some enterprise as "science" is not a value judgment. Dostoevsky's insights into the human condition are as deep as those of Darwin, but they have a radically different status. As Chomsky puts it: "We will always learn more about human life and human personality from novels than from scientific psychology."[2] Literature and science are complementary rather than in competition, and domains which lend themselves to scientific investigation are few. Vision and knowledge of language are such areas, consciousness and free will are (probably) not. The former constitute "problems" about which we can devise explanatory theories in much the same way as we devise theories of particles or genes in the natural sciences; the latter are "mysteries," whose understanding in any depth may well lie beyond our intellectual powers (1975: ch. 4). It is plausible to assume that spiders are incapable of understanding the geometry of the elegant webs they construct. It is equally plausible that we have comparable limits to our understanding, and that understanding free will lies beyond those limits. Those domains about which we can construct theories of the kind characteristic of the natural sciences are said to fall within the scope of "naturalistic inquiry." Knowledge of language is such a domain.

Modularity

Language may be what makes us human, but humans are remarkably complex, and the human mind/brain[3] is notoriously the most complex entity known. Fortunately this complexity can be broken down into more manageable chunks, where each chunk constitutes an appropriate domain of investigation and theory construction. While they can be related, physics and chemistry, botany and zoology are distinct domains; and within any one of them there are finer subdivisions, so that respiration and reproduction, or the circulatory system and the olfactory system are treated separately. This attempt to divide and conquer is seen most clearly in "modular" analyses of the mind. The human mind is argued to be modular in that vision and audition, face recognition, and the number sense are all separable faculties governed by their own generalizations and principles. Chomsky's work over several decades has provided a wealth of evidence that the language faculty constitutes a separate module in this sense, akin in many respects to any other organ of the body (Chomsky 1975, 1984). Moreover, he has provided more, and more rigorous, evidence about the precise internal structure of this module than has been provided for any other domain, except perhaps vision. That is, there are two different notions of modularity: one according to which the language faculty is a module of the mind, distinct from moral judgment, music, and mathematics; another according to which the language module itself divides up into submodules, relating to sound, structure, and meaning. Evidence for both kinds of modularity comes from the independence one from the other of the various modules, as seen most clearly in double dissociation.

Double dissociation

One can be blind without being deaf, deaf without being blind, and so on for all the faculties with which we are endowed. Because our ears and eyes are separate organs, the dissociation of deafness and blindness is unsurprising, even though the cause of deafness or blindness may in some cases be due to damage to a different organ, the brain. That is, we expect the failure of a particular component to lead to a particular deficit, even if, in the case of the brain, the complexity is so great that we may see a variety of different symptoms arising from the failure of a single part. Moreover, the workings of these various components are independent of intelligence, of the working of the "central system" in Fodor's (1983) term. In the case of sight this is well understood: no one any longer expects the misfortune of blindness to correlate with IQ, but the same appears to be true of language.

A striking example of such dissociation is provided by the case of Christopher (Smith & Tsimpli 1995), a man who lives in sheltered accommodation because he cannot look after himself, who cannot solve problems of the intellectual complexity of noughts and crosses (tic-tac-toe), but who can nonetheless read, write, speak, and understand some twenty or so languages. An example of submodular dissociation within the language faculty can be seen in the fascinating case of MC (Froud 2000), who can read nouns and verbs of arbitrary complexity, but who cannot cope with "function" words like *after, not, the,* or *because,* at all.

Such cases show us that our knowledge of language is both more complex and more isolable than might appear at first sight. It is time to look in some detail at precisely what this knowledge consists of, as this is the area in which Chomsky has made the greatest technical advances, and also the area which underpins the philosophical and psychological claims that have made him famous (or infamous) in the rest of academe.

Knowledge of language

Our knowledge of English (or any other language) enables us to produce and understand any of an indefinitely large number of sentences and, additionally, we can make judgments of well-formedness about sentences we have never previously encountered. Consider an example of the order of words possible in simple sentences of English containing an adverb like *occasionally*. All the examples in (1) are equally acceptable but (2), despite the fact that it is perfectly easy to understand, is immediately perceived as odd:

(1)   a. Occasionally John speaks French.
        b. John occasionally speaks French.
        c. John speaks French occasionally.

(2)   John speaks occasionally French.

With other kinds of adverb, such as *fluently*, the range of possibilities is more limited and the contrasts even starker. The example in (3) is fine, but those in (4) are of marginal acceptability and (5), like (2), is ungrammatical:

(3)   John speaks English fluently.

(4)   a. Fluently John speaks English.
        b. John fluently speaks English.

(5)   John speaks fluently English.

If you are a linguist and your theory of word order entails that English speakers should find (2) and (5) as acceptable as (1) and (3), then you are wrong, and your analysis must be replaced by a better one. A corollary of this emphasis on seeking testable explanations is that the central concern of linguistics, as of the other natural sciences, is *evidence* rather than just *data*; this emphasis in turn entails that idealization is necessary: not everything can be considered.

In presenting all these examples I have been assuming that you will agree with my judgments: that (1) and (3) are acceptable forms of speech, for instance. In fact, a major and innovative characteristic of Chomsky's linguistics is its exploitation of the previously neglected fact that we are able to recognize immediately that some sentences – like (5) – are ungrammatical: we have what one might call "negative knowledge." Hamlet can tell Ophelia that "I loved you not," and we can understand him easily enough, but we know we have to say "I didn't love you"; similarly, Othello can ask Desdemona "Went he hence now?", though we know we have to rephrase it in current English as "Did he go?" Such knowledge is not restricted to the literary idiom. We can say equally well either of the sentences in (6):

(6)   a. I asked the way to the school.
        b. I inquired the way to the school.

But whereas (7a) is fine, the analogous (7b) is odd, as indicated by the prefixed asterisk:

(7)   a. I asked the number of people in the class.
        b. *I inquired the number of people in the class.

We should be as puzzled by the fact that we have these intuitions as by the fact that apples fall down not up, or that the sea has waves. Newton was not the first to notice apples falling, but his insight that *why* apples fall is in need of an explanation led ultimately to his theory of gravity. Chomsky was not the first to notice the elementary facts I have cited here, but his insight that our intuitions (our judgments) can tell us something profound about the human mind/brain is of comparable importance. As the biochemist Albert von Szent-Györgi put it: "Discovery consists of seeing what everybody has seen and thinking what nobody has thought."

I have appealed to various facts about our knowledge, but even deciding what the facts are is itself frequently unclear and dependent on other theoretical commitments. Not everyone agrees with the judgments given for (6) and (7), and it is not obvious whether the examples in (4) are to be assimilated in terms of grammaticality to those in (3) or (5), or neither. If, like me, you find them of intermediate status, there is an immediate and perhaps surprising consequence: it is not possible to group sentences exhaustively into those which are grammatical and those which are ungrammatical, as there is a third category which is neither one thing nor the other.

We turn now to take a closer look at what "knowledge of language" consists of, beginning with the fundamental distinction between "competence" and "performance."

Competence, performance, and idealization

To be able to read this book you have to know English. It also helps if the light is on. Turning the light out might stop you reading – your performance. It presumably wouldn't affect your knowledge of English – your competence (Chomsky 1965). Slightly more subtle evidence for this dichotomy can be gleaned from a variety of sources, but two kinds are particularly straightforward: the fact that our linguistic knowledge ranges over an infinite domain, and the fact that we can make mistakes. Consider first infinity, and take the proposition in (8):

(8)   You should have pessimism of the intellect and optimism of the will.

The aphorism is due to the Italian thinker Antonio Gramsci, and has been quoted more than once by Chomsky (1992b: 354) "No-one has ever said it better than Gramsci . . . *You should have pessimism of the intellect and optimism of the will.*" As it encapsulates Chomsky's attitude rather well, I have quoted his report myself (Smith 1999), and there is no *linguistic* reason why my students in turn shouldn't quote me quoting Chomsky, quoting Gramsci . . . and so on, resulting in a sentence which is arbitrarily long. If there is no longest sentence, just as there is no highest number, the set of sentences of your language is potentially infinite, even if the set you can actually get round to uttering is finite. There may of course be non-linguistic reasons for not indulging in the repeated quotation suggested here: the desire for originality, the fear of exhaustion, a finite life-span. But these are nothing to do with the grammar of English, or whatever language in which you choose to couch the report. Assuming – uncontroversially – that the mind/brain is finite, it must then be the case that there is some set of rules, a generative procedure[4] for producing such sequences out of their parts.[5]

Equally cogent evidence for the distinction between what we know and what we do with what we know comes from the phenomenon of mistakes, both pathological and "normal." Slips of the tongue are commonplace and may even provide evidence about linguistic structure (Fromkin 1973), but their interest here is more elementary: the recognition that something is a mistake entails the existence of a norm from which it is a deviation; equivalently, that there is a mismatch between competence and performance. Such mistakes occur sporadically in all speakers, as a function of tiredness, carelessness, inebriation, and so on; in certain cases of pathology they may become all pervasive. If someone has a stroke and resulting (partial) loss of language, their speech may be so replete with mistakes that they are hard or impossible to understand. In some such cases the brain damage resulting from the lesion may have destroyed the subject's grammar; in others it may simply have rendered it inaccessible. In the latter case the patient may make a full recovery and regain the ability to use the language he or she appeared to have lost. As no one recovers from a stroke able to speak a language different from any they knew before, it is safe to conclude that their knowledge of language was all the time intact, despite their temporary inability to exploit it.

Generative linguistics is about competence, but it should not be forgotten that performance can provide crucial evidence for that competence. It is also important to emphasize that no kind of evidence is particularly favored in constructing linguistic theories. It is sometimes thought that evidence derived from psychological experimentation, or from brain scans,[6] or from pathological cases of the sort referred to above, has some kind of priority or greater weight than purely "linguistic" evidence: i.e. evidence based on judgments of native speakers. This is a fallacy, as in general the latter is richer than the former, and allows the construction of theories with a deeper deductive structure.

If one is looking for evidence, certain facts are irrelevant, though it is a serious problem to decide which ones. In general, the role of scientific experimentation is to get us closer to the truth, to the ideal, by eliminating irrelevant extraneous considerations. In other words idealization reveals that which is real, but which is usually hidden from view by a mass of detail. Most scientists accept the reality of the inverse-square law, whether it is being used to explain the intensity of the light reaching us from a star, of the sound reaching us from a jet engine, or the attractive force of a magnet, even though the messiness of experiments means that their measurements never mirror it exactly, giving "a distortion of reality" in Chomsky's phrase (cited in Smith 1999: 12). Consider an example of idealization in the linguistic domain.

First-language acquisition takes place within a particular window of opportunity known as the critical period (Smith 1998), which lasts for a few years and ends (at the latest) at puberty. Given what we know about this critical period, it sometimes comes as a shock to read that first-language acquisition is idealized to "instantaneity" (Chomsky 1986: 52). How can a process that extends over several years be sensibly treated as though it took no time at all? The paradox is only apparent, not real. Although there is a striking uniformity across children learning their first language in respect of the stages of develop-ment they go through, they do nonetheless differ from each other. For instance, in the course of mastering the system of negation, one child may form negative sentences by using an initial *no*, while another may use a final *no*, giving the contrast in (9):

(9)   a. No like cabbage.
        b. Like cabbage no.

Despite this developmental difference, both children will end up with the same system of negation in which they use the correct adult form in (10):

(10)   I don't like cabbage.

As far as we can tell, the early difference in the children's systems has *no* effect at all on the grammar they end up with. If the focus of our interest is on what's known as "the logical problem of language acquisition" – children's transition from apparently having no knowledge of a language to being able to speak and understand it like adults – then we have support for the idealization to instantaneity, which says that the different stages children go through in the language-acquisition process are of no import to their ultimate psychological state. Of course, it may turn out that this surprising claim is false. It might be that sufficiently sophisticated tests of grammaticality judgment, or investigations of neural firing, or subsequent historical changes in the language concerned, showed that the two children's grammars were crucially different, and different in ways that could explain other mysterious facts about knowledge of language. It's possible, but there is (as yet) no evidence, and the idealization is accordingly justified: it leads us to an understanding of one of the variables in the real system we are studying.

Levels of representation

A large part of the Chomskyan enterprise has been devoted to making explicit exactly what our "knowledge of language" consists of. To find out, it is necessary to look at the notion "level of representation."

As we saw in the discussion of modularity, the language faculty can be viewed from the inside or from the outside. From the outside it has to provide an interface with other components of the mind/brain; from the inside it has to relate meanings to pronunciations, semantics to phonetics. The formal properties of the mechanisms effecting this latter relation are to a considerable extent a reflection of the need to make the products of the language faculty "legible" to these other systems. In particular, the complexity of the inner workings of the grammar can be seen on analysis to be largely the side-effects of the need to interact with non-linguistic systems, and the linguistic system itself is as simple as is possible: grammars of natural languages are a "perfect" solution to the problem of relating sound to meaning (Chomsky 2000a: 9f). We return to this striking suggestion after we have looked at the internal structure of the grammar.

The first distinction that needs to be made is that between the lexicon and the "Computational System," basically the difference between what you have to store in memory and what you can create anew as the occasion demands. You have to remember that *cat* means a certain kind of animal, but you do not have to remember – and in principle could not remember – the potentially infinite set of sentences about cats that you are capable of producing or understanding.

From the earliest work in generative grammar (Chomsky 1951, 1955, 1957a) the notion "level of representation" has been central, where different levels of representation are postulated to capture generalizations of different kinds about sentences. To express regularities about pronunciation and the sound structure of sentences, the grammar exploits the level of representation called Phonetic Form (PF). To capture generalizations about meaning and the logical properties of sentences, it exploits the level of semantic representation called Logical Form (LF). The existence of ambiguous sentences like (11):

(11)   Picasso painted his models nude.

means that the relation between the LF and the PF is many to one: such sentences will have the same phonetic form but different logical forms. Similarly, distinct sentences that mean the same thing, like those in (12):

(12)   a. All the children came.
          b. The children all came.

entail that the relation between PF and LF is likewise many to one: such sentences will have the same "logical form" but different "phonetic forms." The implication of this many–many relation is that the mapping from sound to meaning is indirect, mediated by the syntactic structure of the sentences involved. In the same way, the partial similarity (and partial difference) between quantifiers such as *every* and *each* is described by assuming distinct semantic specifications for them in the lexicon. This accounts directly for the semantic contrast in (13) and indirectly for the contrast in grammaticality in (14):

(13) a. Each child came.
      b. Every child came.
(14) a. The children each came.
      b. *The children every came.

In order to give an adequate description of these semantically conditioned differences of syntactic behavior, it is necessary to have a level of LF at which the precise meaning of every expression is specified.

The complexity of syntax

Apart from variations in technical terminology, so much has always been commonplace. What was striking about Chomsky's work from the beginning was the sophistication – and complexity – of his *syntactic* representations. In particular, he argued at length for the necessity of having more than one level of representation within the syntax, postulating the famous distinction between "deep structure" and "surface structure." This terminological contrast didn't feature explicitly in the earliest work, but it is implicit both there and in any framework which exploits the notion of "transformational derivation."[7] In Chomsky's current (minimalist) framework (Chomsky 1995c; Uriagereka 1998), neither of these syntactic levels is actually necessary, but seeing why involves first looking at the various rule types that are used in a grammar. It is, however, worth noting now that a minimalist approach is essentially just scientific common sense. Chomsky's claim that linguistic theory should postulate only those notions (e.g. levels of representation) that are "either conceptually necessary or empirically unavoidable" is taken by scientists as so obvious as not to need saying.

Rules

We have already seen that rules are necessary to characterize the infinite possibilities provided by natural language, but they have a number of other useful properties. Levels of representation are *defined* by the rules that yield them as their output. Rules let us capture significant generalizations that go beyond lexical idiosyncrasy (all verbs have a past tense, not just the verb *evolve*); and they make possible an account of semantic compositionality – the fact that the meanings of larger entities is made up of the meanings of smaller ones: the meaning of *I don't like cabbage* is built up out of the meanings of *I*, *not*, *like*, and *cabbage*. It follows from these properties that sentences are not just strings of words but have structure. This is most obvious when the same sequence of words has two different interpretations depending on the relations between them, as in the ambiguous *black cab driver* which can mean either "a black driver of cabs" or "a driver of black cabs." The difference can be shown by using brackets to set off the *constituents* out of which sentences are constructed: in the present case, as shown in (15):

(15)   a. [black [cab driver]]
         b. [black cab [driver]]

Linking two or more words together as a constituent is not an innocent exercise: it predicts that the same combination will recur, explicitly or implicitly, in other expressions. In (16a), the sequence *many people* is a constituent which shows up in a different position in (16b):

(16)   a. Many people are in the room.
         b. There are many people in the room.

Separating the two elements (*many* and *people*) of this constituent gives rise (in this case) to ungrammatical sequences of the kind in (17):

(17)   a. *Many there are people in the room.
         b. *How many are there people in the room?

Similarly, a constituent can typically be replaced by a "pro-form," such as *they*, in (18a), or an empty category as in (18b):

(18)   a. There are many people in the room but *they* are hiding.
         b. Many people are in the room but – are hiding.

where the dash shows the position of the "understood" empty subject of *hiding*.

    To account for facts of this kind Chomsky and linguists working within his paradigm postulate two different kinds of rule: one that "merges" two words to form a larger constituent: e.g. *many* and *people*; and another that may "move" such a constituent to a different position: e.g. moving *many people* (but not just *many*) to the front of the sentence.[8] Such rules operate under well-defined conditions: the relation between *many people* and *they*, or between *many people* and the empty –, can obtain only in certain circumstances.[9] In (19a) the item *they* may (but need not) be taken to refer to *many people*, but in (19b) this is impossible:

(19)   a. Many people think they are intelligent.
         b. They think many people are intelligent.

In fact, we clearly know far more than this even about such simple sentences as those given. Corresponding to the statements in (16), we have such questions as those in (20):

(20)   a. Are many people in the room?
         b. Are there many people in the room?

The first can be answered appropriately as in (21):

(21)   Many people are in the room and many people aren't in the room

(where, for instance, half are indoors and half are in the garden). A comparable
answer to the second, as in (22), is anomalous:

(22)   There are many people in the room and there aren't many people in
         the room.

We still have the same constituents – *many people, in the room*, and so on, but
the interpretations are different.

   All of us have knowledge of this kind, even though most of us are not aware of
it, and none of us can spell out this knowledge in full detail. The notion of such
unconscious or "tacit" knowledge has been anathema to many philosophers
(Quine 1972), but the issue has been bedevilled by often arbitrary stipulations
as to what constitutes "knowledge." The important point is that humans can
produce and understand any of an infinite number of largely novel sentences,
and can make systematic judgments about their well-formedness, and we need
to explain these abilities. The explanation in terms of merge and move may be
wrong, but it is currently both the most inclusive and the deepest in terms of
the deductive structure of the theory involved.

Displacement

The possibility of movement of items is invoked to account for what is
often called the "displacement property" of language (Chomsky 2000a: 12f):
constituents are pronounced in places other than where they are interpreted.
The simplest kinds of example in English are provided by the contrast between
statements on the one hand, and questions and focus constructions of the kind
seen in (23) on the other:

(23)   a. These delegates might elect the best candidate.
         b. Which candidate might these delegates elect?
         c. The best candidate, these delegates might elect

The basic intuition about such examples is that the phrase containing *candidate*
is in all cases the object of *elect*, even though it appears either at the beginning
of the sentence or after the verb. *Elect* is a two-place predicate: it needs a subject
and an object, respectively *these delegates* and *the best candidate* in (23a), so
that the failure of either to appear results in ungrammaticality: all the strings in
(24) are unacceptable:

(24)   a. *these delegates elected
         b. *elected the best candidate
         c. *elected

To account for this, *elect* is said to *select* an object to its right, and this object may then remain where it is, or be displaced, as in (23b).[10] This selectional difference simultaneously accounts for the contrast with, on the one hand, verbs like *giggle*, which allow no object, as witness the impossible (25), or, on the other hand, verbs like *divide* which can be used with or without an object, as in (26):

(25)   Don't giggle me.

(26)   a. The amoeba divided.
         b. They divided the spoils.

In fact (25) is sometimes produced by children (Bowerman 1987), though it is not likely to be acceptable to anyone reading this – another instance not only of our "negative knowledge," but of our intriguing ability – in the absence of any obvious evidence – to progress from a grammar which allows (25) to one which does not. This is a classic example of poverty of the stimulus: we know more than the environment provides evidence for. It is implausible to suggest that every child who comes up with examples like (25) is explicitly corrected by parents or peers, yet the child pattern is common and the adult intuition is robust.

Interestingly, all languages allow for statements and questions of the kind in (23), but in some languages (such as Chinese and Japanese), the object stays in the same place and doesn't get displaced (Chomsky 1995c: 69), giving rise to sentences like (27):

(27)   These delegates might elect which candidate?

which is itself acceptable as an echo-question in English: that is, a question repeating with incredulity something already suggested. We thus have a situation in which there are two different syntactic structures in two different languages, but with the same interpretation. That is, at some level of representation – presumably LF – both (23b) and the Chinese equivalent of (27) have the same logical structure.

That is, just as we have overt and covert syntactic categories (*they* versus nothing in (18)), we have the possibility of overt (visible) and covert or invisible movement of some categories. The parallel interpretations of (23b) and (27) are captured by saying that in English the movement seen in (23b), giving the syntactic and logical representation, is "overt," whereas the same displacement in Chinese etc. is "covert." In the jargon, these are referred to as before and after "Spell-out": movement before spell-out is visible – as in English; movement after spell-out is invisible – as in Chinese. That the movement is comparable in the two cases is evidenced by a wealth of syntactic facts as well as the intuitively obvious identity of interpretation, where such identity is taken to entail identity of representation at some level.

Empty categories

The idea that there should be phonologically empty words of the kind mentioned here has either outraged or bewildered many members of the linguistic community. Yet the development of a theory of empty categories has been important in allowing linguists to capture interesting generalizations, to simplify the structure of grammars, and ultimately to provide evidence about the innate endowment that the child brings to the task of first-language acquisition.

Traditional descriptions of language frequently refer to "understood" elements, which are not visible (or audible), but whose presence it is convenient to assume. This tradition was adopted and formalized in the transformational treatment of the subject of coordinate sentences like (18b), as well as for imperatives and a variety of other constructions. More recently, it has been widely extended, with interesting implications for the structure of the grammar. Consider the pair of sentences in (28):

(28)   a. John wants Bill to go.
         b. John wants to go.

It is intuitively obvious that in (28a) Bill is to go and in (28b) that John is to go. Making that intuition grammatically explicit can be effected by assuming that in each case *go* has a subject, even though that subject is invisible in (28b), whose structure is then something like (29):

(29)   John wants [ec] to go.

where "ec" stands for an "empty category," construed as referring to the same person that *John* does, as is explicit in the synonymous *John wants himself to go*.

An empty category is in general one that has syntactic properties but is not pronounced. With sentences as simple as these the gain from assuming empty categories is scarcely overwhelming, but in more complex cases, one can begin to see how benefits accrue. For me, and perhaps most speakers of English, a sentence like (30a) typically allows the alternative pronunciation shown in (30b), where *I am* contracts to *I'm*:

(30)   a. I am the greatest.
         b. I'm the greatest.

Stating the precise conditions under which such contraction is possible is not straightforward – (31b) is simply ungrammatical:

(31)   a. John is planning to come at the same time as I am.
         b. *John is planning to come at the same time as I'm.

(31a) is interpreted as meaning "John is planning to come at the same time as I am *planning to come.*" The italicized words are redundant and so are typically not pronounced, even though they are "understood," and have a syntactic existence in the form of an empty category. This suggests an explanation for the impossibility of (31b): contraction cannot take place adjacent to an empty category; *am* is adjacent to an empty category, left by the omission of *planning to come*, so (31b) is excluded (Lightfoot, this volume).

Another initially mysterious contrast, illustrated in (32), succumbs to the same explanation:

(32)   a. Tell me whether the party's tomorrow.
         b. Tell me where the party is tomorrow.
         c. *Tell me where the party's tomorrow.

Why is (32c) ungrammatical? An answer is suggested by a consideration of the kind of echo-question seen in (27), *They elected which candidate?*, and further illustrated in (33):

(33)   a. The party's *where* tomorrow?
         b. The party's *when* tomorrow?

In these examples *where* and *when* appear in the same position as the ordinary locative or temporal phrases that they question, as seen in (34):

(34)   a. The party's in the hangar tomorrow.
         b. The party's at 11 o'clock tomorrow.

The next stage of the argument should be clear – the structure of (32b) is as shown in (35):

(35)   Tell me where the party is [ec] tomorrow

with an empty category marking the place from which *where* has moved, and blocking the contraction of *is* to *'s*.

I-language and E-language

It is time to take stock. We uncontroversially have knowledge of language, manifest in our ability to produce and understand any of indefinitely many sentences, in our ability to make judgments of well-formedness and, more importantly, of ill-formedness: we can recognize previously unheard mistakes or deviations from the patterns of our native language. It is important to note that the strength of the argument from the existence of mistakes does not rest on the identification of a common language shared by the speaker and the hearer. If you hear someone speaking a different dialect of your language you do not assume that they are making mistakes in pronouncing words slightly differently, or in using different vocabulary or grammar. For me, it's not a mistake to say *pavement* rather than *sidewalk*, or to make *sort* rhyme with *bought*: that's just the way I speak my variety of (British) English. Similarly, I use the forms in (36) whilst others use those in (37) to convey the same message:

(36)   a. I jumped out of the window.
         b. I jumped off the table.
(37)   a. I jumped out the window.
         b. I jumped off of the table.

But this raises a basic issue that differentiates Chomsky's linguistics from that of all his predecessors: his concentration on the language of the individual rather than the language of the social or political group in which that individual resides. For much of the time the difference doesn't matter, but there are important philosophical implications of the difference, encapsulated in the terminological difference between "I-language" and "E-language" (Chomsky 1986).

When generative grammar was being first developed (Chomsky 1955, 1957a), a language was defined as a set of sentences, generated by the rules of a grammar. Example (3) (*John speaks English fluently*) would be generated, and so be part of the language; (5) (*John speaks fluently English*) would not be generated, and so would not be. Chomsky's early work included a demonstration that any such definition of "language" could not have a decisive role to play in linguistic theory. The idea that the E-language, some definable entity *e*xternal to the individual and that corresponds to the everyday idea of "English," could be the focus of theory construction is not tenable. If such a social or supra-personal construct was coherent and consistent, it might be the appropriate domain for political, mathematical, or logical statements, but if it is supposed to reflect the human capacity for language, it is neither coherent nor definable.[11] By contrast, I-language, an individual's internal possession, with its explicitly psychological status, is the appropriate domain for statements about personal knowledge, and is also coherently definable. It is uncontroversial that untutored speakers can make grammatical judgments of the kind I have been appealing to throughout this discussion: someone who failed to be sensitive to a difference between (3) and (5) would simply not know English. Chomskyan linguistics aims to characterize explicitly what underlies that ability. In contrast, it is not at all obvious that there is a coherent domain of theoretical investigation in which the geopolitical notion of "English" should figure. For me, both the sentences in (38) are possible:

(38)   a. Nothing, I had for breakfast.
        b. Nothing did I have for breakfast.

For some of my colleagues only one of them is acceptable (Cormack & Smith 2000). It is an interesting research question to tease out the differences between our respective grammars; but it doesn't make much sense to ask which of us is correct, or which is "English." In brief, the apparently narrower domain of I-language – the mentally represented grammar of an individual – is amenable to scientific investigation in a way that E-language is not. The subject matter of linguistics is (tacit) *knowledge*, and no single individual has or could have knowledge of all the varieties of any language in the traditional lay sense of the term.

As we have seen, linguists attempt to formulate aspects of our knowledge of language in the form of rules that both make explicit what we know and thereby make predictions about what else can occur in our own languages and in human language more generally. In principle, such predictions make falsifiable claims, but it is important to note that no serious theory adopts the kind of naïve falsificationism supposedly proposed by Popper (1963). Individual analyses of particular data will be refined or rejected in part on the basis of their conformity with such predictions, but the guiding intuitions behind the theory can often be maintained despite apparent falsification. This apparently cavalier attitude is a direct function of the idealization inherent in producing any scientific explanation. In linguistics as in physics, what is important is to explain some subset of the data, rather than describe everything.

Legibility

A theory of language provides a link between sound and meaning, between representations of the pronunciation and representations of the logical properties of words and sentences. Accordingly, a grammar – the I-language – must define the two levels of representation, PF and LF, and specify the link between them. Ideally, there should be no other levels and the complexity of this link should be minimal. This suggests two questions which it had previously either been impossible to address seriously or perhaps even to formulate. First, how good a solution to this conceptual problem of linking sound and meaning is a human language? Is it right to suggest that the grammars of natural languages are in some sense optimal? Second, what are the relations between the language faculty and other systems of the mind/brain? In particular, can any perceived deviations from optimality in the first be attributed to conditions imposed by the second?

Chomsky addresses these issues in terms of the question: "how 'perfect' is language?", with the answer, surprising for a biological system (2000a: 9),[12] that it is very close to perfect. What this means is that any deviations from conceptual necessity manifested by the language faculty (that is, the I-language) are motivated by conditions imposed from the outside. Chomsky calls these "legibility conditions": conditions imposed by the need for other systems of the mind/brain to use representations provided by the language faculty. This refers in particular to the need for the articulatory and perceptual systems to exploit PF representations, and for the conceptual system to exploit LF. Against such a background, movement or "displacement" processes of the kind seen in (23) or (38), or in the different positions occupied by *Clinton* in *They elected Clinton* and *Clinton was elected*, appear to be conceptually unnecessary. Why do natural languages exploit such devices which are completely foreign to the artificial languages of logic and mathematics? One tentative answer is that displacement may plausibly be motivated by the need to structure information for optimal communication. To elaborate a little: the "focus" example in (23c) is probably motivated by the desire to make more salient one particular entity in the discourse by putting it in initial position. The subjects one wishes to talk about are likely to be differentially accessible to one's interlocutor, depending on how recently they have been mentioned, how prominent they are in the environment, and so on. Putting a constituent like *the best candidate* in initial position then increases its accessibility, and makes fruitful communication more likely. If this is indeed the correct account then it looks as if a property of the language faculty is imposed from outside the system, from another part of the mind/brain: from the "central system" in Fodor's (1983) terminology.[13]

Chomsky does not stop there, but attempts to link this apparent imperfection of language to another. Natural languages are full of phenomena that give rise to problems for second-language learners and irritation for philosophers. There are morphological complexities like declensional paradigms and irregular verbs, which appear to have no real meaning of their own and to be semantically useless. They are another imperfection, necessitating the postulation of uninterpretable features – that is, features with no semantic interpretation. However, current syntactic theory makes systematic use of such uninterpretable features: their function is to drive the movement processes that we have just seen to be motivated from outside the language faculty. If such conjectures are on the right lines, they allow the interesting possibility of reducing two kinds of apparent imperfection to one. In fact, if the argument is correct, the imperfections are indeed only apparent. Given the constraints that other systems of the mind/brain impose on solutions to linking sound and meaning, there may be no other alternatives, so conceptual necessity explains the form of the grammar overall.

Although we may differ in our ability to deploy our knowledge of language, that knowledge is largely the same from person to person. As far as is known, we all see the same way: across the species we have the same visual system; similarly, across the species, we all have the same linguistic system. The case of language is somewhat different from that of other putative modules in that it is evident from the existence of languages other than our own that a certain amount of language *is* acquired on the basis of interaction with the environment: it is "learnt." However, the most fundamental aspects of language are universal and can hence be factored out of the learning equation. In these areas we do not expect there to be differences between individuals, whether they are speakers of different languages or the same language. To give a simple example: we do not need to *learn* that our language contains nouns and verbs: all languages contain nouns and verbs. What we need to learn is which noises our language associates with particular examples of them.

Acquisition

Principles and parameters

So some of the intricate and complex knowledge characteristic of adult grammar is putatively innate, but some of it is obviously "learnt." More accurately, it is attributable in part to the role of the ambient environment: languages differ along various dimensions, and it is obvious that we are not born knowing that the words *tortoise* and *turtle* pick out chelonians, or that English puts the subject before the verb, whereas Welsh puts it after. In recent years, the idea that linguistic theory should be "explanatory" has been focused on explaining how our knowledge of language can be acquired, given the (claimed) poverty of the stimulus.[14]

In the last twenty years, for the first time in the history of language study, there is now a reasonable chance of solving "Plato's Problem" – how it is we can know so much given that the evidence is so impoverished.[15] The solution is Principles and Parameters. The idea is that the child is born knowing the principles which determine the so-called design features of language: the existence of particular categories such as Noun and Verb, the possibility of Merge and Move, the universality of structure dependence, the conceptual structure of possible predicates like CAUSE and LOCATION (Bloom 2000), and much more.

A central aspect of Principles and Parameters theory is that it explicitly exploits the idea that there is a cascade effect so that knowledge can develop without being learned. There is evidence that children acquiring their first language home in on the correct word order extremely early. Before they can speak themselves, children have worked out that English places the verb before its object, so we have examples like *eat this* rather than *this eat*. In the jargon this is usually referred to as being a reflex of the fact that English is "head-first": the head verb *eat* precedes its complement *this*. Once this elementary fact has been established, children also know a number of other facts about English: that we say *fond of tortoises* rather than *of tortoises fond*, *the idea that penguins are cute* and not *that penguins are cute's idea*. They do not need to have heard such examples to have the knowledge. They are born with the principle and with some specification of the range of variation in possible human languages, and on being presented with data they need merely to pick out which of these possible languages is the one that they are being exposed to. The process is one of selection (Chomsky 1980; Piattelli-Palmarini 1989) from an antecedently defined set, rather than instruction about an unconstrained system. One kind of evidence for this theory comes from the interesting category of "mistakes that children do not make." Over-generalizations of the kind *three sheeps comed* are pervasive in the morphology, but comparable analogies typically do not occur in the syntax. Observing that in a sentence like (19a) (*Many people think they are intelligent*) the pronoun *they* may or may not be dependent on *many people*, the child typically does not extend the possibility to (19b) (*They think many people are intelligent*) where the *they* may *not* be dependent on *many people*. That these mistakes just don't appear suggests that children are predisposed to interpret the input they are exposed to in particular ways: the principles and parameters are there from the beginning.

Typology

The theory of parametric variation identifies precisely those aspects of language (apart from the morphophonological makeup of individual items in the lexicon) which it is necessary for the child to acquire on the basis of experience. The theory then has as a natural corollary that these aspects are precisely those by reference to which languages can differ one from the other, and hence the theory simultaneously provides an account of possible typological variation among languages. In each case, the locus of this variation is the set of functional categories – categories like Determiners, Tense and Complementizer. This is not superficially obvious, but consider again the contrast between (23b) and (27), where in different languages WH words (*who*, *which*, etc.) may either move to the front of the sentence or stay where they are. In the case of English and similar languages where the WH phrase moves, there is a technical question as to where it moves to and why it moves at all. The answer to the first question is that it moves to a position called the "Specifier" (Spec) of the Complementizer Phrase (CP), the answer to the second is that it does so because (in English but not in Chinese) the C is "strong" and acts like a magnet attracting the item to it. The technical details are spelt out in the relevant literature (Uriagereka 1998). Suffice it here to say that all sentences have a CP, but that this position may be either empty or filled. It is typically, though optionally, filled in subordinate "complement" clauses as in (39), where the complementizer *that* or the complementizer phrase *which candidate* is shown in italics, and the parentheses indicate optionality:

(39) a. I know (*that*) they elected the best candidate.
      b. I know *which candidate* they elected.

That the two items are in the same position is indicated by the impossibility of having both of them together, as shown by the unacceptability of (40):

(40)   *I know that which candidate they elected.

On the most economical assumptions about the rules of the grammar, it must be that in (23b) *which candidate* has moved to the same position as in (39b), hence both must share the same landing site for the "moved" element: viz. Spec CP. From this it follows that quite radical differences between languages can be accounted for in terms of properties of functional categories, despite the involvement of substantive elements like nouns and noun phrases. More particularly, the differences are limited to the presence of specific features on functional categories within the lexicon. The lay intuition that the basic differences between languages reside in their vocabulary has been given substance by being recast in an explicit theoretical framework.

Universals and evolution

If a substantial part of our knowledge of language is innate, and if any child can learn the language it is immersed in with equal facility, it follows that many aspects of our knowledge are universal. So much is now generally accepted (with some disagreement about the details of what is innate). It is nonetheless still something of a shock for many to read that one can gain insight into English by studying Japanese (Chomsky 2000a: 53–4), or any other language; and of course vice versa. The logic is clear: suppose that a phenomenon in language A can be adequately described by using either of two devices – d_1 or d_2 – but the comparable phenomenon in language B can only be adequately described by one of them, say d_1, then theoretical parsimony demands that one use d_1 for both languages, rather than d_1 for one and d_2 for the other. On further analysis it should also turn out that this choice makes appropriate further predictions, but not always: the poverty of the inflectional system (of English, for instance) may make it impossible to test some hypotheses in that language, whereas they can be easily tested in another (Cole & Hermon 1981; Smith 1999).

We have seen that knowledge of language is rich and intricate, but is in some sense perfect. Moreover, it is largely innate and common to the species, and hence is presumably genetically determined. This rather surprising combination of properties is explicable perhaps only if one can mount an explanation for them in terms of evolution. If our ability to develop language is genetically determined, but our relatives – from chimpanzees to mushrooms – have no comparable language faculty, then it must have evolved. But now there is a problem, as Chomsky is widely quoted as denying that natural selection could have produced human language. Furthermore, as there are supposed to be only two possible explanations for evolution, namely "God or natural selection," Chomsky must either be appealing to divine providence or be a mystic. As has recently been documented in great detail (Jenkins 2000), Chomsky's position is *not* that natural selection has played no role in the evolution of language, but that natural selection is only one factor. In all evolution, whether of language, the eye, or an antibody, an essential contribution is also made by physical and developmental factors working on the variation provided by random mutation. The criticism of Chomsky with regard to evolution is based on a simplistic analysis of the range of possibilities available, and of his position on them. Properties of language have evolved. Natural selection must have played a role in this evolution, but so too have elementary physical constraints, such as the size of the human head. Many other factors have also, presumably, been involved, such as the adoption of a trait in one domain for use in another: an example might be the exploitation of discrete infinity by both the number sense and the language faculty. Our knowledge is vanishingly small in this domain, but the questions are coherent, the issues are empirical, and the problem of unifying the various bits of our knowledge with the rest of the natural sciences is standard.

It is appropriate to end on a note of unification. Linguistics cannot be *reduced* to any other science, but its findings can be unified with those of psychology, biology, and ultimately neurology. The lead in this unification is provided by linguistics, because its theories are the most fully developed. Overwhelmingly, this is due to Chomsky.

2   Plato's Problem, UG, and the language organ

David Lightfoot

> The empiricist view is so deep-seated in our way of looking at the human mind that it almost has the character of a superstition.
>
> Chomsky (*The Listener* May 30, 1968)

Plato's Problem

Plato's Problem was expressed generally by Bertrand Russell: "How comes it that human beings, whose contacts with the world are brief and personal and limited, are nevertheless able to know as much as they do know?" The problem arises in the domain of language acquisition in that children attain infinitely more than they experience. Literally so, we shall see: they attain a productive system, a grammar, on the basis of very little experience. So there is more, much more, to language acquisition than mimicking what we hear in childhood, and there is more to it than the simple transmission of a set of words and sentences from one generation of speakers to the next. There is more to it than a reproduction of experience and, in maturity, our capacity goes well beyond what we have experienced.

Consider some subtleties that people are not consciously aware of. The verb *is* may be used in its full form or its reduced form: people say *Kim is happy* or *Kim's happy*. However, certain instances of *is* never reduce, for example, the underlined items in *Kim is happier than Tim is* or *I wonder what the problem is in Washington*. Most people are not aware of this, but we all know subconsciously not to use the reduced form here. How did we come to this? The question arises because the eventual knowledge is richer than relevant experience. As children, we heard instances of the full form and the reduced form, but we were not instructed to avoid the reduced form in certain places; we had no access to "negative data," information about what does *not* occur. Yet, all children typically attain the ability to use the forms in the adult fashion, and the ability is quite independent of intelligence level or educational background. Children attain this ability early in their linguistic development. More significantly, children do not try out the non-occurring forms as if testing a hypothesis, in the way that they "experiment" by using forms like *goed* and *taked*. The ability emerges perfectly and as if by magic. And it emerges despite limited relevant experience, in a way that might have intrigued Plato.

Another example. Pronouns like *she, her, he, him, his* sometimes may refer back to a noun previously mentioned in a sentence (1a–c). However, one can only understand (1d) as referring to two men, Jay and somebody else; here the pronoun may not refer to Jay, unlike in (1a–c).

(1)   a. Jay hurt his nose.
        b. Jay's brother hurt him.
        c. Jay said he hurt Ray.
        d. Jay hurt him.

As adults, we generalize that a pronoun may refer to a preceding noun *except* under very precise conditions (1d). But then, how did we all acquire the right generalization, particularly knowledge of the exception?

Recall the nature of our childhood experience: we were exposed to a haphazard set of linguistic expressions. We heard various sentences containing pronouns; sometimes the pronoun referred to another noun in the same sentence, sometimes to a person not mentioned there. Problem: because we were not informed about what *cannot* occur, our childhood experience provided no evidence for the "except" clause, that pronouns sometimes do not corefer. That is, we had evidence for generalizations like "*is* may be pronounced *z*" and "pronouns may refer to a preceding noun," but no evidence for where these generalizations break down.

As children, we came to know the generalizations and their exceptions, and we came to this knowledge quickly and uniformly. Yet our linguistic experience was not rich enough to determine the limits to the generalizations. We call this the problem of the *poverty of the stimulus*. This is "Plato's Problem" and it has shaped much of grammatical theory in the work of Chomsky and others. Children have no data that show them that *is* may not be reduced in some contexts and they have no data showing that *him* may not refer to Jay in (1d). These two small illustrations are examples of the form that the poverty-of-stimulus problem takes in language.

There are two "easy solutions" to the poverty-of-stimulus problem; neither is adequate. One is to say that children do not overgeneralize, because they are reliable imitators. That is, children do not produce the reduced *is* in the wrong place or use a pronoun in (1d) wrongly to refer to Jay, because they never hear language being used in this way. In other words, children acquire their native language simply by imitating the speech of their elders. We know this approach is not tenable, because everybody constantly says things that they have never heard. We express thoughts with no conscious or subconscious consideration of whether we are imitating somebody else's use of language. This is true of the most trivial speech: in saying *I wanna get a ticket for the game that's here on Wednesday*, one is using a sentence that one has almost certainly not heard.

Sometimes it is said that children form new sentences "by analogy" with what they have heard, but this simply conceals the problem: it does not account for why some analogies are drawn and others not. The problem is to explain why a reduced *'s* in *Tim's happy* provides an analogical basis for contracting the first *is* in *Kim is happier than Tim is*, but not the second. Why do the sentences (1a–c) not provide an analogical basis for coreference between *Jay* and *him* in (1d)? Children converge on specific generalizations and not on other logically possible ones, in ways that cannot be explained by a general notion of induction or analogy.

A variant on this approach is that children learn not to say the deviant forms because they are corrected by their elders. Some aspects of language are taught in schools: spelling conventions, socially stigmatized forms, some kinds of technical vocabulary. However, language emerges without the aid of teaching; many people are illiterate but nonetheless have a productive capacity to use language. Furthermore, the appeal to instruction does not explain language acquisition. First, it would take an acute observer to detect and correct the error. Second, where linguistic correction is offered, young children are highly resistant and just don't get the correction. Third, in the examples discussed, children do not overgeneralize and therefore parents have nothing to correct; this will become clearer when we discuss experimental work on young children.

So the first "easy" solution to the poverty-of-stimulus problem is to deny that it exists, to hold that the environment is rich enough to provide evidence for where the generalizations break down. The problem is real and this "solution" does not address the problem.

The second "easy answer" also denies that there is a problem, but it denies that there is anything to be learned, and holds that a person's language is fully determined by genetic properties. Yet this answer also cannot be right, because people speak differently, and many of the differences are environmentally induced. There is nothing about a person's genetic inheritance that makes her a speaker of English; if she had been raised in a Dutch home, she would have become a speaker of Dutch.

The two "easy answers" either attribute everything to the environment or everything to the genetic inheritance. Neither position is tenable. Instead, language emerges through an interaction between our genetic inheritance and the linguistic environment to which we happen to be exposed. English-speaking children learn from their environment that the verb *is* may be pronounced *iz* or *z*, and native principles prevent the reduced form from occurring in the wrong places. Likewise, children learn from their environment that *he*, *his*, etc. are pronouns, while native principles entail where pronouns may not refer to a preceding noun. The interaction of the environmental information and the native principles accounts for how the relevant properties emerge in an English-speaking child.

I'll sketch the relevant principles in a moment. A modern Plato might tease native principles apart from learned elements and claim that the native principles reflect knowledge attained in a previous life, that the knowledge was rendered subconscious when the soul drank from the River Lethe, the river of forgetting, just before birth. However, Chomsky assumes that native principles are encoded somehow in genetic material. This involves a kind of Mendelian genetics. In the mid nineteenth century, Mendel postulated genetic "factors" to explain the variable characteristics of his pea plants, without the slightest idea of how these factors might be biologically instantiated. Similarly, linguists seek to identify information which must be available independently of experience, in order for a grammar to emerge in a child. We have no idea whether this information is encoded directly in the genome or whether it results from epigenetic, developmental properties of the organism; it is, in any case, native. As a shorthand device for these native properties, I shall write of the linguistic genotype, that part of our genetic endowment which is relevant for our linguistic development. Each individual's genotype determines the potential range of functional adaptations to the environment (Dobzhansky 1970: 36), and we assume that the linguistic genotype (what linguists call "Universal Grammar" or "UG") is uniform across the species (short of pathological cases). That is, linguistically we all have the same potential for functional adaptations and any of us may grow up to be a speaker of Catalan or Hungarian, depending entirely on our circumstances and not at all on variation in our genetic make-up.

Since children are capable of acquiring any language to which they happen to be exposed between infancy and puberty, the same set of genetic principles which account for the emergence of English (using "genetic" now in the extended sense indicated) must also account for the emergence of Dutch, Vietnamese, Hopi, or any other of the thousands of languages spoken by human beings. This plasticity imposes a strong empirical demand on hypotheses about the linguistic genotype; the principles postulated must be open enough to account for the variation among the world's languages. The fact that people develop different linguistic capacities depending on whether they are brought up in Togo, Tokyo, or Toronto provides a delicate tool to refine claims about the nature of the native component.

Chomsky's approach to Plato's Problem, outlined in the first chapter of *Aspects of the Theory of Syntax* (1965), is to say that there is a biological entity, a finite mental organ, which develops in children along one of a number of paths. The paths are determined in advance of any childhood experience. The language organ that emerges, the grammar, is represented in the brain and plays a central role in the person's use of language. We have gained some insight into the nature of people's language organs by considering a wide range of phenomena: the developmental stages that young children go through, the way language breaks down in the event of brain damage, the manner in which people analyze incoming speech signals, and more. At the center is the biological notion of an internal, individual language organ, a grammar.

The nature of grammars

Children acquire a productive system, a grammar, in accordance with the requirements of the genotype. If asked to say quite generally what is now known about the linguistic genotype, one might say that it permits finite grammars, because they are represented in the finite space of the brain, but that they range over an infinity of possible sentences. Finite grammars consist of a set of operations which allow for infinite variation in the expressions which are generated. The genotype is plastic, consistent with speaking Japanese or Quechua. It is modular, and uniquely computational.

By "modular" I mean that the genotype consists of separate subcomponents each of which has its own distinctive properties that interact to yield the properties of the whole. These modules are, in many cases, specific to language. Research has undermined the notion that the mind possesses only "general principles of intelligence" that cover all kinds of mental activity. One module of innate linguistic capacity contains abstract structures that are compositional (consisting of units made up of smaller units) and that fit a narrow range of possibilities. Another module encompasses the ability to relate one position to another within these structures by movement, and those movement relationships are narrowly defined. Another module is the mental lexicon, a list of word forms and their crucial properties.

To see the kind of compositionality involved, consider how words combine. Words are members of categories like noun (N), verb (V), preposition (P), adjective/adverb (A). If two words combine, the grammatical properties of the resulting phrase are determined by one of the two words, which we call the *head*; the head *projects* the phrase. So, if we combine the verb *visit* with the noun *Chicago*, the resulting phrase *visit Chicago* has verbal and not nominal properties. It occurs where verbs occur and not where nouns occur: *I want to visit Chicago*, but not *the visit Chicago* nor *we discussed visit Chicago*. So the expression *visit Chicago* is a verb phrase (VP), where the V *visit* is the head projecting to VP. This can be represented as a labeled bracketing (2a) or as a tree diagram (2b). The verb is the head of the VP and the noun is the *complement*. (This is the novel, bottom-up approach to phrase structure of Chomsky [1995c: 244ff.].)

(2)　　a. $_{VP}[_V$visit $_N$Chicago]

　　　　b.　　VP

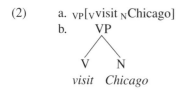

　　　　　　　V　　N
　　　　　　visit　Chicago

In general, two categories *merge* to form a new category. So an "inflectional" element like *will* might merge with the VP *visit Chicago*, to yield the more complex expression *will visit Chicago*, with the structure of (3). The inflectional *will* heads the new phrase and projects to a phrasal category IP. This means that *visit Chicago* is a unit (VP), which acts as the complement of *will*, but *will visit* is not a unit; that is, there is no single node which dominates *will visit* and nothing else in this example.

(3)　　　　$_{IP}[_I$will $_{VP}[$visit Chicago]]

The units defined by these trees are the items that the computational operations manipulate; they are the items that move and delete and that receive indices. Non-units are not available to these operations.

Let us return now to the problem of the reduced *is*. A computational operation attaches the reduced *is* to the preceding word as a "clitic." This makes *'s* as integral a part of that word as a plural-marking *-s*. Just as the plural *-s* is pronounced differently in *cats*, *dogs*, and *palaces*, similarly the reduced *is* in *Pat's here, Doug's sad and Alice's happy*. However, a silent, understood element also attaches clitic-like to a host to the left and the host must be a full phonological word. In an expression like *Kim is happier than Tim is*, there is no silent, understood element following the first *is*, which therefore may be reduced. The fact that there is a silent, understood element following the second *is* ("happy") means that it must be a full, phonological word and may not be reduced.[1] The same holds for *'ve*, *'re*, and the reduced forms of *am, will, would, shall,* and *should*. Poets make linguistic jokes from these principles: the Gershwins were famous for contraction jokes and in *Girl Crazy* (1930) a chorus begins *I'm bidin' my time /'Cause that's the kind of guy I'm.*

Is may be reduced in (4a), where there is no silent, understood element that needs a host, but not in *I wonder what the problem is in Washington*, which has the structure of (4b). Here *what* has moved from the position indicated, is understood in the position *x*, and reduction is not possible. So now we have an answer to the problem sketched at the outset: a reduced *is* is a clitic and may not host a silent, understood element, which also has clitic-like properties.

(4)　　a. The problem is in Washington.

　　　　b. I wonder what$_x$ the problem is x in Washington.

Clitics are little words which occur in many, perhaps all languages, and have the property of not being able to stand alone. Part of what a child growing a grammar needs to do is to determine the clitics in his or her linguistic environment, knowing in advance of any experience that these are small, unstressed items attached to an adjacent element. This predetermined knowledge (which I describe here informally) is contributed by the linguistic genotype and is what the child brings to language acquisition. So hearing a reduced form like *It's cold in here* and knowing that it is equivalent in some way to *It is cold in here* suffices to show the child that *'s* is a clitic; the child also knows in advance of any experience that understood elements require an appropriate phonological host, a full phonological word.

Under this approach, the child is faced with a chaotic environment and scans it, looking for clitics . . . among many other things, of course (Lightfoot 1999). This is the answer that we provide to our initial problem and it is an answer of the right shape. It makes general claims at the genetic level (clitics and their behavior are predefined; understood items are hosted by full, phonological words) and postulates that the child arrives at a plausible analysis on exposure to a few simple expressions like *It's cold in here*. The analysis that the child arrives at predicts no reduction for the underlined *is* in *Kim is happier than Tim is*, *I wonder what the problem is in Washington*, and countless other cases, and the child needs no correction in arriving at this system. The very fact that *'s* is a clitic, defined in advance of any experience, dictates that it may not occur in certain contexts, where it would host an understood item. It is for this reason that the generalization that *is* may be pronounced as *'s* breaks down at certain points and does not hold across the board, and the analysis must generalize to clitics in all languages.

Consider now the second problem, the reference of pronouns. They taught us in school that pronouns refer to a preceding noun, but the data of (1) show that that isn't always right. As we saw, in (1d) *him* may not refer to Jay; in (1b) *him* may refer to Jay but not to Jay's brother. The best account of this complex phenomenon seems to be to invoke a native principle which says that pronouns may *not* refer back to a local nominal element, where "local" means contained in the same clause (IP) or in the same noun phrase (NP).

In (5) I give the relevant structure for the corresponding sentences of (1). In (5b) the NP *Jay's brother* is local to *him* and so *him* may not refer back to that NP – we express this by indexing them differently. On the other hand, *Jay* is contained inside the NP and therefore is not available to *him* for indexing purposes, so those two nouns do not need to be indexed differently – they may refer to the same person and they may be coindexed.[2] Again we see the constituent structure illustrated earlier playing a central role in the way in which the indexing computations are carried out. In (5d) *Jay* is local to *him* and so the two elements may not be coindexed; they do not refer to the same person.

In (5c) *Jay* is not local to *he*, because the two items are not contained in the same clause: *Jay* and *he* may refer to the same person or to different people. In (5a) *his* is contained inside an NP and may not be coindexed with anything else within that NP; what happens outside the NP is not systematic; so *his* and *Jay* may corefer and do not need to be indexed differently.

(5)   a. $_{IP}$[Jay$_i$ hurt $_{NP}$[his$_{i/j}$ nose]]
        b. $_{IP}$[$_{NP}$[Jay$_i$'s brother]$_k$ hurt him$_{i/j}$]
        c. $_{IP}$[Jay$_i$ said $_{IP}$[he$_{i/j}$ hurt Ray]]
        d. $_{IP}$[Jay$_i$ hurt him$_j$]

We could have illustrated this principle equally well with data from French or from Dutch, because the principle applies quite generally to pronouns in all languages. If we assume a native principle, available to the child independently of any actual experience, language acquisition is greatly simplified. Now the child does not need to "learn" why the pronoun may refer to Jay in (5a) or (5b,c) but not in (5d). Rather, the child raised in an English-speaking setting has only to learn that *he*, *his*, *him* are pronouns, i.e. elements subject to our principle. This can be learned by exposure to a simple sentence like (1d/5d), uttered in a context where *him* refers to somebody other than Jay.

One way of thinking of the contribution of the linguistic genotype is to view it as providing invariant principles and option-points or "parameters" (Chomsky 1981a,b). There are invariant principles that understood elements cliticize on to a full phonological word and that pronouns are not locally coindexed. Meanwhile, there are options that direct objects may precede the verb in some grammars (German, Japanese) and may follow it in others (English, French), that some clitics attach to the right and some to the left. These are parameters of variation and the child sets these parameters one way or another on exposure to her particular linguistic experience. As a result, a grammar emerges in the child, part of the linguistic phenotype. The child has learned that *'s* is a clitic and that *her* is a pronoun; the genotype ensures that an understood item is not attached to *'s* and that *her* is never used in a context where it refers to a local nominal.

Here we have looked at two specific acquisition problems and considered what ingredients are needed for their solution. Now let us stand back and think about these matters more abstractly.

The acquisition problem: the poverty of the stimulus

The child acquires a finite system, a grammar, which generates structures that correspond more or less to utterances of various kinds. Some structural principle prevents forms like **Kim's happier than Tim's* from occurring in the speech of English speakers, as we have seen. Children are not exposed to pseudosentences like this and informed systematically that it is not said. Speakers come to know subconsciously that it cannot be said and this knowledge emerges somehow, even though it is not part of the input to the child's development. It is not enough to say that people do not utter such forms because they never hear them. This argument is insufficient because people say many things that they have not heard, as we have noted. Language is not learned simply by imitating or repeating what has been heard.

This poverty-of-stimulus problem, Plato's Problem, defines our approach to language acquisition. Over the last forty years, much of the linguistic literature has focused on areas where the best description cannot be derived directly from the data to which the child has access, or is underdetermined by those data. If the child's linguistic experience does not provide the basis for establishing a particular aspect of linguistic knowledge, there must be another source for that knowledge.

This is not to say that imitation plays no role, just that it does not provide a sufficient explanation. Nobody denies that the child must extract information from her environment; it is no revelation that there is "learning" in that technical sense. Our point is that there is more to language acquisition than this. Children react to evidence in accordance with specific principles. Learning of the kind that takes place in schools or in psychologists' laboratories involves generalization, association, induction, conditioning, hypothesis forming and testing, etc., but this does not play any significant role in explaining children's acquisition of language.

The problem demanding explanation is compounded by other factors. Despite variation in background and intelligence, people's mature linguistic capacity emerges in fairly uniform fashion, in just a few years, without much apparent effort, conscious thought, or difficulty; and it develops with only a narrow range of the logically possible "errors." Children do not test random hypotheses, gradually discarding those leading to "incorrect" results and provoking parental correction. In each language community the non-adult sentences formed by very young children seem to be few in number and quite uniform from one child to another, which falls well short of random hypotheses. Normal children attain a fairly rich system of linguistic knowledge by five or six years of age and a mature system by puberty.[3] In this regard, language is no different from, say, vision, except that vision is taken for granted and ordinary people give more conscious thought to language.

These, then, are the salient facts about language acquisition, or more properly, language growth. The child masters a rich system of knowledge without significant instruction and despite an impoverished stimulus; the process involves only a narrow range of non-adult forms and it takes place rapidly, even explosively between two and three years of age. The main question is how children acquire so much more than they experience.

A grammar represents what a speaker comes to know, subconsciously for the most part, about his or her native language. It represents the fully developed linguistic capacity, and is therefore part of an individual's phenotype. It is one expression of the potential defined by the genotype. Speakers know what an infinite number of sentences mean and the various ways in which they can be pronounced and rephrased. Most of this largely subconscious knowledge is represented in a person's grammar. The grammar may be used for various purposes, from everyday functions like expressing ideas, communicating, or listening to other people, to more contrived functions like writing elegant prose or lyric poetry, or compiling and solving crossword puzzles, or writing an article about Plato's problem.

I do not want to give the impression that all linguists adopt this Chomskyan view of things. People have studied language with quite different goals in mind, ranging from the highly specific (to describe Dutch in such a way that it can be learned easily by speakers of Indonesian), to more general goals, such as showing how a language may differ from one historical stage to another (comparing, say, Chaucerian and present-day English). However, the research paradigm sketched here (and in Chomsky 1959, 1965, 1975, etc.) has been the focus of much activity over the last forty years and it construes a grammar as a biological object, the language organ.

The analytical triplet

A grammar, under this view, is a psychological entity, part of the psychological state of somebody who knows a language. For any aspect of linguistic knowledge, three intimately related items are included in the account. First, there is a formal and explicit characterization of what a mature speaker knows; this is the *grammar*, which is part of that speaker's phenotype. Since the grammar is represented in the mind/brain, it must be a finite system, which can relate sound and meaning for an infinite number of sentences.

Second, also specified are the relevant principles and parameters common to the species and part of the initial state of the organism; these principles and parameters make up part of the *theory of grammar* or *Universal Grammar*, and they belong to the genotype.

The third item is the *trigger* experience, which varies from person to person and is embedded in an unorganized and haphazard set of utterances, of the kind that any child hears (the notion of a trigger is from ethologists' work on the emergence of behavioral patterns in young animals and, as in those domains, consists of abstract structures, "cues" in the sense of Lightfoot 1999). The universal theory of grammar and the variable trigger together form the basis for attaining a grammar; grammars are attained on the basis of a certain trigger and the genotype.

(6) is the explanatory schema, with general biological terminology in (6a) and the corresponding linguistic terms in (6b). The triggering experience causes the genotype to develop into a phenotype; exposure to a range of utterances from, say, English allows the UG capacity to develop into a particular mature grammar. One may think of the theory of grammar as making available a set of choices; the choices are taken in the light of the trigger experience or the "PLD," and a grammar emerges when the relevant options are resolved.

(6)   a. linguistic triggering experience (genotype → phenotype)
        b. Primary Linguistic Data (Universal Grammar → grammar)

Each of the items in the triplet – trigger, UG, and grammar – must meet various demands. The trigger or PLD consists only of the kinds of things that children routinely experience and includes only simple structures. The theory of grammar or UG is the one constant and holds universally such that any person's grammar can be attained on the basis of naturally available trigger experiences. The mature grammar defines an infinite number of expressions as well-formed, and for each of these it specifies at least the sound and the meaning. A description always involves these three items and they are closely related; changing a claim about one of the items usually involves changing claims about the other two.

The conditions of language acquisition make it plain that the process must be largely inner-directed . . . which means that all languages must be close to identical, largely fixed by the initial state. The major research effort since has been guided by this tension, pursuing the natural approach: to abstract from the welter of descriptive complexity certain general principles governing computation that would allow the rules of a particular language to be given in very simple forms, with restricted variety. (Chomsky 2000a: 122)

The grammar is one subcomponent of the mind, which interacts with other cognitive capacities or modules. Like the grammar, each of the other modules may develop in time and have distinct initial and mature states. So the visual system recognizes triangles, circles, and squares through the structure of the circuits that filter and recompose the retinal image (Hubel & Wiesel 1962). Certain nerve cells respond only to a straight line sloping downward from left to right, other nerve cells to lines sloped in different directions. The range of angles that an individual neuron can register is set by the genetic program, but experience is needed to fix the precise orientation specificity (Sperry 1968). In the mid 1960s David Hubel, Torsten Wiesel, and their colleagues devised an ingenious technique to identify how individual neurons in an animal's visual system react to specific patterns in the visual field (including horizontal and vertical lines, moving spots, and sharp angles). They found that particular nerve cells were set within a few hours of birth to react only to certain visual stimuli, and, furthermore, that if a nerve cell is not stimulated within a few hours, it becomes inert. In several experiments on kittens, it was shown that if a kitten spent its first few days in a deprived optical environment (a tall cylinder painted only with vertical stripes), only the neurons stimulated by that environment remained active; all other optical neurons became inactive because the relevant synapses degenerated, and the kitten never learned to see horizontal lines or moving spots in a normal way.

In this view, learning is a selective process: parameters are provided by the genetic equipment and relevant experience fixes those parameters. A certain mature cognitive structure emerges at the expense of other possible structures that are lost irretrievably as the inactive synapses degenerate. The view that there is a narrowing down of possible connections out of an overabundance of initially possible ones is now receiving more attention in the light of Hubel and Wiesel's Nobel Prize-winning success. For the moment, this seems to be a more likely means to fine tune the nervous system as "learning" takes place, as opposed to the earlier view that there is an *increase* in the connections among nerve cells.

Piattelli-Palmarini (1986, 1989) draws a helpful analogy with recent work on immunology. The commonsense view was that the immune system developed antibodies as a kind of learning process, triggered by exposure to bacteria; an organism would produce antibodies to counter the attack. However, Niels Kaj Jerne won his Nobel Prize for showing that this commonsense view is incorrect: antibody formation is a selective process, not instructive. Organisms contain immense numbers of antibodies; the antigen selects and amplifies specific antibodies that already exist. "Looking back into the history of biology, it appears that wherever a phenomenon resembles learning, an instructive theory was first proposed to account for the underlying mechanisms. In every case, this was later replaced by a selective theory" (Jerne 1967; see also 1985).

So human cognitive capacity is made up of identifiable properties that are genetically prescribed, each developing along one of various pre-established routes, depending on the particular experience encountered. These genetic prescriptions may be highly specialized, as Hubel and Wiesel showed for the visual system. They assign some order to our experience. Experience elicits or triggers certain kinds of specific responses but it does not determine the basic form of the response.

This kind of modularity is very different from the view that the cognitive faculties are homogeneous and undifferentiated, that the faculties develop through general problem-solving techniques. In physical domains, nobody would suggest that the visual system and the system governing the circulation of the blood are determined by the same genetic regulatory mechanisms.

Of course, the possibility should not be excluded that the linguistic principles postulated here may eventually turn out to be special instances of principles holding over domains other than language, but before that can be established much more must be known about what kinds of principles are needed for language acquisition to take place under normal conditions. Similarly for other aspects of cognitive development. Only then can meaningful analogies be detected. Meanwhile,

we are led to expect that each region of the central nervous system has its own special problems that require different solutions. In vision we are concerned with contours and directions and depth. With the auditory system, on the other hand, we can anticipate a galaxy of problems relating to temporal interactions of sounds of different frequencies, and it is difficult to imagine that the same neural apparatus deals with all of these phenomena . . . for the major aspects of the brain's operation no master solution is likely. (Hubel 1978: 28)

Real-time acquisition of grammars

In the domain of language, ingenious colleagues at the University of Maryland have shown that the distinctions discussed at the beginning of this chapter do not result from learning and that the hypothesized genetic constraints seem to be at work from the outset. The experimenters constructed situations in which children would be tempted to violate the relevant constraints. The fact that children conform to the hypothesized constraints, resisting the preferences they show in other contexts, is taken to be evidence that they have the constraints under investigation and they have them at the earliest stage that they might be manifested (Crain 1991).

Stephen Crain and Rosalind Thornton developed an elicitation task that encouraged children to ask questions like *Do you know what that's up there?* They hypothesized that children would generally show a preference for the reduced *'s* form whenever this was consistent with their grammars. This preference is revealed in a frequency count of legitimate forms, like *Do you know what that's doing up there?* Comparing the frequency of the reduced forms in these contexts with non-adult reduced forms would indicate whether or not children's grammars contained the hypothetical genetic constraint. If the genetic constraint is at work, there should be a significant difference in frequency; otherwise, not.

Thornton and Crain conducted an experiment to elicit a long-distance question. The target productions were evoked by the following protocols.

Protocols for rightward cliticization

(7)   Experimenter: Ask Ratty if he knows what that is doing up there.
        Child: Do you know what that's doing up there?
        Rat: It seems to be sleeping.

(8)   Experimenter: Ask Ratty if he knows what that is up there.
           Child: Do you know what that is up there?
           Rat: A monkey.

In (7) the child is invited to produce a sentence where *what* is understood as the object of *doing*: *do you know what$_x$ that is doing x up there?* Therefore, *is* may be cliticized because it is not needed to host the silent, understood item *x*; *x* is hosted by *doing*. However, in (8) the child produces a sentence where *what* is understood as the complement of *is*, i.e. between *is* and the following item: *do you know what$_x$ that is x up there?* (cf. *That is a bottle up there*). Here *is* is needed in its full form in order to host *x*; no adult would say **Do you know what that's up there?*, with the reduced form (cf. *That's a bottle up there*).

Thornton and Crain found that young children behaved just like adults, manifesting the hypothetical genetic constraint. The children tested ranged in age from 2 years, 11 months to 4 years, 5 months, with an average age of 3 years, 8 months. In the elicited questions there was not a single instance of the reduced form where it is impossible in adult speech. Children produced elaborate forms like those of (9), but never with the reduced form of *is*.

(9)   a. Do you know what that black thing on the flower is? (4 years, 3 months)
         b. Squeaky, what do think that is? (3 years, 11 months)
         c. Do you know what that is on the flower? (4 years, 5 months)
         d. Do you know what that is, Squeaky? (3 years, 2 months)

There is, of course, much more to be said about grammars and their acquisition, and there is an enormous technical literature (Crain & Thornton 1998). Meanwhile, we have an approach to the riot of differences that we find in the languages of the world and even within languages. As children, our linguistic experience varies tremendously; no two children experience the same set of sentences, let alone the same pronunciations. Nonetheless, the approach we have sketched enables us to understand the universality of our development, why we categorize the linguistic world so similarly and can talk to each other despite variation in childhood experience.

The organ

So the human capacity for natural language results from – and is made possible by – a biologically determined organ specific both to this domain and to our species. Efforts to teach human languages to individuals of other species, even those closest to us, have uniformly failed. While a certain capacity for arbitrary symbolic reference can be elicited in some higher apes (Premack 1980, 1990; Premack & Woodruff 1978) and perhaps even in other animals, human-type syntactic systems are well beyond the capacity of non-humans . . . just as humans, even with intensive training, are incapable of free flight.

The functional properties of our language capacity develop along a regular maturational path, such that it seems more appropriate to see our linguistic knowledge as "growing" rather than being "learned." As with the visual system, much of the detailed structure we find is "wired in," though triggering experience is necessary to set the system in operation and to determine some of its specific properties. The deep similarity among the world's languages supports the notion that they are the product of a common human faculty. The manual languages which develop in Deaf communities independently of one another or of the language of the surrounding hearing community share in these fundamental properties. The profound structural similarities between signed and spoken languages, including not only the basic principles of organization but the specific path of their development, the brain regions associated with their control, and other factors, are neither the result of shared history nor shared properties of gestural and articulatory/acoustic/auditory modalities, but rather they derive from shared biology (Newport 1999; Supalla 1990).

The development of structurally deficient pidgins into the essentially normal linguistic systems found in creoles supports the richness of the genotypic system involved in linguistic development. Pidgins change significantly as they become creoles and this is an automatic result of transmission through the natural language acquisition process in new generations of children (Bickerton 1999; DeGraff 1999; Lefebvre 1998). Less dramatic linguistic changes from one generation to another within the history of, say, English can also be understood sometimes through ideas of the linguistic genotype. Certain aspects of language change take place in fits and starts and that characteristic bumpiness of change can be understood as a matter of parameters being reset at certain critical points in linguistic history (Lightfoot 1999).

The language faculty has properties typical of a bodily organ, a specialized structure destined to carry out a particular function. Some organs, like the blood and the skin, interact with the rest of the body across a widespread, complex interface, and all organs are integrated into a complex whole. Often the limits to an organ are unclear, and anatomists do not worry about whether the hand is an organ or one of its fingers. It is clear that the body is not made up of cream cheese, and the same seems to be true of the brain.

The language organ is not to be interpreted as having an anatomical localization comparable to that of the kidney, at least not at this stage of knowledge. Our understanding of the localization of cognitive function in brain tissue is much too fragmentary and rudimentary to support a claim along those lines. Certain cortical and subcortical areas can be shown to subserve functions essential to language, in the sense that lesions in these areas disrupt language functioning (sometimes in remarkably specific ways), but an inference from this evidence to a claim that "language is located in Broca's (and/or Wernicke's) area" is unwarranted. Even the claim that language functions are located in the left cortical hemisphere seems to be an oversimplification (Kosslyn et al. 1999). At this stage, linguistic capacity is better understood in functional rather than anatomical terms, along the lines that I have indicated. Even if it were to emerge that there is no clear distinction between language-related and non-language-related brain tissue, it would still be useful to treat the language capacity as a discrete human biological system in functional terms.

The domain-specificity of the language faculty is supported by the many dissociations that have been observed between control of language structure and other cognitive functions. If a system operates independently of other systems, it is a candidate for modular status. So with the senses, one can be deaf without being blind, and vice versa, which supports the claim that hearing and sight are products of distinct systems. Neil Smith (2003) provides an excellent discussion of this point. He discusses a linguistic savant, Christopher. Christopher's hand–eye coordination is severely impaired and his psychological profile shows "moderate to severe disability in performance tasks, but results close to normal in verbal tasks." Despite low general intelligence, he has an astonishing capacity to pick up languages; see also Smith & Tsimpli (1995). Some kinds of aphasia show the reverse, and likewise Specific Language Impairment (SLI; for an overview, see Joanisse & Seidenberg 1998). SLI children are cognitively normal but fail to develop age-appropriate linguistic capacities (Bishop 1997). Researchers have postulated a range of grammatical deficits (Clahsen et al. 1997; Gopnik 1997; van der Lely 1996) and Levy & Kavé (1999) offer a useful overview.[4]

Smith points to other dissociations:

Just as intelligence and language are dissociable, so also is it possible to separate linguistic ability and Theory of Mind, with autistic subjects lacking in the latter but (potentially, especially in the case of Asperger's Syndrome [Frith 1991]) language being retained within normal limits. Some Down Syndrome children provide a contrary scenario, with their Theory of Mind being intact, but their linguistic ability moderately to severely degraded. (2003)

Similarly we find "submodular" dissociations within the language organ, suggesting that grammars have their own internal modules. Smith points to dissociations between the lexicon and the computational system. Christopher's talent for learning second languages "is restricted largely to mastery of the morphology and the lexicon, whilst his syntactic ability rapidly peaks and then stagnates . . . [A] reverse dissociation [is] found in the case of children with Spinal Muscular Atrophy, who seem to develop a proficient syntactic rule system but have correspondingly greater difficulty with lexical development (see Sieratzki & Woll 2002)" (Smith 2003). Edwards & Bastiaanse (1998) address this issue for some aphasic speakers, seeking to distinguish deficits in the computational system from deficits in the mental lexicon.

We also know that focal brain lesions can result in quite specific language impairments in the presence of normal cognitive abilities, and vice versa. Friedmann & Grodzinsky (1997) argue that agrammatic aphasics may lack certain functional categories. Ingham (1998) describes a young child in similar terms, arguing that she lacked one particular functional category.

This modular view runs contrary to a long tradition, often associated with Jean Piaget, which claims that language is dependent on prior cognitive capacities and is not autonomous and modular (Piaget & Inhelder 1968; Piattelli-Palmarini 1980 for critical discussion). This claim is undermined by the kinds of dissociations that have been observed. Bellugi et al. (1993) have shown, for another example, that Williams Syndrome children consistently fail to pass seriation and conservation tests but nonetheless use syntactic constructions whose acquisition is supposedly dependent on those cognitive capacities.

Conclusion

Recent theoretical developments have brought an explosive growth in what we know about human languages. Linguists can now formulate interesting hypotheses, account for broad ranges of facts in many languages with elegant abstract principles. We understand certain aspects of language acquisition in young children and can model some aspects of speech comprehension.

Work on human grammars has paralleled work on the visual system and has reached similar conclusions, particularly with regard to the existence of highly specific computational mechanisms. In fact, language and vision are the areas of cognition that we know most about. Much remains to be done, but we can show how children attain certain elements of their language organs by exposure to only an unorganized and haphazard set of simple utterances; for these elements we have a theory which meets basic requirements and we have, at some level, a solution to aspects of Plato's Problem. Eventually, the growth of language in a child will be viewed as similar to the growth of hair: just as hair emerges with a certain level of light, air, and protein, so, too, a biologically regulated language organ necessarily emerges under exposure to a random speech community.

From the perspective sketched here, our focus is on internal, individual grammars ("I-language" in the terminology of Chomsky 1986), not on the properties of a particular language or even of general properties of many or all languages. A language under this view is an epiphenomenon, a derivative concept, the output of certain people's grammars (perhaps modified by other mental processes). A grammar is of clearer status: the finite system that characterizes an individual's linguistic capacity and is represented in the individual's mind/brain. No doubt the grammars of two individuals whom we regard as speakers of the same language will have much in common, but there is no reason to worry about defining "much in common," about specifying when the outputs of two grammars constitute one language. Just as it is unimportant for most work in molecular biology whether two creatures are members of the same species (as emphasized, for example by Monod [1972: ch. 2] and by Dawkins [1976]), so too the notion of a language is not likely to have much importance within this biological perspective. Of course, there is more to the study of language than the biological perspective provides and other lenses focus differently on different phenomena.

3   Grammar, levels, and biology

Howard Lasnik

Introduction

Language is an immensely rich phenomenon, presenting vast challenges for the linguist, the scientist of this phenomenon. Among the most central, and most difficult, questions are ones concerning the nature of the capacity we all have to speak a language. Just what is this capacity, and how does it arise in the individual? We thus have (among many others) the two following related questions:

– What is the correct characterization of someone who "knows a language" (in general terms, who has command of a systematic connection between sound and meaning)?
– How does that systematic connection arise in the individual?

For the first of these questions, the linguist hopes to account, in an explicit way, for the speaker's ability to put together and understand sentences, including ones new to the speaker (and often new to *all* speakers), and for the speaker's ability to judge potential sentences as "acceptable" (*John left*) or "unacceptable" (*Left John*). For the second question, a particularly difficult one given how complex the capacity seems to be and how quickly it is acquired, the linguist seeks to discover what aspects of the capacity are determined by the child's experience, and how this determination ("language learning") takes place. For a half century, Noam Chomsky has been developing a theory of language that deals with these two questions, by positing explicit formulations of human language capacity in terms of a productive "computational" system, most of whose properties are present in advance of experience, "wired in" in the structure of the human brain. Thus, Chomsky conceives of his enterprise as part of psychology, ultimately biology.

From Noam Chomsky's earliest theories of language to his most recent, simplicity has been a guiding concern, pervading all of his analyses. Throughout, this drive towards simplicity has had two major motivations. First, there is the standard, virtually universal, gamble that scientists make: that the world, and the portion of it they are investigating, is simple. Second, in the case of a cognitive system like language, the assumption of simplicity at least helps provide the basis for answering the question of how the part of the system that must be acquired is acquired.

Chomsky (1965) proposes criteria of adequacy for theories of language that relate to how successfully these two questions are answered. "Descriptive adequacy" is the criterion for hypothesized answers to the first question ("grammars"), as explicated in the following passage:

A grammar can be regarded as a theory of a language; it is *descriptively adequate* to the extent that it correctly describes the intrinsic competence of the idealized native speaker. The structural descriptions assigned to sentences by the grammar, the distinctions that it makes between well-formed and deviant, and so on, must, for descriptive adequacy, correspond to the linguistic intuition of the native speaker (whether or not he may be immediately aware of this) in a substantial and significant class of crucial cases. (1965: 24)

The second question concerns "explanatory adequacy":

To the extent that a linguistic theory succeeds in selecting a descriptively adequate grammar on the basis of primary linguistic data [the information available to the child in the process of language acquisition HL], we can say that it meets the condition of *explanatory adequacy*. (1965: 25)

The learner's task is seen as choosing the correct grammar from all the (biologically) possible ones. This means that the linguist's model of the component of the human mind concerned with language acquisition (the "language acquisition device") must show how the correct grammar is selected from among the possible ones.

Generative grammar as a theory of language

Chomsky called his approach "generative grammar." By the term "generative," borrowed from mathematics, he meant simply that he intended to formulate explicit answers to the questions outlined above.[1] The particular explicit answer Chomsky provided was in terms of the mathematical formalism of set theory. Any remotely adequate theory will have to account for the fact that there is no limit on the number of sentences in any human language. Below, we will consider two attempts to deal with this property.

Already in his first detailed piece of linguistic analysis, Chomsky (1951) was explicitly concerned with descriptive adequacy, even though not under that term:

A grammar of a language must . . . correctly describe the "structure" of the language (i.e., it must isolate the linguistic units, and, in particular, must distinguish and characterize just those utterances which are considered "grammatical" or "possible" by the informant . . . (1951: 1)

And explanatory adequacy (though again, not under that term) is fundamental in Chomsky's magnum opus, *The Logical Structure of Linguistic Theory* (*LSLT*, 1955):

We are antecedently interested in developing a theory that will shed some light on such facts as the following:

1 A speaker of a language has observed a certain limited set of utterances in his language. On the basis of this finite linguistic experience he can produce an indefinite number of new utterances which are immediately acceptable to the speech community. He can also distinguish a certain set of "grammatical" utterances, among utterances that he has never heard and might never produce. He thus projects his past linguistic experience to include certain new [sentences] while excluding others. (1955: 61)

That is, based on finite, and quite limited, input, the child creates a productive system that goes far, indefinitely far, beyond that data.

Explanatory adequacy in Chomsky's sense concerns language acquisition. Theories that seek to attain explanatory adequacy must posit some innate structure in the mind. This is surely indisputable; while a human being can learn language, a rock, or a gerbil, cannot. The research question, ultimately a question of biology, concerns just what this innate structure is. Chomsky (1965) poses the issue this way:

To learn a language . . . the child must have a method for devising an appropriate grammar, given primary linguistic data. As a precondition for language learning, he must possess, first, a linguistic theory that specifies the form of the grammar of a possible human language, and, second, a strategy for selecting a grammar of the appropriate form that is compatible with the primary linguistic data. As a long-range task for general linguistics, we might set the problem of developing an account of this innate linguistic theory that provides the basis for language learning. (1965: 25)

This task became more and more central in Chomskyan work of the 1970s, 1980s, and 1990s.

On first examination, human languages appear to be almost overwhelmingly complex systems, and the problems, for the linguist, of successfully analyzing them, and for the learner, of correctly acquiring them, virtually intractable. But if the system is broken down into smaller parts, the problem might likewise be decomposed into manageable components. In fact, on this divide and conquer ("modular") approach, by the 1980s, languages began to seem much simpler, as I will discuss later. To illustrate modularity with a few simple examples, it is uncontroversial that an utterance is made up of sounds (or gestures more generally when we include signed languages). However, while the acoustic signal itself is continuous, it turns out to be crucial to analyze it in terms of discrete elements, "phones," in order to capture basic regularities. Further, analysis into phones does not suffice for linguistic description. *An aim* and *a name* are phonetically indistinguishable, but are quite different linguistic events. Analysis of the sequence of phones into words is thus necessary. But even analysis into a sequence of words does not, in general, capture all the salient properties of an utterance in a human language. Consider the following famous example, first discussed by Chomsky in the 1950s:

(1)   Flying planes can be dangerous.

A moment's reflection reveals that this one string of words is two different sentences, a phenomenon Chomsky called "constructional homonymity" and that is now generally called "structural ambiguity." The two sentences combined in (1) have the following paraphrases:

(2)   They (the objects) can be dangerous.

(3)   It (the activity) can be dangerous.

Structure, the categorization and grouping of the words, is necessary if we are to provide an adequate description of such an example as (1). A similar example is given in (4):

(4)   Mary saw the man with binoculars.

The seeing is with binoculars, or the man has binoculars. The required characterizations of a sentence in all these different terms (including phones, words, phrase structure) are at the heart of Chomsky's theory of *levels*:

> A language is an enormously complex system. Linguistic theory attempts to reduce this immense complexity to manageable proportions by the construction of a system of *linguistic levels*, each of which makes a certain descriptive apparatus available for the characterization of linguistic structure. A grammar reconstructs the total complexity of a language stepwise, separating out the contributions of each linguistic level. (1955: 63)

Chomsky sometimes referred to these levels as "levels of representation," a name that became standard, so I will use it here. But it should be pointed out that the name can be misleading, since its use inevitably leads to confusion with the standard philosophical notion "representation" which concerns a relation between linguistic expressions and portions of the world. Chomsky's levels of representation are completely language internal. Perhaps a more accurate term might have been "levels of structure."

Levels of representation in a theory of language

Levels of representation fit into the theory in the following way:

> We define, in general linguistic theory, a system of levels of representation. A level of representation consists of elementary units (primes), an operation of concatenation by which strings of primes can be constructed, and various relations defined on primes, strings of primes, and sets and sequences of these strings. Among the abstract objects constructed on the level **L** are **L**-markers that are associated with sentences. The

L-marker of a sentence *S* is the representation of *S* on the level **L**. A grammar for a language, then, will characterize the set of **L**-markers for each level **L** and will determine the assignment of **L**-markers to sentences. (1955: 5–6)

Phones are the primes at one level, morphemes at another, words at yet another, and so on.

The child learning a language is assumed to bring knowledge of the levels to bear on the task of learning. That is, the child must learn properties of the language at each level, but knows the levels in advance, hence, knows what to look for. The levels are part of "Universal Grammar," a wired-in part of the language acquisition device that constitutes part of a human being's genetic endowment. Of course, the *linguist* does not know in advance of research what the levels are. Determining them is a scientific question, one of biological psychology. Chomsky has devoted considerable attention to determining just what the levels of representation are in the human language faculty. In *LSLT*, the levels were considered to be phonetics, phonemics, word, syntactic category, morphemics, morphophonemics, phrase structure, transformations. Each was motivated by at least an informal argument. The "interface" level, phonetics, was justified by an argument from simplicity, a recurrent theme in Chomsky's work from the 1950s to the present: the characterization of the levels is simplified if we posit a "lowest" level of phonetics **Pn**, whose primes are phonetic symbols, which ultimately relate to the acoustic and articulatory properties of the sounds of human language.

Although *LSLT* was concerned most centrally with syntax, Chomsky formulates a complete theory of grammar from sound "upwards." And, in fact, his contributions to phonology (the component of language closest to sound) were arguably just as influential in the 1950s and 1960s as his contributions to syntax. In *LSLT*, he formulated a model that incorporates phonology in a specific way. In particular, he proposed that the next "higher" level above phonetics is phonemic representation, described as follows:

The first really significant linguistic level is the level **Pm** of phonemes. The essence of phonemic theory is contained in the definition of the mapping ϕ^{Pm} that carries strings of phonemes into strings of phones. (1955: 159)

There are classic arguments for this level, which is related to sound but is more abstract than the level of phonetics. One class of arguments involves situations where two clearly distinct phones must be treated as if they were the same for many purposes. Consider, for example, the regular English noun plural ending. It is sometimes realized as [z], as in the word *sons*. But it is also realized as [s], as in *books*. Nonetheless, the ending is felt as the same item. Further, there would be a tremendous loss of generality if the two forms were kept completely distinct, since their occurrence is completely predictable. When the noun ends with a sound with the phonetic property "voiced," the plural ending is realized as [z] (itself a voiced sound). When the noun ends with a voiceless sound, the plural ending is [s], the voiceless variant of [z]. Thus, the generalization cannot be stated in **Pm** or in **Pn**, but rather in the mapping from **Pm** to **Pn**. In **Pm**, the plural ending is uniform, even though **Pn** makes a distinction. This type of mapping, "assimilation" (voicing assimilation in this instance), is extremely common in the languages of the world.

The converse situation also arises, where one phone clearly has two distinct sources. A classic example, frequently discussed by Chomsky, concerns the pair of words *writer* and *rider* (see also Dresher, this volume). In most English dialects, the central consonant in both is the same, an alveolar flap usually symbolized as [D]. However, the former word obviously relates to *write*, with a final [t], while the latter relates to *ride*, with a final [d]. Phonemically, we have /t/ and /d/; the distinction is neutralized in the mapping from **Pm** to **Pn**.

One very important debate in the early days of generative grammar was over a question of levels: is there a level of representation intermediate between phonetics and phonemics? Chomsky, following and extending the argument of Halle (1959), concluded that there is not. Chomsky (1964) observed that much work in structuralist phonology maintained, either implicitly or explicitly, a level of representation that he labeled "taxonomic phonemics." This level is required to meet four conditions, one of which Chomsky calls "biuniqueness." Biuniqueness demands a one-to-one correspondence between phonemes and phones, thus, in effect, demanding a high degree of what might be called "concreteness in phonological representations." The substance of Halle's argument is that one seemingly simple and general phonological process of Russian would have to be split into two separate phonological rules if the intermediate level demanding biuniqueness is postulated. As Chomsky observes (1964: 90), "the only effect of assuming that there is a taxonomic phonemic level is to make it impossible to state the generalization." Chomsky points out similar facts from other languages as well, concluding (1964: 91) that "the effect of the biuniqueness condition is to complicate the grammar, that is to prevent it from achieving descriptive adequacy." As noted above, an appeal to simplicity was and is a significant factor in Chomsky's arguments for particular theories and analyses. And if a certain degree of abstractness is the cost of simplicity, Chomsky has always been immediately willing to accept that contract.

Arguments from simplicity can cut both ways. The preceding argument concluded that a particular level should *not* be posited. But, as noted above, in *LSLT* Chomsky also presented simplicity arguments *for* particular levels. One such case, not yet discussed, involves morphophonemic representation. In the case of taxonomic phonemics, the argument was that we would need to posit extra rules if we assumed such a level. For morphophonemics, the argument is virtually the reverse:

We may introduce a level of representation solely because it enables us to replace a great many rules by a single rule about a single element of this new level. Morphophonemic representation provides a good example of this. Suppose that English sentences are represented in terms of morphemes and phonemes. Instead of associating with each morpheme a set of phoneme strings, . . . along with the conditions dictating the occurrence of each, it is often possible to rewrite each morpheme as a string of invented elements called morphophonemes in such a way that a relatively small number of statements about the phonemic forms that these assume in various contexts will suffice to determine many conversions of morphemes into phonemic representation. (1955: 114–15)

Chomsky's illustration of this point centers on a semi-regular pluralization process in English, by which a stem-final [f] in the singular alternates with [v] in the plural (as in *wife–wives*). Thus, we might describe these facts with rules such as the following (where $\hat{\ }$ is the symbol for concatenation and *pl* is the plural morpheme):

(5)   a. *wife^pl* → */wayv/^pl* (ultimately, "wives")
       b. *wife^X* → */wayf/^X*   (where $X \neq pl$)

(6)   a. *leaf^pl* → */liyv/^pl*   (ultimately, "leaves")
       b. *leaf^X* → */liyf/^X*   (where $X \neq pl$)
       etc.

Chomsky argues that a much simpler description can be obtained in terms of morphophonemes, in particular, the morphophoneme *F*. The morphophonemic representations of *wife* and *leaf* are as in (7) and (8) respectively.[2]

(7) $w\hat{\ }a\hat{\ }y\hat{\ }F$

(8) $l\hat{\ }i\hat{\ }y\hat{\ }F$

The morphophonemes can be converted into phonemes by such rules as:

(9)   a. $F\hat{\ }pl \rightarrow /v/\hat{\ }pl$

(10)   b. $F\hat{\ }X \rightarrow /f/\hat{\ }pl$

The simplification is that the relationship is stated once and for all, rather than for each individual word that partakes in the alternation.[3]

Levels of representation in syntax

Chomsky maintains that this line of reasoning extends to syntax:

The same kind of argument can be used to motivate and justify the introduction of a level of phrase structure. If there were no intervening representations between *Sentence* and words, the grammar would have to contain a vast (in fact, infinite) number of conversions of the form *Sentence* → *X*, where *X* is a permissible string of words. However, we find that it is possible to classify strings of words into phrases in such a way that sentence structure can be stated in terms of phrase strings, and phrase structure in terms of word strings, in a rather simple way. (1955: 115–16)

The level **P** of phrase structure differs from the "lower" (sound-related) levels considered thus far in significant respects. First, markers at those lower levels are simply strings of symbols. **P**-markers, on the other hand, must be **sets** of strings; the appropriate set of strings, as will be seen immediately below, provides the necessary structural information about a sentence. The phrase structure of a given sentence clearly cannot be adequately represented by just a string of phones or phonemes. But just as clearly, a string of words or morphemes is similarly insufficient, as already discussed above in connection with (1). Now consider even a very simple sentence such as (11).

(11)   The woman studied the book.

All the processes that depend on the structure of a sentence (semantic, phono-logical, and syntactic processes) demand to know more than that (11) is a string of the five words *The*, *woman*, *studied*, *the*, and *book*, in that order; or that it is a string of the six morphemes – *the*, *woman*, *study*, *past tense*, *the*, and *book*, in that order. In addition, it is necessary to know that *The woman* comprises a unit of structure, a "constituent'; that *the book* also is a constituent, and one of the same type as *The woman* (call it NP [Noun Phrase]); that *studied the book* is a constituent, and of a different type (call it VP [Verb Phrase]); that the two occurrences of *the* are of the same type (call it Determiner); that *woman* and *book* are of the same type (Noun); that *studied* is of a different type (Verb); that the entire sequence is a Sentence. The required set of strings thus includes those in (12).

(12)   The⌢woman⌢studied⌢the⌢book
         Sentence
         NP⌢VP
         NP⌢V⌢NP
         Det⌢N⌢V⌢Det⌢N
         etc.

This set of strings constitutes the **P**-marker of sentence (11), given a particu-lar (oversimplified) *phrase structure grammar*, one specifying that a Sentence consists of an NP followed by a VP; a VP consists of a V followed by an NP; etc. In now standard notation:

(13)   Sentence → NP VP
         VP → V NP
         NP → Det N
         Det → the
         N → *woman*, *book*, etc.
         V → *studied*, etc.

That is, VP is rewritten as (or consists of) V followed by NP, etc. A symbol that cannot be rewritten is a *terminal symbol*. The string consisting solely of terminal symbols is the *terminal string*. **P**-markers are perspicuously represented as constituent structure "trees" as in (14).

(14)

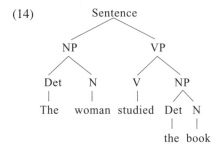

A **P**-marker must indicate what substrings of the terminal string are constituents, and for the ones that are, what the "labels" of the constituents are. In *LSLT*, the fundamental predicate characterizing these relations is the *is a* relation. In the (simplified) example above, the following *is a* relations hold:

(15)   *The* is a Det
        woman is an N
        studied is a V
        the is a Det
        book is an N
        The woman is an NP
        the book is an NP
        studied the book is a VP
        The woman studied the book is a Sentence

One of the most fundamental properties of human language is its infinitude: there is no upper bound on the length of sentences, hence no upper bound on the number of sentences. In all human languages, ever longer sentences can be constructed by embedding one sentence inside another, as illustrated in (16).[4]

(16)   a. Mary reads books.
        b. John thinks Mary reads books.
        c. Susan said John thinks Mary reads books.
        etc.

Chomsky has proposed two major distinct ways of instantiating this embedding property. The first, formalized in *LSLT*, merged one complete phrase structure of the sort in (14) into another. This kind of operation, combining two (or more) P-markers into a new more complex "derived" P-marker, is called a "generalized transformation." Metaphorically, a generalized transformation grafts one tree onto another. As I will discuss below, Chomsky has returned to this mechanism in his recent "minimalist" work. Alongside generalized transformations, there are "singular transformations," which apply to P-markers and derived P-markers. They apply to one tree.

Transformations as the connection between underlying and superficial syntactic structure

Chomsky showed how singular transformations can explain the relatedness between, for example, statements and corresponding questions:

(17)   a. Susan will solve the problem. $\Rightarrow$ Will Susan solve the problem?
        b. John is visiting Rome. $\Rightarrow$ Is John visiting Rome?

The members of each pair come from the same initial P-marker, with singulary transformations producing the divergent surface shapes. One of the great triumphs of the analysis of such pairs in *LSLT* is that it was able to use the same singular transformation for the interrogative sentences in (17) and the superficially very different one in (18).

(18)   Susan solved the problem. $\Rightarrow$ Did Susan solve the problem?

This was a significant achievement since the relations are felt by native speakers to be parallel, an otherwise mysterious fact. Chomsky also showed how in numerous situations, even properties of individual sentences cannot be adequately characterized without recourse to the descriptive power of singulary transformations. There was, thus, considerable motivation for this new device relating more abstract "underlying" structures to more superficial surface representations. In fact, one of the major conceptual innovations in the entire theory is the proposal that a sentence has not just one structure, closely related to the way it is pronounced, but an additional abstract structure (potentially very different from the superficial one), and intermediate structures between these two. This is fundamental to all the analyses in the Chomskyan system.

The organization of the syntactic portion of the grammar is as follows: application of the phrase structure rules creates a P-marker, or, in the case of a complex sentence, a set of P-markers. Then successive application of transformations (singularly and generalized) creates successive phrase structure representations ("derived P-markers"), culminating in a final surface representation. The syntactic levels in this theory are that of phrase structure and that of transformations, the latter giving a "history" of the transformational *derivation* (the successive transformational steps creating and affecting the structure). The representations at these levels are the P-marker and the T-marker respectively. The final derived P-marker is the input to phonological interpretation, and the T-marker is the input to semantic interpretation.[5]

Levels in Chomsky's "standard theory"

Chomsky (1965), henceforth *Aspects*, presented a revised conception of the grammar, based on an alternative way of constructing complex sentences, one that Chomsky argued was an advance in terms of simplicity and explanatory adequacy over the one in *LSLT*. In the *LSLT* framework, the phrase structure rules produce simple monoclausal structures, which can then be merged together by generalized transformations. Generalized transformations are thus the recursive component of the grammar, the one responsible for the infinitude of language. The alternative is that the phrase structure rule component itself has a recursive character. Consider again the complex sentences in (16), repeated here:

(19)　　a. Mary reads books.
　　　　b. John thinks Mary reads books.
　　　　c. Susan said John thinks Mary reads books.
　　　　etc.

By adding a recursive "loop" to the set of phrase structure rules in (13), we directly create the possibility of ever longer sentences. The rule in (20) provides this loop.

(20)　　VP $\Rightarrow$ V Sentence

By (13), a Sentence contains a VP; and by (20), a VP contains a Sentence. Thus, by repeated application, we can construct a sentence inside a sentence inside a sentence . . . (21) is the phrase structure "tree" for (19b) given the augmented phrase structure rules.

(21)

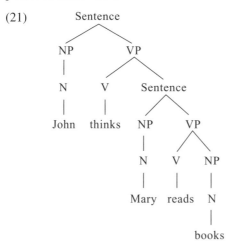

(19c) would be similar, but with one more level of embedding, resulting from one more application of (20).

Under this approach to sentence embedding, unlike that in *LSLT*, there is one unified structure underlying a sentence prior to the operation of any transformations. This structure is the result of application of the phrase structure rules and "lexical insertion transformations" which insert items from the lexicon into the skeletal structure. Chomsky argued in *Aspects* that this underlying structure, which he there named "deep structure," is the locus of important generalizations and constitutes a level in the sense discussed above. Chomsky's major arguments for this new level were that it resulted in a simpler overall theory, and at the same time it explained the absence of certain kinds of derivations that seemed not to occur (or at least seemed not to be needed in the description of sentences of human languages). Taking the second of these points first, Chomsky argued that while there is extensive ordering among singulary transformations (situations where a derivation produces an unacceptable sentence if two transformations are applied in reverse order), " there are no known cases of ordering among generalized transformation although such ordering is permitted by the theory of Transformation-markers" (1965: 133). Further, while there are many cases of singulary transformations that must apply to a constituent sentence before it is embedded, or that must apply to a "matrix" sentence after another sentence is embedded in it, "there are no really convincing cases of singulary transformations that must apply to a matrix sentence before a sentence transform is embedded in it . . ."

As for the first argument, Chomsky claimed that the theory of transformational grammar is simplified by this change, since the notions "generalized transformation" and "Transformation-marker" are eliminated entirely. The P-markers in the revised theory contain all of the information of those in the *LSLT* version, but they also indicate explicitly how the clauses are embedded in one another, that is, information that had been provided by the embedding transformations and T-markers.

This change in the theory of phrase structure, which has the effect of eliminating generalized transformations, also has consequences for the theory of singulary transformations. As indicated above, in the *Aspects* theory, as in *LSLT*, there is extensive ordering among singulary transformations. In both frameworks, the set of singulary transformations was seen as a linear sequence: an ordered list. Given the *Aspects* modification, this list of rules applies "cyclically," first operating on the most deeply embedded clause, then the next most deeply embedded, and so on, working "up the tree" until they apply on the highest clause, the entire generalized P-marker.[6] Thus, singulary transformations apply to constituent sentences "before" they are embedded, and to matrix sentences "after" embedding has taken place. "The ordering possibilities that are permitted by the theory of Transformation-markers but apparently never put to use are now excluded in principle" (1965: 135).

How syntax relates to semantics

An important question for any syntactic theory is how syntax relates to semantics: what the precise connection is between form and meaning. In *LSLT*, the T-marker contains all of the structural information relevant to semantic interpretation. Katz and Postal (1964) proposed a severe restriction on just how this structural information could be accessed. In particular, they postulated that the only contribution of transformations to semantic interpretation is that they interrelate P-markers. As Chomsky puts it, (generalized) transformations combine semantic interpretation of already interpreted P-markers in a fixed way. In the revised theory, which came to be called the "standard theory," the initial P-marker, now a "deep structure," then contains just the information relevant to semantic interpretation. To summarize the model:

> the syntactic component consists of a base that generates deep structures and a transformational part that maps them into surface structures. The deep structure of a sentence is submitted to the semantic component for semantic interpretation, and its surface structure enters the phonological component and undergoes phonetic interpretation. The final effect of a grammar, then, is to relate a semantic interpretation to a phonetic representation – that is, to state how a sentence is interpreted. (1965: 135–6)

To carry out this program, following Katz and Postal (1964), Chomsky proposed that the many seemingly "meaning-changing" optional transformations of *LSLT* be replaced by obligatory transformations triggered by a marker in the deep structure. To take one example, earlier I noted that in *LSLT*, simple questions and the corresponding statements are derived from the same initial P-marker. In the revision, those initial P-markers would be very similar but not identical. The former would contain a marker of interrogation that would both signal the difference in meaning and trigger the inversion that results in the auxiliary verb appearing at the front of the sentence.

At this point in the development of the theory, the model can be graphically represented as follows, with deep structure doing the semantic work formerly done by the T-marker:

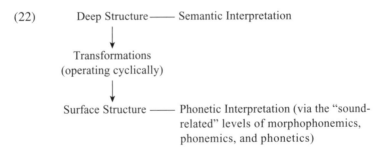

(22)   Deep Structure——— Semantic Interpretation
           ↓
           Transformations
           (operating cyclically)
           ↓
           Surface Structure ——— Phonetic Interpretation (via the "sound-
                                 related" levels of morphophonemics,
                                 phonemics, and phonetics)

There were already questions about deep structure as the sole locus of semantic interpretation. To take just one example, Chomsky (1957a) observed that in sentences with quantifiers, the derived structure has truth conditional consequences. (23a) may be true while (23b) is false, for instance if one person in the room knows only French and German, and another only Spanish and Italian.

(23)　　a.　Everyone in the room knows at least two languages.
　　　　　b.　At least two languages are known by everyone in the room.

In the theory of (1957a), this is not problematic, since semantic interpretation is based on the T-marker. However, in the *Aspects* framework, there is a problem, as Chomsky acknowledges. He speculates that the interpretive difference between (23a) and (23b) might follow from discourse properties, rather than grammatical ones. The problem came to loom larger and larger, leading to a theory, elaborated by Chomsky (1970), in which both deep structure and surface structure contribute to semantic interpretation. In this so-called "Extended Standard Theory" the contribution of deep structure concerns "grammatical relations" such as subject of and object of. The contribution of surface structure concerns virtually all other aspects of meaning, including scope, as in the examples mentioned just above, anaphora, focus, and presupposition.

Alongside these questions about deep structure as the sole locus of semantic interpretation, there were also challenges to its very existence. Postal (1972) argued that the best theory is the simplest, which, by his reasoning, included a uniform set of rules from semantic structure all the way to surface form, with no significant level (i.e. deep structure) in between.[7] And McCawley (1968) explicitly formulates an argument against deep structure on the model of Halle's argument against a level of taxonomic phonemics. McCawley's argument is based on the interpretation of sentences with *respectively*, such as (24).

(24)　　Those men love Mary and Alice respectively.

He argues that in a theory with deep structure, two rules, instead of one, will be needed to determine the meaning of such sentences.

Chomsky considers this argument, but rejects it, claiming that it rests on an equivocation about exactly what the relevant rule(s) would be on the theories in question. Chomsky does, however, accept McCawley's contention that it is necessary to provide some justification for the postulation of deep structure. But he observes that the same is true of surface structure or phonetic representation, or, in fact, any theoretical construct. How can such a justification be provided?

There is only one way to provide some justification for a concept that is defined in terms of some general theory, namely, to show that the theory provides revealing explanations for an interesting range of phenomena and that the concept in question plays a role in these explanations. (1970: 64)

As far as Chomsky was concerned, this burden had been met, especially by the *Aspects* analysis of the transformational ordering constraints discussed above.

Levels in the "Government–Binding" model

As already noted, the semantic role of deep structure was seriously diminished in the Extended Standard Theory. It was to be diminished even further. Recall that the semantic contribution of deep structure in EST is limited to determination of grammatical relations. In deep structure, grammatical relations are transparently represented, while in derived structure, they often seem not to be represented at all. Following Chomsky (1965), let us suppose that the "subject" grammatical relation is assigned to an NP immediately dominated by Sentence, and the object relation to an NP immediately dominated by VP. Consider again (19a), with the following approximate structure:

(25)

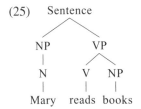

The NP *Mary* is configurationally determined as subject and the NP *books* is configurationally determined as object. But there are sentences in which the grammatical relations are parallel to these, but whose derived structures seemingly do not support these determinations. "Subject-raising" sentences are one instance, and interrogatives are another:

(26)   John seems to be a nice fellow. (cf. It seems that John is a nice fellow.)

(27)   a. What does Mary read?
        b. Who does John think reads books?

In these examples, arguments appear displaced from their basic positions, those responsible for their understood grammatical relations. For instance, in (27b), *Who* is the understood subject of *reads books* but in surface form it is in initial position of the entire complex sentence. Thus, the rules determining grammatical relations, a fundamental aspect of semantic interpretation, apparently need access to deep structure. However, a technical innovation in the early 1970s obviated this dependence on deep structure interpretation. On the basis of a variety of phenomena, Chomsky (1973a) argued that when an item moves, it leaves behind a "trace" marking the position from which it moved.[8] Given "trace theory," Chomsky (1975) suggests that surface structure can be the input for all semantic interpretation. Recall that the obstacle to such an approach was that movement operations seemed to destroy the configurations necessary for the determination of grammatical relations. But once traces are posited, this is no longer obviously so. Chomsky summarizes the situation as follows:

to understand the sentences we have been discussing we must surely . . . know the position in the initial phrase marker of the phrase that has been moved. Thus consider again [(28)], derived by NP-preposing from [(29)]:

(28)   John seems [$_s$ t to be a nice fellow]

(29)   _ seems [$_s$ John to be a nice fellow]

To understand the sentence [(28)] we must know that "John" is the subject of the embedded sentence. The initial phrase marker provides this information, but the surface structure (it appears) does not . . . In fact, it was precisely such considerations as these that motivated the principle of the standard theory that deep structures (our "initial phrase markers") determine semantic interpretation.

But notice that under the trace theory of movement rules, the motivation disappears. The position of the . . . trace in surface structure allows us to determine the grammatical relation of "John" in [(28)] as subject of the embedded sentence. Similarly, in the other cases . . . There is a great deal [of] evidence that surface-structure information contributes to the determination of meaning. Thus, it seems reasonable to postulate that *only* surface structures undergo semantic interpretation . . . (1975: 95–6)

Suppose we use the term "Logical Form" for the syntactic representation that interfaces with semantics. In the theory just outlined, surface structure is Logical Form (LF). However, in the late 1970s, arguments were put forward that transformational operations of the sort successively modifying deep structure, ultimately creating surface structure, also apply to surface structure, creating an LF that is distinct from surface structure. May (1977) argued extensively for an operation moving quantifiers from their surface positions to positions more transparently representing their scope, with the traces of the moved quantifiers ultimately interpreted as variables bound by those quantifiers. May showed how sentences with scope ambiguities receive multiple LF representations under such an approach. For example, a sentence like (30) has the two LF representations in (31), depending on the order in which the two quantifiers are raised. Subscripts mark the association of quantifier with trace.

(30)   Some student solved every problem.

(31)   a. some student$_i$ [every problem$_j$ [t_i solved t_j]]
        b. every problem$_j$ [some student$_i$ [t_i solved t_j]]

(31a) represents the reading of (30) in which *some student* has wider scope than *every problem*, and (31b) represents the reading in which *every problem* has wider scope. Note that unlike the transformational operations mentioned earlier, applications of "Quantifier Raising" (QR) exhibit no phonological displacement. All the expressions in (30) are pronounced in their surface-structure position, on either reading. The model of grammar making this possible is schematized in (32), where deep structure is now "merely" the starting point of the syntactic derivation. It has been stripped of its previous direct role in semantic interpretation.

(32)

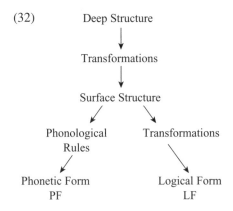

When a transformation operates between deep structure and surface structure, it will have an effect on the phonetic output, since surface structure feeds into PF. On the other hand, a transformational application between surface structure and LF will have no phonetic effect, since LF does not feed into PF. QR in (31) is an example of the latter type of "covert" transformational operation.

The overt movement process instantiated in (27) above, usually called WH-movement (since interrogative expressions in English often begin with the letters *WH*), was assumed to have a covert analogue as well. For instance, under the plausible assumption that overt WH-movement positions an interrogative operator in its natural position for interpretation (with the trace it leaves behind in the natural position for a variable bound by the operator), in sentences with multiple interrogatives, such as (33), at the level of LF all are in sentence-initial operator position, as illustrated in (34).

(33)   Where should we put what?

(34)   what$_i$ [where$_j$ [we should put t_i t_j]

(34) is then rather transparently interpreted as:

(35)   For which object x and which place y, we should put x at y.

Huang (1981/82, 1982) presented one of the most powerful arguments for the existence of covert WH-movement. Chomsky observed in the early 1960s that it is difficult to move an interrogative expression out of an embedded question (a question inside another sentence):

(36)   *Why$_i$ do you wonder [what$_j$ [John bought t_j t_i]]

If (36) were acceptable, it would mean "What is the reason such that you wonder what John bought for that reason?" Huang showed that in Chinese, where interrogative expressions do not seem to move, their interpretation apparently obeys the same constraints that the movement in a language like English obeys. So, in Chinese an example like (37) is possible but one like (38) is impossible on the relevant reading:

(37)   ni   renwei   [Lisi weisheme mai-le shu]
         you think   Lisi why   bought book
         "What is the reason such that you think Lisi bought a book for that reason?"

(38)   (*)ni   xiang-zhidao [Lisi weisheme mai-le sheme]
            you wonder   Lisi why   bought what
         "What is the reason such that you wonder what Lisi bought for that reason?"

Hence, this movement constraint seems to obtain even when there was not any "visible" movement. This argues that even though you cannot hear the "why" moving, it really is moving and that is why it is obeying movement constraints. But this movement is "covert," occurring in the mapping from surface structure to LF, hence not contributing to pronunciation.

The theory with the architecture in (32) was developed in great detail in Chomsky (1981a) and came to be known as the Government–Binding (GB) theory.[9] In this theory, deep structure, by now generally called "D-structure,"[10] has lost its significance as an interface with semantics. It is simply the level that begins the syntactic derivation. And surface structure, now called S-structure, is the "branch-point" in the derivation, leading, on one branch, towards PF, the phonetic interface, and on the other, towards LF, the semantic interface. However, it was acknowledged in Chomsky (1981a) that there are semantic phenomena, principally involving anaphoric relations, that seem to require crucial reference to surface structure. One such phenomenon concerns anaphoric connection between pronouns and full NPs. Consider the following pair:

(39)   John thinks he won.

(40)   He thinks John won.

In (39), *he* can be (though need not be) used to denote John: *John* and *he* can be "coreferential." But in (40), *He* cannot be used to denote John: *John* and *He* are necessarily "non-coreferential" in this instance. Coreference between two NPs is standardly represented by coindexing them (that is, by giving them the same numerical subscript). Thus, we have the grammatical (41) vs. the ungrammatical (42):

(41) $John_1$ thinks he_1 won.

(42) $^*He_1$ thinks $John_1$ won.

The descriptive generalization involves the structural relation "c(onstituent)-command," which is itself based on "inclusion." "Inclusion" is the relation in a given structure between, for example, S, on the one hand, and NP and VP, on the other. That is, S includes both NP and VP. Based on these notions, the structural relation c-command is defined as follows:

(43)   In a given structure, a category X c-commands another category
         Y if every category which includes X also includes Y.

In particular, one NP c-commands another if every category which includes the former NP also includes the latter NP. The condition proscribing coreference in (40) is stated in (45), based on definition (44).[11]

(44)   One NP binds another NP if the former c-commands the latter and
         the two NPs are coindexed (have the same index).

(45)   A pronoun may not bind a full NP.

Consider (39), in light of definition (44). If *John* and *he* are to be coreferential, they will have to be coindexed. Then *John* binds *he* in (41), since *John* both c-commands *he* and is coindexed with it. Note that this is allowed by (45), since the pronoun does not bind the full NP. If, on the other hand, the two NPs were reversed, as in (42), the pronoun binds the full NP. (45) thus accounts for the ungrammaticality of that example (on the specified interpretation).

What Chomsky (1981a) observed is that while *overt* movement can obviate potential violations of (45), corresponding hypothesized *covert* movement cannot. Consider the following example, in which the indicated coreference is blocked by (45):

(46) $^*He_1$ likes everyone that $John_1$ knows.

Many dialects of English have a process of "Topicalization" by which an NP can be moved to the front of the sentence. Applying this movement transformation to the direct object in (46) yields the following:

(47)   Everyone that John₁ knows, he₁ likes.

Significantly, coreference between *John* and *he* is now possible. So far, this is as expected, given the basic GB model, since the LF of (47) is presumably indistinguishable from its surface structure in relevant respects, and in that surface structure, shown in (48), *he* no longer c-commands *John* as it did in deep structure. This can be seen in the phrase structure tree for (47), where the fronted NP is assumed to be adjoined to the original S:

(48)

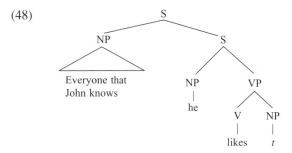

The problem is that the application of QR to (46) yields an LF indistinguishable from (48), the surface structure and LF of (47). Incorrectly, (46) is predicted to allow coreference, if LF is the sole input to semantic interpretation. In Chomsky's next development in his theory, the minimalist program, this problem becomes acute, as will be seen below.

Levels in a minimalist model

Given the diminishing role of deep and surface structure in the theory, Chomsky began to consider the possibility that neither is actually a level of representation. Chomsky (1993a) advances a "minimalist program" for linguistics, which carries still further the successive simplifications in the theory from the 1950s through the 1980s. He argues that if a language is to relate sound to meaning at all, it requires the "interface" levels of LF and PF, the former interfacing with the conceptual-intentional system of the mind, and the latter with the articulatory-perceptual system. Neither D-structure nor S-structure is conceptually necessary in this way.[12] This motivates a shift to a model that is reminiscent of Chomsky's original one in the 1950s, with structure building done by generalized transformations. The derivation begins with a "numeration," a set of lexical items selected from the lexicon. The lexical items are inserted "on-line" in the course of the syntactic derivation. The derivation proceeds "bottom-up" with the most deeply embedded structural unit created first, then combined with another lexical item to create a larger phrasal unit, and so on. Furthermore, singulary transformational operations are interspersed with these generalized transformational operations, again roughly as in the much earlier model. Recall, though, that Chomsky (1965) presented a powerful argument against such a model, that it allowed derivations that never actually occur in human languages. The model with recursion in the base excluded those unwanted derivations. However, on closer inspection, it was not actually elimination of generalized transformations that had this limiting effect. Rather, it was the stipulation that transformations operate strictly cyclically, starting on the most deeply embedded clause and proceeding monotonically up the tree. Chomsky (1993a) observed that a condition with the same effect can be imposed on the operation of generalized transformations and their interaction with singulary transformations. This condition, often called the "extension condition," simply requires that a transformational operation "extends" the tree upwards. This guarantees the same sort of monotonic derivations as those permitted by Chomsky (1965). The one remaining *Aspects* argument against generalized transformations can also be straightforwardly addressed. Chomsky had argued that eliminating generalized transformations yields a simplified theory, with one class of complex operations jettisoned in favor of an expanded role for a component that was independently necessary, the phrase structure rule component. Further, that simplification was a substantial step towards answering the fundamental question of how the child selects the correct grammar from a seemingly bewildering array of choices. Eliminating one large class of transformations, generalized transformations, was a step towards addressing this puzzle. This was a very good argument. But since then, numerous discoveries and analyses have indicated that the transformational component can be dramatically restricted in its descriptive power. In place of the virtually unlimited number of available, highly specific, transformations of the theories of the 1950s and early 1960s, we can have instead a tiny number of very general operations: Merge (the generalized transformation, expanded in its role so that it creates even simple clausal structures), Move, Delete. The complex apparent results come not from complex transformations, but from the interactions of very simple ones with each other, and with very general constraints on the operation of transformations and on the ultimate derived outputs. The 1965 argument can then be reversed on itself: eliminate phrase structure rules! This model, similar in significant respects to the original one in the 1950s, can be graphically represented as in the following diagram, where the point of "spell-out" is where the derivation splits off on one branch towards PF, ultimately phonetics, while the transformational derivation itself (the "syntactic" portion of the derivation) continues on towards LF, ultimately semantics:

(49)   Numeration (the selection of lexical items)

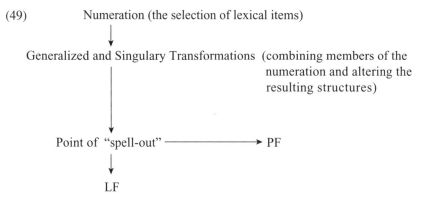

Generalized and Singular Transformations (combining members of the
                                          numeration and altering the
                                          resulting structures)

Point of "spell-out" ─────────────▶ PF

          LF

A major technical goal of the minimalist program is to reduce all constraints on representation to "bare output conditions," determined by the properties of the systems external to the language faculty (but still internal to the mind) that PF and LF must interface with. Internal to the computational system, the desideratum is that constraints on transformational derivations will be reduced to general principles of economy. Derivations beginning from the same lexical choices (the numeration, in Chomsky's term) are compared in terms of number of steps, length of movements, etc., with the less economical ones being rejected. Lexical items are assumed to be composed of "features," some of which need to be "checked" in particular configurations. This is what drives movement, since, all else being equal, a derivation with an instance of movement is less economical than one without. Further, moving less material is more economical than moving more material. This latter point provides a direction for resolving the near paradox (under minimalism) that covert operations do not seem to affect anaphoric possibilities, as illustrated by (46) above. Suppose movement is always driven by the need for some feature F to be checked. Then, as Chomsky (1995a) puts it,[13]

The operation Move, we now assume, seeks to raise just F. Whatever "extra baggage" is required for convergence involves a kind of "generalized pied-piping." In an optimal theory, nothing more should be said about the matter; bare output conditions should determine just what is carried along, if anything, when F is raised.

For the most part – perhaps completely – it is properties of the phonological component that require pied-piping. Isolated features and other scattered parts of words may not be subject to its rules, in which case the derivation is canceled . . . (1995a: 262–3)

Thus, overt movement will almost invariably be of a whole word or phrase. Covert movement, on the other hand, does not feed into phonology, so just the crucial features will move, leaving the larger category behind. By this line of reasoning, in the case of (46), *John* will remain in the c-command domain of *he* at LF, correctly resulting in non-coreference.

It is interesting to observe that while the several stages of the theory have all agreed that surface structure (or its minimalist descendant "spell-out") is the sole input to phonological interpretation, there have been quite distinct claims about the connection to semantics. The successive models posited the following representations as the interface:

(50)   a. *LSLT* model   T-marker
        b. *Aspects* model   Deep Structure
           (the "standard theory")
        c. Extended Standard Theory   Deep and Surface Structure
        d. Government–Binding (GB)   LF (via S-structure)
        e. Minimalism   LF (via a continuous
                                      transformational derivation
                                      beginning with the numeration)

Note that in all of these models except the first, we find one (or two) specific syntactic structures that feed into semantic interpretation. In the *LSLT* model, on the other hand, the interface is the T-marker, which includes *all* of the syntactic structures created in the course of the derivation. Now recall that the minimalist approach to structure building is much more similar to that in *LSLT* than to any of the intervening models. This suggests that interpretation in the minimalist model also could be more like that in the *LSLT* model, distributed over many structures. Interestingly, already in the late 1960s and early 1970s, there were occasional arguments for such a model of interpretation even within the Extended Standard Theory, and for phonological interpretation as well as semantic interpretation. For example, Bresnan (1971) argued that the phonological rule responsible for assigning English sentences their intonation contour applies cyclically, following each cycle of transformations, rather than at the end of the entire syntactic derivation. There were similar proposals for semantic phenomena involving scope and anaphora put forward by Jackendoff (1969).[14] In his work of the very late 1990s,[15] Chomsky suggests a more general instantiation of this distributed approach to phonological and semantic interpretation, based on ideas of Epstein (1999) and Uriagereka (1999). At the end of each cycle (or "phase" in Chomsky's most recent work), the syntactic structure thus far created is encapsulated and sent off to the interface components for *all* phonological and semantic interpretation. Thus, while there are still what might be called PF and LF components, there are no *levels* of PF and LF. Epstein argues that such a move represents a conceptual simplification, and both Uriagereka and Chomsky provide some empirical justification.

The simplifying developments in the theory leading towards the minimalist approach have generally led to greater breadth and depth of understanding of both how human languages work and how they are acquired by children. This success has led Chomsky to put forward the audacious proposal that the human language faculty might be a "perfect" solution to the problem of relating sound and meaning, given the boundary conditions provided by other modules of the mind. Much further research is, of course, needed to determine whether this bold proposal is sustainable.

4   How the brain begets language

Laura-Ann Petitto

I first met Noam Chomsky through a project that attempted to get the baby chimp Nim Chimpsky to "talk." At nineteen, with the certainty of youth, I knew that I would soon be "talking to the animals." Nim was the focus of our Columbia University research team's Grand Experiment: could we teach human language to other animals through environmental input alone with direct instruction and reinforcement principles? Or would there prove to be aspects of human language that resisted instruction, suggesting that language is a cognitive capacity that is uniquely human and likely under biological control? Nim was affectionately named "Chimpsky" because we were testing some of Chomsky's nativist views. To do so, we used natural sign language. Chimps cannot literally speak and cannot learn spoken language. But chimps have hands, arms, and faces and thus can, in principle, learn the silent language of Deaf people.

By the early 1970s, a surprising number of researchers had turned to learning about human language through the study of non-human apes. Noam Chomsky had stated the challenge: important parts of the grammar of human language are innate and specific to human beings alone. Key among these parts is the specific way that humans arrange words in a sentence (syntax), the ways that humans change the meanings of words by adding and taking away small meaningful parts to word stems (morphology), and the ways that a small set of meaningless sounds are arranged to produce all the words in an entire language (phonology). The human baby, Chomsky argued, is not born a "blank slate" with only the capacity to learn from direct instruction the sentences that its mother reinforces in the child's environment, as had been one of the prevailing tenets of a famous psychologist of the time, B. F. Skinner. Nor are babies born with innate knowledge of a specific language, which had been one caricature of Chomsky's innateness views of the time. What is innate in the baby, instead, is tacit knowledge of the finite set of possible grammars that world languages could assume (the finite set of units and the relations among them that make up a sentential string, and the finite ways that they move to form different arrangements in sentences). Innately equipped with this tacit knowledge of the finite set of possible language units and the rules for combining them, the baby listens to the patterns present in the specific language sample to which she is being exposed, and "chooses" from her innate set of possible grammars the grammar she is hearing. Chomsky's brilliant theoretical proposals on these topics had so captured the imagination of the international public – and we were all so much in the thick of arguing for or against the innateness of language and other forms of higher human cognition – that history would soon come to call this period the "Chomskyan Revolution."

My departure from Project Nim Chimpsky in the mid 1970s to attend graduate school in theoretical linguistics at the University of California, San Diego, was bittersweet. It had become clear that while Nim had some impressive communicative and cognitive abilities, there was a fundamental divide between his knowledge and use of language and ours. No one can "talk to the animals" by sign or otherwise. Nim's data, along with our close analyses of data from all other chimp language projects, unequivocally demonstrated that Chomsky was correct: aspects of human language are innate and unique, requiring a human biological endowment.

Guided (and inspired) by Noam Chomsky's theoretical formulations of human syntax and morphology, we discovered that chimpanzee and human syntax are fundamentally different. While apes can string one or two "words" together in ways that seem patterned, they cannot construct patterned sequences of three, four, and beyond ("words" and "signs" are homologous). After producing a "matrix" two words, they then – choosing from only the top five or so most frequently used words that they can produce (all primary food or contact words, such as *eat* or *tickle*) – randomly construct a grocery list. There is no rhyme or reason to the list, only a word salad lacking internal organization. Remarkably, moreover, chimps never produce word morphology. They do not seem to have any understanding of a basic word stem, nor of modifying its meanings by adding small meaningful word parts ("morphemes") that we bind or "affix" in highly patterned ways to word stems. If they were to naturally acquire the word *fruit* (which they don't) they would not readily acquire *fruity*, *fruitful*, *unfruitful*, *fruitfulness* . . . Born with no capacity at all to make the stem/affix distinction, they never – unlike human children, who quite quickly develop the ability to understand and use affixed terms – develop it later.

Add to this picture the fact that the actual physical forms of chimp lexical productions vary from one time to another in very unsystematic ways. This is not a matter of chimps having bad or immature "pronunciation" of their lexicon, nor is it due to differences between the hands of chimps and humans. Instead, their lexical productions are not patterned and their production errors are random – not drawn from the finite set of units from which all of their words and sentences are built. This fact never changes over chimp development. In short, chimps lack sign phonology. It has always interested me that despite the controversial abilities attributed to chimpanzees in the "Ape-Language Wars" over the decades, no researcher has ever dared to claim that any chimp has mastered the phonological aspect of human language organization. This deeply telling fact is returned to below.

Alas, the whole story is even worse than irregularities in chimpanzees' syntax, morphology, and phonology: the very *meanings* of their words were "off." For one thing, chimps cannot, without great difficulty, *acquire* the word *fruit*. While apes seem to have some capacity to associate words with concrete things and events in the world they inhabit, unlike humans, they seem to have little capacity to acquire and readily apply words with an *abstract* sense. Thus, while chimps can associate a small set of labels with concrete objects in the world (*apple* for apples, *orange* for oranges), they have enormous difficulty acquiring a word like *fruit*, which is a classification of both apples and oranges. There is no tangible item in the world that is literally fruit, only instances or examples of this abstract kind-concept that seems to exist only in human heads.

For another thing, chimps do not *use* words in the way we do at all. When we humans use the common noun *apple* in reference to that small round and juicy object in the world that we eat, we do not use it to index (pick out) only one object in the world (say, a specific red apple on a table), nor do we use it to refer to all things, locations, and actions globally associated with apples. Instead we use the label to "stand for" or *symbolize* the set of related objects in the world that are true of this particular kind-concept in our heads. Crucially, we also know the range or scope over which word kind-concepts may apply: for example, the label *apple* symbolizes a set of related *objects* and therefore this label is used only in reference to objects, not actions. (We further know how kind-concepts such as *apple* act in a sentence, i.e. what forms it can accept, like the noun plural marker -*s*, and what forms it cannot accept, like the verb present progressive marker -*ing*.) Although chimps can be experimentally trained to use a label across related items (such as the use of the sign *apple* while in front of a red apple or a green apple), children learn this effortlessly without explicit training, and chimps' spontaneous label-usage respects none of the above underlying constraints. Chimps, unlike humans, use such labels in a way that seems to rely heavily on some global notion of *association*. A chimp will use the same label *apple* to refer to the action of eating apples, the location where apples are kept, events and locations of objects other than apples that happened to be stored with an apple (the knife used to cut it), and so on and so forth – all simultaneously, and without apparent recognition of the relevant differences or the advantages of being able to distinguish among them. Even the first words of the young human baby are used in a kind-concept constrained way (a way that indicates that the child's usage adheres to "natural kind" boundaries – kinds of events, kinds of actions, kinds of objects, etc.). But the usage of chimps, even after years of training and communication with humans, never displays this sensitivity to differences among natural kinds. Surprisingly, then, chimps do not really have "names for things" at all. They have only a hodge-podge of loose associations with no Chomsky-type internal constraints or categories and rules that govern them (Seidenberg & Petitto 1979, 1987; Terrace et al. 1979). In effect, they do not ever acquire the *human* word *apple*.

My disappointment with chimpanzee language was, however, balanced by the prospect of pursuing an intriguing hypothesis. Because humans can readily acquire both signed and spoken natural languages, they must, I reasoned, possess *something* at birth *in addition to* mechanisms for producing and perceiving speech sounds that makes this possible. I wanted to discover what this elusive "something" could be.

By the mid 1970s, linguistics and psychology (especially adult psycholinguistics and child developmental psycholinguistics) were abuzz with excitement over Chomsky's "language acquisition device" (LAD). As stated in general terms above, the LAD assumes innate knowledge of a set of universal and specifically linguistic elements and relations. Armed with such knowledge, the young child can (i) narrow the range of possible grammars consistent with a partial (and often defective) set of sentences (the "primary linguistic data") and (ii) fix on a theory (a grammar) for the specific native language to which it is exposed. My specific questions focused on mechanisms: if such a LAD exists, precisely how might the human brain embody it? How might innate, specifically linguistic knowledge of the set of basic elements and relations be encoded in neural tissue? I knew that attempts to understand this would provide a key to what *biologically* distinguishes human language (including human minds and brains) from the communication of other animals.

The biological foundations of human language

It is not surprising that most linguists, along with most of those who think about the biological foundations of language, closely associate language with speech. For most of us, speech comes early and remains the primary modality for linguistic expression. It is a mistake, however, to associate language and speech too closely. Natural languages must be defined more abstractly, and the science of language must be able to deal with evidence from other modalities. An excellent reason for thinking this is that signed languages are acquired at the same rate as verbally expressed ones. They also reflect the same universals ("principles"). So, language must be defined in a way that applies as easily to sign as it does to speech. To someone like me, who is interested in both the development of language and its neural embodiment, this fact raises intriguing questions.

A superficial reading of Chomsky's early and current work – both formal and informal – might give the impression that he, like many others, closely associates language and speech. In his formal work, for example, he calls one of the "interfaces" of the language faculty "phonetic form" (PF) [recently: PHON].

Informally, when arguing against philosophers who seem often to think of the words of languages as marks on a page, he points out that speech is certainly prior to marks on page or stone, and that words are sounds in the head. But a closer reading – confirmed by many inspiring discussions that I had with Chomsky beginning in the early 1980s when I was a doctoral student at Harvard – indicates that he has a much more abstract characterization of language and its acquisition in mind.

Chomsky is also famous for insisting that his formal view of linguistic computation is not a view of "real-time" neural processes. Moreover, he strongly resists the ideologues who want to tell us that mental processes are "nothing but" neural processes. So, those who study his work might get the impression that he dislikes neural and brain evidence. But this impression too is wrong. His basic view is that the neural investigation of language is still in its very early stages and at the moment the linguist is in a much better position to tell the neurophysiologist what to look for than the other way around. He welcomes good studies and evidence on the matter. One purpose of this chapter is to describe what is, I hope, some evidence of this sort.

Studies of very early signed-language acquisition offer an especially clear window into the biological foundations of all of human language. Spoken and signed languages utilize different perceptual modalities (sound versus sight), and the motor control of the tongue and hands are subserved by different neural substrates in the brain. Comparative analyses of these languages, then, promise insights into the specific neural architecture that determines early human language acquisition in our species. If, as has been argued, very early human language acquisition is under the exclusive control of the maturation of the mechanisms for speech production and/or speech perception (Locke 2000; MacNeilage & Davis 2000), then spoken and signed languages should be acquired in radically different ways. At the very least, fundamental differences would be predicted in the maturational *time course* and *structure* of spoken versus signed language acquisition, presumably due to their use of different neural substrates in the human brain.

I have conducted comparative studies of monolingual hearing children (groups acquiring English, and others French) and monolingual deaf children (acquiring American Sign Language, ASL, or Langue des Signes Québécoise, LSQ) from ages birth through 48 months. I have also conducted studies of young bilinguals in "typical" contexts, such as babies acquiring French and English. These bilinguals were compared to two extraordinary cases of childhood bilingualism: bilingual hearing babies acquiring a signed and a spoken language from birth, as well as bilingual hearing babies acquiring two signed languages but no spoken language. Further, I have conducted comparative studies of how the human brain processes highly specific aspects of natural language structure in profoundly deaf adults processing signed language as compared to hearing adults processing spoken language, using modern Positron Emission Tomography (PET) brain-scanning technology. The empirical findings from all of these studies are clear. They show surprising similarities in the overall time course and structure of early signed and spoken language acquisition as well as in their neural representation in the human brain. Below, I briefly summarize each set of key findings and offer a hypothesis about some of the neurological mechanisms that permit human language acquisition to begin. Then I suggest some implications for Chomsky's view of language.

Milestone data

Monolingual signing versus speaking babies

Deaf children exposed to signed languages from birth acquire these languages in the same stages and at the same times as hearing children who acquire spoken languages. The stages include the "syllabic babbling stage" (6–10 months) as well as other developments in babbling, including "variegated babbling" (ages 10–12 months), "jargon babbling" (ages 12 months and beyond), the "first word stage" (9–14 months), the "first two-word stage" (17–26 months), and the grammatical and semantic developments beyond.

Signing and speaking children also exhibit remarkably similar semantic, discourse, and pragmatic complexity in their development. For example, analyses of young ASL and LSQ children's social and conversational patterns of language use over time, as well as their expressions' conceptual content, categories, and referential scope, demonstrate unequivocally that their language acquisition follows the identical path seen in age-matched hearing children acquiring spoken language (Petitto 2000).

Bilingual hearing babies acquiring a signed and a spoken language

Recent work focuses on two very unusual populations that provide data rich with theoretical implications: hearing children in bilingual, "bimodal" (signing–speaking) homes, and hearing children who are not exposed to spoken language at all in early life, only to two signed languages. First, the bilingual *hearing* children exposed to *both* a signed and a spoken language from birth (e.g. one parent signs and the other parent speaks) demonstrate no preference whatsoever for speech, even though they can hear. For example, these speaking–signing bilingual children acquiring French and LSQ produced their first word in French and their first sign in LSQ at the same time. Indeed, each of these signing–speaking children's languages are acquired on an identical timetable, and this timetable is the same as for other bilingual children acquiring, for example, French and English from birth; it is even the same, remarkably, as the timetable for monolingual children! And contrary to fears of confusing children by exposing them too early to two languages, bilingual children simultaneously exposed to two languages from birth achieve their linguistic milestones on the same timetable as monolinguals, revealing no language delay or confusion (Petitto et al. 2001; Charron & Petitto 1991; Holowka, Brosseau-Lapré & Petitto 2002; Kovelman & Petitto 2002, 2003; Petitto & Holowka 2002; Petitto & Kovelman 2003; Petitto, Kovelman, & Harasymowycz 2003). But the findings from the signing–speaking children provide us with data that have particularly clear theoretical implications. If speech *per se* were neurologically privileged at birth, then these children might have been expected to glean any morsel of sound that they could get, perhaps even turning from the visually signed input. Instead, they acquire both the signed and the spoken languages to which they are exposed on an identical maturational timetable.

Second, and perhaps even more surprising, are data from a study I was fortunate enough to undertake of an extraordinary group of bilingual children. Although these children could hear, their profoundly deaf parents had exposed them *exclusively* to two *signed* languages from birth through early childhood, with no spoken language input. For example, in one family, the deaf mother was from the United States and signed ASL and the deaf father was from Québec and signed LSQ. These children achieved all milestones in their two signed languages on the same timetable as each other and in the identical manner observed in all other bilingual and monolingual children (Petitto 2000). Moreover, this same pattern of development was also observed in yet another particularly interesting group of children – a group of hearing monolingual babies who were exposed exclusively to one signed language (no speech). Here, as above, these children achieved all of the classic language milestones in sign language on the same timetable as hearing babies acquiring speech, including babbling on their hands, but not vocally because they had never been exposed to speech (Petitto et al. 2001).

Summarizing so far, entirely normal language acquisition occurs in profoundly deaf children exposed only to signed languages, hearing bilingual babies acquiring a signed and a spoken language simultaneously, and, most remarkably, hearing children without any spoken language input whatsoever, only signed language input. These data clearly provide no support for the prevailing hypothesis that normal human language acquisition in all children is determined primarily by the maturation of the mechanisms to hear and produce speech. Interestingly, the hearing bilingual babies who were presented at birth with a tacit choice (speech versus sign) attended equally to these two input signals, showed no preference for speech whatsoever, and achieved every language milestone equally and on the same timetable as monolinguals. Moreover, the hearing babies exposed exclusively to signed language exhibited normal language acquisition (albeit in sign) and did so *without* the use of the brain's auditory and speech perception mechanisms, and *without* the use of the motor mechanisms used for the production of speech.

Structural data

Homologies in signing and speaking babies

Researchers trying to understand the biological roots of human language have naturally tried to find its "beginning." The regular onset of vocal babbling – *bababa* and the other repetitive, syllabic sounds that infants produce – has led researchers to conclude that babbling represents the initial manifestation of human language acquisition, or, at least, of language production. Babbling – and, by extension, early language acquisition in our species – has been said to be determined by the development of the anatomy of the vocal tract and the neuro-anatomical and neurophysiological mechanisms subserving the motor control of speech production. In this view, baby babbling is at first a fundamentally motoric behavior, rather than a linguistic activity. Here, babies learn language by pairing these motoric forms – through learned associations – with meaningful words in the environment (e.g. MacNeilage & Davis 2000). The existence of babbling has been further used to argue that the human language capacity is exclusively linked *neurologically* at birth to innate mechanisms for producing speech in the development of language in a child, or ontogeny (Liberman & Mattingly 1989). It has also been presented as proof that human language evolved over the period of human phylogenetic development exclusively from our species' incremental motoric ability to control the mouth and the jaw muscles (Lieberman 2000).

In 1991, my graduate student Paula Marentette and I reported a surprising discovery, the existence of babbling on the hands of profoundly deaf babies (Petitto & Marentette 1991). Through intensive qualitative analyses of the hands of young deaf babies exposed to sign as compared to hearing babies exposed to speech (ages 10 to 14 months), we found a discrete class of hand activity in deaf babies that was structurally identical to vocal babbling observed in hearing babies. Like vocal babbling, manual babbling possesses (i) a restricted set of "phonetic" units (unique to signed languages) and (ii) syllabic organization. It is also (iii) used without meaning or reference. This babbling hand activity was also different from all babies' other hand activity, be they deaf or hearing. Its structure was particularly distinct from all babies' communicative gestures, or the deaf babies' attempts to produce real signs.

The discovery of babbling in the silent modality of the hands disconfirmed the view that babbling is neurologically determined wholly by the maturation of the ability to talk. Instead, it confirmed a claim central to Chomsky's theory: that early language acquisition is governed by tacit knowledge of the abstract patterning of language that is biologically endowed in the species, and that this governance is so powerful that it will "out" itself by mapping onto the tongue if given the tongue, or the hands if given the hands – all the while preserving linguistic structures across the two modalities. The deep commonalities between the linguistic patterns expressed on the tongue in hearing children's vocal babbling and those seen on the hands of deaf children's silent babbling (independent of the tongue) teach us that Chomsky's prophetic emphasis on language's core underlying principles and patterns (not the peripheral ability to talk) are the organizing force behind our extraordinary capacity for language.

It is crucial that the Petitto & Marentette (1991) study discovered the existence of syllabic organization in the deaf babies' silent hand babbling. Like spoken language, the structural nucleus of the "sign" (identical to the "word") in signed languages is again the syllable. Although the precise quantitative properties of this rhythmic activity were not known at the time (see below), in signed languages, the sign-syllable consists of the rhythmic closing and opening (and/or the rhythmic hold–movement/movement–hold) alternations of the hands/arms. This sign-syllabic organization has been analyzed as being structurally homologous with the closing and opening of the mouth aperture in the production of consonant–vowel, CV (closed–open) mouth alternations in spoken language. The convergence of similar syllabic structures unique to babbling, be it on the hands or the tongue, suggested once again that something other than peripheral factors, such as the mouth and jaw, was driving this fundamentally linguistic behavior in young humans. Something else was guiding this powerful convergence of structure on two radically different modalities. Discovering what this was would bring us closer to discovering the underlying brain mechanisms (should they exist) that could make possible Chomsky's formal proposals about early language acquisition – his LAD.

A key clue about where to look emerged from the study of deaf babies' hand babbling. When they produced hand babbling, their hands seemed to move with a different rhythm than their other hand movements – those that all babies make. But was this difference real? Maybe babies exposed to signed languages simply used their hands more than babies exposed to speech. So my colleagues and I conducted a quantitative study of young baby hands using innovative technology, called "Optotrak"— optoelectronic position-tracking – in an attempt to identify the *quantitative rhythmic properties* that underlie all babies' hand activity. But to test the strength of our own views, we wanted to put them through the hardest possible test. So we examined the hands of typical young hearing babies acquiring spoken language and that rare group of babies mentioned above: hearing babies exposed only to signed languages from birth (no speech). Both groups of babies were equal in all respects, except for the modality of language input. If babbling (and, by extension, early language acquisition) is determined by the development of the control of the mouth alone, then both groups of babies' hand activity should be the same. Alternatively, if babbling is a linguistic activity that reflects babies' sensitivity to specific patterns at the heart of human language and their capacity to use them, then the two groups of babies' hand activity should differ. Indeed, as Chomsky had argued in his LAD, if babies are born with tacit knowledge of the core patterns that are universal to all languages, even signed languages, then the linguistic hypothesis predicts that differences in the form of language input should yield differences in the hand activity of the two groups. In biological terms, tacit knowledge was construed as the baby's sensitivity to specific patterns at the heart of human language – in particular, the rhythmic patterns that bind syllables, the elementary units of language, into baby babbles, and then into words and sentences.

The precise physical properties of babies' hand activity were measured by placing tiny light-emitting diodes (LEDs) on their hands. The LEDs transmitted light impulses to cameras that, in turn, sent signals into the Optotrak system. This information was then fed into computer software that provided us with the timing, rate, path movement, velocity, frequency, and sophisticated 3-D graphic displays of all baby hand activity. Optotrak computations were calculated "blind" to videotape reference to the babies' hands (we did not see the babies' hands in the first part of the study, only the lighted dots on the computer screen). Independently, on-line videotapes were made of all babies for post-Optotrak analyses. This method, then, provided the most accurate and rigorous quantitative analysis of moving hands to date, and an advance over previous subjective classification of baby hands from videotapes.

The quantitative Optotrak analyses revealed that hearing sign-exposed babies produced two types of hand activity, while the hearing speech-exposed babies only produced one. Sign-exposed babies produced a significantly different type of *low-frequency* rhythmical hand activity, with a frequency around *1 Hertz*, and another type of *high-frequency* rhythmical hand activity, with a frequency around *2.5–3 Hertz* – the type that the speech-exposed babies used nearly exclusively! Further, sign-exposed babies' low-frequency hand activity corresponded to the rhythmical patterning of adult sign-syllables and, after lifting the "blind," videotape data revealed that this hand activity alone exhibited the qualitative properties of silent linguistic hand babbling.[1]

Remarkably, a dramatic dissociation of two hand-movement types (linguistic vs. motoric) was carved onto a single manual modality differentiated by different rhythmical frequencies. This could only occur if babies find salient, and can make use of, the rhythmical patterning underlying human language. This evidence indicates that specific rhythmical patterns underlie baby babbling, and these reflect highly specific rhythmical sensitivities that babies must be born with. These sensitivities correspond to highly specific aspects of the patterning of natural language and almost certainly constitute one of the central biological mechanisms by which babies discover the patterns of their native grammar in the linguistic stream around them (Petitto et al. 2001; Petitto et al. 2004).

In a new twist on a classic theme, we further wondered just how similar very early language *perception* is across sign and spoken languages. By around 4 months, all babies have the universal capacity to discriminate categorically all the phonetic-syllabic units found in the world's spoken languages (such as [ba] and [pa]), even those that they have never heard. But by around 14 months, most babies have lost this universal capacity and have instead gained an increased sensitivity to detect the phonetic contrasts in their native language. In order to test the neural basis of this capacity – is it a general acoustic or a specific linguistic capacity? – we built an infant-controlled Habituation Laboratory and showed hearing *monolingual* babies (never exposed to sign) moving images of hands. But these hands were phonetic-syllabic units in ASL (below). As with speech, we found that these babies demonstrated categorical discrimination of ASL hand phonetic-syllabic units at age 4 months, which they lost by 14 months (Baker, Isardi, Golinkoff & Petitto 2003; Baker, Sootsman, Golinkoff & Petitto 2003). Intriguing results were then seen in hearing *bilingual* babies (never exposed to sign) who looked like our young monolinguals at age 4 months. But at age 14 months they showed a linguistic "advantage": they demonstrated increased sensitivity to phonetic units over their monolingual peers, suggesting that experience with multiple languages can serve as a "perceptual wedge," keeping open longer the capacity to discriminate a wider range of phonetic units than their monolingual peers (Norton, Baker & Petitto 2003). Here, from the new perspective of infant language perception, these results provide compelling support that the sensitivity to phonetic-syllabic contrasts is a fundamentally linguistic (not general acoustic) process and part of the baby's biological endowment.

Before closing this line of studies, we decided to take one last look. This time we examined only the everyday hearing baby learning a spoken language. Again we asked, "is babbling a linguistic versus a motoric activity?" But now we also wanted to understand *when* the human language capacity emerges in early life and – crucially, for me, because of a research desire that was born after my work with Nim – to find *what* its neural basis is. Our challenge was answering these questions in a way that would not hurt or unsettle young babies.

To gain another perspective on these issues, we carried out another study. It is a notable fact that adults tend to talk out of the *right* side of their mouths. This seems to be due to the fact that our brain's *left* hemisphere is doing the lion's share of our language-processing. (We do not see this right mouth asymmetry when we speak to others because our brains correct the uneven image.) Intrigued by this fact of cerebral organization, we wondered whether baby babbling might be produced more out of the right side of infants' mouths, thereby reflecting the involvement of their left hemisphere's language-processing centers.

Encouraged by the availability of a non-invasive measure (below) to assess the laterality of mouth movements in adults, we applied it for the first time to baby mouths. This also gave us an opportunity to find out whether there was evidence of laterality in other forms of mouth activity. Specifically, would babies produce smiles out of the *left* sides of their mouths (reflecting the involvement of their *right* hemisphere's emotion-processing centers)? And would babies produce non-babbling vocalizations somewhere in between the left and right sides of their mouths?

Ten babies were studied at the onset of their babbling stage, five English babies and five French. This was an important study design consideration to ensure that no language-specific effects were being revealed on babies' mouths. The standard measure of mouth laterality – called the "Laterality Index" – was used, which has been used around the world in the study of adults, especially adults after suffering a neuropsychological trauma (e.g. from a stroke) to determine what brain tissue had been impaired and spared. We found that babies babbled out of the right side of their mouths, smiled out of the left, and produced non-babbling vocalizations somewhere in between. This study was the first to demonstrate left-hemisphere cerebral specialization for babies while babbling which, in turn, suggests that language functions in humans are lateralized from a very early point in development (Holowka & Petitto 2002).[2]

Summary: significance of studies of early signed and spoken language acquisition

Summarizing these studies of sign–speech homologies, it seems clear that despite modality differences, signed and spoken languages are acquired in virtually identical ways. The differences observed between children acquiring a signed language versus children acquiring a spoken language are no greater than the differences observed between hearing children learning one spoken language, say, Italian, versus another, say, Finnish. These findings cast serious doubt on the core hypothesis in very early spoken language acquisition that the maturation of mechanisms for the production and/or perception of speech exclusively determine the time course and structure of early human language acquisition. They also challenge the hypothesis that speech (sound) is critical to normal language acquisition, and the related hypothesis that speech is uniquely suited to the brain's maturational needs in language ontogeny. What these data suggest, as Chomsky had hypothesized, is that language does indeed have innate computational systems. But here is the added observation that language will co-opt whatever provides it with an opportunity to develop in accordance with its innate agenda. This innate agenda seems perfectly happy to accept and use language on the hands (if presented with signed language) or the tongue (if the ambient language is a spoken one). That this should be true is stunning testimony to the power of this innate agenda, that is, the brain's specified neural sensitivity to a core set of patterns underlying human language, and the corollary fact that an innate agenda must exist in the first place. But, again, where is this "patterning" taking place?

Testing hypotheses about the biological–neurological foundations of language with PET studies of signing and speaking adults

The left hemisphere of the human brain has for over one hundred years been understood to be the primary site of language processing (Wernicke 1874). As in early language acquisition, the fundamental explanation for this fact has been that language functions processed at specific left-hemisphere sites reflect its dedication to the motor articulation of speaking or the sensory processing of hearing speech and sound. Contemporary functional imaging studies of the brain have provided powerful support for this view, including those demonstrating increased regional cerebral blood flow (rCBF) in specific portions of the left hemisphere when searching, retrieving, and generating information about spoken words (specifically, in the left inferior frontal cortex, called the LIFC). This view is especially evident regarding the left Planum Temporale (PT), and to a lesser extent the right PT, which participates in the processing of the meaningless phonetic-syllabic units in all spoken language. The left PT forms part of the classically defined Wernicke's receptive language area, receiving projections from the primary auditory afferent system, and is considered to constitute a *unimodal* secondary auditory cortex (for a complete report of these issues and the present PET study under discussion, see Petitto et al. 2000). These data and studies do not, however, resolve the fundamental question of whether these brain sites involved in language processing are devoted to speaking and hearing, or whether they constitute tissue that is better thought of as dedicated to aspects of the patterning of natural language. For these data and studies do not exclude the possibility that areas of the brain thought to be "devoted" to speech perception and production are also those employed in human sign languages.

The existence of natural signed languages provides key insights into whether language processed at specific brain sites is due to the tissue's sensitivity to sound *per se*, or to the patterns encoded within it. In a study to test this, we measured rCBF while deaf signers underwent PET brain scans, which we co-registered with their MRI anatomical brain scans. Vital to this study's design was our examination of two highly specific levels of language organization in *signed languages*, including the generation of signs (lexical level) and phonetic-syllabic units (sublexical level; meaningless parts of signs). As I mentioned before, this level of language organization is found in all the world's languages (be they signed or spoken) and comprises the restricted set of meaningless units from which a particular natural language is constructed.[3] If the brain sites underlying the processing of words and parts of words are specialized specifically for sound, then deaf people's processing of signs and parts of signs should engage cerebral tissue *different* from that classically linked to speech. Conversely, if the human brain possesses sensitivity to aspects of the patterning of natural language, then deaf signers processing these specific levels of language organization may engage tissue *similar* to that observed in hearing speakers.

We studied two entirely distinct cultural groups of deaf people who used two distinct natural signed languages. Five were native adult signers of American Sign Language (ASL; used in the United States and parts of Canada) and six were native adult signers of Langue des Signes Québécoise (LSQ; used in Québec and other parts of French Canada). ASL and LSQ are grammatically autonomous signed languages; our use of two distinct signed languages constitutes another significant design consideration, unique to the present research, introduced to provide independent, crosslinguistic replication of the findings within a single study. We further compared these eleven deaf people to ten English-speaking hearing adult controls who had no knowledge of signed languages.

Two main findings emerged from this Petitto et al. (2000) study. First, *both* the deaf people processing genuine signs and the hearing controls processing words exhibited clear cerebral blood flow increases within the identical brain region, the left inferior frontal cortex (LIFC). This finding demonstrated that one component of processing human language (something as abstract as lexical search and retrieval) was housed at a specific brain site. Because both language on the hands and language on the tongue were processed at the same brain site, it supported a surprising hypothesis: there exists tissue in the human brain dedicated to a *function* of human language *structure* independent of speech or sound.

The second major discovery involved tissue universally viewed as being literally tied to sound processing, again the Planum Temporale or PT, especially the processing of the small phonetic-syllabic units that make up a spoken word. Here we witnessed robust activation in the profoundly deaf people's PT while they were processing meaningless parts of signs (phonetic-syllabic or sublexical parts of a sign on the hands). This was the remarkable thing: how could there be activity in sound tissue in the brains of profoundly deaf people who never heard sound? The activity could not be due to processing based on any auditory representations as they are traditionally understood – the transduction of sound waves, and their pressure on the inner ear, into neural signals. In witnessing these specific results, we demonstrated neural activity in what has hitherto been thought to be exclusively auditory cortex by using purely visual stimuli – but, crucially, the visual stimuli were linguistic. Thus, rather than being dedicated exclusively to sound (as had been thought for generations) it must be that this tissue is instead dedicated to linguistic *patterns* in the input – specifically to the patterns inherent in rhythmically contrasting phonetic-syllabic units – be they patterns on the hands or the tongue. In short, we found the biological instantiation of a key level of Chomsky's "hierarchical" levels of language organization: phonology.

Finally, we randomized the MRI anatomical brain scans of all of these deaf and hearing subjects, flipped the x-axis so that no one knew if they were looking at the subjects' left or right hemispheres, and then computed the gray- and white-matter tissue volumes in all of these brains' classic sound tissue (primary and secondary auditory cortices) – without ever knowing the hearing status of the brains being analyzed. In a nutshell, we found that there were no differences in the gray-matter volumes in the deaf and hearing peoples' sound tissue (meaning that there was no cell loss in the sound tissue of profoundly deaf people as compared to hearing people) and no differences in the white-matter volumes between the groups (meaning that there was no loss of neuronal input to this sound tissue). Surprisingly, like hearing people, there was a greater left-versus-right-hemisphere asymmetry in the sound tissue of the deaf people (for a full report of these findings see Penhune et al. 2003). How could this be? Why doesn't sound tissue shrivel up and die in deaf brains? Here, as above, it must be that such tissue is sensitive to specific linguistic patterns in natural language (not sound) and the on-going processing of sign language provides the tissue with just those linguistic patterns to keep it alive and kicking!

Together such facts demand that those who study language and its acquisition introduce hypotheses of the mind/brain that make sense of how this is possible.

Adaptive phonological differentiation

When examining the sublexical level of language organization of signed and spoken languages we find striking commonalities: both employ a highly restricted set of units organized into regular structured patterns – patterns that amount to rapid rhythmically alternating maximal contrasts. This suggests an hypothesis (albeit in a nascent form) that speaks to how visual images might activate auditory brain tissue. And it might at least focus further research efforts, for example, to explain what exactly it is about the neurons of the human PT and their connections to other systems in the head that gives the specific multimodal linguistic-pattern-responding character it has. The PT can be activated either by sight or sound because, I suggest, this tissue (or at least a part of it) has specific neurons or groups of neurons working in concert that, when activated by appropriate input patterns, responds selectively to specific distributions of complex, low-level units in rapid rhythmic alternation. These distributions are those that, informally, we think of as natural-language phonological structure. To be sure, PT tissue does also, in general, deal with sensory *sound* input – the

PT is typically employed in hearing humans in processing non-linguistic sound inputs, and its homologue in the brains of some apes apparently performs only this task. But, due to some yet unknown factor, PT tissue in humans has a sensitivity to certain specific patterns found only in natural languages. This actually may be one key neural difference between the chimpanzee and human brain and provides an intriguing experiment in nature regarding how far a creature could get in language without it: chimps can hear speech but have no brain power to find in the stream of sounds around them the finite set of units and their patterns that make up a language's phonological inventory. From this, we can predict just about how far they'd get without this capacity: no syntax, no morphology, and, of course, no phonology. But, with decent memory and association powers, they would be able to pick out or refer to things in their here and now with list-like global association. Voilà. This is just about what chimps do.

Crucially, the PT is apparently *not* neurally sensitive to any and all rhythmically alternating acoustic input containing contrasts. Music, for example, provides complex multifaceted rhythmical signals that engage brain tissue at multiple cerebral sites yet, in general, contemporary scientists agree that the PT (especially the left PT) is not the brain site for processing these different forms of rhythmically alternating contrasts (for a review see Zatorre & Binder 2000).[4] To summarize, the hypothesis is that the left PT site contains, in addition to other forms of specialization, specialization for highly specific, maximally contrasting rhythmical patterns in the input. These patterns are found exclusively in specific aspects of natural language – specifically, phonetic-syllabic units and their distributional patterning.

If this is correct, there is an initial *biologically guided* capacity (what I called the innate agenda, above) to find salient, and to attend to particular aspects of, input streams involving phonetic-syllabic contrasting units, which after several months of life can (given relevant input) become attuned to whatever sorts of sensory input are capable – consistent with the internal agenda – of activating it. Thus, experience with specific phonetic-syllabic units in the input stream provided by – in the case of humans – sound or vision to a young baby literally changes and "adapts" the baby's biological perceptual and attentional mechanisms to be sensitive to patterns in the given modality or modalities. This "guiding" capacity amounts to a neurally set agenda (a system that "looks for" certain patterns) and leads to the child's ability to discover, and to utilize, elementary units of language structure. Without such an internal agenda, the child's mind would not recognize the patterns needed for linguistic development. Nim's mind, lacking what Chomsky calls a "language faculty," would not and could not find that pattern in the input stream. It would never become salient. The PT neurally embodies a small part of the tacit knowledge of the set of basic elements and relations that Chomsky proposed must be contained in a child's LAD.

On the neural tissue underlying human language acquisition

Returning to the question with which I began my research – how does the brain permit the radical change in the morphology of its expressive and receptive mechanisms for language found in speech and sign, and what is the genetic basis for this stunning equipotentiality? – I think we have found at least some answers. The various studies discussed above suggest that the brain at birth cannot be working under rigid genetic instruction to produce and receive language via the auditory-speech modality. If this were the case, then the nature of signed and spoken language acquisition – including the nature of the maturational time course and early language structures – as well as the cerebral organization of sign and speech in the adult brain should be different. Clearly, it is not. The fact that the brain can tolerate variation in language transmission and reception, despite different environmental inputs, and still achieve the target capacity (being a speaker of a natural language, perhaps several), provides support for a genetic component underlying language acquisition that is nevertheless biologically "flexible" (neurologically plastic). I hypothesized that PT tissue constitutes a key brain site that contributes to launching human language acquisition and have suggested that it gains its vital role in the establishment of nascent phonological representations in all humans through a process that I have termed "Adaptive Phonological Differentiation." This process "guides" the newborn's attention to find salient specific aspects of the input stream with specific rhythmical contrasts that correspond to key aspects of natural language structure: elementary phonetic-syllabic units and their sing-song distributional patterning (prosody). Drawing from the baby Optotrak findings mentioned above, I further suggest that this PT tissue tunes the infant's perceptual systems to find salient, and to attend to, (initially) maximally-contrasting, rhythmically-oscillating bundles of about 1.2–1.5 seconds. Armed with this honed sensitivity, the baby's mind can, in turn, begin to "select" the restricted set of elementary phonetic units and combinatorial regularities of their native language(s). The precise timing is unclear, but it is known that they begin the production of these elementary units at around six months (see also Jusczyk 1999).

The same processes must be at work when a baby is confronted at birth with two or more natural languages, whether spoken or signed. Here the newborn's sensitivity to specific rhythmical and distributing patterning must provide it with the means to detect two related but different rhythmically contrasting linguistic patterns. The development of this capacity surely serves as a basis upon which bilingual babies tacitly build up representations of their two distinct phonological systems. (Petitto et al. 2001; see also Holowka, Brosseau-Lapré & Petitto 2002; Petitto & Holowka 2002 for a discussion of the processes that make possible human bilingual acquisition). Again, exact timing in the case of multiple languages is unclear, but this process is certainly well underway by age 6 months, exhibiting regular growth and expansion in the capacity to detect distinct forms of systematic rhythmical-temporal and distributional patterns over time. So, whether one language or many, a baby's innate mechanisms will – irrespective of whether the input is from eye or ear – guide it to find specific patterns in the input stream and, when its internal systems find them, they "instruct" motor systems to produce "output" informed by them.

Chomsky may not have encountered languages on the hands early in his life but, remarkably, his "abstract" theory of the LAD allowed for the flexibility in modality we have seen in this chapter. And while he assumed the LAD must be biologically instantiated in some way, he did not have any idea of how it is written into neural tissue. I think we now have some idea of how a small, but crucial, part of it is.

5   Chomsky and Halle's revolution in phonology

B. Elan Dresher

Introduction

Chomsky and Halle's approach to phonological theory, as with other components of generative grammar, represented a sharp break with the main currents of American linguistics that immediately preceded them. The differences were conceptual as well as technical. Accounts of the development of phonology emphasize technical issues, such as arguments over the existence of a "taxonomic phonemic level," or whether it is permissible to "mix levels" in a phonological analysis. Lying behind discussion of these issues, however, were assumptions about psychology and the practice of science. Indeed, throughout the development of phonology, major changes came about not only through technical breakthroughs, but also by reinterpreting the significance of existing technical devices. This was also the case with Chomsky and Halle's innovations.

In this chapter I discuss Chomsky and Halle's contributions to phonological theory by putting their views in the context of the theories that prevailed before them. I will also try to connect the technical issues to the larger conceptual ones concerning the nature of language acquisition and the mind.[1] I will be treating Chomsky and Halle's contributions together, without attempting to distinguish who contributed precisely which ideas. Their early work in generative phonology, culminating in the major work *The Sound Pattern of English* (Chomsky & Halle 1968, henceforth *SPE*), was done jointly.

Nevertheless, some indication of what each brought to the enterprise can be gleaned from Chomsky's 1957b review of Jakobson and Halle's *Fundamentals of Language* (Jakobson & Halle 1956). Chomsky finds that "much can be said" for Jakobson and Halle's approach to phonology. In particular, he approved of the hypothesis that the sound systems of all languages could be characterized in terms of a limited number of universal distinctive features. Second, he preferred their approach to identifying phonemes over others then current. They assigned two segments to the same phoneme if they have the same feature specifications. Most other approaches to phonemic analysis prevailing at the time assigned sounds to phonemes if they are in complementary distribution (or in free variation) and phonetically similar, appealing to a notion of similarity that is difficult to define. Finally, Chomsky seconds the authors' emphasis (advanced over the years by Jakobson) on the importance of extending phonological theory to account for language acquisition, disorders, and other aspects of linguistic behavior.

On the other side, Chomsky observes that many of Jakobson and Halle's proposals need to be made more explicit and precise before they can be empirically tested. He further proposes an amendment to their conception of how phonemes are related to speech. He found their requirement that the distinctive features assigned to phonemes be present in their correct sequence in the phonetics too strict. He proposes that distinctive feature specifications form instead an "abstract underlying system of classification related, perhaps indirectly, to the physical facts of speech." Finally, Chomsky proposes that general criteria of simplicity play an important role in the evaluation of particular phonological analyses.

One can say, then, that Chomsky and Halle's theory of generative phonology was a synthesis of Jakobson and Halle's theory of distinctive features and phonemic analysis, revised in the light of Chomsky's emphasis on formal explicitness, simplicity, and abstractness and autonomy of mental representations.

Rules and derivations

When first introduced, the centrality of *rules* in Chomsky and Halle's approach to phonology appeared revolutionary. A grammar of a language must merely *list* many things – for example, the English word *tide* begins with a *t*, ends with a *d*, and has a vowel sound represented by *i*. A person who knows English but who happens never to have encountered this word cannot derive this information. It is a particular fact about English that must be learned and committed to memory.

Other facts about the pronunciation of this word are more systematic. For example, the *t* in *tide* is pronounced with a puff of air, called aspiration (represented as t^h), in contrast to the *t* in *style*, which is not aspirated. Any speaker of English told that *tide* begins with *t* would automatically know that the *t* must be pronounced with aspiration. That is, the aspiration of *t* is not an idiosyncratic fact that must be listed in the lexical entry of *tide*, but can be encoded in a rule. Thus, the lexical, or *underlying*, form of the word *tide* need only specify that the initial sound is a /t/, where slant brackets represent *phonemic* forms; this form is then subject to the rule of aspiration, which derives the *phonetic*, or *surface*, form [t^h] (where square brackets represent phonetic forms).

The vowel written *i* is a diphthong, phonetically [aːj], where ː indicates that the vowel is long, and *j* represents a glide. The length of the vowel is predictable: *tide* ends in a *d*, which is a voiced sound, and in English, stressed vowels lengthen before voiced sounds. Thus, the vowel of *bid* is longer than the vowel of *bit*, which ends in a voiceless sound, *t*. Similarly, the diphthong in *tight* is shorter than in *tide*. In some dialects, such as Canadian English, the first part of this diphthong is pronounced with a higher and more centralized tongue position before a voiceless consonant, and is phonetically transcribed as [ʌj]. Therefore, speakers of these English dialects need only learn that the diphthongs in *tide* and *tight* are both /aj/. General rules then apply to lengthen /aj/ to [aːj] before voiced sounds and to raise it to [ʌj] before voiceless sounds.

One might suppose, as it generally was in pre-generative phonology, that the distribution of the various phonetic realizations, or *allophones*, of a phoneme could be represented by an unordered set of statements. The diphthong /aj/, for example, appears as [aːj] before voiced sounds (a process we will call Lengthening) and as [ʌj] before voiceless sounds (Raising).

Chomsky and Halle proposed, however, that rules must be *ordered* if they are to give correct results and be statable in the simplest, most general way. Consider, for example the words *ride* and *write*. They undergo the rules of Lengthening and (in the dialects under consideration) Raising. The rules can be written as follows:[2]

(1)   Lengthening $V \rightarrow [+\text{long}]/\underline{\quad}$ (glide) $\begin{bmatrix} C \\ +\text{voiced} \end{bmatrix}$

(2)   Raising $/a/ \rightarrow \Lambda/\underline{\quad}$ glide $\begin{bmatrix} C \\ -\text{voiced} \end{bmatrix}$

These rules also apply in *rider* and *writer*. In the pronunciation of North American English, the *t* and *d* in these words are pronounced with an alveolar "flap," in phonetic transcription [ɾ], a quick tap of the tongue rather than a sustained occlusion.

(3)   Flapping $\{t,d\} \rightarrow ɾ / V$ (glide) $\underline{\quad} \begin{bmatrix} V \\ -\text{stressed} \end{bmatrix}$

The result of applying the three rules is shown below.

(4)   A simple derivation

	writer	*rider*
Underlying	/rajtər /	/rajdər /
Lengthening	–	raːjdər
Raising	rʌjtər	–
Flapping	rʌjɾər	raːjɾər
Phonetic	[rʌjɾər]	[raːjɾər]

Note that the Flapping rule must follow the other two rules. If Flapping were to apply first, an incorrect form would be generated: as shown in (5), *writer* would be pronounced just like *rider*, which is not the case in this dialect.[3]

(5)   An incorrect derivation

	writer	*rider*
Underlying	/rajtər/	/rajdər/
Flapping	rajɾər	rajɾər
Lengthening	raːjdər	raːjdər
Raising	–	–
Phonetic	*[raːjɾər]	[raːjɾər]

Therefore, the basic architecture of the phonological theory of *SPE* can be diagrammed as in (6).

(6)   Basic architecture of phonological component (*SPE*)[4]

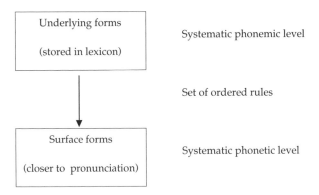

Underlying forms

(stored in lexicon)

Systematic phonemic level

Set of ordered rules

Surface forms

(closer to pronunciation)

Systematic phonetic level

In hindsight, one might wonder why the rather simple model in (6) would have ever been considered revolutionary. None of the basic ingredients were novel: not the idea of two basic levels, nor even the idea of a derivation mediated by ordered rules. However, in the context of phonological theory in America in the 1950s, it represented a significant new departure. To see why this was so requires a brief excursion to the nineteenth-century origins of modern phonetics and phonology.

Two levels: broad and narrow transcription

That at least two levels of representation are required to represent the sounds of a language was becoming apparent already in the nineteenth century. Phonologists and phoneticians realized that a degree of precision in the representation of sounds was required that was unattainable using conventional alphabets. They aimed to develop a system in which one sound was always represented by one symbol (unlike English, where the sound [s] is sometimes represented by <c> as in <city>, and sometimes by <s>, as in <sit>), and in which one symbol is used for only one sound (again unlike English, where the letter <c> sometimes represents [s], and sometimes [k] (<electricity>). This movement ultimately led to the development of the International Phonetic Alphabet (IPA), a transcription system that approaches the goal of a one-to-one relation between sounds and symbols. This type of transcription came to be known as *narrow transcription*, because it records very fine distinctions between speech sounds.

It quickly became apparent that a narrow transcription is not a practical way to transcribe particular languages. For example, consider English *t* in words like *stop, top, hat, not you, trap*, and *writer*. When looked at closely, these [t]s are all different: unaspirated [t] in *stop*; aspirated [tʰ] in *top*; unreleased [t⁻] in *hat* (optionally: it may also be released and aspirated); palatalized [tʲ] in *not you*; retroflexed [ţ] in *trap*; and flapped [ɾ] in *writer*. These are only some of the realizations of English *t*. Detailed examination of other sounds of English reveals that they, too, are not unitary sounds but groups of sounds, distinguishable by separate phonetic symbols. The IPA has a way of distinguishing all these sounds, and this is desirable if we wish to give an accurate transcription of what each variant actually is. But it would be very cumbersome and quite impractical to actually attempt to use this type of transcription as a way of writing English.

More important, a narrow transcription fails to do justice to some basic facts about the sound system of English. For there is something correct about the intuitions of speakers that the sounds listed above are all "variants of *t*." A transcription system that treats [t] and [tʰ] as being as different from each other as each is to [p] or [n] is missing something important: the English spelling system, for all its faults and quirks, does a better job at capturing the way sounds actually pattern in English. Thus, alongside narrow transcription there developed the notion of a *broad* transcription, which is designed to abstract away from predictable variations and alternations in sounds.

In the above example, [t] and [tʰ] are allophones of the same phoneme /t/, whereas [n] in *nip* is an allophone of a different phoneme, /n/. We know that /t/ and /n/ are different phonemes in English because they are in *contrast*: *tap* and *nap* are different words in English, as are *fit* and *fin*. So one function of a broad transcription is that it abstracts away from allophonic variation and represents only contrastive differences of sounds.

Rule-governed behavior in sound systems is not limited to allophonic variation. Consider the English plural -*s*. Following a voiced sound it is pronounced [z], as in *dogs, beds, bees, sins*, and *dolls*. Following a voiceless sound, it is pronounced [s], as in *cats, ropes*, and *sticks*.[5] Since this alternation between [s] and [z] is rule-governed and entirely predictable, it is plausible to suppose that the regular plural morpheme has a single lexical representation, say /z/, and that English speakers apply a rule devoicing /z/ to [s] following a voiceless sound.

English *s* and *z*, however, are not merely allophonic variants of a single phoneme in English. When these sounds do not immediately follow a consonant, they contrast, as in *sip* vs. *zip*, and *bus* vs. *buzz*. Therefore, the phonological rules in (6) also include rules that change one underlying phoneme into another, in addition to rules that create allophones of a phoneme (without changing phonemic identity). In the case of the plural, the English spelling system again more closely approximates a broad than a narrow transcription, consistently writing the regular plural as <s> even when it is pronounced [z]. Similarly, the final segment in *electric* is consistently written with a <c>, whether it is pronounced [k], or [s] (as in *electricity*), or [š] (as in *electrician*).

Whereas a narrow transcription should ideally be universal, a broad transcription is language particular, reflecting the patterning of sounds in particular languages.

Narrow transcription in phonological theory

Students of phonology brought up in the tradition of generative grammar will readily identify broad transcription with Chomsky and Halle's systematic phonemic level and narrow transcription with the systematic phonetic level. Indeed, the model in (6) appears to be a natural translation into phonological theory of the two types of transcription. However, some difficulties had to be overcome in arriving at the model in (6). The first of these concerns the nature of the phonetic level: to what extent is it truly a "systematic" level of representation?

Leonard Bloomfield (1887–1949), and the American linguists who followed him, known as the post-Bloomfieldians, maintained that a phonetic level corresponding to a narrow transcription cannot be supported as a legitimate linguistic representation because it is not systematic, but arbitrary. According to Bloomfield, such a transcription is dependent on the background and perception of the transcriber: some transcribers will notice and note down certain subphonemic distinctions, but others that are less familiar to them will go unrecorded, particularly as they are not crucial to marking contrastive sounds in the language.

For example, an English-speaking transcriber might record that the *t* in the English word *two* is aspirated, because the distribution of aspirated and unaspirated /t/ in English is systematic. But there are many other aspects of this sound that may or may not be noted: whether the sound is dental (made with the tongue against the teeth) or alveolar (tongue against the alveolar ridge); whether the lips are rounded (as they are in *two*) and, if so, how much; whether the tongue is released quickly and simultaneously with the puff of air, or whether the tongue lags a bit, creating an affricated (tending to [t^s]) or palatalized [t^j] sound; and so on.

Since a linguistic representation must be based on more than just the whims of individual transcribers, Bloomfield concluded that there is no principled level of phonetic representation corresponding to a narrow transcription.

As pointed out by Chomsky (1964), this argument rests on the assumption that there is no universal theory of phonetic representation. Lacking such a theory, it would appear that a phonetic representation has no principled basis. However, a universal feature theory, of the sort initiated by Prague School linguists and developed in works such as Jakobson, Fant, and Halle (1952), Jakobson and Halle (1956), and subsequently revised by Chomsky and Halle (1968), can serve as the basis for a phonetic transcription. The universal set of distinctive features is designed to discriminate all and only those aspects of sounds that are contrastive in the languages of the world. *SPE*, for example, uses twelve distinctive features to represent the consonant sounds of English.[6] The existence of a universal set of phonetic features constrains what can go into a phonetic representation. No such theory existed in American linguistics, so there was no basis for a systematic phonetic level.

How, then, are the sounds of a language to be represented in a linguistic description? We are left with broad transcription, or, in terms of (6), the systematic phonemic level. However, the systematic phonemic level is too remote from the surface phonetics, that is, too abstract, to serve as the only level of phonological representation.

Consider the English vowel system. In English, unstressed vowels tend to reduce to schwa [ə] in many contexts:

(7)   English vowel–schwa alternations

Tense vowel		Reduced		Lax vowel		Reduced	
Canádian	[ej]	Cánada	[ə]	Asiátic	[æ]	Ásia	[ə]
managérial	[ij]	mánager	[ə]	telégraphy	[ɛ]	télegraph	[ə]
horízon	[aj]	horizóntal	[ə]	medícinal	[ɪ]	médicine	[ə]
custódian	[ow]	cústody	[ə]	photógraphy	[a]	phótograph	[ə]
sulfúric	[juw]	súlfur	[ə]	prodúction	[ʌ]	próduct	[ə]

Thus, [ə] is an allophone of every English vowel phoneme. It follows that a phonemic representation of the above words should include unreduced vowels only; reduction to schwa would then be a rule-governed allophonic variation.

Bloch (1941) argued that while such a system is indeed elegant, it poses problems for a learner (as well as a linguist unfamiliar with the language). What happens when learners come across a schwa whose unreduced version is unknown to them, as in words like *sofa* or *of*? Or even *manager*, if they haven't heard a related form such as *managerial*? If there were a "lower" phonetic level of representation, a learner could at least represent the phonetic form of such words with a schwa, while deferring a decision as to which underlying phoneme to assign it to. But, having rejected a phonetic level, post-Bloomfieldian theory had no recourse to such a level of representation. The consequence is that learners (and linguists) would be unable to assign any phonological representation to such utterances.

Moreover, according to Bloch, the only data relevant to phonemic analysis are "the facts of pronunciation," that is, the distribution of surface allophones, and not, for example, the existence of morphologically related forms. This assumption severely limits the evidence one can use in arriving at a phonological analysis. It presupposes an analyst who has no access to the fact that the word *manager* is related to *managerial*. Such an analyst would not be in a position to know that the final schwa of the former is related to the stressed vowel of the latter.

Thus, without a systematic phonetic level, the post-Bloomfieldians needed a new level of representation that was much less abstract than the systematic phonemic level, and that did not suffer from the arbitrariness they attributed to phonetic representation. In structuralist terminology, this level was simply called the phonemic representation, and the more abstract systematic phonemic level was called the morphophonemic representation. In the terminology of Chomsky (1964), the new level is called the taxonomic phonemic level. The post-Bloomfieldian conception of the phonological component was thus as in (8).

(8)   Levels in post-Bloomfieldian American structuralist phonology

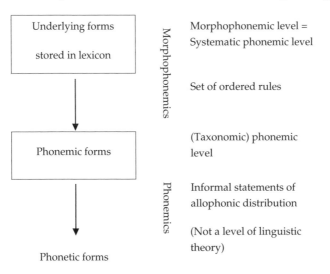

The new (taxonomic) phonemic level

Bloch's argument assumes that language learners must be able to encode utterances into phonemes based only on the distribution of surface sounds, or phones. Of course, learners of a language must acquire not only the phonological system, but the rest of the grammar as well, including the morphology and syntax. However, it became an entrenched assumption of American structuralist linguistics that acquisition of language went "bottom-up," from phones to phonemes, from phonemes to morphemes, from morphemes to syntax, and so on. Though this assumption had no empirical support whatsoever, it had important consequences for the development of phonological theory.

One consequence was the dictum that it is impermissible to "mix levels" in developing a phonemic analysis. That is, a phonemic analysis must be justifiable solely on the basis of allophonic distribution, making no appeal to "higher" levels such as morpheme identity. As Chomsky (1964) showed, this assumption had disastrous consequences for the generality and simplicity of the phonological analysis.[7]

An example is Hockett's (1951) discussion of a hypothetical language with no underlying contrast between voiced and voiceless consonants: all consonants are voiceless except word-medially between vowels, where they are voiced. This is a fairly common situation, and the natural assumption is that a phonemic representation should indicate only voiceless consonants, since voicing is predictable. Hockett considers the case of two sequences of words in such a language, *pat adak* and *padat ak*. In the standard analysis, these words would have the phonemic representations shown in (9), where # represents a word boundary separating the words.

(9)   Consonants voiced only word-medially between vowels

	a.	b.
Phonemic	/ #pat#atak# /	/ #patat#ak# /
Voicing	#pat#adak#	#padat#ak#
Phonetic	[patadak]	[padatak]

Hockett argues that there is a problem with this analysis. The word boundaries do not correspond to any sound, or even to a regular absence of sound or pause. If one hears (9b) [padatak] one would not know, on phonetic grounds alone, whether it derives from /patat # ak/ or /pata # tak/. Of course, one could determine this if one knew something about the lexicon: one might find, for example, that there is a stem / patat-/ with the appropriate meaning but no stem / pata/. But performing such a look-up is to "mix levels." In Hockett's interpretation of phonemic theory, the phonemic representation must not rely on the proper positioning of word boundaries. If boundaries are omitted from the phonemic representation, then both utterances in (9) are represented as / patatak/. But now we cannot account for the different distribution of voiceless and voiced consonants in (9a) and (9b); the only solution, according to Hockett, is to represent voiced consonants as such in phonemic representation. Rather than the phonemic forms in (9), we would posit / patadak/ for (9a) and / padatak/ for (9b). This result appears to be incompatible with the original concept of a phoneme. Moreover, the generalization that the voicing of consonants is predictable and therefore need not be learned on a case-by-case basis is lost.[8]

The attempt to constrain the phonemic level so as to keep it closer to the surface phonetics led to the requirement that the phonemic level meet a number of further conditions. Their effect was to ensure that there be a one-to-one relation (*biuniqueness*) between allophones and phonemes: given an allophone, it should be possible to unambiguously assign it to a phoneme; and given a phoneme, it must be clear what allophone instantiates it in any given context. The # boundaries in (9) violate biuniqueness, because phonetic [padatak] can derive either from /patat # ak/ or /pata # tak/. Like the prohibition on mixing of levels, these conditions resulted in a loss of generalizations, with no compensatory gain in descriptive or explanatory force.

Consider again the interaction of Flapping and rules affecting the /aj/ diphthong shown above in the *writer/rider* example (4), repeated here.

(4)   A simple derivation

	writer	*rider*
Underlying	/ rajtər /	/ rajdər /
Lengthening	–	raːjdər
Raising	rʌjtər	
Flapping	rʌjɾər	raːjɾər
Phonetic	[rʌjɾər]	[raːjɾər]

It is clear in (4) that [ɾ] is a predictable allophone of both / t/ and / d/, and there is no difficulty in formulating rules to account for its distribution. However, this simple derivation fails a number of conditions that the post-Bloomfieldian linguists placed on phonemic representations.

First, the phonemes / t/ and / d/ have a common allophone, [ɾ]. This amounts to a *partial overlapping* of the two phonemes, which violates the biuniqueness condition. The problem with overlapping is that it is not possible, upon inspection, to decide which phoneme an allophone belongs to. Of course, if we could appeal to morpheme identity we would know that the [ɾ] of *writer* belongs to / t/, because of *write*, and that the [ɾ] of *rider* belongs to / d/, because of *ride*. But this again violates the constraint against mixing of levels.

Another problem with this analysis from the point of view of post-Bloomfieldian theory is that there is a mismatch between the location of the phonemic and the phonetic contrast in *writer* and *rider*: forms that are phonemically different only in their fourth member (/t/ vs. /d/) are phonetically different only in their second member ([ʌj] vs. [aːj]). According to Chomsky (1964), this mismatch is a violation of the condition of *linearity*.

This example shows also that the notion of *minimal pair* is not a self-evident one. A minimal pair is a pair of words that differ in a single phoneme. Minimal pairs are often used to show that two sounds contrast in a language. For example, we can demonstrate that [s] and [z] contrast in English by adducing minimal pairs such as *sip* and *zip*, or *bus* and *buzz*. Since the only difference in these words is the [s] vs. [z], we conclude that they belong to distinct phonemes. However, a similar test would show that [aːj] and [ʌj] are distinct phonemes in English, since *writer* and *rider* appear to be minimal pairs distinguished in their second elements, not their fourth.

As Chomsky (1964) points out, minimal pairs are thus not evident from the surface, but require that we take into account various kinds of information. In the case of *sip* and *zip* there are no further facts that contradict the conclusion that the distinction is simply between /s/ and /z/.[9]

According to the logic of post-Bloomfieldian phonemics, then, we would have to transcribe *writer* as /rʌjrər/ and *rider* as /raːjrər/. In effect, the phonemic level would fail to capture any of the generalizations about English sound patterns discussed above. It would fail to note that [ɾ] is a predictable allophone of /t/ and /d/, and that [ʌj] and [aːj] are predictable allophones of /aj/.

Finally, we have seen that the rules in (4) have to be ordered; ordering was not permissible in American structuralist phonemics. The relationship between a taxonomic phoneme and its allophones had to be statable as a set of unordered distributional statements.

What, then, of the generalizations about sound patterning that are thereby excluded from the phonemics? Where in the grammar, for example, do we represent the fact that there is a single regular English plural, or that the sounds of *write* are systematically related to the sounds of *writer*, or that the stressed vowel in *managerial* is related to the final schwa in *manager*? American structuralist theory had a place for all these generalizations: the morphophonemic component.

Morphophonemics

In *Menomini Morphophonemics*, Bloomfield presented an analysis that resembles a generative derivation: starting from underlying representations, a series of rules apply in order to yield phonemic representations. This type of analysis, and morphophonemics itself, had a marginal status in structuralist theory. There was very little theorizing done in this area, as opposed to the attention devoted to phonemic theory. In contrast to the latter, morphophonemics had a freewheeling, anything-goes character, which led, as it turns out, to interesting and insightful analyses.[10] Why was there such a contrast between the two components? The answer lies in the degree of "reality" attributed to each of these levels.

As we have seen, the taxonomic phonemic level was the lowest linguistic level recognized in the theory. By assumption, it had to be a level that could plausibly be attributed to speakers, including those just learning the language. In keeping with the very restricted conception of psychology and learning that prevailed at the time, learners were credited with only the most basic ability to perform operations of grouping and classification. The various constraints placed on the phonemic level were designed to allow a phonemic representation to be easily discovered from the phonetic input available to such a learner.

By contrast, morphophonemics was not given a psychological interpretation. Morphophonemic representations were not necessarily considered to be things that speakers had. According to Anderson (1985: 276), Bloomfield considered morphophonemic description to be "an elegant artifact, providing a uniform and concise account of a complex set of facts, but not to be confused with the actual language capacity of speakers. Only the phonemic forms, and the morphological fact of relations between them, could be considered to have that status."[11]

It is significant that Chomsky's first work in linguistics, his MA thesis (a later version of his BA thesis), is titled *Morphophonemics of Modern Hebrew*. His later contributions to generative phonology essentially adapted the techniques used in morphophonemics – rules and derivations – and placed them at the center of phonological theory (and other components of grammar). To make this move, however, Chomsky and Halle had to overcome the arguments in favor of the taxonomic phoneme. Having shown that the "elegant fiction" of the morphophonemic component was actually real, they now had to show that the taxonomic phoneme, the rigorous core of phonological theory, was a fiction.

Against the taxonomic phoneme

As we saw above, there is no empirical support for a taxonomic phonemic level that adheres to the various conditions and restrictions imposed by the post-Bloomfieldians, suggesting that such a level is *unnecessary*. In a famous argument, Halle (1959) demonstrated that such a level is also *undesirable*, because it leads to a loss of generalizations.

Imagine, then, a phonology with three significant levels: a morphophonemic (systematic phonemic) level that was not in dispute; a systematic phonetic level based on a universal distinctive feature theory; and mediating between them, the taxonomic phonemic level (10).

(10)   Three-level phonological component

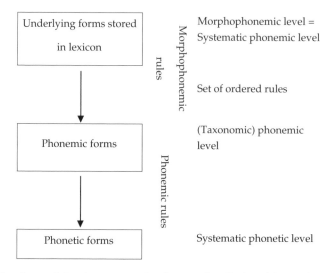

In Russian, voicing is a contrastive feature that distinguishes pairs of obstruent phonemes. Thus, phoneme /t/ is distinct from /d/, /k/ is distinct from /g/, /s/ contrasts with /z/, and so on. There is a rule that voices word-final obstruents if a voiced obstruent follows in the next word. Thus, we find [m'ok l,i] "was (he) getting wet?," with a *k* preceding the sonorant *l,*, but [m'og bɨ] "were (he) getting wet," where *k* voices to *g* before voiced obstruent *b*. The voicing rule that changes *k* to *g* changes one phoneme to another, and so it must be a morphophonemic rule, applying as in (11a).

(11)   Russian voicing applying twice

    a. Morphophonemic voicing

Systematic phonemic	// m'ok bi //	// ž'eč bi //
Voicing	m'og bi	–
Taxonomic phonemic	/ m'og bi /	/ ž'eč bi /

    b. Allophonic voicing

Taxonomic phonemic	/ m'og bi /	/ ž'eč bi /
Voicing	–	ž'eǯ bi
Systematic phonetic form	[m'og bɨ]	[ž'eǯ bɨ]

Three obstruents, / c /, / č /, and / x /, do not have corresponding voiced consonants. However, voicing also applies to these segments as well. We have [ž'eč l,ɨ] "should one burn?," with voiceless č before the sonorant *l*,, but [ž'eǯ bɨ] "were one to burn," where ǯ is the voiced counterpart to č. Because [ǯ] is not a phoneme in its own right, but exists only as an allophone of /č/, this application of voicing is an allophonic rule, and must be assigned to the component that maps phonemic forms into phonetic forms (11b).

Halle argued that the derivation in (11) needlessly splits the voicing rule into two (or, alternatively, applies the same rule twice). However, there is no evidence that voicing applies differently in these cases, or that the change occurs in two stages rather than just once. Having a taxonomic phonemic level makes it impossible to capture the generalization that there is one voicing rule at work here, applying equally to all the segments in its purview.[12]

Without the taxonomic phonemic level, the grammar takes on the form of (6), with only two significant levels of representation: the systematic phonemic, or lexical, level and the systematic phonetic level.

Grammar as a system of knowledge

One of Chomsky's most fundamental contributions was to reposition linguistics as a field with implications for the nature of mind and learning. This reorientation required a new way of looking at linguistic description, one that was diametrically opposed to that prevailing in American linguistics up to that time.

Bloomfieldian philosophy of science and psychology

Leonard Bloomfield introduced a particularly radical form of behaviorism and scientific empiricism to linguistics. This view included an approach to science in general, and to psychology in particular, that together had a great influence on the development of phonological theory.

With respect to science, Bloomfield and his followers took a view that was influential in the 1920s and 1930s, known as Operationalism, that all science must be framed in terms of statements that describe basic operations, such as reports of how long it takes an object to travel a certain distance. Putting the focus on operations seemed to make the "content" of science out to be observable matters (measurements and experimental techniques) rather than obscure-looking "hidden" entities and principles. Theoretical terms and theory itself, it was thought, could be treated as codes or shorthand for observations and techniques. Such an approach is incapable of characterizing most important scientific theories, and the main body of philosophy of science soon abandoned Operationalism.

In American linguistics, however, this general orientation remained influential, and provided a theoretical underpinning to the bottom-up approach to linguistic analysis. The scientist (here, the linguist) begins with basic data, that is, a set of utterances in a language (a *corpus*). These utterances appear to observers (linguists) as a stream of speech. Observers then perform basic operations to analyze the speech stream: they can *segment* an utterance into individual sounds, or phones; and they can *classify* the phones into phonemes. These operations can then be repeated at a higher level of analysis, segmenting and classifying strings of phonemes into morphophonemes, then into words and phrases, and so on.

American linguistics in fact took this approach even farther than other fields, making it an aim of linguistic theory to devise *discovery procedures* that would automatically apply the techniques of segmentation and classification to any corpus and produce an analysis. As Chomsky (1957a) argued, no other science has hoped to arrive at such procedures, which in effect would be an algorithm for arriving at the correct theory in a particular domain, using only the restricted "data" that operationalist ideology allows.[13]

These general views about science were complemented by a set of assumptions about psychology, which amounted to a radical form of behaviorism. Bloomfield and his circle believed that there was no point in attributing a "mind" to any organisms, including humans.[14] Rather, behavior is a set of responses to stimuli. Language, then, is simply another form of behavior, verbal behavior, a set of learned responses, or habits.

It followed, on this view, that linguistics had nothing to contribute to psychology proper. The big questions of psychology – how learning takes place, for example – were held to be the province of psychologists. The special mandate of linguistics was to study verbal behavior proper – to describe (and merely that) the way utterances are put together and used (primarily, it was assumed) in communication. Thus, linguists in this framework were given to say that linguistics should be free of psychology, and should make no assumptions about psychology. This statement, given the above, was quite obviously disingenuous. What was meant, however, is that linguists need not get involved in psychological speculation, beyond the background assumptions sketched above. That is, internal to a linguistic description there is no need to invoke psychology. Nevertheless, the analysis is couched in a framework that is heavily indebted to a specific model of psychology.

The combination of scientific and psychological assumptions that formed the background of neo-Bloomfieldian linguistics placed narrow limits on the types of linguistic theory that could be entertained. Moreover, they tended to draw the focus of inquiry away from evaluating how successful particular theories were in accounting for the facts of language – capturing significant generalizations, accounting for how language is acquired, and so on – and emphasized instead conformity to what were in effect a priori and unmotivated restrictions on the form of a linguistic theory, whatever the consequences might be for particular analyses.

Chomsky's philosophy of science and psychology

Chomsky's approach represented a radical break with Bloomfieldian thought both with respect to science and psychology. With respect to science, Chomsky began with the premise that a linguistic description is a hypothesis about how the data is organized, and thus is a scientific theory of the grammar. He pointed out that no other science has developed, or even seeks to develop, discovery procedures – a set of automatic procedures applied to basic data that results in a theory of the data. Rather, scientists arrive at hypotheses about nature however they can. What can be expected of a scientific theory is not an account, let alone justification, of how it was arrived at, but criteria for assessing how good a theory it is. That is, rather than discovery procedures, linguists should be concerned with developing evaluation procedures, means by which to compare competing theories (grammatical descriptions) with a view to determining which is the better theory.

With respect to psychology, Chomsky argued that behaviorism chose the wrong target. There is not, and likely will not be, a theory of human behavior.[15] But it may be possible to characterize aspects of cognition, or *knowledge*, that contribute to behavior. He therefore proposed that the proper object of linguistics is not verbal behavior, which is the product of diverse systems, but rather knowledge of language. Chomsky proposed that a grammar is actually a theory of the knowledge that native speakers have of their language.

Learnability and Universal Grammar

If a grammar is an account of knowledge, the question immediately arises as to how native speakers come to have this knowledge. As he has argued at length (notably in Chomsky 1975), one cannot consider learning in a domain apart from the cognitive principles that the learner brings to it. In the case of language, where many considerations point to a specialized ability shared by all humans, there is no general learning theory we can appeal to. Rather, linguistic inquiry itself must determine, first, what is actually acquired, and second, what cognitive principles learners employ. The answer to the first question will be a grammar of the language that has been acquired. The answer to the second question is a set of universal principles collectively called Universal Grammar (UG). Whether a particular grammar is easy to learn or difficult depends on the combination of accessibility to relevant data and the nature of UG.

SPE begins with the sentence, "The goal of the descriptive study of a language is the construction of a grammar." Much of *SPE* is devoted to constructing the phonological part of the grammar of English. Freed from restrictions on the relation between phonemes and their surface allophones and from the requirement that morphological relations may not enter into a phonological analysis, the phonology of English that emerges in *SPE* is radically different from previous accounts.

As the opening sentence indicates, *SPE* is much more concerned with the particular grammar of English than with how this grammar could be acquired. Nevertheless, the phonology of English presented in *SPE* is set within a general theory of phonology which is intended to provide a first attempt at a theory of UG in the domain of phonology.

The main mechanism proposed by *SPE* for guiding a learner to the correct grammar is the *evaluation measure*. The evaluation measure, assumed to be part of UG, assigns a higher value to a rule that uses fewer features over a rule that uses more features. This measure reflects the fact that features capture natural classes: therefore, the fewer features, the more general the class. A rule that applies to a more general class is generally preferred to one that delimits a narrower class. That is, a simpler rule is preferred over a more complex one.

While such an evaluation measure can guide a learner in making local decisions between similar rules that differ in their formal simplicity, it is of little help in allowing a learner to choose between sets of rules, or even entire competing grammars. With respect to this problem, there are parallels in the early development of phonological and syntactic theory. In both cases, the theories inherited from structuralism were too descriptively limited: they did not possess the resources to provide a descriptively adequate account of their subject matter. In both cases, therefore, the emphasis at first was on expanding the descriptive resources of linguistic theory. In the case of syntax, this meant exploring the power of transformations; in the case of phonology, the power of derivations and the rule formalism introduced by *SPE*.

In syntax, a concern with constraining the theory arose in the late 1960s and eventually came to dominate thinking in the field, at least in the part of the field associated with Chomsky. By this time, however, Chomsky had largely given up working on phonology, and was not involved with subsequent developments.[16] Many of these developments took as their starting point the theory of *SPE*. Here I will only highlight certain issues that particularly pertain to learnability.[17]

Abstractness of phonology

The underlying forms posited by *SPE* are in general rather abstract with respect to their phonetic surface forms. Much ink has been shed over the extent to which such abstractness is learnable, or whether there should be constraints on abstractness.[18] It is an empirical question whether phonological systems obey constraints limiting the "distance" between underlying and surface forms. If they do, we expect to find evidence for this from the patterning of the phonology itself. However, in some cases proposals to constrain abstractness have tended to be based not on empirical evidence, but, rather, on a priori assumptions concerning what is learnable.

There is no particular reason to suppose that there is a simple relation between abstractness and learnability. Consider again, for example, the derivation in (4). The rule of Flapping contributes to create a considerable mismatch between the underlying and surface forms, as we have seen. At the same time, Flapping obscures the contexts of Raising and Lengthening, by making it appear that Raising applies before a voiced consonant (the flap [ɾ]) in *writer* and that Lengthening fails before a voiced consonant in the same form. This derivation is ruled out by theories that place restrictions on abstractness. Kiparsky (1973), while not ruling out such derivations, proposed that rules that are *opaque* by his definition (i.e. contradicted by surface forms) are difficult to learn. Intuitively, one might expect this to be so: a learner who has not yet acquired the rule that raises /aj/ to [ʌj] before voiceless consonants might be misled by hearing forms like *writer* ([rʌɾər]), where the raising has taken place, though the following consonant is voiced on the surface.

Nevertheless, it is not obvious that this grammar is difficult to learn. The rules of Raising and Centralization apply without complicating factors in the words *write* and *ride*, as well as many other words of English. Similarly, the rule of Flapping applies transparently in many words, such as *sit* ~ *sitter* and *dad* ~ *daddy*. A learner who has learned this much of the grammar already has the main ingredients of the derivation except for the relative ordering of Flapping and the other rules, which must be acquired on the basis of forms like *writer* and *rider*.[19]

Just as it is not the case that abstractness necessarily leads to learnability problems, neither is it the case that reducing abstractness necessarily makes learning easier. For example, in Seri (Marlett 1981) there is a set of vowel-initial words that behave as if they begin with a consonant. Marlett proposes that such words have an underlying initial consonant, designated C, which is deleted toward the end of the derivation. This is an abstract analysis, because it posits a segment that is present in underlying and intermediate representations that is never audible at the surface.

Marlett and Stemberger (1983) present a different analysis. They adopt a nonlinear theory of phonology in which phonological representations consist of different tiers. One of the tiers is a CV-tier, or "skeleton," which relates segmental features to syllable structure. Rather than posit an abstract underlying consonant, they propose that the exceptional verbs have an initial C position on the CV-tier that has no counterpart on the feature tiers. The two analyses are presented schematically in (12).

(12)   Two analyses of Seri exceptional verbs

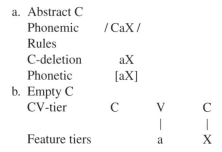

a. Abstract C
   Phonemic   / CaX /
   Rules
   C-deletion   aX
   Phonetic   [aX]
b. Empty C
   CV-tier   C   V   C
                         | |
   Feature tiers   a   X

Marlett and Stemberger comment that the Empty C analysis is superior to the Abstract C analysis because it is less abstract, since the empty C is present at the surface. However, if we focus on learnability and ask what would lead a learner to posit the empty C in (12b), we find that it is exactly the same evidence that would lead the learner to an abstract C in (12a). Since abstractness is a relation between levels of a derivation, it is no surprise that one can reduce abstractness by enriching representations. In (12), the "vertical" relation between a phonemic C and its null phonetic realization is replaced by a "horizontal" relation between a C on one tier and a null representation on the feature tier(s). The analysis in (12b) raises interesting issues about the nature of representations, but does little to advance the problem of learnability.[20]

Markedness and other substantive principles

While abstractness in itself is not necessarily a special problem for learnability, when combined with the otherwise rather loosely constrained apparatus of *SPE* a real problem for learnability does arise. In short, the theory of *SPE* does not provide an adequate answer as to how learners are able to arrive at the actual grammar of their language and not any number of other grammars.

One shortcoming of the *SPE* theory, recognized within *SPE* itself, is that the theory is overly formal: the evaluation measure counts only the number of symbols in a rule, without taking account of intrinsic properties of features or of phonological processes. Thus, a three-vowel system with vowels / i a u / is very common, but one with the vowels / ü ɛ æ / is unheard of. Similarly, a rule changing *i* to *u* is much more common than one changing *i* to *ɨ*, even though *u* differs from *i* by two features ([back] and [round]) and *ɨ* differs from *i* by only one feature ([back]). To remedy this fundamental theoretical inadequacy Chomsky and Halle introduce a theory of markedness. Taking up and extending ideas from the Prague School, they propose that certain feature values and combinations are *unmarked*, or default, whereas others are *marked*, and entail a greater cost to the grammar. By making phonological rules and inventories sensitive to markedness considerations, one can explain why certain segments are more common than others, and why certain rules are more highly valued than other rules with the same number of symbols. Markedness theory contributes to learnability by giving further structure to the hypothesis space of possible grammars.[21]

Asymmetries in intrinsic content also arise in the relationship between phonological changes and their contexts. For example, rules assimilating one or more features of a segment to features in the environment are very common. An extension of markedness theory would also take account of the *naturalness* of rules.

I have suggested that various proposals to limit abstractness have not improved the learnability of grammar. On the contrary, it can be argued that abstractness of the right sort actually improves learnability, by working together with markedness and naturalness to limit the choices available to a learner.

Dresher (1981b) adduces an argument along these lines from Old English. The verb *eotan* "to eat" can be shown to have the underlying stem vowel /e/. This vowel is raised to [i] in the present indicative second and third person singular forms *ites* and *iteθ*. Dresher proposes that the suffixes in these forms derive from underlying /+is/ and /+iθ/, respectively, and the forms in question are derived by means of two rules, given informally in (13) and (14). The derivations are shown in (15).

(13)   *e*-Raising
        Stressed *e* raises to *i* when an *i* follows in the next syllable.

(14)   *i*-Lowering
        Unstressed *i* lowers to [e] when it follows a light syllable (a syllable containing a short vowel and followed by a single consonant).

(15)   Derivation of forms with stem vowel *i*

Underlying	/et+is/	/et+iθ/
e-Raising	itis	itiθ
i-Lowering	ites	iteθ
Phonetic	[ites]	[iteθ]

This analysis is supported by a web of other evidence (see Dresher 1985 for details). Assuming here the correctness of the analysis, the question we wish to answer is how a learner of Old English could arrive at it. In particular, what would lead a learner to suppose that the suffixes are /+is/ and /+iθ/ when they always appear as [+es] and [+eθ]?

Learners would know that unstressed *e* does not in general cause raising of a preceding *i*: there are many words like the present subjunctive *eten* "we / you (pl.) / they eat." It is possible that raising in the present singular is simply an exception, conditioned by morphology, just as the English vowel change from *foot* to *feet* must be attributed to an irregular rule that operates in the plural. While such an analysis cannot be excluded, the assumption of *SPE* is that it is not preferred by the learning theory. In the formulation of Postal (1968), the *SPE* theory incorporates the Naturalness Condition.

(16)   The Naturalness Condition (Postal 1968)
        Phonological classifications are preferred to morphological or arbitrary classifications at all levels of the phonology.

The Naturalness Condition instructs the learner to seek a phonological solution before falling back on a morphological one.

   In a learning theory which values simple and natural rules learners could proceed from the change to make hypotheses about the context. The raising of / e / to [i] involves a change of one feature, [–high], to [+high]. The most favored context for such a change is in the vicinity of another [+high] feature. In our case, there is no such segment visible on the surface; however, the vowel -*e* in the suffixes -*es* and -*eθ* is only one feature away from a high vowel, namely -*i*. Thus, even lacking other evidence, learners equipped with a learning theory of the kind sketched above may suspect at an early stage that the suffix vowel in -*es* and -*eθ* may be a disguised /i/. In this case, the suspicion will be supported by evidence from other parts of the phonology.

   Notice that this solution would not be possible without abstractness. By allowing a certain distance between phonemic and phonetic forms, we can take advantage of rule ordering to formulate rules that are maximally simple and natural. In this way, abstractness contributes to learnability.

6 Universal aspects of word learning

Lila Gleitman and Cynthia Fisher

> Suppose instead of saying *Dutch* we had said *Clashes with the wallpaper; I*
> *thought you liked abstract work, Never saw it before, Tilted, Hanging too low,*
> *Beautiful, Hideous, Remember our camping trip last summer?*
> (Chomsky 1959; Review of B. F. Skinner's *Verbal Learning*)

Most of the action in linguistic theory under Chomsky's aegis has focused on questions of how words are put together into sentences rather than on the words themselves. Fair enough: the universal hallmark of human language is its parametrically organized combinatorial structure. In linguistic systems, the individual word classes (for instance, the nouns, the verbs, the complementizers) play particular and crucial structural roles; rules and parameters directly implicate these classes. But what about the items that comprise these classes? It has been widely maintained that these individual atoms or particles of language play no central role in its core, or, to use recent terminology, in "language narrowly conceived" (Hauser, Chomsky & Fitch 2002). No distributional property of English worth its salt is dependent on whether some particular noun – let us say *elephant* rather than *rhinoceros* or *gnu* – appears in it.[1] Rather, what words seem to be relevant to is the conceptual system that interfaces with language. In this latter domain, relevant to "language broadly conceived," the difference between an elephant and a gnu really matters.

Similarly, the linguistic-theoretical study of language acquisition has focused primarily on the nature and setting of syntactic parameters rather than on the evolving character of the lexicon (e.g. Manzini & Wexler 1987; Lightfoot 1999; Baker 2001). Again, this is no surprise. Acquisition of the combinatorial features of a language poses a classical poverty-of-the-stimulus problem, requiring the learner to extract abstract organizing principles from input structured only (or almost only) as morpheme sequences (see, particularly, Chomsky 1986). In contrast, a first intuition is that acquiring words and their meanings can be fully accounted for by a procedure that associates the forms (say, the sound "elephant") with their meanings (here, the concept ELEPHANT) in consequence of observing the referential contingencies for the word's use (say, visible presence of an elephant). Here is this claim, as put by John Locke (1690):

(1) If we will observe how children learn languages, we shall find that . . . people ordinarily show them the thing whereof they would have them have the idea, and then repeat to them the name that stands for it, as "white," "sweet," "milk," "sugar," "cat," "dog," (Book 3, IX, 9)

In this chapter we will revisit lexical learning in aspects that seem to be relevant to Chomsky's program for understanding language and its users. We will focus on four broad issues. First, we show that the method of word-to-world pairing advocated by Locke in (1) is too weak, taken alone, to account for the robustness of word learning. Second, we discuss further data sources – *linguistic* data sources – that in principle can enrich and constrain this acquisition procedure. Third, we describe what is known of the circumstances in which children recruit and exploit these various data sources. Fourth and finally, we allude to the accumulating evidence that the word-learning procedure leaves its footprint in the mature mental representation of language: grammars are heavily lexicalized, in part because the learning procedure for words has – necessarily – built complex (syntactically organized) lexical structures.

Before beginning, we want to make clear the sense of "word learning" that we will discuss. We restrict ourselves to the *mapping problem*: how one comes to know, if exposed to French, that *chien* is the phonological form that expresses the concept DOG while *voir* expresses TO SEE; whereas if exposed to Italian, that it is *cane* and *vedere*. We leave aside altogether the question of where the concepts themselves come from, stipulating only that, to a useful approximation, these concepts are in place to support the word-learning procedure. That is, acquiring the meaning for *dog* and *see* requires that the learner antecedently be able to entertain these concepts[2] (Fodor 1983). Our question – the mapping problem for vocabulary acquisition – is how the child decides which sound goes with which meaning.

The robustness of learning to input variation

Locke's dictum (1) is that the correlation between word use and the specifics of the reference world is both necessary and sufficient to account for word learning. It follows from this that words could not be acquired (the mapping problem could not be solved) except under conditions in which words were uttered in the presence of their referents. We ask in this section whether this precondition is met in children's learning environment; and, if it is, whether this precondition is sufficient as well as necessary.

The contingencies for a word's use

Perhaps the central difficulty with Locke's approach was noted by Chomsky (1959), who challenged empiricist speculation on just this point; hence the epigraph to the present chapter. The trouble is that one does not always or even particularly often say "Dutch" on viewing a Rembrandt painting. Conversation, even from mothers to babies, is not a running commentary on the objects, events, properties, and relations presently on exhibit in the world. No mother carefully utters "open" every time she opens the door; worse, "open" is frequently uttered – even systematically so – when the door is shut ("Help! I'm locked in this bathroom! Please someone come and open the door!"). In the next main section of this chapter we will document this "stimulus-free" property of language use. The problem is not that utterances have no relevance to matters at hand. It is rather that the concept *relevance* is so broad that it places very little constraint on what is likely to be said, given some circumstance. We should note that the issues here look even more ominous from the perspective of Quine (1960), who famously noticed that indefinitely many construals can be put on any observation of the world (say, a rabbit-observation). Chomsky's objections seem more to the point, as he grants constraints on interpretation deriving from human conceptual structure and from conversational relevance; and yet *still* the word-to-world contingencies appear to be so flexible as to render learning by observation intractable.

Cross-situational observation

The standard response to the problem just discussed is that the child doesn't have to learn from a single observation. Rather, over successive observations, probabilistic relations between word and world will converge to support word learning. After all, in the end *elephant* is uttered more in elephant situations than in zebra situations (Pinker 1984). One potential pitfall for a learning device reliant on these correlations is the ornate differentiating series of observations that would be required if it is not to go hopelessly wrong, a difficulty that Locke seems to acknowledge by his very choice of examples: in (1) whiteness is an attribute of both the sugar and the milk, and sweetness of both the sugar and (if one is lucky) one's mother. An even more difficult problem is that such a procedure does not seem to comport well with the actual learning facts. For one thing, a statistical learning procedure that maps between word sounds and events must be errorful over its course, involving significant backtracking and revision, and so predicts some proportion of howlers along the way. Children should sometimes mix up the milk and the sugar with their mothers, at least in speech acts. Moreover, vocabulary acquisition should overall be a slow process, since an accumulation of observations is required to warrant conclusions about each item (and the more variable the word-to-world circumstances, the slower should be the learning). Yet learning proceeds at rates up to ten new items per day, almost completely without the predicted howlers. Children seem to be drawing the right conclusions about the meanings and referents of words based on one or a very few exposures. In Carey's (1978) terms, they are "fast mappers."

Populations deprived of information; colorless green ideas

Just as no child receives all the sentences of English as the condition for learning its grammar, so no child observes all the potential referents as a condition for acquiring word meanings. Totally disjoint dog observations underlie individuals' acquisition of the word *dog*. You see Fido and Spot, I see Rex and Ginger, yet for each of us a generalization results such that we *consensually* partition the whole world into the dogs and the non-dogs. The British Empiricists were among the first to ask just how far observational environments could diverge, to support the learning of the same word. They suggested that relevant test beds for the learning by observation hypothesis can come from populations who are systematically deprived of certain opportunities to observe the world. Here is this suggestion, as offered by David Hume:

(2)...wherever by any accident the faculties which give rise to any impression are obstructed in their operations, as when one is born blind or deaf, not only the impressions are lost, but also their correspondent ideas; so that there never appear in the mind the least trace of either of them. (1739/1978: 49).

For example, the congenitally blind do not observe redness or seeing. Therefore by hypothesis they could not acquire the concepts RED and SEE. It follows, if word learning requires a mapping between instantiations of a concept and the hearing of a word (*qua* phonological object), then a blind child would have no basis for learning the meaning of words that express vision-related concepts. Two cases studied by Landau and Gleitman (1985) were vision verbs (*look*, *see*) and color nouns and adjectives (*color*, *green*, *red*). Sighted blindfolded three-year-olds told to "Look up!" turned their faces skyward, suggesting that they interpreted *look* to implicate vision in particular. This interpretation isn't true of the blind: a blind three-year-old given the same command raises her hands skyward instead of her face, suggesting that for her the term is connected to the manual sense.

So far so good for Locke and Hume: the difference in observational opportunities leads the blind and sighted to different interpretations of the same term. Successful communication from mother to blind child using this term often occurred just when the objects to be "looked at" were in the learner's hands, licensing a physical contact interpretation of blind looking. However, several common verbs used by the mother to the blind child shared the property of being uttered – and even more systematically than *look* – when the child had a relevant object in hand, including *hold*, *give*, *put*, and *play*.

Moreover, the blind child's interpretation of *look* goes beyond manual contact. An informative manipulation was to say "You can touch that table but don't look at it." If *look* means *touch* to the blind, this command is incoherent and therefore cannot be obeyed; but instead the blind child gingerly taps or scratches at the table in response to this command. Subsequently told "Now you can look at it," the child explores the surfaces of the table manually. Based on this kind of evidence, Landau and Gleitman (1985) concluded that blind *look* (a) semantically differs from sighted *look* by implicating a different sense modality, but (b) semantically resembles sighted *look*, and differs from *hold*, *touch*, etc., in being a term of perception. To be sure, in order to look a blind person must touch; but that does not imply that *look* means – or "just means" – *touch*. (And predictably, "You can look at this table but don't touch it" elicits confused complaints from the blind child.)

Summarizing, we can easily account for the blind child's failure to map *look* onto the visual modality from an orthodox associative perspective on word learning that focuses on the necessity of extralinguistic observation. But this perspective cannot so easily explain how blind – and sighted – learners hit upon *looking* as a perceptual rather than as a contact term. Again, these findings suggest that word-to-world pairing is insufficient as a full explanation of word learning. Both populations know too much, from too little information about the world. Chomsky (1986) termed this "Plato's Problem."

The blind child's understanding of color terms offers a similar insight: Landau and Gleitman's (1985) blind preschool-aged informant knew that (a) *color* is the supernym for a subset of adjectival terms including *green* and *red*, but not *clean* and *happy;* and (b) the color terms apply only to concrete objects. Asked "Can a dog be blue?" the blind child at five years of age responded with different color terms: "A dog is not even blue. It's gold or brown or something else." Asked "Can an idea be green?" the child responded "Really isn't green; really just talked about – no color but we think about it in our mind." That is, *blue* may not be an actual attribute of dogs; but *green* is a category error as applied to ideas. These findings display the remarkable resilience of semantic acquisition over variations of input: lacking the ordinarily relevant observations that support solution of the mapping problem for visual terms, the blind are not helpless to do the same. But then what is the foundation for this learning?

Hard words

Many of the words that mothers frequently utter to their infants are so divorced from straightforward perception that it is hard to see how observation could possibly be available to support their acquisition. Even supposing (somewhat controversially) that the learner by the age of two or three is capable of understanding the concept we express as *think*, it is quite difficult to imagine circumstances, short of visits to the Rodin Museum, that would bring it to mind as what a conversation is about. If we point to some group of people who truly are thinking, and contrast them with another set of people who truly are not thinking, what good can it do the learner to gaze upon these contrasting people-sets? Their thinking is happening inside their heads, invisible to any observer. Items of this sort have posed important challenges to the view that the mapping problem can be accomplished by a machinery responsive solely to the observable contingencies for a word's use. "Show them the thing . . ." seems a very much less compelling method for this kind of item than it does for the elephants.

More generally, the trouble with verbs and other predicate terms is that they're abstract, and therefore much less obviously displayed in the flow of events. Verb meanings depend not only on the events in view, but also on a choice of perspectives on events (Clark 1990; Gleitman 1990; Gleitman, Gleitman, Miller & Ostrin 1996; Pinker 1989, *inter alia*). At the extreme, perspective-changing verbs like *chase* and *flee* pose a problem of principle for any theory of lexical acquisition that relies solely on word-to-world mapping. Verbs within these pairs describe the same events, differing only in their focus on the perspective of one or the other participant in that event. This focus difference is unobservable, residing only in the speaker's head. As further examples, one cannot say of a scene that one of its participants is *giving* if nobody *gets*, and every time one *puts* the cup on the table, the cup also *lands* on the table (Gleitman 1990).

Inconvenient facts about word learning

Children do not learn every word they hear. Input frequency does not even begin to explain this fact. Perhaps we need no complex theory to explain why no child's first word is *the* despite its frequency in maternal speech. But a timing difference for object terms versus action terms (and its surface correlate, nouns versus verbs) requires a little further theorizing. Many studies show that children's early production vocabulary is dominated by concrete nouns – names for objects and people in particular (see for reviews Gentner & Boroditsky 2001; Woodward & Markman 1998). This is true in languages other than English, even in languages like Italian that possess surface properties conducive to verb learning, including the omission of inferable noun phrases. The same bias toward learning object names is present in the earliest language comprehension as well. Novel words presented in object-manipulation contexts cause one-year-olds to focus on the kinds of similarity across objects that can indicate shared category membership (Waxman & Markow 1995). When a new word is presented, the object-kind interpretation is often so salient that it's difficult to get children to arrive at any other interpretation (Bloom 2000; Gentner 1982).

At first glance, this bias does not seem to be in conflict with the observational theory of word learning. It could be – this surely is true in the limit – that some concepts are more difficult to entertain than others, and therefore are simply unavailable to the infant mind. The relational notions that verbs typically express might be harder to grasp, or less salient to infants, than are notions of object kind. If the relevant world observations are potentially available but uninterpretable, then the words can't be learned. This account of the late appearance of verbs relative to nouns would thus accord perfectly well with the Lockian prediction. However, there is a different account of this striking, universal, input–output disparity for the efficient acquisition of nouns and verbs: the acquisition of nouns and verbs may require different kinds of information, and the information sources themselves may become available at different developmental moments. We turn now to evidence for just such a position.

Linguistic and conceptual supports for vocabulary acquisition

How can the robustness of word learning be understood in the face of the vagaries of ordinary experience and the vast array of reasonable interpretations of what has been said? We will argue that vocabulary acquisition is not of a piece. Some words are *necessarily* learned before others. The initial learning of concrete nouns sets in motion a process that makes possible the efficient learning of less concrete words; bits of the lexicon and grammar of the exposure language are acquired in a succession of causally interlocking steps. Learners construct the linguistic ladder, so to speak, while they are climbing it.

> *Word-to-world mapping: showing them "the thing" suffices for some words, but not for* think – *or* thing

Some words are less obscure than others in the flow of experience made available for our inspection. Evidence for systematic variations in the recoverability of various words' meanings from world context alone comes from studies by Gillette, Gleitman, Gleitman, and Lederer (1999). Their interest was in understanding how information structure in the input influences solution of the mapping problem, apart from whatever role developmental differences in mentality may play. Therefore they used *adults* to simulate vocabulary learning *under various informational circumstances*.

The first step in these investigations was to understand the limits of word-to-world pairing: solving the mapping problem by using observed scenes as the sole clue. To do so, the investigators showed their adult subjects brief videoclips (about 45 seconds in length) of mothers and toddlers playing with toys and conversing. The soundtracks were removed from these video clips, and a "beep" was inserted in each clip at the moment when the mother had uttered a particular target word. The targets were the 24 nouns (e.g. *ball, hand, hat*) and 24 verbs (e.g. *push, come, look*) most frequently produced by mothers in the corpora from which these clips were drawn. For each word, the adult observers were told they would see six videotaped occasions of the same word's use in a row.

Thus they had some opportunity for cross-situational observation. Their task was to identify each "mystery word" using this accumulating evidence. With only these scene observations as evidence, adults correctly identified three times as many of the mothers' nouns (about 45 percent) as of their verbs (about 15 percent).

Success rates in this task could be predicted by other adults' judgments of the imageability (concreteness) of each word. On average, the common nouns in the mothers' speech were judged more imageable than the common verbs, and variability in judged imageability was a better predictor than the noun/verb distinction of which words were successfully induced from observation of the scenes. The most concrete of the target verbs (e.g. *throw*) were identified more frequently than the most abstract. Those judged most abstract, including *think* and *know*, were never guessed correctly by any subject. Subsequent studies have begun to refine the notion of concreteness that determines which words are relatively easy to learn from observation alone. For example, Kako and Gleitman (in prep.) found that words for basic-level categories of whole objects (e.g. *elephant*) are strikingly easier to identify based on observations of their circumstances of use alone than are abstract nouns (e.g. *thing*) or part terms (e.g. the elephant's *trunk*).

These findings (see also Snedeker & Gleitman in press) yield a simple explanation for the probabilistic noun advantage in infants' first vocabularies. The adult subjects in Gillette et al.'s (1999) studies had already grasped the concepts lexicalized by all the English words to be guessed in the study. Nevertheless, only the most concrete words were successfully identified from observing the extralinguistic contexts alone. The most concrete words, including a useful vocabulary of names for things, are just those for which linguistically unaided observation is likely to be informative.

These data confirm that the solution to the mapping problem may start with Locke's procedure but cannot end there. Observation of the thing is sufficient for the acquisition of some (e.g. *elephant*) but not all of our words (e.g. *thing*, *trunk*, *think*). The true beginner can only try to observe elements in the world that systematically covary with the use of particular words. This leads to success in those cases in which the word's meaning is concrete enough to be readily observable in the flow of events: mostly nouns, but also a heterogeneous set of other words.

Sentence-to-world mapping

How does the child move beyond an initial concrete, largely nominal, vocabulary? To learn less concrete (less observable) terms, the learner needs other kinds of evidence – linguistic evidence, bootstrapped from (*grounded by*) the previously acquired vocabulary of concrete words.[3]

The view known as *syntactic bootstrapping* proposes that the interpretation of verbs and other predicate terms is guided by information about the structure of the sentence in which the verb appears (Landau & Gleitman 1985; Gleitman 1990; Fisher 1996). Most generally, this view proposes that word learning after the first steps proceeds by sentence-to-world pairing rather than merely by word-to-world pairing.

To illustrate, let us return to the Gillette et al. (1999) "human simulations" described earlier. These investigators repeated their experiment, asking adults to identify verbs spoken to young children based on various combinations of linguistic and extralinguistic information. Adults were much more accurate in guessing which verb the mother said to her child when given information about the sentences in which the verb had occurred. When given a list of the nouns that occurred in the sentence (alphabetized to remove word-order information), along with the scene in which the verb was produced, subjects' guesses were significantly more accurate than when given the scene alone. Subjects also profited from more explicit syntactic information about the verbs' original contexts of use, even when denied observation of the scene: presented only with a set of sentences in which all the content words were replaced with nonsense words (e.g. Can ver GORP litch on the fulgar?; much as in Carroll's poem *Jabberwocky*), subjects were significantly more accurate in guessing the verbs than when they saw the scenes, or even when they saw the scenes plus an alphabetized list of cooccurring nouns. When presented with the complete sentence contexts, with only the verb replaced by a nonsense word (e.g. Can you GORP Markie on the phone?), subjects' guesses were quite accurate even without access to the scenes, and nearly perfect with both sentence and scene.

Why would syntactic information so strongly guide semantic inferences? Verbs vary in their syntactic privileges (i.e. the number, type, and positioning of their associated phrases). These variations are systematically related to the verbs' meanings (Chomsky 1981a; Fisher, Gleitman & Gleitman 1991; Gleitman 1990; Grimshaw 1990; Jackendoff 1983; Rappaport, Hovav & Levin 1988; Pinker 1989, *inter alia*). A verb that describes the motion of an object will usually occur with a noun phrase that specifies that object; a verb that describes an action on an object will typically accept two noun phrases (i.e. be transitive); a verb that describes the transfer of an object from one position to another will take three arguments. Similarly sensible patterns appear for argument type: *see* can take a noun phrase as its complement because we can see objects, but also can take a sentence complement because we can perceive states of affairs.

Such syntactic–semantic correspondence patterns show striking regularities across languages (Baker 2001; Croft 1990; Dowty 1991). These crosslinguistic regularities have long been taken to be primary data for linguistic theories to explain, leading to principles such as the *theta criterion* and the *projection principle* (Chomsky 1981a), which jointly state that the nouns in sentences must be licensed by the right kind of predicate (one that can assign them a thematic or "theta" role), and that clause structure must be projected from lexical entries. Similarly, unlearned constraints linking thematic roles such as *agent* and *theme* to grammatical functions like *subject* and *object* have been proposed to explain crosslinguistic regularities in the assignments of semantic roles to sentence positions. Causal agents, for example, overwhelmingly appear as grammatical subjects across languages (Baker 2001; Keenan 1976).

Based on these systematic links between syntax and meaning, the adults in Gillette et al.'s (1999) studies, or a suitably constructed young learner, can consult each verb's sentence structure to glean information about its meaning. The observed sentence structure, by specifying how many and what types of arguments are being selected by the verb, provides a kind of "linguistic zoom lens" to help the learner detect what is currently being expressed about an ongoing event or a state or relation. The set of such structures associated with a verb, across usages, is a complex function of its full expressive range (we discuss these issues further on p. 138, below).

Linguistic evidence aids identification of abstract nouns as well. Kako and Gleitman (in prep.) found that the inductive advantage for basic-level object kinds was reduced when linguistic information was added to or substituted for the scene information (*Sorf the RENCK's reb?* or *See the RENCK's trunk?*). Consistent with this finding, several prior studies have found that abstract, superordinate, or part nouns are typically introduced into the conversation in informative *linguistic* contexts (e.g. *This is the bear, here are his ears; Here's a dog, a cat, and a horse, they're all animals;* see Shipley, Kuhn & Madden 1983; Callanan 1985).

Inferences from syntax to meaning will presumably differ in their mechanics for abstract nouns and for verbs. To a considerable degree, however, sentence structures will be informative insofar as they convey information about the predicate-argument structure of their meanings, for argument-taking nominals of various sorts (e.g. *John's shoe; the fact that Bill likes ham*), nominal arguments of known verbs (e.g. *feeding the ferret*), unknown verbs (e.g. *she adores ham*), or other argument-taking predicates (e.g. *the cat is on the mat*).

Summary: the information base for word learning

The "Human simulation" studies just discussed tell us about the information structure of the input: more than one kind of information is available for vocabulary learning, and these information sources are more or less informative depending on the kind of word being learned. For the case of basic-level names for things, reference is fairly easy to determine from unaided inspection of the scene, whereas there is almost no information to be gained from these words' licensed positions in sentences (other than the fact that they are nouns). It is easy to see why. Tens of thousands of English nouns appear in the linguistic context "the gorp," so this context hardly narrows the search-space for mapping; in contrast, it is relatively easy to observe, say, a horse or a flower or a fork in the situational context. The meanings of more abstract words, including most verbs, are harder to identify in the flow of events, but have more informative linguistic contexts. At the far end of this abstractness continuum are the credal verbs, such as *think* and *know*, for which the situational observation is of almost no value, while the linguistic-syntactic information is hugely informative for these very cases (Gillette et al. 1999; Snedeker & Gleitman in press).

Children's use of multiple cues in word learning

Important as it is to determine the potential informativeness of the multiple cues to word meaning available in the input, it still remains to demonstrate how and when learners are responsive to them.

The meanings to be communicated, and their systematic mapping onto linguistic expressions, arise independently of exposure to any language

In advance of language learning, infants during the first year of life naturally factor their representations of events into conceptual predicates and arguments (Bloom 2000; Fisher & Gleitman 2002). Some of the most striking evidence that the structure of human cognition yields a language-appropriate division of our thoughts into predicates and arguments comes from learners who are isolated from ordinary exposure to a language and therefore have to invent one on their own.

Most deaf children are born to hearing parents who do not sign, and therefore the children may not come into contact with gestural languages for years (Newport 1990). Deaf children with no available language model spontaneously invent gesture systems called "Home Sign" (Feldman, Goldin-Meadow & Gleitman 1978; Goldin-Meadow 2003). Remarkably, though these children are isolated from exposure to any conventional language, their home sign systems partition their experience into the same pieces that characterize the elements of sentences in Italian, Inuktitut, and English. Specifically, home sign systems have nouns and verbs, distinguishable from each other by their positions in the children's gesture sequences and by their distinctive iconic properties. Moreover, and especially pertinent to the issues that we have been discussing, sentence-like combinations of these gestures vary in both the number and positioning of the nouns as a function of what their verbs mean. Systematically appearing with each verb in a child's home sign system are other signs spelling out the thematic roles required by the logic of the verb: the *agent* of the act, the *patient* or thing affected, and so forth.

The nature of this relationship is easy to see from a few examples: Because "crying" involves only a single participant (the crier), a verb with this meaning appears with only one nominal argument. Because "tapping" has two participants, the tapper and the thing tapped, such verbs appear with two nominal arguments. Because "giving" requires a giver, a getter, and a gift, this verb shows up with three nominal phrases. As mentioned earlier, these semantic functions of the nouns vis à vis the verbs are known as their *thematic* or *semantic* or *theta roles* (Chomsky 1981a). The same fundamental relationships between verb meaning and nominal arguments surface in much the same way in the speech of children who are acquiring a conventional language, and in the gestures of linguistically isolated children who must invent one for themselves.[4]

In addition, the nouns occurring with each verb do not appear haphazardly to either side of the verb. The isolated deaf children adopt systematic gesture orders, such as routinely signing undergoers immediately before verbs, (transitive) agents following verbs, and intransitive actors before verbs. Thus, a home signer who produced "Snack$_{<theme>}$-Eat-Susan$_{<agent>}$," might also produce "Susan$_{<actor>}$-Move Over" and "Cheese$_{<theme>}$-Eat" (Goldin-Meadow 2003). Apparently, just as no child has to learn to factor experience into predicates and arguments, no child has to learn to use word order systematically to specify the semantic role played by each element.

In sum, linguistically isolated children construct, out of their own thoughts and communicative needs, systems that resemble the languages of the world in at least the following universal regards: all have words of more than one kind, at minimum nouns and verbs, organized into sentences expressing predicate-argument relations. The number of noun phrases is predictable from the meaning of the verb; the positioning of the nouns expresses their semantic roles relative to the verb. Thus, the fundamental structure of the clause in both self-generated and more established communication systems derives from the non-linguistic conceptual structures by which humans represent events, coupled with strong preferences for "flattening" these conceptual structures into linguistic expressions. This "cognitivist" interpretation of the origin of language in child conceptual structure motivates all modern linguistic treatments of verb semantics that we know of (Baker 2001; Chomsky 1981a; Dowty 1991; Fillmore 1968; Jackendoff 1983; Rappaport-Hovav & Levin 1988). The same cognitivist approach figures in most psychological theories about learning of both syntax and lexicon, whatever the other disagreements of their proponents (e.g. Gleitman, Gleitman et al. 1988; Pinker 1989; Slobin 2001; Tomasello 2000). Indeed, both "nativist" and "learning-functionalist" wings of the language-learning investigative community have seized upon the transparency and universality of such form-to-meaning correspondences in language acquisition as uniquely supporting their learning positions in particular. (After the battle, the opposing generals retreated to their tents to celebrate their victory.)

Young children use the structure of a sentence to guide interpretation of new verbs

Here we discuss evidence that young language learners, much like the infant language inventors that we just discussed, exploit form-to-meaning correspondences as a rich source of evidence about the lexicon.

The case of argument number   Particularly well studied has been early sensitivity to noun-phrase number as a cue to verb interpretation (Fisher 1996, 2002; Naigles 1990; Lidz et al. 2003; Naigles & Kako 1993). For example, Naigles (1990) showed that children as young as 25 months of age interpret new verbs in accord with the number of their noun-phrase arguments. The children watched a video-taped event in which two actions occurred simultaneously: in one composite display, a bunny pushed a duck into a bending posture, while the bunny and duck bent their free arms at the elbow. Each child heard this display described by either a transitive ("The bunny is gorping the duck!") or an intransitive sentence ("The bunny and the duck are gorping!"). Following this training, the two subevents of the composite scene were shown separately on two side-by-side monitors, and the children were exhorted to "Find gorping!" One screen showed the causal event in which the bunny bent the duck; the other showed the non-causal event in which both animals bent their arms. Children who had heard the transitive training sentence looked longer at the causal event, while children who had heard the intransitive sentence looked longer at the non-causal event.

Similar syntactic evidence can persuade young children to alter their interpretation of a familiar verb. Naigles, Gleitman, and Gleitman (1992) asked preschoolers to act out sentences using a toy Noah's Ark and its associated characters. The informative trials were those in which a verb was presented in a new syntactic environment, as in *Noah brings to the ark* or *Noah goes the elephant to the ark*. Young children adjusted the interpretation of the verb to fit its new syntactic frame, for example acting out *go* as "cause to go" (a.k.a. "bring") when it was presented as a transitive verb.

Compare these results with the innovations of the deaf home signers who invented their own manual communication systems. In both cases, children map participants in a conceptual representation of an event one-to-one onto noun arguments in sentences. Elsewhere we have proposed (Fisher 1996, 2000a; Gillette et al. 1999) that children might first arrive at this structure-sensitive interpretation of a sentence in a simple way – by aligning a representation of a sentence with a structured conceptual representation of a relevant situation.

In this way a child might infer that a sentence with two noun arguments must encode some conceptual relationship between the referents of the two nouns, while a sentence with only one noun argument might describe a state, property, or act of its single referent. This simple structure-mapping could take place as soon as the child learns to identify some nouns, and can represent them as parts of a larger utterance.

The centrality of argument number as a learning cue is further clarified by recent studies that emphasize two important issues. One is that sensitivity to argument number makes its appearance astonishingly early in language acquisition, often before the child has uttered a single verb. The other is that this sensitivity can be demonstrated even in stripped-down experimental settings that remove all alternative evidence.

In a recent series of studies (Fisher 1996, 2002) children aged two, three, and five years heard novel verbs in the context of (videotaped) unfamiliar causal events; the verbs were presented either transitively or intransitively. The sentences contained only ambiguous pronouns, as in *She's pilking her over there* versus *She's pilking over there* so that the sentences differed only in their number of noun phrases. The children's interpretations of the novel verbs were tested by asking them to point out, in a still picture of the event, which character's role the verb described (*Who's pilking (her) over there?*). Children at all three ages were more likely to select the causal agent in the event as the subject of the transitive verb. Just as for the adult judges in the Gillette et al. (1999) studies, these findings provide evidence that the *set of noun phrases* in the sentence – even without information about which is the subject – influences young children's interpretations of verbs. Recently these findings have been extended to children as young as 21 months of age. Fisher and Snedeker (2002) showed 26- and 21-month-olds side-by-side videotaped events. One screen displayed a novel caused-motion event involving two people, and the other displayed a novel independent motion event involving only one person. As they watched each pair of scenes, the children heard either a transitive (*He's pilking him!*) or an intransitive sentence (*He's pilking!*). Children who heard the transitive sentence looked longer at the two-participant caused-motion event, while children who heard the intransitive sentence tended to look equally at the two events (both of which displayed possible referents for an intransitive verb).

The findings reported so far are consistent with the view that there is a bias to map one-to-one between the set of arguments of the verb and the set of participants in the event, in children acquiring an established language as well as for linguistic isolates inventing their own sign systems. But perhaps, in the case of children learning an established language, the early honoring of this simple mapping from participant number to noun-phrase number is an effect of language learning rather than the reflection of some unlearned bias. Do children simply exploit the most stable cues to mapping made available in the language they hear, rather than relying on an unlearned bias for one-to-one mapping?

To investigate this issue, Lidz, Gleitman, and Gleitman (2003) asked preschoolers to act out novel combinations of verbs and syntactic structures in two languages: English (as in Naigles et al. 1992) and Kannada, a language spoken in southwestern India. Kannada permits pervasive argument dropping, rendering the relationship between argument number and noun-phrase number relatively variable in typical input sentences. Kannada also has, however, a causative morpheme that only occurs with causative verbs. The critical sentences pitted argument number (two nouns vs. one) against causative morphology (explicitly marked as causal or not). Kannada-speaking three-year-olds ignored the presence or absence of the causative morpheme, relying only on the number of noun-phrases in the sentence they heard. In contrast, Kannada-speaking adults' enactments were influenced by both morphology and argument number. The adult findings again demonstrate that language learners ultimately acquire whichever cues to sentence meaning the exposure language makes available. But strikingly, they also show that children are not totally open-minded: they appear to find some formal devices (argument number) more potent than others (inflectional morphology).

It is important to notice that the count-the-nouns procedure taken by itself is coarse at best and fallible at worst. This is because *nouns in the sentence* and *arguments of the verb* are by no means the same thing. Often, for example, there are too few nouns to match up with the event participants. This is for several systematic reasons, including incorporation phenomena of many kinds, and the possibility of argument omission. In many languages, sentence subjects can be omitted if they are recoverable from context and prior discourse; in some languages, including Chinese, Japanese and Korean, a verb's direct objects can be omitted as well. Violations of any simple noun-counting principle are also obvious in the reverse direction, for example when a language (like English) requires a subject even for argumentless predicates (*It is raining*). And in any language, complex noun-phrases (*John's sister, a horse of a different color*) contain more than one noun, and sentences can contain adjunct phrases (*with Ginger, in the morning*), again yielding more noun phrases than argument positions.

Despite the complexity of the relationship between nouns in sentences and the subcategorized arguments of the verb, several sources of evidence suggest that ordinary sentences provide strong probabilistic information about the participant structures of verbs. For example, in the human simulations of Gillette et al. (1999), adults benefited from simply being given an alphabetized list of the nouns in each sentence in which the mothers had produced a particular verb. In this case the adults (like the hypothetical learner) could not tell which nouns were arguments of a verb and which were adjuncts, yet this linguistic hint aided recovery of verb meanings from scenes. Li (1994; see also Lee &

Naigles 2002) analyzed speech to young children in Mandarin Chinese, and found that although mothers often did omit noun phrases in sentences, maternal utterances still supported a systematic distinction among semantically and syntactically distinct classes of verbs. Though arguments can be omitted, transitive verbs still occur with two nouns in the sentence more often than intransitive verbs do, and systematically so.

Beyond argument number   Experimental studies of novel verb learning by young children have focused on argument number, in part because this is an easily detectable cue to sentence interpretation. But clearly there's more linguistic evidence for lexical learning than argument number. Landau and Gleitman (1985) argued, based on analysis of a blind child's lexical development, that the child's observation that *look* and *see* appeared in sentence complement structures made sense of her seemingly effortless acquisition of the perceptual nature of these verbs, while purely observational evidence yielded no clear way to discriminate these from object-contact verbs like *touch* and *hold*. One can, for example, *see that the sky is falling*, and *look how I'm doing this*, but not *touch that the sky is falling*. Argument type, like argument number, provides a powerful source of information for lexical learning.

Differences in argument type and number systematically map onto a semantic cross-classification of the verb lexicon, as revealed by naïve adults' judgments of semantic relatedness among verbs (Fisher et al. 1991). Verbs that accept sentences as their complements describe relations between their subjects and an event or state; these include verbs of cognition (*know*, *think*), perception (*see*, *hear*), and communication (*explain*, *say*). Verbs that take three noun-phrase arguments describe relations among the referents of those three noun phrases, typically transfer of position (*put*, *drop*), possession (*give*, *take*), or information (*explain*, *argue*). Later studies using the Fisher et al. procedure documented that these regularities could be recovered from a sample of English sentences produced in spontaneous child-directed speech in English (Lederer, Gleitman & Gleitman 1995) and Mandarin Chinese (Li 1994). Verbs' syntactic behavior, including both argument type and number, thus provides a source of information that systematically cross-classifies the set of verbs in much the same way within and across languages, pointing to dimensions of semantic similarity. Indeed, it is this *cross-classification* – the set of structures associated with a single verb or small verb class – that accounted for subjects' accuracy in the *Jabberwocky* (syntax-only) condition of the Gillette et al. (1999) human simulation experiments.

Can young children, like these adults, profit from the full range of syntactic structures they might observe with each verb? Considerable evidence tells us that they are quite good at learning about the sentence structures in which particular verbs occur (Gordon & Chafetz 1990; Snedeker, Thorpe & Trueswell 2001;

Tomasello 2000); such findings suggest that they may well be capable of taking advantage of probabilistic evidence, presented across multiple sentences, for the range of sentence structures assigned to each verb. Moreover, a computer simulation of syntactic learning from a sample of child-directed English (Brent 1994) suggested that subcategorization frames for verbs could be recovered, based on very little prior syntactic knowledge (a few function words): an analysis of verbs' lexical contexts provided useful information for distinguishing among verbs that are transitive or intransitive, or that take verbal or sentential complements (as in *John likes to fish*).

Beyond the first primitive mapping of two-noun sentences onto two-participant relations, mapping rules that are language-specific also come into play, further enriching the informational base and thus further increasing the efficiency and precision of predicate-term acquisition. The earliest-appearing of these is probably the interpretation of word order in multi-argument sentences: Hirsh-Pasek and Golinkoff (1996) reported that English-learning 17- to 19-month-olds were sensitive to word order in transitive sentences containing familiar verbs (*Cookie Monster is tickling Big Bird* vs. *Big Bird is tickling Cookie Monster*): they looked longer at a video screen on which the subject of their test sentence was the agent of the target action. Children aged 21 and 26 months show the same sensitivity to English word order when presented with made-up verbs and unfamiliar actions (Fisher 2000b). Young children acquiring a free word-order language quickly acquire the semantic implications of case-marking morphology (e.g. results for Turkish learners reported in Slobin 1982).

Children also develop more subtle language-specific expectations about the meanings of classes of words in their language; Slobin (2001) has termed this phenomenon "typological bootstrapping." For example, Talmy (1985) described systematic differences in the typical meanings of motion verbs in languages like Spanish (verb-framed languages) and English (satellite-framed languages). Spanish motion verbs tend to encode direction (*enter, ascend*), while in English, path information is relegated to a prepositional phrase, and verbs are more likely to encode manner (*walk in, run up the hill*). Native speakers of Spanish and English learn these tendencies, and develop slightly different expectations for the likely semantic content of a new verb (Naigles & Terrazas 1998; for further discussion see Choi & Bowerman 1991; Fisher & Gleitman 2002; Landau & Gleitman 1985).

The particular nouns that typically occur with each verb also undoubtedly guide the child's interpretation: *drink* and *eat* are not only transitive verbs; they systematically select animate subjects and different direct-object nouns (the potable and edible items). Data from "human simulations" suggest that this sort of information is helpful in both noun and verb learning (Gillette et al. 1999; Kako & Gleitman in prep.; see Pinker 1989 for the initial statement of this proposal). Quite young children have access to this sort of information as well: two-year-olds look at a picture of a glass of juice (rather than of a non-potable object) when they hear the familiar verb *drink* (Fernald 2003), and successfully induce the referent of a new word introduced in an informative context as the object of a familiar verb (e.g. *She's feeding the ferret!*) (Goodman, McDonough & Brown 1998).

Summary

In the course of lexical development, children have opportunities to observe each verb's typical subcategorization frames, its typical nominal arguments, and the kinds of scenes or events that pertain when the verb is invoked. Although much work remains to be done to specify how each source of information is detected and used by children, and how multiple sources of information interact in development, we argue that all of these sources of information converge to make vocabulary learning efficient and nearly errorless.

Central to this so-called *syntactic bootstrapping* view is the interaction of multiple cues for word learning, trading off in different ways for different classes of verbs. This position does not *replace* observation of situations with linguistic observations. Ultimately, word learning is a mapping problem. The learner must identify what (in the world, or at least in a human's conception of the world) the surrounding community of speakers means by each word. Though our arguments focus on the ambiguity of referential settings – and thus the need for linguistic evidence to make vocabulary learning stable – the observations that give semantic content to words are observations of the non-linguistic world. Sentence structures are relevant only to a subset of the dimensions of verb meaning, those that affect the number and type of arguments associated with the verb, and the temporal structure of the event it names (Fisher et al. 1991; Grimshaw 1990; Rappaport-Hovav & Levin 1988). In contrast, the various manners of motion encoded by *slide*, *roll*, and *bounce* have no direct reflection in sentence structure (Fillmore 1968). When *push* comes to *shove*, only observations of the manner (and comparative violence) of actions in the world will suffice to differentiate syntactically and semantically related verbs.

Lexical learning and the structure of linguistic knowledge

We have summarized evidence that, in order to acquire word meanings, child learners amass all sorts of specific knowledge about individual words: their contexts of use, their lexical-distributional properties (e.g. the association of *bake* with *cake*) and the full range of their syntactic behavior. All this evidence is required, in different degrees for different words, to converge on their meanings. The result is a knowledge representation in which detailed syntactic and semantic information is linked at the level of the lexicon. What happens to all this information, collected to solve the mapping problem? Is it disassembled, rather as a building scaffold is dismantled once the beams and bricks are in place? We think not.

Experimentation on sentence comprehension in older children and adults suggests the continued linking of linguistic distributional knowledge to particular lexical items. Native speakers learn not only which sentence structures each verb can grammatically combine with, but also how often each verb occurs in each structure. Adults retrieve this information as soon as they identify a verb, and use it to bias online sentence interpretation (Garnsey et al. 1997; Trueswell & Kim 1998). Snedeker et al. (2001) demonstrated that both children and adults resolved the ambiguity of such sentences as *Tickle the frog with the feather* and *Choose the frog with the feather* as a function of the frequency with which these verbs naturally occur with noun-phrase versus verb-phrase modification. On-line parsing decisions by adults and by children as young as five are influenced by detailed and frequency-sensitive knowledge about the syntactic behavior of each verb.

These findings from the psycholinguistic literature mesh naturally with computational approaches to parsing that also represent syntactic representations as strongly lexicalized: in Lexicalized Tree Adjoining Grammar, for example, the syntactic possibilities of a language are represented by a finite set of tree structures that are linked with individual lexical items, and a small set of operations by which trees can be joined (Joshi & Srinivas 1994). This apparatus permits the statement of syntactic dependencies (such as subcategorization) and semantic dependencies (such as selection restrictions), and yields a natural treatment of non-compositional idioms (*kick the bucket*). Such approaches are based on a claim similar to the one we derive from examination of the learning procedure: an adequate description of the syntactic combinatorial principles of a language is unworkable if kept separate from the lexicon and lexical learning. Similarly, independent evidence from crosslinguistically based theoretical linguistics supports a view of language in which significant structural properties reside in the lexical component of the grammar (Borer 1984; Chomsky 1995c).

General and particular, and the requirement
for universal grammar

The manifest specificity of lexical organization that we have discussed throughout has often been taken as supporting a picture of language and its learning that can avoid appeals to unlearned constraints on the construction of grammars. For example, Tomasello (2000) and Goldberg (1995) have proposed construction-based accounts of language representation and acquisition, suggesting that children simply learn, word by word and construction by construction, how to express each idea. According to this view, a more general and flexible grammar grows slowly from this piecemeal knowledge through general cognitive principles of induction and generalization. Proponents of such theories emphasize variability and exceptions in the syntax–semantics mapping rules, and argue that no constraints beyond those of the human cognitive/conceptual apparatus are needed to account for the nature of human languages, and the facts of language development.

However, we believe that this is a mistake. Although syntax must be represented in the lexicon – to explain how we know, with such exquisite detail, which structures each verb appears in, and how we learn the meanings of the verbs in the first place – strong universal constraints on the alignment of syntax and semantics are needed to explain the full set of facts. One issue, compellingly discussed by Mark Baker (2001), is the uniformity of clause-level structures within languages:

We do not find languages in which the verb meaning "hit" comes before the object, English-style ("The child might hit his parent"), and the verb meaning "kiss" comes after it, Japanese-style ("The child might his parent kiss"). The word order of the object and the verb is thus not learned purely by learning . . . individual verbs but must be somehow keyed into the process of learning the verbs as a class. (2001: 80)

If the organizational structure for predicate–argument structures could be anything at all, with the learner simply picking up these facts on an item-by-item basis, it would be hard to explain why each language organizes these structures so regularly, across verbs. The same is true for the basic semantic–syntactic linkages, even in languages at the extremes of linguistic diversity, as Baker shows by comparing languages such as English and Mohawk. In all the languages of the world, though with occasional quirks and exceptions, not only do all the core participants in the action denoted by the verb get expressed grammatically (the "theta criterion"), but the causal verbs put their agents in subject position, the undergoers systematically surface as objects, the complements of mental verbs surface as clauses, and so forth. These linguistic properties shared across cultures and language families, however otherwise diverse, imply strong restrictions on how we factor experience into predicates and arguments, and what aspects of the conceptual predicates and arguments are reflected in the organization of the clause. Children, being creatures like us, expect language to be organized in accord with such principles and therefore they can learn it.

Part II

Chomsky on the human mind

7   Empiricism and rationalism as research strategies

Norbert Hornstein

Introduction

A major influence on Chomsky's approach to the study of mind has come from rationalist philosophers such as Descartes. Like these thinkers, Chomsky's work can be usefully seen in opposition to empiricist approaches to mind articulated by thinkers such as Locke.[1] The aim of this chapter is to provide a conceptual backdrop against which one can locate some of Chomsky's claims. I try to do this by outlining the different ways that the empiricist and rationalist traditions (actually, idealized versions of each) try to reconcile an apparent tension in epistemology (the theory of knowledge). The tension comes in trying to combine a theory of mind with a theory of truth to yield an account of how it is possible for humans to know anything, i.e. have true beliefs in some domain, especially true beliefs about the "outside world."[2] The two traditions endorse very different conceptions of the relation of minds to the world. However, it is possible to construct a shared conception of what the epistemological project amounts to that plausibly animates the details of the particular proposals that have been advanced. Doing this, I believe, allows for a better evaluation of the intuitions that drive these programs and thereby permits one to more fully appreciate some of Chomsky's main philosophical proposals. In what follows, I will try to outline these general conceptions. I will then try to relate them to some of the concerns that Chomsky has raised in his linguistic and philosophical writing.

How you know

There are at least two kinds of questions that one can ask concerning the nature of knowledge: (a) What can be known? and (b) How does one come to know anything? Often these questions arise together with the limits of knowledge circumscribed on the basis of its mechanics. However, despite their links, the second question is largely independent of the first. In what follows, I focus on the second. Answering it involves elaborating a theory of belief formation, a theory of truth, and an account of the interaction of the two.

More specifically, an epistemology is here taken as trying to account for how beliefs arise, how they relate to each other, and how they relate to the world. How beliefs arise and relate to each other is the province of a psychology of mind. How beliefs relate to the world concerns a theory of truth. Epistemology tries to combine the efforts of each of these two theories to provide a story that explains how it is possible to have true beliefs. Thus, for our purposes here, a theory of knowledge consists of three subparts: (i) a psychology or theory of mind, (ii) a theory of truth, and (iii) a theory of how (i) and (ii) combine to allow some beliefs to be true. We shall see that the rather different psychological theories developed within the empiricist and rationalist traditions can be seen as responding to the demands of the two different strands in an overall theory of knowledge so conceived; empiricists responding to the exigencies of (ii) and rationalists reacting to the requirements of (i).

Before delving into details, let's slightly elaborate each of (i)–(iii) above. A core part of a theory of mind involves outlining how beliefs arise and interrelate. As such, it concerns itself with categorizing various kinds of beliefs, e.g. simple versus general, abstract versus concrete, sensory versus cognitive, composite versus elementary, etc. Second, a psychology tries to say how beliefs are generated, e.g. they arise from sense experience, from operations on more basic ideas, they are inborn, etc. Looked at in this way, a theory of mind requires a psychology which categorizes the varieties of our beliefs and outlines a set of mental mechanisms and operations as a result of which our beliefs can be said to arise and interconnect.

The second ingredient required for an epistemology is an account of truth. Such a theory says what truth is a property of. In particular, it tries to say what it is for a belief to be true or for some idea to refer. Various kinds of theories have been explored in this regard. Two major variants have been realist theories of correspondence and non-realist quasi-verificationist approaches. The most important property of the former is its radically non-epistemic nature. The picture animating the realist account is a sharp distinction between beliefs on the one hand and the world on the other. Beliefs are true insofar as they "match" or "fit" the world. Unpacking what "fitting" or "matching" amounts to is an important focus of such approaches.

It helps to understand what is meant by saying that truth is radically non-epistemic by contrasting realist theories with their non-realist counterparts. Non-realist approaches take truth as intimately connected to our epistemic abilities or our methods of inquiry. On this view, truth is the outcome, under some possibly idealized conditions, of our investigative or cognitive capacities and/or procedures. To say that some belief is true is to say that it is as highly valued as it can be along certain epistemic dimensions, e.g. coherence, naturalness etc. Outlining what these epistemic dimensions are and saying what sort of idealizations are appropriate is a central task of this approach. However, where this

view of truth contrasts with the former is in seeing truth as related to our cognitive powers in some (however attenuated) way. For the realist our cognitive
powers are what they are and the world is however it happens to be. There is no
conceptual link between the former and the latter as there invariably is within
non-realist conceptions.

The last part of a theory of knowledge elaborates the "fit" between the psychological theory of mind and the theory of truth. By mixing and matching the
various accounts of mind with alternate theories of truth, one develops different
epistemologies and provides varying answers to the question of how true belief
is possible.

In what follows, three combinations will be discussed: (a) an empiricist
psychology coupled with a realist conception of truth, (b) a rationalist theory of
mind coupled with a realist conception of truth, and (c) a rationalist psychology
joined with a non-realist view of truth. We will see that each combination has
its own charms. Hopefully, consideration of these views will also allow us to
better understand some of Chomsky's concerns.

The empiricist mind

Empiricist theories of mind (a version of Locke's theory underlies what follows) take beliefs to be complex entities made up of simpler parts, call them
"ideas," joined together by diverse mental operations. Ideas come in two varieties, simple and general. The latter are formed from the former by an operation
of abstraction. Taking simple ideas as inputs, abstraction yields a general idea
by intersecting the properties of the input simple ideas. In this way, the properties of general ideas are dependent on (and derived from) simple ideas. Note
that by being intersective, abstraction is a subtraction operation in the sense
that it deletes what is not common to the members of the group of simple ideas
upon which the operation acts. Importantly, abstraction does not add anything
to properties of a general idea that is not part of the simple ones that yield it.

Simple ideas arise via sensation. They come in two varieties; those caused
by primary qualities and those stimulated by secondary qualities. The former
conform to the contours of the stimulating quality and "resemble" them. The
latter do not. Rather they are products of the mind and do not closely "resemble" those features of the external world that cause them to arise. A good part
of empiricist reflections on the mind revolves around demarcating the border
between primary and secondary qualities as it is the relation of ideas to primary
qualities that is at the foundation of empiricist epistemology.

All simple primary ideas are formed (or fashioned or molded) in the mind
by the action of the environment through the medium of the senses. The terms
"formed," "fashioned," "molded" are meant to evoke the notion that the features
of the simple idea are *very* closely related to the properties of the stimulus

situation. Simple ideas (at least those formed by primary qualities) directly (and accurately) reflect features of the environment as transmitted via the senses. The leading picture or metaphor is the mind as a wax tablet. The mind receives these simple ideas via sensation in much the way that hot wax receives the imprint of an object impressed upon it. In the latter case, the contours of the imprint are closely related to the physical properties of the imprinting object. In a similar way, empiricists urge, the properties of a simple idea in the mind can be traced to the properties of the physical stimulus. In the case of minds, however, the "wax" is multi-modal and potentially able to receive inputs through each of the senses. A simple idea is consequently a multi-dimensional item, the inputs to each sense forming or molding one of the dimensions of the "idea." Some of these inputs reflect the molding effects of primary qualities. One epistemological project is to figure out how to distinguish those simple ideas that are indeed "molded" by their causers and those that are not. This is *not* something that the mind does naturally for us. It requires conscious effort and rigorous attention. This said, however, once the ideas are appropriately categorized, there remains one set, the simple primary ideas, that link minds to the world via a resemblance relation grounded in a particular causal mechanism: for these ideas the external stimulus molds the specific features of the idea that arises in the mind.

Observe that on this sort of account, simple primary ideas closely reflect the physical properties of the environmental stimuli that produce them. They reflect the environment because the medium on which the environment acts is receptive and passive. With this view in hand, an account of mental contents reasonably proceeds via an account of the structure of the environment and the stimuli it produces. What is distinctive about empiricist theories is the emphasized causal connection posited between the structure of our simple primary ideas and that of the stimulus. With regard to simple primary ideas, minds are passive and whatever structure they have is due to the molding effects of experience.

Behaviorism is a plausible outcome of empiricism so construed; for if a radical form of empiricist psychology is correct, then one gains little by concentrating on the properties of minds rather than those of stimuli. Put another way, since the structure of (key) simple ideas is a reflection of the features of the environment and since it is much harder to examine minds than environments it makes sense to concentrate one's attention more on the structure of stimuli, which are easily observed, than on minds, which are not. The crucial point about behaviorism is not its idiosyncratic disavowal of the mental but the view that key sectors of the mental are a mere reflection of the properties of the physical stimulus. In this sense, behaviorism is continuous with empiricist characterizations of the mind as passive and receptive.

Given this sort of empiricist view of how simple ideas arise, it is relatively clear in what abstraction consists. It is a second-order operation over the imprinted properties of the simple ideas. In effect, it is a generalization of the features of simple ideas. For this sort of procedure to work, there must be a relatively large data set to work on, a large number of simple ideas that are fodder for the abstraction operation. The operation consists in taking what is (sufficiently) common among the relevant simple ideas and dropping the differences.[3] Note that if this is how general ideas arise, then the structure of such an idea is also closely bound to the properties of the physical stimulus: the formation of the general idea is determined by the common properties of the individuals in the abstraction set and these individuals, it has been observed, are just simple ideas (some of) whose features are intimately connected to those of the physical stimulus. As such, the structure of some general ideas is also closely circumscribed by the properties of the stimuli that give rise to the simple ideas.

Once we have general and simple ideas, various additional mental operations can relate them to form beliefs. For example, predication can take a general idea like "apple" and predicate to it the general idea "red" to form the belief "apples are red." Other operations might combine general ideas to form yet more complex general ideas, e.g. "Red apples" and more complex beliefs, e.g. negations of a belief, conjunctions of beliefs, etc. The intricacies of this process are not critical for current purposes. What is important is the close relation that exists between the properties of the world (the stimuli) and the structure of some of our ideas and beliefs that an empiricist psychology of mental operations advances. Learning, the acquisition of ideas and beliefs, is a direct function of the environmental stimulus situation. A central concept is that of a formative stimulus and the leading picture of the mind is a blank, passive, highly receptive multi-modal, repository of environmental input. We will return below to how these psychological ideas can be exploited in an account of true belief.

The rationalist mind

Rationalist theories of mind markedly contrast with the one above. The main difference lies in a firm rejection of the idea that experience exercises a shaping effect on the structure of mental contents. Environmental stimuli, for rationalists, are not stimuli that structure the contents of the mind. Rather, they are triggers or occasions for the formation of ideas or beliefs. In other words, though experience is causally necessary in explaining how beliefs arise in the mind it does not function the way it does within empiricist models to shape mental content and structure. In particular, the idea that sensory input is (in some way) *similar* to the idea that it gives rise to (the way a wax impression is to the thing that formed it) is largely rejected. There need be very little similarity between sensory triggers and the ideas/beliefs to which they causally relate.

An analogy might help to make the rationalist view of mental operations clearer. Ideas in the mind are like drawings in a dark, unlit room. Acquiring an idea is like illuminating a picture in the dark. Experience is like flipping on a light switch. Before the light switch is flipped, the pictures are invisible. Thus, light-switch flipping is necessary to the pictures becoming visible. However, flipping on the light does not fashion or form the picture but allows one to see what is there quite independently. Nor is there anything very "similar" between what brings the pictures to visibility – the act of turning on the lights – and what appears as a result of this action. The flipping of the light switch allows one to see what is already there. It does not construct the pictures that are seen.

For rationalists, then, experience activates ideas that already inhabit the mind, it does not form them. Consequently, the relation between experience and the structure of one's beliefs and ideas, on this kind of account, can be very remote. As the analogy emphasizes, what appears as a result of turning on the light is a function of what pictures there are hanging on the wall, not on how one flips the switch.

Two features of this perspective are noteworthy. First, experience *is* required in accounting for the emergence of mental structures. To return to the analogy, the pictures remain invisible unless the light comes on. The rationalist who posits rich innate mental structures need not (and did not) dispense with a causal role for experience. She or he just assigns a different role to experience than the empiricist does. Second, the role that rationalists assign to experience is that of a triggering stimulus, a cause that activates ideas and beliefs whose structures are (largely, if not wholly) what they are prior to the influence of the triggering stimuli.

Not surprisingly, this view of the role of experience dispenses with the idea that the mind is like a blank wax tablet constructed by experience. Rationalist psychology pictures the mind as a highly structured active entity. The mind does not passively reflect experience but actively participates in interpreting it. Given a rationalist view of the role of experience in generating ideas, it is no longer possible to be confident that what is "in" the mind (even "simple" ideas) is a faithful record of what is external to it (in the environment).

Note further that given this sort of view, general ideas need not be seen as arising via abstraction. The reason is that for a rationalist there is no reason for ideas that are triggered to be closely related to the stimuli that trigger them. Therefore, it is possible to accept the notion that general ideas are (to a considerable extent) simply fixed natively in the mind. The same holds for beliefs. For a rationalist, it is unnecessary to distinguish simple ideas from general and ideas from beliefs *as regards origins*. As a matter of historical fact, the innate ideas rationalists proposed were by and large rather abstract. Ideas concerning particulars arose from the interaction of general ideas and sensory experience. However, the details are irrelevant for present purposes. What is important is the differences between rationalist and empiricist psychologies. The differences reside in (a) the different causal roles each assigned to experience, formative stimuli for empiricists, triggering stimuli for rationalists, (b) the different explanations of how beliefs arise, (c) the different views of how structured the mind is prior to experience and how active the mind is in manipulating stimuli, passive, blank and receptive or active, structured and participatory; and (d) the different attitudes towards "similarity" as characterizing the causal relation between environmental sensory input and the mental products resulting from sensory experience.

A reprise

In the presentation so far, I have outlined two different views of how minds are structured. The views have been presented as incompatible. This is clearly misleading. The mind need not be exhaustively empiricist or rationalist in nature. A combination of mechanisms drawn from each tradition is possible and even likely. However, considering the non-mixed cases is instructive and I will continue to contrast the two approaches as if they were exclusive.

One more point: in the presentation, I have heavily relied on analogies to convey the differences between formative stimuli that structure ideas and triggering stimuli that merely reveal prior structure. The main contrasts can be made without the analogies. What is conceptually central to empiricism is the contention that the structure of the mind is closely related ("similar"), via operations like imprinting and abstraction, to (at least some of) the structure of the environment. Thus, in accounting for the contents of belief, one must look to the properties of the stimulus. The central feature of an empiricist approach is the *kind* of causal link – a formative one – postulated to exist between the contents of thought and the structure of the environment.

Rationalists differ in substantially distancing mental structures from the causes that allow them to become mentally active. There need be nothing similar between the cause and the ideas or beliefs that it gives rise to. As such, for rationalists, there is little of interest in psychologies based on abstractive and inductive mechanisms.

In sum, both empiricists and rationalists provide a role for experience. They differ in what they see this role to be.

True belief

Before discussing the relative merits of these two approaches, let's consider what account of knowledge (or true belief) we get by combining them with a realist conception of truth. So our first question is: given an empiricist psychology and a realist conception of truth, how is knowledge (true belief) possible?

Recall that for a realist, truth consists in correspondence between mental objects like beliefs and the non-mental properties of the world. As such, a belief will be true only if the ideas which comprise it all denote/refer to entities in the world in the appropriate way. So, for example, the belief represented by the proposition "Apples are green" is true only if the property denoted by "green" is a subset of the properties which combine to form the general idea denoted by "apple." Further, on an empiricist account, this will hold just in case all the individual apple-ideas have as part of their sensory imprint particular ideas of green.

Recall that general ideas arise for an empiricist through abstraction over the set of particular ideas. The general idea can have no properties absent from each of the particular ideas. As such, general ideas refer *in virtue* of the particular ideas that they are related to via the abstraction operation. This feature is the key ingredient in an empiricist psychology and it has an interesting property in the context of an overall epistemology. It provides the outlines of a *mechanical (causal) model* that explains how *people* are able to successfully refer and hold true beliefs by explaining how it is that *ideas* can refer; in particular, how simple (primary) ideas refer and how via abstraction general ideas can as well. If beliefs are seen as combinations of such ideas, then it also provides an account of how it is that some beliefs (the ones formed in the right way) can be true.

This point is of some importance, so let me put it another way. For the empiricist, people are able to refer because they have ideas that refer. An empiricist psychology explains *how* ideas can refer in the course of describing how they *arise*. Recall that the properties of simple ideas faithfully track properties of the world. Experience shaping a passive receptive medium accounts for the possibility of reference and truth. Ideas "latch onto" the world because they are impressions of it. As simple (primary) ideas are analogous to wax impressions, they can refer to what is impressed upon them in much the same way that a wax impression of a key can be used to identify or denote the key used to make the wax impression. Similarity between impression and impressor has quite a concrete meaning in cases such as this. For the empiricist, this notion is fully generalized, its chief virtue being a causally robust account of reference.[4]

The empiricist account of general ideas as products of abstraction makes their capacity for reference continuous with the account provided for simple ideas. Once again, how they arise causally accounts for how they can refer. Abstraction "adds" nothing not already contained in the simple ideas that are fodder for the inductive process. Thus, abstraction does not alter simple ideas in ways that affect a general idea's capacity to refer. Abstraction allows general ideas to retain their links to the world via the links that simple ideas establish.

With this much in place, the rest of the story is conceptually clear. Beliefs are complex relations among ideas. They will be true only if the parts refer and relate as the proposition expressing the belief indicates. Some of these relations will result in true beliefs, some false. How the true beliefs can be true ultimately rests on the relations that simple ideas have to their formative stimuli.

The virtues of this sort of account are pretty clear. It provides a mechanical-causal model of true belief in its account of the aetiology of ideas. In a psychological guise, empiricists, in effect, offer a causal theory of reference and truth. There are not many of these accounts to be had, so this sort of account does have its charms. The difficulties begin when one starts to seriously evaluate the plausibility of the learning theory.

Problems with empiricism

The main problem with empiricism resides in its psychology, in particular, the very tight connection postulated to hold between the structure of our ideas and beliefs and the structure of the experiential input from the world. The problems arise when one considers in detail how an empiricist psychology might account for the highly abstract, detailed, and structured knowledge that humans have in some domains such as language and mathematics. The problem that knowledge of language (or of geometry, a rationalist favorite) poses is that in these domains the structure of our ideas and beliefs is not well described as tracking (being similar to) stimulus input. The connection between beliefs attained and experience available to fix these beliefs is very remote. In fact, on careful inspection, it appears that the kinds of experience relevant to forming the requisite ideas/beliefs does not exist in the stimuli available to the individual who acquires the relevant knowledge. The structures of many (if not most) of our ideas and beliefs go far beyond the properties of the experience that we are subject to. As such, the causal link between the environment and our beliefs, so vital to the inductive premises of empiricist psychology, is broken. If correct this undermines empiricist epistemology by undermining its psychology. For an illustration of the problem, consider the language case.[5]

Knowledge of language is a paradigm case of knowledge in the sense that a native speaker has complete and systematic mastery of a large body of very complex facts. So an interesting epistemological question is how it is that one comes to acquire knowledge of one's native language. The central fact about language acquisition is that children are able to learn their native languages rapidly and on the basis of degenerate, deficient, and inadequate data gathered from the ambient environment. More precisely, children acquire a knowledge of language despite the following inadequacies in the linguistic data set that they have access to.[6]

(a) The linguistic evidence a child has is imperfect; it includes slips of the tongue, incomplete thoughts, misstatements, etc.

(b) The knowledge of his or her native language that the native speaker attains extends to an open-ended set of objects. There is no real upper bound on the number of sentences native speakers can use and understand. This despite the fact that the linguistic stimuli to which a child is exposed are merely finite. This implies that children must postulate rules on the basis of a limited number of example outputs of these rules. In sum, there is an inductive gap between what is attained (a rule) and the linguistic input to this acquisition process (sentences/utterances conforming to this rule).

(c) There is considerable evidence that the knowledge attained by the native speaker includes features for which there is virtually *no* evidence in the data that a child has access to in the course of acquisition.

Of these shortcomings (c) is the most problematic. It implies that *no* inductive account can possibly explain knowledge of language, as there is no inductive base on which to found such an account. Let me elaborate a bit as the point is crucial.

Points (a) and (b) together can be taken as indicating difficulties for a traditional empiricist approach to language. Recall that for an empiricist the reliability of our beliefs depends on the qualities of the environmental stimuli on which they are based. What (a) and (b) point out is that the data base may be more misleading than one might initially suppose. However, (a) and (b) do not in themselves pose an insurmountable obstacle. What they point out is that one needs to be a little sophisticated in how one exploits the environmental input. An empiricist psychology will have to statistically massage the inputs in order to overcome the hurdles posed by (a) and (b). (a) poses a standard kind of sampling problem. So long as the linguistic input is not systematically misleading it will be possible to use the data to overcome the problem of imperfect "sentences" that (a) notes.

(b) may prove to be more challenging. What is attained are rules. The evidence are bits of spoken/produced language. The problem is to figure out how to generalize from instances of a rule to the rule. This is not an entirely trivial problem but it is the sort of problem that empiricists are comfortable addressing.[7]

Neither (a) nor (b) force us to deny that our ideas and beliefs about language are formed by experience. (c) poses a much more significant problem. It claims that for large parts of a native speaker's attested linguistic knowledge there is *no* relevant experience available at all on the basis of which the relevant ideas/beliefs could be induced. If this is so, then not even a sophisticated empiricist theory can suffice, for there is no way to fashion an inductive link between our ideas/beliefs and any relevant linguistic input. This points to the conclusion that some of a native speaker's linguistic knowledge is already in the mind – it is innate – and is not formed/structured by environmental inputs. Note, once again, that this does not imply that experience is irrelevant to our coming to have this knowledge. Instead, that experience triggers, rather than forms, the relevant mental structures that underlie this knowledge.

Note that once innate beliefs are needed, they can be used to mitigate the problems raised by (a) and (b) above. We can evaluate inputs against the expectations that the innate beliefs give rise to. We can use our innate beliefs to help get us to rules whose general features are innately provided from instances of these rules. Once innate beliefs are required, they serve to simplify the inductive problem quite generally.

The argument above, the argument from the poverty of the stimulus, is a staple of the rationalist argument against empiricist approaches to knowledge. In more classical rationalist texts the argument is made by considering mathematical rather than linguistic knowledge. However, the point is the same; what we know about numbers, or geometrical figures or sequences, etc. far outstrips the relevant inputs. There is an unbridgeable gap between what we know and whatever evidence we could have used to come to know it. One of the contributions that Chomsky has made to the rationalist position comes in providing one very well worked-out and detailed example of where knowledge attained outruns inputs available. Given that linguistic knowledge is both a mundane and a paradigm case of knowledge (what better example is there of knowledge than knowledge of one's native language?), the failure of empiricist psychology in the linguistic case suggests that the empiricist epistemological project is generally inadequate. Moreover, it suggests that once one begins to look carefully at specific domains of knowledge, it quickly becomes evident that the poverty-of-the-stimulus problem characteristic of the linguistic and mathematical cases generalizes all too easily.

An epistemological consequence

The rationalist critique of empiricist psychology has epistemological repercussions. Recall that what makes an empiricist theory of mind attractive is that it nicely combines with a realist conception of truth to say how it is that ideas can refer and beliefs can be true. The problem is that the psychology required to make this account run is simply inadequate. The question that arises is what happens if we substitute a rationalist approach to the mental. Do we retain a similarly satisfying account of how beliefs can be true?

Not really. Recall that it is the wax tablet model that undergirds the causal account of reference in an empiricist epistemology. The rationalist rejects this psychological model. This makes it impossible for the rationalist to exploit the empiricist's strategy of accounting for how true belief and reference is possible by observing how it is that ideas and beliefs are fixed in the mind. For the rationalist, how beliefs arise is not bound in the right way to the structure of the environment. There is nothing "similar" between stimulus and idea/belief. Thus, there is no way to ground the reference relation in the mechanics of idea/belief fixation. The rationalist's notion of experience as a trigger, and the mind as active and structured, prevents him or her from advancing an account of truth and reference grounded in the aetiology of ideas and beliefs as the rationalist account crucially exploits notions of mind at odds with one needed to get such an account off the ground. As such, the rationalist cannot import the empiricist's account of how true belief and successful reference is possible.

What account does the rationalist provide? There is no real account; only the blunt statement that we are "built" for (some) truth. As Descartes put it, we can have true beliefs because a benevolent God implanted in us some ideas that refer and some beliefs that correspond to reality. Put more bluntly, that some of our ideas refer and some of our beliefs are true is something of a miracle.

There is no "theory" here, just an assertion. Moreover, the anemic nature of the account of true belief can be traced to what is arguably the principal virtue of the rationalist story: the sophisticated nativist psychology. By distancing the aetiology of the structure of ideas and beliefs from the stimuli that prompt them the rationalist cannot then easily turn and use the causal link afforded by environmental stimuli for epistemological purposes.

This feature of rationalist theories may be useful in accounting for a curious sociological fact among philosophers. Empiricism seems to be the default view among philosophers. A general distrust of rationalist claims is quite standard. Part of this may stem from an appreciation of the tension noted here. If one holds a realist conception of truth then it might appear that the only way to avoid a "miracle" theory of knowledge is to adopt an empiricist psychology.

Theories of truth

The above illustrates an interesting tension within an overall epistemology. On the one hand we have empiricism which affords a mechanical account of how true belief and reference is possible, but it does this by adopting a suspect psychological theory. On the other hand, there is rationalism which provides a promising view of the mental but has little to say about how people are able to use ideas to refer and how they can have true beliefs.

A possible resolution to this tension comes from considering the possibility that the problem lies with the theory of truth heretofore held constant. Recall that there are three parts to an overall epistemology: a psychology, a theory of truth, and an account that explains how ideas and beliefs as described by the psychology can refer and be true in the sense offered by the theory of truth. To this point we have considered how to combine two psychologies with a realist conception of truth and found the mixes considered wanting. Perhaps we could avoid these troubles by combining a rationalist theory of mind with a non-realist theory of truth.

Recall that non-realist conceptions of truth allow truth to be tied to our cognitive capacities and investigative procedures. Truth (and reference) on such a view is what our exercised capacities yield, perhaps in the limit. Whether this view can move from metaphor to proposal is unclear. However, the *intuition* that animates it is tolerably clear. Truth is linked to our epistemic capacities and is not radically distinct from them, as the realist maintains. The promise of this view of truth is that it might be combinable with a rationalist view of the mind without requiring a "miracle" view of truth and reference. Let me assign some (very!) tendentious tags to the two combinations we are considering. Call a rationalist psychology combined with a realist theory of truth a "Cartesian" view. Call a rationalist psychology combined with a non-realist view of truth a "Kantian" view.

The central intuition animating the Cartesian is that our capacities for knowledge are in some sense a fortuitous accident. It arises from a brute fact with only God's benevolence to explain it; namely, we are built for truth, at least in some domains of inquiry.[8] The Kantian alternative reverses the slogan: we are not built for truth so much as truth is built by us. It is the output of our capacities (again under perhaps idealized circumstances) and so it is not surprising that we are able to have true beliefs and to refer successfully as this comes down to little more than saying that there are good beliefs versus bad beliefs as judged by our own lights. The good ones are the true ones. After all, what would it mean to say that some belief or other is as good as one might hope (the simplest, most elegant, most explanatory, perfectly predictive and retrodictive, etc.) but is nonetheless false? The Kantian scheme might yield a non-trivial account of true belief by elaborating the cognitive parameters along which beliefs are to be evaluated. Truth will be epistemic superiority along these dimensions.

Some Chomskyan reflections

It is not my aim here to evaluate the alternatives surveyed above. Rather I would like to use the general background issues outlined above to highlight some of Chomsky's concerns.

Chomsky is clearly partial to the rationalist critique of empiricist learning theory. As noted above, his own work in grammatical theory constitutes one of the best-worked-out cases in favor of a rationalist approach to the mind. It is clear from the case of linguistic knowledge that the mind is already highly structured before its encounter with linguistic experience. Though linguistic experience is important for language acquisition, it plays its role in the context of rich mental structures that form part of human biological endowment. This view clearly resonates with rationalist beliefs.

A reflection of this rationalist commitment can be seen in Chomsky's distinction between I-language and E-language. The former is the *i*ndividual, *i*nternal, *i*ntensional system of knowledge that undergirds a person's linguistic capacities

(Chomsky 2000a: 5). The latter marks the sense in which Dutch and German are different languages (Chomsky 2000a: 48).

Chomsky has argued that the latter notion is of little use if one's interest is a scientific theory of language. The E-language notion has never been well defined and has played virtually no role in any naturalistic approach to explaining linguistic phenomena. Despite this it has great staying power. Why so? It is (at least in part) a reflection of empiricist commitments that many find hard to shake off. Consider how these empiricist commitments require a construct such as E-language.

Given an empiricist psychology, one's internal states reflect the properties of the environment that one is exposed to. It is clear that people attain linguistic competence. As such, they must have *learned* their native languages. But, given empiricist views of learning, this means that a native speaker's psychological state must have tracked some mind-external properties. Which? Those of the E-language. The picture that emerges is something as follows (cf. Chomsky paraphrasing Dummett, Chomsky 2000a: 48):

[Language] is a particular social practice "in which people engage," a practice that "is learned from others . . ." [Language] . . . exists "independently of any particular speakers"; every individual speaker "has" such a language, but typically has only a "partial, and partially erroneous, grasp of the language."

Typically, this learning is characterized in crudely behaviorist terms. Quine's discussion of this process in *Word and Object* serves to illustrate this:

The child's early learning of a verbal response depends on society's reinforcement of the response in association with the stimulation that merits the response, from society's point of view, and society's discouragement of it otherwise. (1960: 82)

In short, the need for E-languages seems to be just the sort of object required once one adopts an empiricist approach to acquisition.

The problem, as Chomsky notes, is that there is "no useful general sense in which we can characterize "language" so that Dutch and German are two distinct "languages," which people know only "partially" and "erroneously." Moreover, the lack of such a general notion is a "commonplace" of empirical work within linguistics (Chomsky 2000a: 48). Furthermore, as Chomsky has argued in great detail, the general picture of learning that requires notions like E-language has very little to recommend it empirically.

In short, the current debate over which notion of language to adopt for naturalistic investigation, I-language versus E-language, reflects the themes that animated the earlier divergent empiricist and rationalist approaches to mind.

Chomsky believes that what holds for linguistic competence holds much more generally. It is clear that in many domains our attained capacities far outstrip the data that cause them to arise. The poverty of the stimulus is easily detected in almost every domain. This holds for various perceptual domains such as vision and hearing and cognitive domains such as our concept of number, cause, and perceptual body. It most likely also extends to our science-forming capacities where, it has been regularly noted, theory also far surpasses the inputs/data that undergird it. Though we know very little about the science-forming "module" of the mind, there is little reason to resist the conclusion that it too is partially based on innate features given the under-determination of its outputs (theories) by its inputs (data in some domain) (Chomsky 2000a: 82).

Chomsky suggests that part of the success of empiricism lies with the terminology used to discuss the relevant issues. He suggests that we dispense with the notion that knowledge development is due to learning. Rather, knowledge "grows"/"matures" in us much the way that bones do or the way that puberty does. Acquisition of knowledge on this suggestion is not something that we do, rather it is something that happens to us and whose course of development is largely due to the nature of our internal (biological) constitutions.

This switch in metaphors clarifies the rationalist conception of the mind. It refocuses the role of the environment in the development of various competencies that arise in us by highlighting the inner dynamics of an unfolding native constitution. Note that the growth metaphor leaves intact important causal links to the environment. One does not grow without the right nutrients. However, there is no temptation when thinking of growth to downplay the structure of the grower in charting the course of development, as there seems to be when one thinks of acquisition in terms of learning instead of growth.

Chomsky suggests a second area for terminological revision: dump the idea that linguistic competence is a kind of "ability." As he notes, once one sees language in E-language terms as a social practice whose development in the child is tied to the shaping effects of community and environment, "it is tempting to understand knowledge of language as the learned ability to engage in such practices . . ." (Chomsky 2000a: 48). The "ability" view contrasts with the conception of language as a

generative procedure that assigns structural descriptions to linguistic expressions, knowledge of language being the internal representation of such a procedure in the brain (in the mind, as we may say when speaking about the brain at a certain level of abstraction). From this point of view, ability to use one's language (to put one's knowledge to use) is sharply distinguished from having such knowledge.

Once again, the suggested terminological change rests on the inadequacy of the empiricist theory of the mental that lurks behind the term "ability." Empiricists, for the reasons outlined earlier, are partial to concepts that reduce the distance between a manifest capacity and the shaping effects of the environment that are presumed to underlie it. Notions such as ability, behavior, E-language, and learning all carry empiricist resonances. To overcome the subtle empiricist influence the use of such terms can have, Chomsky urges that we replace them with others more congenial to the rationalist picture of our mental life.

A second area which reflects Chomsky's rationalist concerns relates to his skepticism concerning how the epistemological project outlined in earlier sections has been conceived. The project outlined above revolves around the question of how *beliefs* can be true and *ideas* refer. Chomsky (2000a: 148–50) suggests that this is not a well-formulated question as it is not ideas that refer (at least in ordinary usage) but people who refer by using ideas in various (context-dependent) ways.

The question "to what does the word X refer?" has no clear sense, whether posed for Peter, or (more mysteriously) for some "common language." In general a word, even of the simplest kind, does not pick out an entity of the world, or of our "belief space". . . . (Chomsky 2000a: 181).

In ordinary usage, . . . person X refers to Y by expression E under circumstances C, so the relation is at least tetradic; and Y need not be a real object in the world or regarded that way by X. More generally, person X uses expression E with its intrinsic semantic properties to talk about the world from certain intricate perspectives focusing attention on particular aspects of it, under circumstances C . . . (Chomsky 2000a: 150)

Similarly, it is not beliefs that are true but assertions made by individuals under specific circumstances that employ beliefs. The problem then is not how to set up a correspondence between ideas and objects but to explain particular kinds of language use. Chomsky explicitly notes the rationalist flavor of this view of the semantic enterprise. Quoting from Cudworth, he summarizes a rationalist position with which he sympathizes:

An approach to semantic interpretation in such terms has a traditional flavor. Seventeenth-century rationalist psychology held that innate "cognoscitive powers" enable people "to understand or judge of what is received by the sense," which only gives the mind "an occasion to exercise its own activity" to construct "intelligible ideas and conceptions of things from within itself" as "rules," "patterns," "exemplars," and "anticipations" that provide relations of cause and effect, whole and part, symmetry and propostion, characteristic use . . . unity of objects and other Gestalt properties, and in general "one comprehensive name of the whole." (2000a: 181ff.)

As the above quote makes clear, Chomsky, following the observations of earlier rationalist thinkers (and some modern philosophers like Goodman), believes that it is unlikely that there will be a mechanical account of such "referential" activity, contrary to what the empiricist vision might suggest. What counts as having successfully referred is context dependent and subject to a variety of idiosyncratic concerns and interests. It would be surprising if anything very general unified all these instances of reference once one gets beyond the cognitive resources that these various referential uses exploit. The same goes for asserting truly. If this is correct, then the entire project of trying to ground epistemology in some sort of mechanical causal theory that animates the empiricist program is simply misconceived.

An expression such as "I painted my house brown" is accessed by performance systems that interpret it . . . and articulate it while typically using it for one or another speech act, on the productive side. How is this done? The articulatory-perceptual aspects . . . are still poorly understood. At the conceptual-intentional interface the problems are even more obscure, and may well fall beyond human naturalistic inquiry in crucial respects. (Chomsky 2000a: 125)

Observe, if Chomsky's arguments are even roughly correct then this removes the main difficulty with the rationalist alternative to empiricism noted above, viz. that it provides no compelling account of how beliefs can be true and ideas refer. Put another way, the main virtue of the empiricist approach was its promise of a non-trivial account of true belief and reference. If this promise cannot be fulfilled, then there is little left to recommend the empiricist perspective.

A third area where Chomsky's rationalism appears is in his discussion of problems ripe for naturalist inquiry. Chomsky draws an important distinction between problems and mysteries. He has observed that there are some areas that yield to naturalistic inquiry and many, the vast majority, that do not. The former are filled with *problems*, questions that can be attacked and understood using the procedures of scientific inquiry. In other domains the standard techniques of scientific inquiry gain no traction and all we are left with are pseudo-questions whose potential answers are as mysterious as they have ever been.

Among the aspects of the mind are those that enter into naturalistic inquiry; call them the "science-forming faculty" (SFF). Equipped with SFF, people confront "problem situations," consisting of certain cognitive states . . . questions that are posed, and so on . . . Often SFF yields only a blank stare. Sometimes it provides ideas about how the questions might be answered or reformulated, or the cognitive state modified, ideas that can then be evaluated in ways that SFF offers (empirical test, consistency with other parts of science, criteria of intelligibility and elegance etc.). (Chomsky 2000a: 82–3)

Chomsky notes that we should expect that some domains of inquiry will prove efficacious and some not. After all, if the mind is richly structured, then there is reason to expect that this structure would impose limits on the domains in which naturalistic inquiry can be successfully pursued. Given the rationalist view that what underlies our deepest and most complex capacities is a highly structured mind, it is reasonable to think that there will be intrinsic limits to what we can know and that therefore there may well be some domains within which naturalistic inquiry will never gain a real foothold.

Like other biological systems, SFF has its potential scope and limits; we may distinguish *problems* that fall within its limits and *mysteries* that do not. (Chomsky 2000a: 83)

> There may well be many . . . questions that are not subject to empirical inquiry in the manner of the sciences . . . if humans are themselves part of the natural world, and thus have specific biological capacities with their scope and limits, like every other organism. (Chomsky 2000a: 73)

This idea resonates with the Cartesian view outlined above. Recall that the crucial intuition behind the Cartesian view is that knowledge is a fortuitous accident. We can gain significant knowledge only if our minds are built for truth in one or another domain. Only then is deep insight possible. However, if the overlap between mind and the world is accidental, then there is no reason to believe that it will be generally applicable to any question that might interest us or even be of importance to us. Limits to knowledge are inherent given this picture of things.

> The successful natural sciences . . . fall within the intersection of SFF and the nature of the world; they treat the (scattered and limited) aspects of the world that we can grasp and comprehend by naturalistic inquiry, in principle. The intersection is a chance product of human nature. (Chomsky 2000a: 83)

This contrasts with both the empiricist view of matters and the "Kantian" perspective briefly parodied above. For the former, the mind is an all-purpose device whose structure is a function of what inputs it receives. The mind, being blank, is not predisposed to inquiry in any direction. One domain is neither better nor worse than any other. Thus, the distinction between problems on the one hand and mysteries on the other finds no place.

The "Kantian" retains some of the empiricist's viewpoint. For him or her truth is a function of our own capacities and methods of inquiry. As such, it would appear that the possibility of radical failure should be hard to formulate. Mysteries are temporary. With time they should convert to problems. The idea that some problems are intrinsically unsolvable for us, an idea that the Cartesian emphasizes as a real possibility, fits ill with the idea that truth is, in the end, a function of us.

Chomsky (1988b) observes that if humans are no different from other animals then there should be some things that they will do well as they are constructed to succeed in these domains, and some that they will fail at because of their inherent cognitive limitations. As he notes, the failures are the price we pay for our successes. Without a richly structured mind we would be unable to advance theories that far outstrip the data that suggest them. As all interesting theories are vastly underdetermined by the evidence that support them, it would seem that our successful explanations rest, in part, on the resources of our structured minds. However, with all advantages come limitations. If it is indeed the case that our successes are spurred in part by innate gifts of nature, then it is natural to assume that these same structures should act to limit what we can come to know. This has a clear Cartesian resonance.

Conclusion

Chomsky has quite self-consciously located his work in a rationalist setting. Like earlier thinkers, he has stressed the distance between our knowledge and our behavior, between our environment and our mental states, between what we know and how we put our knowledge to use. In a contemporary setting, these rationalist commitments set Chomsky apart from many thinkers still animated by empiricist concerns. The aim of this essay has been to illuminate some of Chomsky's concerns by locating them against the more general backdrop of empiricist–rationalist differences.

8   Innate ideas

Paul Pietroski and Stephen Crain

Here's one way this chapter could go. After defining the terms "innate" and "idea," we say whether Chomsky thinks any ideas are innate – and if so, which ones. Unfortunately, we don't have any theoretically interesting definitions to offer; and, so far as we know, Chomsky has never said that any ideas are innate. Since saying that would make for a *very* short chapter, we propose to do something else. Our aim is to locate Chomsky, as he locates himself, in a rationalist tradition where talk of innate ideas has often been used to express the following view: the general character of human thought is due largely to human nature.

One can endorse this view without saying that humans have specific concepts, like TURNIP or CARBURETOR, independent of experience. Correlatively, it is important to remember that while Chomsky is a nativist about language, he does not think that specific languages are innate. Whether a child ends up speaking Japanese or English, or both, clearly depends on the child's experience. The nativist claim is that all natural languages share core features that reflect the biology of *homo sapiens*. Knowing a language, like having a heart, is a reflection of our biological endowment. Just as humans have internal organs with characteristic traits, they speak languages with characteristic traits. According to Chomsky, linguistic variation is severely constrained by the mental systems that make human language possible. But this is compatible with some linguistic variation across (and within) communities, since the traits of individuals are always products of nature *and* nurture. Diet and exercise affect one's heart, within a limited range of possibilities. Similarly, experience affects the course of a child's linguistic development, within certain parameters.[1]

Thus one can be a nativist about language without saying that humans come into the world equipped with particular languages, like cars come off the assembly line equipped with wheels. Similarly, one can be a nativist about ideas without saying that humans come into the world equipped with particular ideas. Encounters with the world clearly have an impact on the ideas that humans acquire. Nevertheless, biology may well impose substantial constraints on the "space of possible ideas" that are naturally available to humans, much as biology constrains the "space of possible languages" that are naturally available to humans. Moreover, experience can have an impact without "shaping" the ideas that humans naturally employ. If children do not learn languages by generalizing from experience, and a child's history of linguistic stimulation simply drives the child down one of the biologically available linguistic paths, then perhaps the same is true of the acquisition of mental capacities more generally. A nativist perspective is reinforced in so far as mental capacities emerge in young children throughout the species, in settings where experience dramatically underdetermines the knowledge that children attain. As with language, perhaps experience plays the role of triggering innate mental resources in the formation of (at least many of) the ideas that humans naturally employ – ideas that can develop only in a limited number of ways. If so, while experience influences the particular course of idea-formation in any given individual, this is *not* (as empiricists suggest) because individuals seek and find regularities in their experience. Rather, regularities are imposed on experience in accordance with mental structures already in place.

We think this is Chomsky's view, and also the view he finds in certain historical figures who participated in debates about innate ideas. Chomsky's contribution to the traditional debate lies in (i) his articulation and defense of a detailed nativist program in linguistics, showing *how* experience plays only a restricted role in a broadly rationalist account of the acquisition of linguistic knowledge, and (ii) the framework this program suggests, given its empirical success, for the more general study of human cognition. Linguistics – where this includes not just the study of expressions and their properties, but also related work in psycholinguistics – provides a case study of how to investigate *which aspects of human thought are due largely to human nature*. Earlier chapters have addressed (i). We'll try to give the flavor of (ii) by discussing some historically important examples, and then by reviewing some recent discoveries, inspired by the Chomskyan approach to human psychology, about the properties of linguistic expressions that have a direct bearing on logical reasoning.

Experience, mind, the gap

As the previous chapter indicated, Chomsky is part of a rationalist tradition according to which human knowledge is rooted in the cognitive resources used when humans conceptualize their experience. Experience can, and often does, "trigger" the use of these resources. So humans deprived of normal experience may not develop in the usual way, and they may be unable to apply their cognitive resources in the usual knowledge-producing ways. But rationalists maintain that in at least many domains, the knowledge we do achieve goes far beyond our experience in ways that reflect the contours of our cognitive apparatus. From this perspective, the knowledge achieved is not the result of "generalizing" from experience: the *character* of human knowledge owes more to our shared human nature than to our shared human experiences. Knowledge of language is a paradigm example of a domain in which such "poverty-of-stimulus" considerations strongly favor a rationalist approach; see the previous chapter.

Although our cognitive systems surely reflect our experience in some manner, a careful specification of the properties of these systems on the one hand, and of the experience that somehow led to their formation on the other, shows that the two are separated by a considerable gap, in fact, a chasm . . . . The problem, then, is to determine the innate endowment that serves to bridge the gap between experience and knowledge attained. . . . The study of language is particularly interesting in this regard. (Chomsky 1986)

As this quote makes clear, Chomsky sees his "rationalist linguistics" as one branch of a broader – and for the most part, yet to be developed – rationalist psychology; see especially Chomsky (1966, 2002a). A similar program was envisioned by various seventeenth- and eighteenth-century theorists whom Chomsky regularly cites as initiators of the (very much unfinished) cognitive revolution: Descartes, the Port-Royal logicians, Ralph Cudworth, and Herbert of Cherbury. These thinkers maintained that a great deal of human knowledge springs (under the pressure of normal experience) from cognitive resources that humans have *independent of and prior to* experience. In their terminology, human beings have *innate ideas*.

Having introduced this traditional terminology, some caveats are in order. The claim is not (and was not) that humans are born with certain ideas – say, the idea of a triangle, or the idea of a verb phrase – and then just wait for the chance to apply them. Whether humans are *born* with ideas is not important on a rationalist account. The relevant cognitive resources may develop according to a maturational timetable, or they may be triggered by experiences that occur later in life.[2] Moreover, a rationalist need not describe any pre-triggered cognitive resource as, say, an innate idea *of a triangle*. Perhaps a person can be properly said to have an idea *of X* only if the person has had triggering experiences that are "appropriate to" the formation of that idea. If so, then nothing within us prior to experience can be properly described as an idea of X, no matter what we substitute for "X." Rationalists can agree to limit use of the word "idea" in this way. For this is fully compatible with the hypothesis that humans come to have the idea of a triangle (or a verb phrase), across a range of environmental situations, mainly because human cognition has contours that make us apt to acquire such ideas. Indeed, a rationalist need not describe any pre-triggered cognitive resource as an *idea*. Perhaps every idea is an idea *of* something, and so a thinker has an idea only if it is an idea of X, for some particular instance of "X." On this view, all ideas are intentional; they have a specific *content*. A rationalist could adopt this view while granting that mental entities come to have specific contents only under the pressure of experience.[3]

The traditional terminology is thus misleading. Innate ideas need not be inborn; experience is relevant; and whatever is innate need not be an idea, much less an idea of anything in particular. We suspect this is why Chomsky aligns himself with Descartes and other rationalists, but *without* using the phrase "innate ideas" to describe his own views. For Chomsky, the important issues do not concern what counts as an idea. The important issues concern (the size of) the "gap" between experience and knowledge, and how to best characterize the cognitive resources that fill the gap – thereby making it invisible in ordinary life.

In hindsight, it seems clear that many empiricists have rejected rationalist proposals at least in part because of misunderstandings about the crucial features of those proposals. To the best of our knowledge, no empiricist has successfully rebutted the relevant poverty-of-stimulus arguments for a broadly rationalist psychology.[4] One can sympathize with the desire (discussed in the previous chapter) for an account of how humans occasionally come to have veridical and justifiable beliefs about the mind-independent world. But one must guard against letting this desire drive one's psychological theorizing. According to Descartes and Chomsky, questions about how minds are related to the world are hard questions to be faced honestly in light of (i) our best theories of human psychology and (ii) our best theories of the mind-independent world. If our best theories of human psychology turn out to be rationalist theories, then so be it, even if this makes it *really* hard to see how we ever manage to come to have true justified beliefs about the mind-independent world. One can't argue for an empiricist psychology by noting that *if* human knowledge were mainly a product of generalizing from our shared experiences, then it would be easier to account for empirical knowledge.[5]

Why it's called "Plato's Problem"

It might help at this point to focus the discussion on a historically important example, already mentioned, that reveals how far human knowledge can extend beyond experience.

If a triangle is a three-sided figure with perfectly straight lines, then no one has ever seen a triangle, at least not in the ordinary sense that we can and do see rocks, people, and chalk marks. Nor has anyone ever heard, touched, smelled, or tasted a triangle. Nonetheless, humans have the idea of a triangle; and one can know a great many things about triangles. For example, the ancient

Greeks – who also had the idea of a *square*, a *right* triangle, the *area* of a figure, and the *sum* of two areas – knew that the square built on the hypotenuse of a right triangle with equal sides must be equal to the sum of the areas of the (equal) squares built on the shorter sides of the triangle. These ideas correspond to abstract geometric objects that are related as depicted below:

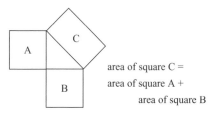

area of square C =
area of square A +
area of square B

DIAGRAM 1

For present purposes, the crucial point about "correspondence" is not that the abstract entities *exist*, but that geometric ideas are not spurious. Since the Pythagorean Proposition is provably correct, it somehow "agrees with" reality. (By contrast, endlessly many similar propositions disagree with reality. Consider the false claim that the square of the hypotenuse equals *twice the sum* of the other squares.)

Rationalists are struck by several features of cases like these. First, in order to entertain the Pythagorean Proposition, one needs to have the relevant ideas. If you met a creature who didn't have the idea of a three-sided figure composed of straight lines, you couldn't tell him *what* the Greeks knew, much less how they came to know it. In one sense, this is a perfectly general point. If you met someone who didn't have any conception of cows, you couldn't tell him that cows are brown. But at least you could show him some cows (distinguishing them from rocks, horses, bulls, etc.); whereas you can't show anyone a triangle.[6] So one question is how humans can even entertain thoughts concerning triangles. How do we come to have the relevant ideas?

A recurrent empiricist suggestion is that thinkers somehow *abstract* ideas from a series of sensory experiences, by representing similarities (and ignoring dissimilarities) across those experiences. Whatever the virtues of this proposal as it applies to acquiring the idea of a cow, it is unclear how the suggestion applies to triangles. How does one abstract the idea of a perfectly straight line from encounters with perceptible objects whose edges are never perfectly straight? Not only are geometric lines not *common* features of experience, they are never manifested in experience at all. A possible reply is that thinkers somehow abstract the *ideal* of a straight line by observing various nearly straight lines that diverge from the ideal in statistically random ways; in effect, one "averages" across a range of perceptible cases. But this raises the question of why humans focus on some averages and not others. Why does our idea of a line abstract away from thickness altogether, as opposed to representing some ideal or average thickness? More generally, why do human thinkers naturally form ideas that correspond to *certain* (averageable) dimensions of perceived entities, but not others?

Shifting back to language for a moment, this is the point of Chomskyan examples like (1–4).

(1)   John ate an apple.

(2)   John ate.

(3)   John is too clever to catch a fish.

(4)   John is too clever to catch.

Assuming that most speakers of English hear sentences like (1–2) before hearing sentences like (3–4), why *don't* they generalize as follows: since (2) means that John ate something or other, (4) means that John is too clever to catch something or other? Of course, speakers don't interpret (4) on analogy with (2). They know that (4) means, roughly, that John is too clever for relevant parties to catch *John*. One can say that speakers interpret (4) on analogy with some other experienced paradigm(s). But this just pushes the question back. Why do speakers analogize along some dimensions but not others? The facts suggest that the explanation will take a rationalist form: the cognitive apparatus brought to experience has a certain *character* in virtue of which human beings are disposed to project from experience to certain characteristic states of linguistic knowledge.

An empiricist account, based on abstraction of ideas from sensory experience, also requires that each thinker who acquires a certain idea has *enough* experience to abstract that idea. Encounters with one or two triangular figures are presumably not a sufficient basis for acquiring an idea that has been "shaped" by experience.[7] Moreover, theorists cannot rest content with the claim that someone *could* abstract the idea of a triangle (or a verb phrase) given *suitable* experience. One has to explain why so *many* thinkers abstract the same idea across the range of *actual* experiential situations. If thinkers of varying intelligence regularly form certain ideas, even when their experience is limited, that is a fact to be explained. So as rationalists have always stressed, if humans can acquire certain knowledge quickly and in the absence of much experience, such knowledge would seem to be a reflection of the cognitive resources humans bring to experience. Plato thus describes his famous thought experiment in which an uneducated servant comes to know the Pythagorean Proposition with *very* little experience (given some prompting by Socrates).[8]

Summarizing the key steps, the servant comes to "see" that doubling the sides of a square quadruples the area, as suggested by the diagram below:

DIAGRAM 2

He also agrees that a square can have any area. (It is striking that this is so obvious. How would you *teach* it to someone not initially disposed to agree?) So for example, a square can have an area twice that of the square we started with; and doubling the sides of a square with area 2 yields a square with area 8.

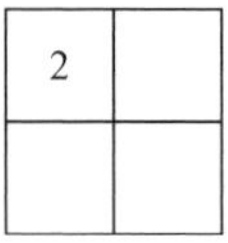

area of each square x = 2
area of the large square = 8

DIAGRAM 3

Socrates then leads the servant to a crucial (but intuitively obvious) lemma: bisecting a square yields two right triangles with equal areas; and so any square, including our square of area 8, can be divided into four right triangles with equal areas.

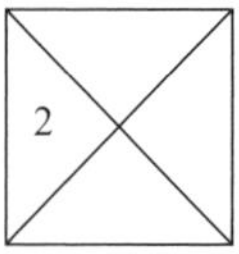

area of the large square = 8
area of each triangle = 2

DIAGRAM 4

If we now extend the figure, by adding a right triangle to create a square of area 4, we have an illustration of the Pythagorean Proposition: the square of area 8 *is* the square of the hypotenuse of a right triangle (with area 2), each of whose sides has a square with area 4:

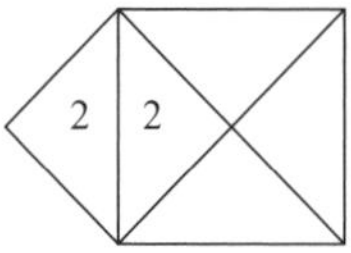

area of the large square = 8
area of the small square = 2 + 2 = 4

DIAGRAM 5

And as Meno recognizes, the same result can be achieved (in the same way) for any right triangle with equal sides.[9]

Faced with the fact that humans can manifest rather esoteric knowledge so quickly, Plato conjectured that humans "recollect" knowledge acquired in some past (immaterial) life in which ideal objects could be apprehended directly. But this is no explanation, absent an account of how immaterial beings apprehend triangles (and then store this knowledge in a form accessible to material beings). So one may as well – and Chomsky does – treat Plato's talk of recollection as a placeholder for unknown cognitive resources from which the knowledge springs. This makes it clear that Plato's "experiment" raises more questions than it answers: what is the best theoretical characterization of the relevant cognitive resources; how do they give rise to the knowledge in question; and in virtue of what do human beings have these resources? But this is hardly an embarrassment. Figuring out which questions to ask is a crucial starting point for inquiry.[10]

It is also striking that the Pythagorean Proposition, like many mathematical claims, is *provable* from compelling principles that are intuitively more basic. One cannot prove that cows give birth to cows, or that heat rises. One discovers, in large part by making repeated observations, that these generalizations are correct. But not only are measurements of perceptible figures unnecessary for geometric knowledge, they are irrelevant. One can't come to know the Pythagorean Proposition, in the way that geometers knew it, by generalizing from thousands of carefully drawn and measured triangular figures. A diligent student might note that the more carefully she draws and measures, the closer she approaches the ideal. But this is not a proof of the theorem. And provable propositions seem to have a distinctive character that is related to the felt *necessity* of such propositions.[11]

If thinkers recognize certain propositions as noncontingent, this suggests that judgments concerning such propositions go beyond experience of the mind-independent world. A related observation (Chomsky 1986) is that the same kind of felt necessity attaches to claims like (5–8).

(5)   If Mary persuaded John to go to college, John intended to go to college.

(6)   If John boiled the soup, the soup boiled.

(7)   If John thinks that Bill likes himself, John thinks that Bill likes Bill.

(8)   If John is too clever to catch, John is too clever for relevant parties to catch John.

And speakers of English know that (9) and (10) are not even *possible* sentences of English.

(9)   Bill thinks that Mary likes each other.

(10)   Who did Mary wonder that saw Bill?

These facts about speakers' capacities to tell that certain strings of words are (not) legitimate English expressions, or that certain English sentences are sure to be true come what may, call for explanation. They invite the hypothesis that humans (unconsciously) deploy various linguistic ideas that spring from underlying cognitive resources, with the result that (5–8) are perceived as analytic while (9–10) are perceived as illicit.

Cartesian ideas

Knowing a language, however, requires experience in a way that knowledge of geometry does not. Again, knowing Japanese differs from knowing English, even if the underlying mental states have much in common. Correlatively, knowing a language requires at least some experience with its vocabulary and certain aspects of its syntax. For example, one has to learn that direct objects typically follow verbs in English, while they typically precede verbs in Japanese; and that Japanese has overt case marking, as in Latin, while English does not. Thus, while Chomsky regularly speaks of Plato's Problem, he does not push the analogy to mathematical knowledge too hard. As his favorite seventeenth-century rationalists argued, symptoms of innate cognitive resources are not limited to our judgments about abstract objects.

In a famous example, Descartes asks what underlies his various judgments concerning a piece of melting wax. The perceptible qualities of the wax – its visual appearance, smell, and so on – change over time. Indeed, Descartes claims, no perceptible feature of the wax remains constant throughout all possible changes in the wax.[12] Descartes concludes that he conceives of the wax as something *with* (changeable) perceptible qualities, even though the wax does not seem to *be* any bundle of perceptible qualities. The wax seems to be something that *underlies* its perceptible qualities. Perhaps this intuitive view is wrong; though for present purposes, the metaphysics doesn't matter. Focus on the question of how we come to have the idea of an extended substance: something that occupies space and is a potential bearer of various perceptible qualities at various times. What *in experience* could provide the basis for the idea that the things we see – like lumps of wax – are things over and above bundles of sensible qualities?[13] Cartesians, seeing no prospects for a plausible answer to this question, conclude that even the ideas humans employ when thinking about concrete perceptible objects are ideas that transcend perceptual experience.

Descartes applied similar considerations to the idea of a thinking thing; and while one can object to both his metaphysical and psychological conclusions, it is easy to see why Chomsky is impressed with the style of argument. Descartes tried to figure out, on the basis of the kinds of judgments we make about thinkers (including ourselves), what human beings naturally assume about thinkers/persons independent of experience. The goal is to characterize the cognitive resources that humans bring to their experience of persons; so Descartes tried, as best he could given the theoretical tools available, to isolate our idea of a person and factor out the contribution of experience. Similarly, Chomsky uses the linguistic judgments of speakers as data for claims about what children assume about language, prior to experience.

For various reasons, moral knowledge was also an important topic in the seventeenth and eighteenth centuries. So much of the discussion about innate ideas concerned the kinds of moral judgments humans are apt to form. Ralph Cudworth and Herbert of Cherbury, mentioned above, held (roughly) that human nature makes a certain range of moral ideas naturally available to anyone who grows up in a normal human environment. And once a thinker starts to form judgments involving these ideas, particular judgments – say, "killing people is wrong" – will be especially compelling. While early formulations of this view were often incautious, and open to easy criticism by empiricists, Chomsky endorses the underlying picture.[14] Human minds develop in accordance with human nature, projecting ideas in response to initial experience; and then humans use those ideas, as best they can, to represent a world that has whatever character *it* has. In certain domains, like geometry and language and morals, these ideas manifest themselves as a special kind of knowledge whose source is "from within."

One might think there is a crucial difference between the "linguistic ideas" that seem to spring from human nature and ideas of perceptible objects. For the latter are at least "directed" towards the language-independent world, even if human judgments fail to represent that world accurately. And one might think that ideas *of* external objects – ideas that are (or at least are intended to be) *about* things independent of those ideas – cannot be innately constrained in the way that the idea of a verb phrase is constrained. But stated this baldly, the objection just restates the denial of rationalism. On Chomsky's own view, there are no linguistic expressions independent of language users; nothing "outside us" is relevant to whether or not our natural linguistic judgments are right or wrong. Correspondingly, an ordinary speaker's idea of a verb phrase is not about some aspect of the external world to which the speaker is attuned. On the other hand, an ordinary person's idea of (say) wax *is* about – or at least is sometimes used to think about – some aspect of the mind-independent world. But the fact that we think about things outside us hardly shows that our ideas owe their character to those external things. And the fact that we occasionally "tune in" to features of the mind-independent world, in ways that let us form *reliable* judgments, hardly shows that our ideas are not predominantly shaped by the cognitive systems that gave rise to them.

From this perspective, we are *fortunate* if we can use our natural ideas to form thoughts that truly reflect mind-independent reality. So one should not assume that humans have a natural capacity to form reliable judgments about *every* aspect of the environment that attracts their attention. Thus, rationalists typically stress that the very capacities that make knowledge possible also impose constraints on what one can know by deploying those capacities. For example, the language faculty imposes constraints on which languages humans can naturally acquire. This leaves open the possibility of "decoding" a non-human language – i.e. a language that does not conform to the principles of universal grammar – by using cognitive systems other than the language faculty; but we could not understand such a language in the way we can understand human languages. Similarly, when acting as scientists, humans *may* be able to construct ideas that lie outside the space of ideas naturally available to them; although Chomsky (1975, 1980, 2002b) suggests, in good rationalist fashion, that whatever cognitive systems underlie our capacity for doing science will also be governed by their own internal principles (see also McGinn 1994a).

That said, Chomsky also thinks that by pursuing the kind of scientific research that linguists pursue, we can begin to understand aspects of how human beings represent and reason about the world. So we conclude this chapter with a brief discussion of two phenomena that seem to straddle syntax and semantics and logic. For such phenomena may provide suggestions about how to (slowly) push beyond the study of linguistic forms, and into the study of why linguistic expressions have the meanings they do (as opposed to other logically coherent but "non-human" meanings), while remaining focused on how human ideas are constrained by our biological endowment.

Beyond mere grammar

As we have emphasized, Chomsky contends that the cognitive apparatus human beings bring to language learning has a certain *character*, given which humans acquire certain characteristic states of linguistic knowledge that go well beyond their experience. To illustrate this point about the language faculty, Chomsky frequently notes that as soon as children are able to combine the words *brown* and *house* to form the expression *brown house*, the composed phrase has semantic properties beyond those attributable to the meanings of the individual words. In particular, children use *That is a brown house* to say that the *exterior* of the house in question is brown; and unless interiors are explicitly mentioned, children will hear *That is a brown house* as a claim about the exterior of the house. (See chapter 10.)

The kind of innate knowledge that Chomsky envisions also includes knowledge of linguistic properties that have been investigated by researchers in the field of formal semantics. Chomsky views formal semantics as a theory about a component of the language faculty that determines certain features of structures generated by the computational system – i.e. the syntax. These structures include expressions of various categories. For example, the category of determiner covers a large class of (intuitively quantificational) expressions like *some, all, no, every, most, at least three, more than three, but less than ten*, and so forth.

There seem to be semantic universals that constrain the contribution of determiners to the meanings of expressions that contain them. One proposed universal property of determiner meanings, known as conservativity (Barwise & Cooper 1981; for introductory discussion, see Larson & Segal 1995; Chierchia & McConnell-Ginet 2000), is illustrated in (11).

(11)   If all cows are brown cows, then all cows are brown.

Speakers of English can know that (11) is sure to be correct, regardless of the situation. Moreover, (11) remains obviously correct if we replace *all* with other determiners like *some, no*, and so on. This suggests the following generalization:

(12)   If [(DET cows) (are brown cows)], then [(DET cows) (are brown)]

In (12), "DET" can be replaced by any natural language determiner to produce an obvious truth. Some examples include those in (13).

(13)   a. If most cows are brown cows, then most cows are brown.
          b. If all but two cows are brown cows, then all but two cows are brown.
          c. If more than three cows are brown cows, then more than three
             cows are brown.

This turns out to be an important fact. To see why, it will help to note that one can specify the meaning of a determiner using (something like) set-theoretic relations. One can think of determiners as names for relations that can hold between sets. For simplicity, let's continue to focus on sentences of the form DET NP VP, where the determiner is followed by a noun (or noun phrase) like *cows* and a verb (or verb phrase) like *are brown cows*; the NP and VP are, respectively, the first and second arguments of the determiner. A sentence of the form DET NP VP is true if and only if the set associated with the first (NP) argument bears the relation named by DET to the set associated with the second (VP) argument. For example, the sentence *All cows are brown* is true if and only if the set of cows is a subset of the set of brown things. So one can think of the determiner *all* as a label for the subset relation. Likewise, *All cows are brown cows* is true if and only if the set of cows is a subset of the set of brown cows. So (11) expresses the following set-theoretic truism: if the set of cows is a subset of the set of brown things, then the set of cows is a subset of the set of brown cows.

The sentence *Some cows are brown* is true if and only if the set of cows intersects with the set of brown things. So one can think of the determiner *some* as a label for the relation of intersection. Likewise, *Some cows are brown cows* is true if and only if the set of cows intersects with the set of brown cows; and if the set of cows intersects with the set of brown things, then trivially, the set of cows intersects with the set of brown cows. Similar remarks apply to all natural language determiners. The generalization indicated in (12) is quite robust. But natural languages also contain quantificational expressions that *would* be counterexamples to (12) *if* these words were determiners. For example, inserting the word *only* into (12) would yield (14), which is not a truism (as indicated by '#').

(14)   # If only cows are brown cows, then only cows are brown.

Suppose there is a brown horse in the conversational context. Then while (11) and (13) remain obviously correct, (14) is false. So to maintain the generalization in (12), one must say that *only* is not a determiner. But this is independently plausible, since *only* (which is arguably an adverb) can appear in a much wider range of syntactic positions than genuine determiners. Consider, for example, *He only likes brown cows* and *Bessie is the only brown cow*.

The availability of words like *only* in natural languages shows that logic alone does not explain the generalization about the conservativity of determiner meanings. Rather, it seems that natural language is intolerant of determiner meanings that would violate (12), though it tolerates such meanings for other kinds of linguistic expressions. So even if actual instances of (12) report logical truths, logic alone does not exclude the possibility of quantificational expressions that would be counterexamples to (12). The relevant generalization evidently holds because of some fact about speakers of human languages, whose mental grammars are subject to a substantive constraint that prohibits certain determiner meanings; see Pietroski (2005) for a proposal.[15]

If this constraint turns out to be a linguistic universal, then it is a likely candidate for innate specification. For what evidence (that children are sensitive to) would allow speakers to *infer* that other speakers use only conservative determiners? The nativist proposal would be that the conservativity of determiner meanings is a reflection of features shared by all natural languages in virtue of human biology. These "core" features of natural languages constitute what Chomsky calls "Universal Grammar" – the initial state of the language learner. A consequence of Universal Grammar is that sentential structures are interpreted in certain ways. If this is correct, then theorists can try to characterize the notion of "natural" consequence that is a by-product of how the human language faculty is organized (see Ludlow 2002). And it seems that the "interpretive" component of Universal Grammar does indeed impose constraints on the meanings of so-called logical words. A child exposed to a particular spoken language has to figure out which sounds in that language are associated with which possible meanings for quantificational expressions like *all*, *some*, and *no*. But the nativist expects a child to know how such words contribute to the truth conditions of sentences (in any natural language) as soon as these words have entered the child's lexicon. For example, the nativist will expect the child to manifest knowledge that all determiner meanings are conservative, as soon as it is possible to test for such knowledge.[16] (We return to words for propositional operators – *and*, *or*, and *not* – presently.)

Other semantic properties of determiners are also viable candidates for innate specification. Although all determiners are conservative, they can be further partitioned into semantic classes that correspond to certain entailment relations among sentences. Consider the impeccable inferences in (15):

(15)   NP: If no <u>cow</u> ate a vegetable, then no <u>brown cow</u> ate a vegetable.
        VP: If no cow <u>ate a vegetable</u>, then no cow <u>ate a green vegetable</u>.

Given the determiner *no*, one can replace a general term like *cow* with a more specific expression like *brown cow* in the first (NP) argument. One can also replace a general term like *vegetable* with a more specific expression like *green vegetable* in the second (VP) argument. To capture this fact, semanticists say that *no* is "downward entailing" in both of its arguments. This is related to the fact that negation generally licenses inferences from claims about sets of things to claims about subsets. For example, if John did not buy a car, it follows that he did not buy a red car; whereas if John bought a car, it does not follow that he bought a red car.

But not all determiners have this feature, as indicated in (16–17):

(16)   NP: If every <u>cow</u> ate a vegetable,
              then every <u>brown cow</u> ate a vegetable.
        #VP: If every cow <u>ate a vegetable</u>,
              then every cow <u>ate a green vegetable</u>.
(17)   #NP: If some <u>cow</u> ate a vegetable,
              then some <u>brown cow</u> ate a vegetable.
        #VP: If some cow <u>ate a vegetable</u>,
              then some cow <u>ate a green vegetable</u>.

The universal quantifier *every* is downward-entailing on its first argument, but not on its second argument. The existential quantifier *some* is not downward entailing on either of its arguments.

The semantic property of downward entailment has important linguistic consequences. For it is connected to several seemingly unrelated linguistic phenomena, including the licensing of so-called negative polarity items (such as *any*, *ever*, and *at all*) and restrictions on the interpretation of *or*. The sentences in (18–20) illustrate that the negative polarity item *any* is licensed by downward-entailing argument positions. For example, *every* is downward entailing on its first (NP) but not its second (VP) argument. And as shown in (19), *any* can appear in the complex NP *cow that ate any vegetable*; but if *any* appears in the complex VP *ate any vegetable*, it sounds odd (given the determiner *every*), as indicated by the asterisk. By contrast, *no* is downward entailing in both of its arguments, and *any* can appear in either argument; while *some* is downward entailing in neither of its arguments, and *any* cannot appear in either argument.

(18)　　NP:　No cow that ate any vegetable became ill.
　　　　　VP:　No cow ate any vegetable.

(19)　　NP:　Every cow that ate any vegetable became ill.
　　　　　VP:　*Every cow ate any vegetable.

(20)　　NP:　*Some cow that ate any vegetable became ill.
　　　　　VP:　*Some cow ate any vegetable.

Similar remarks apply to the complex NP *cow that ever ate vegetables* and the complex VP *ever ate vegetables*. The generalization seems to be that negative polarity items are licensed in downward-entailing environments.

Another striking fact is that if a determiner is downward entailing on one of its arguments, the disjunction operator has a "conjunctive" implication in that argument position. This is illustrated in (21), where *or* has a conjunctive implication when it appears in the first argument of *every*, but not when it appears in the second argument.

(21)　　NP:　If every cow that ate broccoli or asparagus became ill, then
　　　　　　　　(i)　every cow that ate broccoli became ill and
　　　　　　　　(ii) every cow that ate asparagus became ill.
　　　#VP:　If every cow ate broccoli or asparagus, then
　　　　　　　　every cow ate broccoli and
　　　　　　　　every cow ate asparagus.

The conjunctive implication is present for both arguments of *no* and neither argument of *some*. For example, if no cow ate broccoli or asparagus, it follows that: no cow ate broccoli, *and* no cow ate asparagus. But if some cow ate broccoli or asparagus, it does not follow that some cow ate broccoli; nor does it follow that some cow ate asparagus.

One can think of DeMorgan's law for negation, stated in (22), as a special case of a general relation between disjunction and conjunction in downward entailing linguistic environments, as stated in (23).

(22)   not(A or B) ➜ not(A) and not(B)

(23)   For any downward-entailing operator O: O(A or B) ➜ O(A) and O(B)

The generalization in (23) extends to all downward-entailing expressions. But since *every* is downward entailing only in its first argument, the conjunctive implication of disjunction arises only in its first argument. Theorists can thus capture the fact that *every* falls between *no* and *some* with regard to the DeMorgan phenomenon.[17]

In thinking about such facts, it is important to distinguish logical truths – about the interrelations of logical notions like conjunction, (inclusive) disjunction, and negation – from facts about the (natural) meanings of linguistic expressions. The logical truth reported with (22) does not, by itself, tell us anything about the meanings of sentences involving the natural language expressions *not*, *and*, and *or*. In this regard, note that DeMorgan's law would not be germane to sentences of the form *A or B* if the word *or* had an "exclusive" interpretation according to which *A or B* is false if *A* and *B* are both true. This suggests that certain expressions have the property of being downward entailing because speakers of human languages are subject to a substantive constraint involving downward entailment.

This constraint is relevant to at least all of the following: the basic (inclusive) meaning of disjunction words in natural languages, the licensing of negative polarity items, and prohibitions on the imposition of scalar implicatures. The constraint under consideration is another candidate for innate specification. If so, language learners are expected to approach the task of grammar formation equipped with this aspect of logical reasoning. Whatever "errors" of logical inference learners make, we do not expect them to violate DeMorgan's laws, or to produce negative polarity items in the wrong linguistic environments. Recent experimental evidence from studies of child language lends credence to nativist hypotheses. As soon as children can be tested, around the age of three, they obey the licensing conditions on negative polarity items, they compute the conjunctive interpretation of disjunction in downward entailing linguistic environments, and they evince knowledge that determiner meanings are conservative (Chierchia et al. 2001).

This is the kind of inquiry suggested by Chomsky's conception of innate ideas. One tries to learn about the character of human thought by looking for generalizations that are neither logical truths nor plausible candidates for hypotheses that thinkers have empirically confirmed on the basis of data available to them. If young children, with different backgrounds, all respect a (non-logical) generalization G that trained linguists have only recently noticed, this suggests that G is a reflection of human nature. This is then a starting point for further inquiry into how (and why) human nature gives rise to such generalizations. Chomsky – following Plato, Descartes, and others – thus offers a methodology for how to formulate and occasionally answer substantive questions about human thought.

9   Mind, language, and the limits of inquiry

Akeel Bilgrami and Carol Rovane

This chapter explores a very general philosophical and methodological theme in Noam Chomsky's work – the scope and limit of scientific inquiry in the study of mind and language. It is a conspicuous fact about Chomsky that accompanying the vast and driving intellectual ambition of his program in what he conceives as the *science* of linguistics is a notable and explicit modesty about the extent to which he thinks he has given, indeed the extent to which one can give, scientific answers to fundamental questions. This modesty in terms of *breadth* of coverage is in a sense the other side of, and therefore indispensable to, the *depth* of what he has achieved in the area he has covered.

In his work, he seems to offer at least two different sorts of reasons for us to be made modest about ourselves as inquirers. First there is a modesty implicit in his guardedness about claiming for semantics what some other philosophers have claimed for it, and what he himself has claimed only for syntax understood in a broad sense viz., that there is in some interesting sense an explanatory theory to be offered which can be incorporated into the science of linguistics. Second, there are reasons for modesty having to do with the fact that either because of our conceptual limitations or because of faulty formulations of questions, we are in no position to give serious and detailed answers to them. The next two sections will take up each of these in turn.

Is referential semantics possible?

For Chomsky, scientific inquiry into language and into the human mind is possible if it can assume that what is being studied are the "*inner* mechanisms" which enter into the study of thought and expressions and behavior generally. As he says:

The approach is "mentalistic" but in what should be an uncontroversial sense. It is concerned with "mental aspects of the world" which stand alongside its mechanical, chemical, optical, and other aspects. It undertakes to study a real object in the natural world – the brain, its states, and functions – and thus to move the study of the mind [and language] towards eventual integration with biology and the natural sciences. (Chomsky 2000a: 6)

Though eventual integration with biology is the goal, it is a distant goal. In the interim scientists work with the data and the theoretical resources available to them, at a level of description and explanation which it allows them. They have the scientific goals of describing and explaining the language faculty which is present in the entire species as a biological endowment, but at a level of description and explanation which in the interim is bound to be a cognitive and computational level, with the properties of internality, universality, innateness, domain-specificity, among others, all of which Chomsky's own successive theories of grammar over the last few decades have exemplified.

This deep commitment to internalism is presented as being of a piece with what Chomsky says is the naturalistic intractability of semantics as standardly conceived, which relies heavily on reference and more generally on the relations our words and concepts bear to objects, properties, and states of affairs in the *external* world. Two main reasons emerge for this skepticism from a number of interesting remarks over many essays. First, we have extremely rich and diverse conceptions of the things our words refer to, and that infects reference itself, making it a highly mediated and contextual notion. This thwarts scientific generalizations about reference from ranging over all speakers of a natural language and even perhaps over a single speaker at different times. And second, there is no reference without speakers *intending* to refer, and intentionality in general is not a fit subject for naturalistic treatment. Let's look at each of these in turn.

In stressing agents' rich and diverse conceptions of the things they refer to, Chomsky resists a normative as well as a social understanding of the notion of reference. He repeatedly rejects the intuitions urged by both the proponents of twin-earth thought experiments as well as socialized variants of it such as Burge's highly fortified example about his protagonist's arthritis. And he concludes, rightly in our view, that there is no theoretical compulsion to insist that the term *water* used on twin-earth and earth must always have different meanings and reference (for example, even for speakers here and there, who know no chemistry), nor to insist that the term *arthritis* on the lips of Burge's medically ignorant protagonist must mean and refer to what the doctor's term in his society means and refers, rather than to a wider class of ailments.[1] Social and other external relations do not force a uniform norm of meaning and reference of a term on all speakers of a language, such that all departures from it necessarily amount to mistakes. For some departures, instead of thinking of them as violations of a norm, we can think of them as individual ("idiolectical") meanings and references, tied to local contexts of use.

There might be two different referentialist responses to this appeal to the diverse conceptions of things to which we refer with our terms.

The *first* would be to say that despite the diverse conceptions that speakers have, they all *intend* to use a term as others do; they all intend their use of a name like *Hesperus*, or a natural kind term like *water*, to refer to what others, especially the experts, in the community refer to. Or (a somewhat different account) they may *intend* to refer to that thing which was named by the originary baptismal reference-fixing event, or instances of that substance which have the same scientific nature as the substance picked out in the originary, reference-fixing event. These intentions give uniformity to the reference of these terms for all speakers who use them, so no dreaded contextuality arises from the diversity of conceptions speakers might have of the things they refer to. Over many essays (some are found in his [2000a]), Chomsky addresses all these accounts and has trenchant things to say against them. First of all, he points out, the *data* leave underdetermined whether one should think of reference as having this uniformity or think of it instead as being much more contextual and individual. Certainly data about deference among speakers towards experts in the community do not necessarily point to a socially constituted notion of reference because they can be handled quite easily within the idiolectical approach to reference by simply pointing out that the reference of an individual's term changes once one learns from experts and defers to them. And then, he points out, quite apart from data not forcing the issue, none of the *theoretical* or philosophical motivations philosophers have had for stressing such a uniform and decontextualized notion of reference is compelling either. He patiently addresses such motivations (e.g. that only such a notion will account for theory-change as being distinct from meaning-change, and for how one may learn about the world – and not just about what is intended by the speaker – from others' usage of terms) and shows that these things are all easily accounted for within an individualist approach.

But even putting those criticisms aside, his point remains that these accounts achieve their uniformity and transcend particular contexts only by relying on the intentions of speakers and – intentionality being what it is – that puts them outside what is naturalistically tractable in a theory. In fact, both Kripke and Putnam who favor this form of referential semantics are careful to make no claim to a *theory* of reference, leave alone a naturalistic and scientific account of it.

But there is a *second* referentialist response which, realizing the naturalism-thwarting element of the first's appeal to intentions, does not appeal to intentions in its account of meaning and reference. This is the view, owing first to Dretske and much refined and developed by Fodor, which ties reference to causal covariances between mental tokens of a type in the language of thought and objects or properties in the world (Fodor 1975, 1998; Dretske 1981; Frege 1892). On this view, the rich and diverse conceptions of things that speakers may have of the objects referred to are irrelevant because the causal relations posited are uncontaminated by such mediating conceptions. And so the sorts of intentions appealed to by the first response in order to finesse these conceptions of things are unnecessary. There is no question, in any case, of appealing to intentions to refer since we do not and cannot have intentions towards terms in the language of thought, we can only have them towards words we vocalize. Since neither intentions nor conceptions of things play any role, these relations between a term (concept) and an object or property in the world may be the basis of *universal* laws which hold for all speakers who possess the concept and who stand in causal relations with the object or property in question. In fact Fodor (1990) sometimes himself describes the aspirations of such a naturalistic semantics in Newtonian terms. In a sense, this second challenge to Chomsky is the more interesting one because it accepts one half of his overall view (the naturalism and the scientific aspirations for linguistics) and resists the other half (the internalism, or the claim that it is *only* internalistically described phenomena which are scientifically tractable). This referentialist response holds that reference *is* scientifically tractable, and therefore there is a respectable naturalistic version of *semantics*, as well as syntax.

Despite the fact that Chomsky does not explicitly say so, we suspect that he would be unimpressed by this response which, while it does in a very general way allow for naturalism (purely *causal* covariances), it does not offer any specific suggestions for naturalistic inquiry, no specific research programs, no specific hypotheses, no design for specific experiments to test hypotheses. There is only an assertion that the subject of reference has very austere causal covariances underlying it which involve no conceptions, intentions, etc., and that it provides no obstacles to naturalism and the search for general decontextualized scientific laws in the study of semantics. Chomsky's successive theories of universal grammar, all of which restrict themselves to syntax broadly understood, are rich and detailed. Fodor's naturalistic referential semantics is, by contrast, little more than a suggestive idea. It seems very much the suggestion of a philosopher straining to make claims for reference that lie within science, but with no real sense of what science must actually then do in this area of study.

But even putting this important qualm aside, there is another worry much more on the surface of what Chomsky does explicitly say in the many passages where he speaks of our *ordinary* concept of reference: he is bound to ask of Fodor's naturalistic version of "reference," why is this an account of reference? Why is it not to be seen as giving up the idea of reference for causal covariances? He may not have anything against such a naturalization (Chomsky does not in general feel any qualms about changing the subject from common sense to science), so long as it is not claimed that it is reference that we are still talking about. There must be some common features, some shared structure, between reference as ordinarily understood and reference as naturalistically understood in these terms, which makes it clear that the notion is indeed preserved more than nominally.

What makes Fodor particularly interesting as an interlocutor is that he explicitly argues that something deep *is* preserved. His notion of meaning and (intentional) content is based exclusively upon the notion of denotation or reference. (As he says at the beginning of his [1990], "The older I get the more convinced I am that there is no more to meaning and content than denotation.") And, in turn, meaning and content are what go into the explanations involved in what he calls "granny psychology," the psychology which cites content-bearing states in the explanation of intentionally described behavior. One's intentional contents, contents specified in that-clauses (the belief *that water quenches thirst*, say) are individuated strictly by the referents of the component terms, such as the term *water*. Reference, *even after it is naturalistically characterized* in terms of the causal covariances that hold between our mental tokens of *water* and instances of a substance with a certain chemical composition, *continues* to contribute to contents of intentional states such as the one just cited which (in intentional psychology) explain actions of ours in the world, such as drinking water when we are thirsty, etc. And it is part of his claim that this psychology, the psychology whose states are expressed and understood by the grannies of the world, is not to be "eliminated" at all for *another* psychology, which makes no mention of intentional content. Rather, granny psychology *approximates* the truth (or truths) eventually captured in full naturalistic dress when one sees through its chief notions (content, meaning, reference) to what underlies them – the causal covariances.

We have here the real target of Chomsky's skepticism. What he is rejecting is the idea that when we come up with these universal laws based on causal covariances – granting for the moment that these are the deliverances of an interesting scientific research project, which is doubtful – we have come up with something that is in *any way* interestingly *continuous* with intentional psychology as understood in common sense.

Chomsky says many things that make it clear that he would be skeptical. Here are two related arguments that support his skepticism. He does not formulate these arguments in just these terms, but it seems to us that they drive his doubts.

First argument. We are considering a naturalism about reference which also claims that reference plays a vital and exclusive role in the attribution of intentional content and generally in intentional psychology. Now, any view of reference (of our terms or of the concepts which those terms express) should be compatible with the following constraint on the commonsense attribution of intentional content to a subject: if a subject believes something with an intentional content or expresses that belief with that intentional content by uttering a sentence, and that belief (or assertion) is merely false, i.e. if the speaker is merely misinformed about something in the world, it should still follow that he is quite rational in having that belief with that content (or in making that assertion). In other words, *merely being misinformed does not bring with it irrationality or incoherence*. For example, suppose someone is misinformed about the chemical composition of water and he says, "Water is not H_2O" (or has a belief with the content that water is not H_2O). Now if the reference of the term (or concept) *water* is given by the causal covariance between his relevant mental tokens and instances of H_2O, then it strictly follows that he is thinking something inconsistent. But this man is merely misinformed in saying or believing what he does. He is not irrational and logically incoherent. Thus the naturalistic view of reference violates a basic constraint on our commonsense understanding of reference and its role in intentional psychology. A naturalistic psychology based on such an understanding of reference which violates this constraint therefore *fails* to be continuous with ordinary intentional psychology, such as it is.

It should be apparent that this argument echoes, indeed that it more or less is, Frege's argument for sense. Chomsky appeals explicitly to Frege and uses the term "perspectives" instead of "senses."[2] Frege and Fregeans go on to spoil this famous argument and this important constraint on which it is based by demanding all sorts of *further* things of the notion of sense: viz., that senses are abstract objects to which our thinking is related, that to be this they must be expressed in a shared language, etc. – all claims of which Chomsky is critical. We come back to that in a moment.

Second argument. To repeat, we are considering a naturalism about reference which also claims that reference plays a vital and exclusive contributing role in the attribution of intentional content and generally in intentional psychology. Now, any view of reference (of our terms or of the concepts which those terms express) should be compatible with the following constraint on the attribution of intentional content to a subject: if a subject believes or desires something (say, believes that drinking water will quench his thirst or desires that he drink the water in front of him), and there are no familiar forms of psychological obstacles such as self-deception or other less interesting psychological obstacles such as that it is simply too submerged in his thinking, then he knows what he believes or desires. Of course, self-knowledge does not hold ubiquitously of our beliefs and desires precisely because we have many beliefs and desires which we repress or which are too submerged in our psychologies, etc. But we can assume that if these psychological obstacles and censors are not present, then awareness or self-knowledge of the intentional states would be present. Its presence could not be denied by anything but such *internal psychological* obstacles. It could not be denied by philosophical fiat, it could not be denied because Fodor has proposed a certain theory of reference. Let's take an example. Suppose someone is ignorant of chemistry, in particular of the chemical composition of water. And suppose he says (or believes) "Water quenches thirst." If the term or concept *water* in that assertion or belief has the reference it has because of the causal covariance which holds between the mental tokens of the relevant mental type and instances of H_2O, then this subject believes (says) something of which he is quite unaware, i.e. he believes that a substance with a certain chemical composition quenches thirst. He could not possibly be aware of what he believes since he knows no chemistry. But not knowing chemistry is not a *psychological* obstacle of any kind. It is just ignorance about the world. On this view of intentional psychology, this subject, in order to gain self-knowledge of what he himself thinks, would have not to overcome repressions, self-deceptions, and other psychological obstacles, he would rather have to learn *more chemistry*, learn more about the chemical composition of substances in his external environment. Thus, the naturalistic view of reference violates another constraint about our commonsense understanding of reference and its role in intentional psychology. Again, in violating this constraint, a naturalistic psychology, based on such an understanding of reference, therefore, *fails* to be continuous with intentional psychology, such as it is.

Both these arguments are implied by Chomsky's attitude towards reference as it figures in our *commonsense* understanding.

The first, Fregean argument requires that the notion of reference be embedded in the context of various conceptions of an object to which the speaker intends to refer, just as Chomsky has all along explicitly insisted. The conceptions are not separable from the object to which the speaker intends to refer. It's the object, under those descriptions or conceptions, to which the speaker refers. Chomsky tends to assimilate any view which denies this embedding as the "myth of the logically proper name." One function of embedding reference in conceptions is to make rational sense of the speaker who is merely misinformed (in the cases we are discussing, misinformed about various *a posteriori* identities, e.g. the identity of Hesperus with Phosphorus, or of water with H_2O, etc.). Without this embedding, the constraint on intentional psychology that requires that a notion of reference keep continuity with that psychology is violated.

The second argument is only *implied* by some things that Chomsky says. In the first argument, an agent's conceptions of things, or what Frege called senses, were seen to be essential to understanding reference, and to the intentional psychology of agents to which the reference of terms (or concepts) contributes. It is essential, as we said, because without it, someone who was merely misinformed about identities would be viewed as being self-contradictory. What philosophers call "Frege puzzles" about identity are based on this. Someone who does not know that Hesperus is Phosphorus may think that Hesperus is bright and Phosphorus not bright, and we know that the person is not contradicting himself. So we have to introduce senses or conceptions of things ("perspectives") as individuating his concepts and terms, rather than reference, in order to make him come out as rational. But, how would we have to view him if we thought he *was* contradicting himself? The idea would have to be that since both terms referred to the same planet, and since (as Fodor's naturalism insists) reference, not senses and conceptions, individuates terms and concepts (in this case, singular terms and singular concepts, but as we saw the point applies equally to *water*), he must have two contradictory thoughts. He would not of course *know* that he was contradicting himself. It's not as if he knows that Hesperus and Phosphorus are the same object and he is perversely saying knowingly contradictory things about them. Rather, he would be unaware that he was thinking and talking about the same planet, but he *would* be talking about them, and that is why he would be contradicting himself. Self-contradiction in an agent can be made tolerable only if it is accompanied by such lack of knowledge of his self-contradictory thoughts. Thus if senses are left out of the individuation of concepts and the contents of an agent's thoughts, and if individuation of concepts was seen as a matter of reference, the ensuing self-contradiction in his thinking would be tolerable only if it is explained by saying that his ignorance of astronomy would amount to *an ignorance of his own thoughts*, his own intentional (in this case, self-contradictory) psychology. Senses or "perspectives" (unlike reference) therefore make sure not only what the *first* argument demands of them, viz., that people merely misinformed (about identities, in this case) do not come out as having contradictory thoughts, but they also make sure that those thoughts are self-known to the agent. This latter task of senses is what the second argument demands as a constraint on thoughts.[3]

What is it about senses which ensures that they will carry out this second task, that they will see to it that our intentional psychology, i.e. our intentional states, are self-known to us (unless, of course, there are psychological obstacles to it)? As we just saw, to make things tolerable, one is forced to say that one fails to know what one thinks if what one thinks, or elements in one's thinking, such as one's concepts, are individuated by *objects* (such as, in these examples, planets or cities to which our concepts refer). To put it in terms of language, one can fail to know what one is saying if the meanings of one's terms are specified in terms of objects. So if senses are to avoid the problem of leading to lack of self-knowledge of one's thoughts, they must precisely *not* be like the sorts of things which *are* the source of the problem, which can lead to lack of self-knowledge. To put it in a word, senses cannot be like planets and cities, they cannot themselves be *objects* about whose identity we can be misinformed, thinking for instance that there are two senses when there is only one, as we might do with a planet or a city. If they were objects, we would not be able to see them as solutions to Frege's puzzles about identity. They would be subject to similar puzzles themselves. Thus there are no such things or entities as senses or thoughts to which we are related in our thinking in the way that Fodor and other referentialists think we are related to objects such as planets and water in the world. However, Frege, unfortunately, thought that senses *are* objects, abstract ones. But senses can only do the job they are asked to do *by him* in the first argument, they can only do the job that Frege himself wanted them to do (to solve Frege puzzles about identity), if they also do the job they are asked to do in the second argument, which is to make sure that they and the concepts and thoughts they individuate are self-known to the agent. And they can only do this latter job if they are not themselves objects. For if they were objects one might be confused into wondering whether some sense of ours was the same as another just as one might wonder if Hesperus is Phosphorus, or water is H_2O?[4]

It is *this* insight – that thoughts are not objects – which Chomsky explicitly articulates against Frege, and in doing so he implies the force of the second argument given above. He cites much earlier thinkers in support of the insight, saying:

> The basic assumption that there is a common store of thoughts surely can be denied; in fact, it had been plausibly denied a century earlier by critics of the theory of ideas who argued that it is a mistake to interpret the expression "John has a thought" (desire, intention, etc.) on the analogy of "John has a diamond." In the former case, the encyclopedist du Marsais and later Thomas Reid argued, the expression means only "John thinks" (desires, etc.) and provides no ground for positing "thoughts" to which John stands in relation. (Chomsky 1966, 2002a, 1993b: 18)

The insight can now be *generalized* to make the point that is needed against the project of naturalizing intentionality by individuating thoughts and concepts in terms of the external objects and substances with which we stand in causal relations. Thoughts are not objects, as Chomsky following earlier eighteenth-century critics is pointing out. We have just seen that there are no internal or abstract objects such as senses. So Frege's insight of our first argument about the need for senses, conceptions of things, perspectives on things, etc. (which Chomsky endorses) would be undermined if we thought that senses were themselves objects. The second argument ensures that it is not undermined in this way, by posing a constraint which cannot be met if we take senses to be objects. But the claim is more *general* in its significance than that. Our concepts and thoughts are not individuated in terms of internal objects, but equally they are not individuated in terms of external objects either. What the referential semanticist offers, when he tries to finesse an agent's conceptions of things, is precisely this externalist individuation. He tries to make the contents of our thoughts depend on nothing but the external objects with which the concepts which compose them stand in causal relations. In saying this he falls afoul of the two constraints which we identified in the two arguments above, which define our ordinary commonsense understanding of meaning and reference and intentional psychology. Falling afoul of them makes clear that the continuity with granny psychology that Fodor himself seeks would go missing.

And Chomsky's interesting point here is that at a *general* enough level of description of the mistake, *both* Frege *and* Fodor are making the *same* mistake, they are both in their different ways individuating thoughts in terms of objects. That they are doing so differently, in terms of internal[5] and external objects respectively, should not distract from the fact that they make the same mistake at the more general level.

All this is related directly to Chomsky's stance on the subject of reference. Frege, in insightfully exposing the flaws in the idea that concepts are individuated in terms of the external objects posited by the referentialist, introduces the importance of the idea of an *agent's conceptions of things*, but he does not rest with that insight; he goes on to spoil it by viewing these as internal and abstract objects. And on the other side, the naturalistic referential semanticist, also insightfully acknowledges that *conceptions of things would not be the sorts of things that could be naturalistically treatable* (Fodor is explicit about this), but then does not rest with that insight; he goes on to spoil it by individuating thoughts in terms of external objects with which we stand in causal relations, and which he thinks confer naturalism upon reference. Thus the point made by Chomsky (and Reid and du Marsais) can be generalized to say that thoughts are not to be individuated in terms of objects at all, external or internal, and once we do so, we can rest with the two insights that were respectively observed by both Frege and the referential naturalist, and then spoilt by them, when they would not rest there. We have already italicized them above. They are (1) there is no understanding reference to things without there being conceptions that particular speakers have of the things to which they intend to refer, and (2) conceptions of things are not naturalistically treatable. These, as we have seen, are the very insights that Chomsky has all along insisted on in thinking about referential semantics.

Having argued that reference to things is not the sort of thing that comes unaccompanied by the intentions and beliefs (conceptions of things) of speakers, he argues that reference must therefore really be understood as part of the *use* of language. It is not part of the description of the language organ or faculty, of the mechanisms and internal cognitive system that enable the use of language. It is rather part of a description of what is enabled, which goes much beyond a description of the enabling apparatus, involving such things, as we said, as a person's intentions and his richly conceived understanding of what the objects around him are, none of which can be the object of "theoretical understanding" and "naturalistic inquiry," but is rather illuminated by wider forms of understanding which it would be just confusing and conflating to call "theoretical" or "scientific" or "naturalistic." Since the *use* of language has traditionally been seen to fall within pragmatics, Chomsky boldly proposes the revisionary classification of placing reference not in semantics at all, but in pragmatics. He says, "It is possible that natural language has only syntax and pragmatics"; and then he adds, quoting an earlier work by himself which he says was influenced by Wittgenstein and Austin, "it has a 'semantics' only in the sense of the study of how this instrument whose formal structure and potentialities of expression are the subject of syntactic investigation, is actually put to use . . ." (2000a: 132) This redrawing of the traditional boundaries of the trio of syntax, semantics, and pragmatics is by no means arbitrary. The entire earlier discussion of the nature of reference provides the methodological motivation. Given the fact that the central notion of semantics, reference, is caught up with intentionality and the use of language, and given the fact (to put it in his words) that "general issues of intentionality, including those of language use, cannot reasonably be assumed to fall under naturalistic inquiry" (2000a: 132, 45), then it should go into a domain which unlike syntax is avowedly non-naturalistic in the descriptions and explanations it gets: pragmatics.

Philosophers have tended to make the contrast between pragmatics and semantics rest on the distinction not between those areas of language where intentions are and are not involved respectively, but rather between those areas where non-linguistic intentions are involved and those where linguistic intentions are. For philosophers, notions such as reference and truth-conditions which govern semantics need not eschew intentions. After all, one may have an intention to use a sentence with certain truth-conditions. This would be a linguistic intention, unlike an intention to use a sentence to get people to believe something, or do something, etc. For philosophers, it is only the latter which fall outside of semantics and in pragmatics. But it is a mark of Chomsky's deep commitments to a scientific and naturalistic understanding of linguistics that he allows it (and nothing else) to drive his basic classificatory criteria of the various areas of the study of language. Since for Chomsky intentions of any kind are unsuitable for a scientific and naturalistic treatment, the philosopher's attempt to distinguish semantics from pragmatics by appeal to two notions of intention misses the mark. They both fall in pragmatics, and all the rest is syntax, which is now (compensatingly as a result of the *narrowing* of linguistics to only two broad areas) itself to be thought of *more broadly* than philosophers have thought of it, to include some areas of a naturalistically and internalistically treatable semantics in which no notions of reference or of intentionality occur at all.[6]

Is there a mind–body problem?

That leaves us with the other remaining source of modesty listed at the opening of the chapter. It has to do with the fact that (1) we may fail to formulate *clear* questions before trying to answer them, and (2) our cognitive capacities are essentially limited and, so, some of the questions we formulate may not be ones *we* could ever answer. The second kind of question, Chomsky calls "mysteries" and cites the problem of human freedom as an example; and he cites the mind–body problem as an example of the former. Chomsky himself does not say very much about mysteries, except to see them as a direct result of our creaturely limitations. Some philosophers have run together mysteries with ill-formulated questions, and the discussion in this section will try to give a detailed exposition of Chomsky's views and disentangle the issues involved in (1) and (2).

As stated, a central example of this form of modesty can be found in Chomsky's discussion of the so-called "mind–body problem" which, he claims, can no longer be so much as formulated. This claim is bound to meet with resistance from some philosophers who think they have formulated a mind–body problem and, indeed, regard their formulation as a central issue in philosophy of mind. But when we view their problem from the perspective of Chomsky's skepticism about its formulatability, it emerges that the problem is not best regarded as a mind–*body* problem at all. Their problem is really generated by what they claim is the *sui generis* nature of consciousness and this is as much a mind–*mind* problem as it is a mind–body problem. This leaves Chomsky's central point about the unformulatability of the mind–body problem standing. Furthermore, it's not clear what to say about the problem concerning consciousness that these philosophers think of as their mind–body problem. Colin McGinn (1994a), for instance, has argued that this problem is a mystery in Chomsky's (1975, 2000a) technical sense – and many philosophers are likely to find this plausible. If McGinn is right, then this is not an example of an obstacle to inquiry issuing from an ill-formulated question. Rather, we have a well-formulated question that we cannot answer due to our cognitive limitations – what Chomsky calls a "mystery." The rest of this section shows why, from Chomsky's point of view, that is not a sensible conclusion. For, from his point of view, it would require that we have a clearer and more positive conception of consciousness than we do. Hence, like the mind–body problem, the problem of consciousness is also best set aside until it too admits of clearer formulation.

Why does Chomsky claim that we cannot so much as *formulate* a mind–body problem? His reasons are both historical and scientific. According to him, there was a problem that Descartes could and did formulate. But our scientific commitments have changed since then, and it is no longer possible to formulate one.[7]

Potted history of philosophy generally locates the source of Descartes's mind–body problem in his dualistic conception of the mind as an immaterial and extensionless substance. But, according to Chomsky, the real source of his problem was his conception of body as a material substance subject to the mechanistic thesis that causal influence on material bodies requires direct bodily contact in space (contact mechanics). This is what precluded mental influence over bodily events – not the immateriality of the mind but the idea that the only way a mind could exert causal influence over bodily events would be through direct bodily contact in space. Chomsky observes that this mechanistic conception of causation was contradicted by Newton's theory of gravitational attraction. Newton conceived gravitational attraction as a species of action at a distance which does not involve direct bodily contact in space – though, apparently, he did so with reluctance and even intellectual embarrassment. Once motion was reconceived along Newtonian lines, the mechanistic conception of material substance gave way to a much richer and open-ended conception of matter as capable, in principle, of supporting all sorts of properties that couldn't be counted as "material" in the sense that went together with Descartes's contact mechanics. The ultimate consequence of Newton's contribution, then, was to think of the world as having many "aspects," among which are mental aspects, and they are all properties of organized whatever-there-is. We can persist in calling this matter, *but it is no longer something that stands in interesting contrast to the mental*. So, Descartes's problem vanished with the onset of Newtonian physics. However, no one seems to have noticed. And, in consequence, no one has appreciated a more general lesson that Chomsky wants to draw from Descartes and Newton, which is that it is no longer possible to formulate a mind–body problem at all.

Let's apply Chomsky's lesson to what some *contemporary* philosophers take to be their mind–body problem. They locate the source of their problem in the mind – specifically, in the qualitative aspects of consciousness which Nagel tried to capture with the phrase "what it's like." The problem is supposed to be that it is impossible to put consciousness in this sense into perspicuous relation to physical nature. Thus, these philosophers tend to go along with potted history and locate the real source of Descartes's problem about mental–physical causation on the mental side as well, in his conception of the mind as an unextended substance. They focus so exclusively on Descartes's metaphysical conception of the mind as an extensionless substance that they overlook the crucial role that his mechanistic conception of body played in generating his problem. This has led them to overlook, in turn, how changes in the notion of body that were wrought by Newtonian physics dissolved Descartes's problem. Moreover, by ignoring these historical facts, we ignore the more general fact that our physical concepts must always play a central role in generating any serious problem about the relation between mind and body. This is highly significant, because our physical concepts have not proved to be very stable. If they are not stable, then none of the alleged problems raised about the mind–body relation can be stable either. Inevitably, any new version of the problem will, like Descartes's original, employ specific physical assumptions. And, so, like Descartes's, it too may dissolve if there are major developments in the physical sciences. According to Chomsky, this makes it impossible for philosophers to formulate their alleged problem about the relation of mind and body. For they aim to formulate a *perennial* problem that is not going to be either solved or dissolved by the future course of science. But, in order to formulate such a perennial problem, philosophers would have to have *two* well-defined terms – mind *and* body – such that we could see a permanent difficulty about understanding their relation. In Chomsky's view, the latter term simply isn't well defined. It has proved to be a plastic notion that has undergone a succession of profound alterations and developments in the course of the history of the physical sciences. Furthermore, Chomsky holds that it is both historically inaccurate and methodologically unreasonable to concentrate so much on alleged contrasts between the mental and the *physical* per se. The best way to view the problem is in terms of the extent to which various *aspects* of the world are unified – where such aspects include not only the physical and the mental but, also, the optical, the electromagnetic, the chemical, etc.

Some might wonder whether current physical theory provides a way to formulate at least a current, if not a perennial, problem analogous to the problem that mechanistic physical theory generated for Descartes. Here is a crude gesture in that direction. On one interpretation of contemporary physical theory, physics is complete in the following sense: it tells us that everything in the world is constituted of particles and energy, and it specifies all of the laws by which all possible changes in particles and energy ever take place. This leaves no causal role for specifically mental phenomena to play in the physical world. And the same goes for any other phenomena that might be posited by any special science. The point is not that there shouldn't be any special sciences, or that there is nothing for them to do. They can, as they always have done, try to identify and explain various phenomena. The point is that if they succeed in identifying and explaining *real* phenomena, both the explananda and explanantia must ultimately be physical. This is directly implied by the completeness of physics. Therefore, if there are any aspects of mind that we believe could never be understood in this way – as physical phenomena wholly governed by physical forces – we have a current version of the mind–body problem after all. It is a problem about how to reconcile our conviction that current physical theory is true with our conviction that irreducible mental phenomena are real.

This interpretation of contemporary physics, which holds that all of the special sciences should ultimately be reducible to physics, is controversial among physicists themselves, and Chomsky doesn't endorse it. His view is that the special sciences should be free to proceed autonomously, leaving it open whether we will or won't be able to account for their results within physical theory. Although we are sometimes able to provide such an account, there is no guarantee that we will be able to in every case. And Chomsky insists that even when we can, the result may fall well short of *reduction*. He prefers to describe success in this domain as the successful *unification* of a special science with physics. There is no guarantee that such unification can be achieved in every case, any more than reduction. And even when such unification can eventually be achieved, it may have to wait until after our physical concepts themselves have undergone substantial change – as they had to before chemistry could be unified with physics. Therefore, it is always wrong in Chomsky's view to inhibit the course of the special sciences with the requirement that we be able to find a way to account for their findings within *current* physical theory. Yet it was by imposing exactly that requirement that we managed above to formulate a current version of the mind–body problem analogous to Descartes's original. Chomsky would not be moved. The general lesson he draws from Descartes and Newton stands: the instability of physical concepts should make us sensitive to the difficulty of formulating a serious mind–body problem.

Let's consider more carefully the standard formulation that philosophers try to give. We've already indicated that, for them, the problem arises from the *sui generis* nature of consciousness – in particular, its qualitative aspects. The problem is that any particular physical facts can always be imagined to be the same while the qualitative aspects of consciousness are imagined to be different or even, perhaps, altogether absent. (Note that in this formulation, the term "physical" does not refer merely to the subject-matter of physics, but is intended to refer more broadly to a whole range of phenomena which includes chemistry and neurophysiology.) Chomsky's quick reply would be that we won't have a well-formulated mind–body problem until we've been given a coherent account of *both* terms of the problem. But the philosophers who claim to find a problem here don't agree, because they believe that it will persist in the face of *any* evolution of our physical (and here, again, they use this term in the broadest sense) concepts. This is a point to which we will return. But first, a digression about philosophers who, *like Chomsky, deny* that there is any such philosophical problem. We register some important differences between them and Chomsky.

Certain philosophers – call them the optimistic materialists – are unimpressed by the feats of imagination that allegedly generate the philosophical problem (imagining the qualitative facts of consciousness altered while the physical facts remain the same). They see this as nothing more than a reflection of our temporary ignorance about the physical basis of consciousness. And they confidently predict that we will eventually overcome our ignorance. In their view, once we have discovered the physical basis of consciousness, we will find it perfectly natural to identify conscious phenomena with physical phenomena – just as we have come to find it natural to identify heat with molecular motion. And this can be so even if we retain the capacity to *imagine* them coming apart (after all, we continue to be able to imagine defying gravity even though we have come to believe a theory according to which it is impossible). In addition to these optimistic materialists, some dualists might also agree with Chomsky that there is no mind–body problem. The fact that we can't put consciousness into perspicuous relation to the physical world is merely a sign of their distinctness.

It is important to see that, when Chomsky denies that there is a mind–body problem, he isn't aligning himself with *either* of these philosophical positions. He is *not* taking up a metaphysical position like reductive physicalism or dualism. He regards such metaphysical issues as scientific issues that haven't been sufficiently sorted out to be a basis for any significant conclusions about mind or body or their relations. His opposition to the idea that there is a problem springs, as noted, from modesty about whether we can actually *formulate* a clear problem.

What, then, of the philosophers who think they can do this? Colin McGinn is a particularly fitting example since his account of the mind–body problem is inspired by Chomsky. In fact, he sees *all* philosophical problems as mysteries in Chomsky's technical sense. It is philosophy's fate as a discipline to be condemned to mysteries as its subject-matter.

A little more needs to be said to expound Chomsky's (1975) notion of a mystery. A mystery is a problem that we can't solve due to our intrinsic cognitive limitations. In Chomsky's view, we are bound to be subject to such limitations. This is because our cognitive capacities are, au fond, biological, and any biological capacity is bound to have limitations. Furthermore, such capacities and their limitations are bound to vary from species to species. Take, for example, the respiratory capacities of different animals. Mammals absorb oxygen into their systems from the air they breathe. The respiratory capacity by which mammals do this enables them to live wherever there is air to breathe and prevents them from living anywhere there isn't. They cannot live underwater as fish do. Likewise, the particular respiratory capacity by which fish absorb oxygen from water simultaneously enables them to live underwater and prevents them from living out of water. They cannot live in the open air as mammals do. Chomsky applies the same point to cognitive capacities. If an animal is cognitively constituted in such a way as to be able to solve certain sorts of problems, that automatically makes the animal ill-equipped to solve other sorts. The problem that has interested Chomsky the most is the one that children confront in acquiring a human language ("Plato's Problem"). Children are able to solve this problem because each human language is an instantiation of a single underlying universal grammar, and we have innate knowledge of that grammar as well as a capacity to identify instantiations of it. Chomsky speculates that once in place, the language capacity enables us to solve a whole range of problems that are soluble via the same sorts of iterative and recursive structures that characterize human languages – a central and important case being mathematical problems. Other species, such as wasps, obviously lack human language and, hence, cannot deal with the whole range of problems that the capacity enables us to solve. We should not infer that wasps are mindless. The cognitive capacities of wasps are simply different from ours, and enable them to solve the specifically waspish problems that they need to solve. Similarly, there could be other species who stand to us as we stand to wasps – species whose members have cognitive capacities by which they can solve a whole range of problems that we don't have the capacity to solve.

Typically, the cognitive problems that the members of a given species can't solve will lie entirely beyond their comprehension. So, not only is it the case that wasps cannot solve mathematical problems; they cannot cognize the problems to begin with. But Chomsky doesn't think it *has* to be this way, especially not in the human case. He finds it plausible that we human beings actually have the ability to formulate some of the problems that it is beyond our cognitive powers to solve. These problems which we can formulate, but whose solutions lie beyond our cognitive grasp, are mysteries for us. (Though they might be soluble by species with different cognitive capacities.)

McGinn agrees with Chomsky that cognitive capacities are bound to bring in train cognitive limitations, with the consequence that some of the problems we face may not be soluble by us – and, hence, mysteries in Chomsky's sense. According to McGinn, these mysteries are the problems that characteristically engage philosophers. His point is not that philosophers have never confronted problems human beings *are* able to solve. Rather, when a problem becomes tractable, it ceases to be a specifically philosophical problem and becomes instead a topic of scientific investigation. Thus, the real and proper domain of philosophy is the class of perennial problems that human beings can never solve and will always be perplexed by. This way of thinking about philosophical problems is a naturalized descendant of Kant's critical philosophy, a fact to which McGinn expressly draws attention with the label "Transcendental Naturalism." McGinn diverges from Kant in that he sees no reason to suppose that we have *a priori* insight into our cognitive constitution and its built-in limitations. In the place of Kant's *a priori* investigation, he offers an empirical speculation. He speculates that a problem can be solved by human beings only if it can be solved by invoking two related cognitive strategies, namely, *Combining Atoms and devising Lawlike Mappings* – CALM for short. This speculation is partly motivated by some suggestions of Chomsky's about how our language capacity might have acquired wider cognitive application. But it can't be said that we have very much direct psychological evidence that our cognitive abilities are completely circumscribed by the limits of CALM thinking. And McGinn recognizes this. He draws other, less direct evidence for his speculation from the history of philosophy. He asks us: which of the problems that have engaged philosophers eventually became scientifically tractable? Which have continued to resist scientific understanding and, as a result, continued to perplex us in the way that is characteristic of a truly philosophical problem? In his estimation, all the problems that proved to be scientifically tractable yielded to CALM strategies, whereas all the problems that have continued to perplex philosophers didn't. He infers that CALM strategies really do circumscribe the limits of human understanding. And, like Kant, he recommends that philosophers should recognize these limits and stop trying to answer the questions that cannot be answered from within them. If McGinn is right, we face a new end of philosophy.

It stands to reason that Chomsky would be sympathetic to McGinn's account of philosophy.[8] The general spirit of the account is Chomskyan, embracing his naturalistic conception of our cognitive capacities, along with the corollary that there are bound to be limits on human understanding. And Chomsky seems to find truth in McGinn's picture of the characteristic activity of philosophers, which is to wallow in insoluble mysteries rather than get on with the constructive business of science.

However, his sympathy with McGinn must stay at the level of generalities. For one thing, McGinn's speculation about CALM is insufficiently supported to win unqualified endorsement from a working scientist like himself. But the more important dividing issue concerns one of the uses to which McGinn puts the speculation. He uses it in order to formulate the very problem about mind and body that Chomsky claims can no longer be formulated. CALM, remember, is supposed to distinguish the soluble problems from the insoluble, where such insolubility is the mark of the truly philosophical problem. And McGinn regards the mind–body problem as a paradigmatic example of the latter. In fact, he holds that CALM provides a particularly good way to formulate the problem. The problem is that we can't account for *consciousness* in CALM terms, as arising in the material world due to the ways in which physical atoms are combined or due to lawlike mappings among physical phenomena.

It is odd that McGinn should focus on the mind–body problem, given that his overall account of philosophical problems derives so much of its inspiration from Chomsky, and Chomsky goes to such pains to argue there is no such problem. It is even odder that McGinn never addresses this argument. Chomsky cites McGinn's overall account of philosophical problems as mysteries in his sense, but he too passes over in silence this difference between them. Although both of them would clearly prefer to emphasize what they have in common, it proves instructive to sort out this difference between them.

How might McGinn respond to Chomsky on the mind–body problem? Since Chomsky's official position is that we can no longer so much as formulate it, McGinn might simply point out that he *has* formulated it, in terms of CALM. He might buttress this response with the following line of thought: when Chomsky denies that there is a mind–body problem, his main concern is to liberate the mental (and other special) sciences from any theoretical constraints that might derive from the current state of physical theory, his thought being that otherwise we might fall into mistakes similar to the one Descartes made when he thought he needed to account for mind–body interaction within the constraints of mechanistic theory; however, although it is sensible and laudable that Chomsky should thus try to spare future mental science from similar mistakes, his argument doesn't touch the version of the mind–body problem that derives from CALM: CALM is not proposed as a transient constraint that happens to derive from some current theoretical commitment. CALM is proposed as an insuperable constraint on all human thought.

Its hard to say anything in detail about how Chomsky would evaluate this last, highly speculative, proposal of McGinn's, except to repeat what was said above about how little direct empirical support it has. But it should be registered that the speculation seems, on the face of it, wholly non-credible. It seems obvious that it is within our power to conceive physical phenomena in non-CALM terms, specifically, in teleological terms. We do not have in mind the "as if" teleology often invoked in ordinary descriptions of biological phenomena, as when one says that a tree's roots grow downward in order to find water or that the heart pumps blood in order to send nutrients to different parts of the body. Everyone knows that roots and hearts don't really have ends. Nevertheless, what we now take ourselves to *know* about this doesn't exhaust what we can *conceive*. We can (whether plausibly or not) without incoherence conceive that all sorts of physical things might really possess ends. Aristotle certainly did. Moreover, we can conceive this in a non-CALM way. Let's offer an explanation by way of contrast with a CALM conception of what we are calling "as if" ends. Conceived in CALM terms, the possession of an end is the possession of a disposition or lawlike tendency to achieve the end. Call ends in this sense "as if" ends because they are reducible to something that can be described in perfectly non-teleological terms, namely, laws. But now consider minded things. When we conceive minded things as having ends, we don't necessarily conceive them in CALM terms, as having dispositions or lawlike tendencies to achieve their ends. We can conceive them instead as merely *striving* to achieve their ends in a very limited sense that falls short of a lawlike tendency. This is what we mean by a genuine teleological conception, as opposed to an "as if" one – a conception in which behavior is directed towards ends in a way that cannot be reduced to a disposition or lawlike tendency. Of course, the only domain in which we currently find such a non-CALM teleological conception natural and plausible is the intentional activities of minded things. (See the first section of this chapter for a more extended discussion of why intentional activity is neither dispositional nor lawlike.) But the point is that this is *not* because it is somehow beyond our cognitive powers to apply the conception to material things as well.

It is worth registering this point for two reasons. First, it brings out that McGinn's speculation about CALM might turn out to be false. CALM might not be an insuperable cognitive limitation, but a theoretical constraint that *derives from our current theoretical commitment* to giving non-teleological accounts of natural phenomena. And this bears directly on the question whether McGinn has successfully escaped the critical force of Chomsky's argument against those who attempt to formulate a contemporary mind–body problem. If CALM is a mere theoretical constraint that derives from the current state of scientific understanding, then Chomsky is within his rights to suggest that we ignore it – just as Descartes would have done well to ignore the problem that mechanism posed for his account of the mind, on account of the fact that Newton eventually provided an alternative physical theory in which the problem didn't arise. This is not to say that Descartes was in a position to know that this would eventuate. Chomsky's point is that *we* have the benefit of hindsight and shouldn't fall into the same trap.

At this point, McGinn might retreat to a less ambitious position from which he could still try to formulate a serious mind–body problem. For, even if it can't be shown that CALM is an insuperable cognitive limitation, CALM approaches have proved to be a real scientific advance over earlier teleological approaches. So, McGinn might reason, it is a good bet that CALM is here to stay, and yet consciousness could never be accounted for in CALM terms. That counts as a serious problem, Chomsky's lessons from Descartes and Newton notwithstanding.

This brings us to the second reason for raising the possibility of a non-CALM teleological conception. When McGinn was confronted with this possibility, he didn't say he found it inconceivable (even though this is entailed by his own speculation about the limits of our understanding). He was prepared to allow, at least for the sake of argument, that it is conceivable. And he didn't say what most of us these days believe, which is that non-CALM conceptions are not explanatory and, so, will never have a place in a scientific account of the relation of mind and body. Instead, he insisted that the mind–body problem would arise even within a non-CALM teleological framework. According to him, we can no more understand how consciousness could arise out of non-CALM teleological processes than we can understand how it arises from CALM phenomena (McGinn 1994b). This means that McGinn misled us when he stated that CALM provides a good way to formulate the mind–body problem. But the aim here is not to lodge that complaint. The aim is to raise the following question: what alternative formulation can McGinn give, which makes clear what there is in common between CALM conceptions and non-CALM teleological conceptions, and which also makes clear why it is impossible to put the concept of consciousness into intelligible relation to either one? It turns out that he, like most contemporary philosophers, does *not* appeal to any general features of *body* (or the material and physical more generally), but appeals rather to special features of consciousness – in particular, to the idea that the qualitative aspect of consciousness ("what it is like") is sui generis. Of all the things in the world, this is the only thing that can be known only from a *first-person point of view*. Everything else can be known and conceived from a *third-person point of view*. And it is *this* dichotomy between the first person and the third that really makes for the mind–body problem as it is typically understood by contemporary philosophers, including McGinn. The problem arises because we can always imagine the phenomenological facts that we know from a first-person point of view being different or absent, while all of the other facts that we know from a third-person point of view remain the same.

It is understandable that many philosophers would be inclined to think that this formulation of the mind–body problem is untouched by Chomsky's argument to the effect that there is no such problem. He may be right that our physical concepts may change in unanticipated ways. He may also be right that the special sciences, including the mental sciences, should not be constrained by the commitments of current physical theory. But, all the same, our physical concepts will never cease to be concepts of things known from a third-person point of view and, in consequence, the concept of consciousness can never be put into perspicuous relation to them. Those who take this view of the mind–body problem, as arising from the first-person/third person dichotomy, may be somewhat incredulous that Chomsky doesn't see the problem.

Chomsky might point out that the conception of something as knowable from the third-person point of view is not a specifically *physical* conception at all. Many *mental* facts are also knowable from the third-person point of view – for example, facts about intentional attitudes, action and perception. And qualia pose the very same problem in connection with these mental facts that they pose in connection with physical facts. That is, we can always imagine that all of the publicly knowable mental facts remain constant while the facts concerning the qualitative aspects of mental life are permuted or absent – as in the much discussed cases of inverted spectra and zombies. These possibilities follow from the essentially private nature of qualia, as things knowable only from a first-person point of view. And that is not all. If qualia truly are private, then they are epiphenomenal. For, if they had any systematic effects *in the rest of mental life*, that would make them knowable from a third-person point of view – they would not be private. Wittgenstein concluded: so much the worse for privacy. But contemporary philosophers who recognize a mind–body problem do not concur. They are prepared to acknowledge that qualia are known only from a first-person point of view. That is why they think they face a mind–body problem. But all this brings out, on behalf of Chomsky, that this problem is *not* well described as a mind–body problem. It's just as much a mind–*mind* problem – a problem about how to understand the relation of qualia to the rest of mental life. So, if McGinn is right to see consciousness as generating a *mystery*, it shouldn't be regarded as a mystery about the relation of consciousness to *body* per se.

Most philosophers who recognize the qualitative aspect of consciousness would recognize that it generates a mind–mind problem. But they wouldn't see much point in denying that there is a mind–body problem. In fact, they would very likely view *both* problems as special cases of a *single*, more general problem concerning the relation of the qualitative aspects of consciousness to *everything* which is public, where that includes all aspects of the physical world as well as the public aspects of mind. Chomsky, by contrast, wouldn't see much point in lumping everything public together in this way. That makes it seem as if the pressure to find some interesting relation between the qualitative aspects of consciousness and physical facts is as great as the pressure to find some interesting relation between them and other mental facts. But that just isn't so, according to Chomsky. It might seem to be so if we had a physicalist bias according to which everything must ultimately be related to physical facts. But that *is* a bias. We ought not, in Chomsky's view, to prejudge how much unity we will eventually achieve within the sciences. For all we know, the mental sciences might always remain quite independent of the physical sciences. If things were to turn out that way, then no mental phenomena could be put into interesting and perspicuous relation to the physical facts. And, in that case, it would obviously be completely inappropriate to ask that the qualitative aspects of consciousness, in particular, be put into such relation. But this would not constitute a *problem*. It would just be how the world turned out to be.

It might appear that the mind–mind problem still stands and remains pressing. For, from the first-person point of view of consciousness, the fact that there is something it is like seems to go to the heart of our conviction that we are minded. This conviction runs so deep that it leads many neo-Cartesians to *equate* being minded with being the subject of conscious states that have a qualitative aspect. As soon as the equation is made, the mind–mind problem seems to disappear. The role of the qualitative aspects of consciousness in the rest of mental life comes to seem utterly straightforward: they are constitutive of the whole domain of the mental. To view the mind in this way is to see it as essentially private. What we have been describing as the *public* aspects of mind are not aspects of mind at all. They are mere evidence of mentality, the actual existence of which can be settled only from a first-person point of view. The neo-Cartesian conception therefore licenses skepticism about other minds: the limitation on our knowledge of what it's like for others is a limitation on our knowledge of other minds altogether.

Chomsky opposes the neo-Cartesian conception of the mind on numerous grounds. He opposes any attempt to circumscribe the mind by any single criterion, such as consciousness or intentionality. And he finds the criterion of consciousness particularly implausible. It would entail that linguistic knowledge isn't really *knowledge* (on the ground that we are not conscious of it) – something he emphatically denies. Furthermore, it would make any science of the mind impossible. There are also familiar philosophical grounds of opposition issuing from Wittgensteinian considerations. The tie between intentional facts and publicly knowable behavioral facts is closer and deeper than neo-Cartesians allow – indeed so close as to rule out privacy altogether. From this Wittgensteinian perspective, there is neither a mind–mind problem nor a mind–body problem – at least not of the sort we have been discussing.

Perhaps it would be going too far to dismiss privacy altogether. We can allow that there is something it is like to feel a toothache or see peacock green which is knowable only from a first-person point of view, where that brings in train some reasonable doubts about whether we can really know what it is like for others, and even brings in train the less reasonable but nevertheless coherent worry that in some cases there may be nothing it is like. We can do this while insisting that analogous doubts and worries about our knowledge of related intentional facts, such as the desire to visit the dentist or the belief that there are peacocks in the vicinity, are misplaced. If we allow and insist upon all this, we are conceding what McGinn and other philosophers take to be the source of their problem. But it must be stressed that if any problem could be formulated here, it would be a mind–mind rather than a mind–body problem. And it is highly doubtful that Chomsky would regard it as a clearly formulated problem, given the force of the Wittgensteinian considerations against the very idea of privacy.

It has been explained in some detail why Chomsky thinks it is (now) impossible to formulate a mind–*body* problem. The reasons are historical and scientific. His overall views would also give him reason to doubt whether we can formulate a coherent mind–mind problem. Here the reasons are less historical and scientific, and closer to philosophical reasons of the familiar Wittgensteinian sort. Insofar as the alleged problem is supposed to be generated by the fact that there are qualitative aspects of consciousness which are essentially private, there is nothing we can do but apprehend them from our own first-person points of view and, otherwise, remain silent about them. In doing this, we wouldn't have formulated a problem at all. That is the third reason to be modest about the scope of inquiry.

10 Meaning and creativity

James McGilvray

Introduction

Often, philosophers, linguists, and cognitive scientists aiming to construct a theory of meaning for languages focus on how words are used by people to deal with the world. They might assume there is a regular way in which the word *dolphin* is used – that people regularly use *dolphin* to *refer to* or *denote* a class of aquatic beasts. And they might assume that there is a central, core use of words – using *She has a pet dolphin* to *correctly describe* some state of affairs, perhaps. If these assumptions were correct, *dolphin* might then be defined in terms of some regular function(s) it serves in a community of individuals who "speak the same language," understood as "use words in the same way" (cp. Davidson 1967, Sellars 1974; contrast Chomsky 1996a, b, 2000a, Fodor 1998). These assumptions are built into technical terms: "truth (or correctness) conditions," "functional (or conceptual) role," etc. Because these attempts focus on communities, circumstances, things, and so on, I call them "externalist" approaches.

Externalist assumptions are wrong. Chomsky (1959, 1966, 1975, 1980, 1981a, 1986, 1995b, 1996a,b, 2000a), recalling observations that go back to Descartes (see below), repeatedly points this out. Words do sometimes get used by people in similar ways; and they do sometimes come to be related to the world. But they do neither by themselves. Similar uses and relations to the world are products of human actions, of words' free and typically creative use by humans. Because people use words for all sorts of purposes, because the use of language is a form of free action, and because there is little reason to think that there can be a science of free action, there is little reason to think that there can be a naturalistic externalist theory of meaning.

The key to a *naturalistic science* of meaning for human languages lies in adopting an internalist strategy: look inside the head. As other contributors to this volume show, the language organ, an innate biological faculty, produces expressions (sentences) consisting of sounds and meanings. Think of the meanings of sentences as language's conceptual contributions to human cognitive capacities and activities – including referring, inferring, and saying something true. Think, then, of linguistic meanings as a potentially infinite set of internally constituted sentential concepts. These are theoretically defined mental entities that "interface" with other mental systems and that – as we put it in ordinary speech – are used by people to do various jobs. Chomsky informally calls them "meanings" or "perspectives"; formally, they are "LF"s and – recently – "SEM"s (for "semantic interfaces"). Naturalistic sciences of them – thus, of meanings – are in place.

Abandoning externalist assumptions, we also gain insights into human freedom and creativity. Language, offering us internally constituted conceptual material unavailable to other creatures, turns out to be an extremely useful organ. It offers readily accessible conceptual resources to deal with the myriad cognitive tasks of getting along with others and understanding the world. Its contributions begin early; it is automatically acquired at an early age and, with its resources available, the child easily develops common sense (folk physics, folk psychology, etc.) and engages in play and fantasy. Its continuing availability and increasingly sophisticated use in solving all sorts of everyday problems contribute to the cognitive functioning of adults, enabling creative solutions to cognitive tasks as varied as those that confront citizens, gossips, engineers, and artists. So by looking inside the head and not at the extraordinary diversity of ways language is used, the scientist of meaning can stop trying to construct a theory of language use, and the philosopher of mind and interested layman can begin to appreciate how a biological organ plays a crucial role in offering humans the individual and cultural diversity and creativity that are characteristic of the human species. Abandoning the quixotic task of constructing a science of linguistic action and behavior, an internalist and rationalist approach to language and mind makes sense of how language can be so useful, and why humans have such distinctive mental powers.[1]

A word on why this chapter is where it is. Because meanings are defined by appeal to Universal Grammar (UG), a discussion of linguistic meaning alone could be placed in the linguistics section. But because linguistic meanings contribute so much to human creativity and because the way in which they do suits only an internalist and rationalist picture of the mind, it also belongs in a section on Chomsky's view of the human mind. Finally, because language with its unlimited number of concepts is a biological engine that provides for and even encourages a distinctively human form of creativity, and because creativity and the need for it play such important roles in Chomsky's political views, a chapter on meaning and creativity rightly appears immediately before a section dealing with his political views.

Defining linguistic concepts

If linguistic meanings at the interface with other systems are biologically constituted sentential "perspectives," how does one define them? The meanings of sentences are composed from the meanings of their words. So we can begin by asking what the meaning of a word is.

Ordinary dictionaries are little help. They do not define the meanings of words – the relevant "atomic" and/or complex concepts (Chomsky 1996a, b: 24). They assume that a person already has a natural language and access to linguistically expressible concepts. For those who do, dictionaries might do two things. First, *Webster's* and the *Oxford* might inform a person about what sounds people in a population associate with specific meanings. While possibly useful, this is irrelevant to a naturalistic science of meaning. Meaning–sound associations are arbitrary; there is no biological relationship between them. The concept WASH could be as easily associated with the sound "wiggle." Associations reflect what Chomsky calls "Saussurean arbitrariness." These associations are social conventions, of no interest to the natural scientist.

Second, dictionaries might provide hints and prompts. They *hint* by listing in their "definitions" a few terms that point in the direction of a concept. They *prompt* by proffering a context in which a word is used. They display a phrase containing words that, except for the target one, are likely to be familiar; these allow the speaker to create a context of use for the unfamiliar word and produce in their heads a concept that they might use in that context. The full-fledged *Oxford* offers hundreds of thousands of examples of both techniques. Depending on whether a person has already positioned a concept in their mental dictionary or not (i.e. associated a concept with a specific sound and perhaps come to use the associated elements), a hint or prompt might *remind* or *trigger*. Reminding needs no explanation. Triggering is a matter of some prompt generating or producing the concept in one's head; I return to it in a moment. So far, the important thing to notice is that dictionaries work only because people either already have in their active mental dictionaries, or can readily insert into one, the relevant concepts. They do not define; they hint or prompt, leading to reminding or triggering.

Assume for the moment that words as the naturalistically inclined linguist understands them consist of sounds and concepts. A scientific definition of a word must consist, then, in a full theoretical specification of a sound and a meaning. Defining sounds is a job for phonologists and phoneticians (Dresher, this volume). While defining sounds is a fascinating task and there are suggestive parallels with defining meanings/concepts, this is not the occasion to attempt either. The scientist of meaning aims at individual (root) concepts and how these are put together to make sentential concepts. Linguists already know a lot about how the mind puts sentences together, for there has been considerable progress in syntax and morphology – the sciences that deal with how. There has been less progress in getting a grip on individual concepts. But the strategy is clear: as with phonology, syntax, phonetics, and morphology, look inside the head.

One reason to look inside, mentioned above, is that language *use* is out of reach of science, for use is creative. Another is found in poverty-of-stimulus facts. They apply to sounds and meanings too. Over the lifetime of an individual, a person easily acquires thousands of linguistically expressed concepts, each acquisition an example of poverty of the stimulus. Children, given little data, acquire approximately a (root) word a waking hour between the ages of two and eight (Chomsky 1995b). The capacity to activate concepts and quickly associate them with sounds ("learn words") continues into later life. Unlike the full range of linguistic sounds,[2] there do not seem to be temporal barriers (closed "windows of opportunity") to swift acquisition of the concepts expressed in natural languages. While it seems children need to acquire some before others (DOG before CHIHUAHUA), there are no obvious parametric switches set soon after birth that channel the language organ's efforts in a particular direction, excluding others. For concepts, the seventeenth-century Cambridge Platonist Ralph Cudworth spoke of circumstances "occasioning" and "inviting" a concept. To make this possible, he thought, (lexical) concepts must somehow be prefigured (anticipated – he called it "prolepsis") in an "innate cognoscitive power." The nineteenth-century German linguist and philosopher Wilhelm von Humboldt said the mind must have an innate productive "mental instrument" that yields lexical concepts: when prompted by a "signal" from a person's speech, "matching but not identical concepts are engendered" in the mind of the hearer (Humboldt 1999: 152; Chomsky 2002a: 102–3). If so, a naturalistic definition of a lexical concept consists in providing a theory of the relevant mechanisms – the innate machinery – that yield it and others.

Triggering, mental machinery, and theoretical definition

Although the poverty facts indicate that some natural – neither use- nor social-dependent – process is at work, no one really knows how triggering takes place. Some occasion, external or internal, "occasions" the mind's machinery, and a concept is activated. As indicated, the hints and prompts of dictionaries can serve the purpose: similar concepts, or a context of use, trigger a concept and associate it with a sound in a person's mental dictionary. Overheard conversations serve as triggers, as do novels, the efforts of others to inform, poetry readings, pictures, etc. What philosophers call "ostensive definition" – for example, pointing to a metal object with two handles and saying "spokeshave" – might do. Occasions where someone encounters something for the first time might too: a Filipina child might acquire the concept SNOW when getting off a plane in Montréal in January. She might not acquire exactly what another person has, and likely her concept will undergo modifications later. Her *uses* of the concept will certainly be variable; they likely will become more sophisticated too. But these are details. The important point is that she must have a mind biologically like that of others for SNOW to be triggered as readily as it is, and to be like others' SNOW. She must have mental machinery devoted to language, plus machinery (it may be the same) that assembles or packages specific concepts that can be inserted in linguistic derivations to produce sentential concepts. Whether specifically linguistic or not, internal machinery sets the agenda and dictates what counts as a trigger: the mind with the relevant machinery "looks" for some pattern in the input that sets it on a course it "anticipates" already. Laura Petitto's discussion (this volume) of the onset of babbling provides a simple, important, example. Apparently, the language organ is not shaped by experience; it brings concept-forming machinery to experience. In *this* sense, individual concepts are innate, or latent in (the machinery of) our minds. If we are to define them, we must – as with sounds and signs – deal with that machinery.

To avoid confusion, keep in mind that to say that the concepts that typically appear in natural languages are anticipated in the machinery of the mind is not to say that we are conscious of them, when latent *or* active. Nor is it to say that they are "there" ready-formed, with all the features that constitute a specific lexical item already assembled in the form they take in a person's working vocabulary. Certainly it is not to say that they come already linked to things or classes of things in the world. It is to say that they are products of biological machinery capable on an occasion of constituting or "activating" them, yielding items with configurations that when placed at language's interface with other systems can affect human cognitive functioning, thereby affording a capacity to recognize, distinguish, gauge, assess, or otherwise use the concept. Perhaps a specific concept is anticipated in something like the way the human immune system anticipates a range of pathogens: the machinery provides for them. Clearly, like the immune system, the machinery that provides concepts to language does not anticipate *all* concepts. Some concepts are native to other systems. Language cannot process most "qualia" (as philosophers call them), such as colors. Language deals with the *linguistic* concept RED, not with a (specific) *visual* RED that people with a functioning visual system enjoy and that they "attribute" to the surface of an object outside the head.[3] Scientific concepts, furthermore, unlike those that appear in our natural languages, are not virtually built into our biology. They are *not* easily acquired in the way the concepts of natural languages are, but instead require sophisticated understanding of a theory and, typically, a lot of preparation and work.[4] They seem to be created, or invented, by people who construct sciences. Chomsky holds that people have some innate aid in constructing such theories: our "science forming capacity" (1975, 1988b) provides a kind of guidance. But the particle physicist's concept PION is *not* somehow anticipated in us at birth. If it were, the child would readily acquire it.

Note that defining a concept such as PAINT in the way required for a science of language is not defining in the way philosophers traditionally assume.

Defining is not a matter of stating necessary and sufficient conditions on the application or use of a concept – stating under what conditions the transitive verbal concept PAINT is true of an action performed by Vermeer or Sam the house painter. Mathematicians and scientists might sometimes in their work use concepts such as ALEPH-NULL and PION in ways that are regular and determinate enough to give credence to the project of constructing such a definition (really, an idealized proposal for what counts as proper use among the practitioners of the relevant science). But neither they nor anyone else uses PAINT in such a way. Thinking that this is what definition consists in misses a crucial point: the use of linguistic concepts is creative, and can be so just *because* natural language concepts and their internally provided "contents" are anticipated, or innate.

To define a linguistic concept naturalistically is to construct a science of Cudworth's innate cognoscitive power or Humboldt's mental instrument. Describing exactly how linguistic concepts are triggered and put together – describing the operations of our mental instruments – is a scientific project that has only begun. Speculating, although not unreasonably, perhaps the mechanisms perform a kind of mental chemistry. Perhaps what is innate is a relatively small set of really primitive features and a much smaller set of configurations into which they can be put, plus some machinery that when prompted combines features in configured arrays – makes a structured compound, unique in its character. When a person is confronted by something that "needs" a concept of a specific sort (for example, one that embodies what we understand when we understand REFRIGERATOR), the machinery provides it by inserting features in an array. This is a convenient picture of concept acquisition and has the advantage that it allows that the features that are put into configurations, and the configurations themselves, are smaller in number than the hundreds of thousands (or more) root concepts that a human can acquire.[5] The number of acquirable concepts must be large. We must allow for those for which there is yet no need. The ancient Mesopotamian child did not need REFRIGERATOR, even though s/he could easily have acquired it, given the relevant triggering experiences. Like most of us, however, s/he could not have easily acquired the technical concepts of the sciences that detail the principles by which refrigeration works.

Continuing to develop this picture, perhaps we can then think of morphology or the operations of "making words" as adding structure and turning a root concept into an item of a specific lexical category (N, V_{tr}, A . . .). STRUCT becomes the noun concept STRUCTURE, the verb CONSTRUCT, and so on. Perhaps we can think of lexical categories as specific kinds of configurations of features characteristic of the relevant category. If we include morphological operations in the basic computational structure of the language faculty proper, and if as above we think of roots as assembled by internal machinery (which may or may not be a part of the core operations of the language faculty), we can think of root concept and lexical category acquisition as being written into the machinery of the mind. It is a short step to thinking of the "features" that are assembled in root concepts and in morphological configurations (noun, verb, etc.) as "saying" what a concept and further structures added to it contribute to the semantic interface – to sentential meanings. Finally – continuing the theme – we can think of a full theoretical specification of a sentential meaning as describing the contribution that that sentence can make to any cognitive tasks to which it might be put by further systems in the head and, eventually, by the person.

Examples give an idea of some of the features that must somehow come to be included in a word's concept. Verbs come in a set of forms that specify argument places: a verb such as GIVE can be thought of as an array that provides argument places for nouns assigned the features GIVER, RECEIVER, GIVEN. Natural language noun features seem to be configured to answer Aristotle's "causes" (explanations) of the things that the nouns can be used to refer to. They "say," "this is its origin," "this is what it does," "this is what it's made of," and "this is its essence" (Chomsky 1975, 1995b, c; Moravcsik 1975; Pustejovsky 1995).[6] Take HOUSE: perhaps HOUSE's features are something like ARTIFACT ("made by humans"), CONTAINER ("envelopes"), RIGID ("secure materials"), DWELLING "holds humans." In effect, a specification for the noun-concept HOUSE says what a speaker "knows" in Chomsky's "know a language" sense – in effect, what a speaker with the concept HOUSE brings to his or her thought or discourse about houses.

Because this picture of natural language concepts, their acquisition, and their structural and "content" contributions to cognition is convenient and seems consistent with what is understood about the nature and structure of words and how to develop a theory of them, I adopt it. It is at best a reasonable guess.[7] And it is burdened with primitive terminology: no serious linguist expects that the terms for concepts and their defining features that I have been using (SLUG, ARTIFACT) will continue to serve as theoretical vocabulary. We must start somewhere, but – if we are on the right track – theory advances, and we must expect changes and improvements, including a more articulate theoretical terminology, which is likely to be as far removed from the starting point as any advanced science's vocabulary and associated concepts are.

One reason such a vocabulary has not been easy to produce is that it must be integrated within a *full* and *adequate* theory of the language faculty. To see why, let us start with what might still be thought to be the simplest possible task, defining a single "word" or lexical item. Let us assume that a theory of meaning for words says what lexical items are in terms of *features*. Assume too that the features in terms of which a definition will be given are those that will or can play a role in the derivation of a sentence. This is reasonable, for lexical items (or rather, their features) combine – in Chomsky's terminology,

"Merge" – to form "sentences" or "*expressions*" that pair sound-interfaces with meaning-interfaces (sounds with meanings/concepts), and presumably these features make a difference in how an expression's derivation proceeds and/or in what appears at the relevant interfaces. On this assumption, Chomsky (1995c) suggests that lexical features include phonological (sound-specifying), formal (N, V . . .), and "semantic" (ARTIFACT) ones.[8] A set of sets of these three kinds of features is a "*lexical item*."[9] A list of phonological, formal, and "semantic" feature clusters is a list of the features that might compose a lexical item. A theory of what the features are, of how they can be arrayed and arranged, and how they can enter and play a role in a linguistic derivation, is a theory of the lexicon and of the role of lexical features in a linguistic derivation.

Thinking of a theory of the lexicon in this way, we can ask how one would know that a hypothesis about a specific word's features is accurate and adequate. Evidence about a specific lexical item's features in a specific I-language would be needed, of course. That might come, in part, from observing how a person uses a word. But to be sure that we have a good theoretical description of the features of even a single lexical item in a single I-language, we need assurance that the list of features and possible configurations appealed to in giving the description is adequate. That is, one needs a list that is descriptively adequate (yields good theoretical descriptions of lexical items' features) and complete, so that it can – so far as natural languages and their acquisition are concerned – adequately distinguish any specific lexical feature from others. Without this, there is no guarantee that the theory has the right theoretical terms. Furthermore, one needs to consider the role of a lexical item in linguistic processing. If the issue is which features are relevant to defining not a sound, but a meaning – a concept as it appears in a sentence at SEM – the theory will have to say which features can appear at the semantic interface of the language faculty, and how these features "interact" with the features of other lexical items, not just to form phrases and clauses but in more complex ways (consider *fake owl* and *long trip*). That is because it is at that interface – SEM – that the language faculty makes its contribution to a person's cognitive efforts, to a person's attempts to classify, describe, explain, speculate, soliloquize, conjecture, remonstrate, etc. – in effect, to "express thoughts." Obviously, people use linguistic concepts to perform these tasks; if so, a theory of language needs to say what these concepts at an interface "contain" that makes it possible for language to contribute – often remarkably subtly – to the performance of these and other cognitive tasks. Furthermore, it is reasonable to suppose that the language faculty is sufficiently well "engineered" that at the end of the derivation of a sentence, everything that appears at SEM be able in principle to "instruct" other systems – in effect, a feature that appears there must be able to make a difference to (or be "legible" to [Chomsky 1986, 2000a, b]) those other systems. So a theory of the language faculty and the lexicon should speak to this by ensuring that nothing appears in lexical specifications that cannot contribute either to the ways SEMs can be produced (derived) or to "communication" with other systems in the head. But, if so, to be assured that one's list of lexical features is adequate, one must also have in hand an adequate theory of what *any* lexical item can contribute – for *any* actual or possible I-language – to SEMs. The theory of the lexicon cannot be just a theory of one of Harriet's I-languages, much less one of Harriet's "words." It must be a theory that can deal with the lexicons of any I-language, for any natural language (Swahili, Miskito, etc.) either in existence or biologically possible. To have a theory adequate to a specific lexical item is to have one that is adequate to any; it is to have, at the least, a theory of Universal Grammar, or UG. This gives an idea of why it has been difficult to develop a full theoretical vocabulary for lexical concepts. No wonder *Webster's* authors do not define words.

Because humans acquire and use language so readily, it is tempting to think that a theory of meaning should be easy – that it is enough to sit down and ruminate, exercise intuitions about how people use language, talk to friends and colleagues, perhaps read a few articles. Several philosophers have done just these things; and some have made some interesting observations concerning how people use words. But their accomplishment is little different from that of the dictionary scribe. It is useful, sometimes, for some purposes. The important issue is not describing usage and exercising the conceptual powers ("intuitions") of people who have a language, but explaining and describing articulately, in a science, what a language is and what it is about it that lets us use it in the creative ways we so obviously can. That is work in a natural science and – unaided by rich native conceptual resources – it is *very* much more difficult.

"But it's just syntax!"

UG when complete can fully describe all the expressions – including their meanings – that are available in an arbitrary I-language. It will offer a science of linguistic meaning. It will allow one to define anything that appears at any possible SEM. But – someone with lingering hopes of a theory that speaks to language–world relations might say – UG is a (broadly) syntactic theory, and a *syntactic* theory can't offer a theory of *meaning*! It only provides descriptions of syntactic entities,[10] such as abstract versions of [s[DP[DThe] [Nhorse]] [VP[Vkicked] [DP[Dthe] [Nstall]]] – versions that do not even have "words" in them, only theoretical feature-descriptions. How can *these* be descriptions of meanings? Chomsky grants that SEMs are syntactic entities, of course. That is how they are defined. But they are still theoretical descriptions of meanings. Meanings are syntactically defined – but they do just what linguistic meanings should.

A description of what is to be found at SEM is a description of a very rich cognitive resource. As indicated, Chomsky includes "semantic" features among the lexical ones. After derivation, features such as ANIMATE, ABSTRACT, and ARTIFACT "appear" at the (a) interface(s). They are features that, when clustered together in a set along with relevant formal features, are sufficient to distinguish one lexical item's specific linguistic conceptual content – its cognitive contribution at SEM to other systems – from another's. Because Chomsky's term "semantic" for these features suggests to many ears relations to the world, to avoid misunderstanding I will call them "FG-features" ("fine-grained features"). FG-features do not distinguish the noun *bank* from the two forms of verb *bank* (transitive and intransitive). Categorial features (N, V_{tr}, V_{it}) do that. Instead, FG-features capture theory-relevant differences between each instance of *bank* in each category. There are no settled terms for these differences, so I invent enough to make the point. The group of noun *banks* that can be used to refer to a place for holding items of some sort (*financial bank, poker bank, job bank*, etc.) can be thought of as having REPOSITORY FG-features that distinguish members of that group from the members of the BERM *bank* group (the nouns that can be used to refer to sides of rivers, to mounds, to billiard table edges, to cloud configurations, etc.). Both classes of lexical items may also be distinct from the TILT *bank* class – the skew of the airplane as it makes a turn. Probably further terms will be required to distinguish different kinds of REPOSITORY *banks* (financial, job, computer memory, etc.), but the point is clear. In having a lexical item, a person has remarkably detailed and specific linguistic knowledge. If so, and if FG features appear at SEM, and if SEMs contribute to other systems, it should not be hard to begin to see SEMs in a new light, to see them as "conceptual," even though they remain syntactic. In effect, they represent (contain) detailed linguistic knowledge, "information" that appears at SEM. Chomsky mentions many examples without – understandably – being definite about how to represent lexical detail.

Lexical features seem to be adapted to human cognitive purposes – biological (including social, project-related intentional, etc.) interests and needs, not to the needs of logical consistency. Many nouns have *both* ABSTRACT and CONCRETE features (Chomsky 1977a, 1995c, 2000a). If something is conceived as a village (something is described using the concept VILLAAGE) that same thing *can* be conceived as destroyed by a flood, but also as moved, even after a specific concrete instantiation of it has been destroyed. That is because VILLAGE has the options ABSTRACT or CONCRETE, or *both*.[11] So one can say, "Riverdale will be flooded and destroyed in an hour; we'd better rebuild it up the hill." If VILLAGE is also a FG-sub-classification of POLITY, perhaps the same is true of all concepts that have POLITY: TOWN, CITY, STATE, etc. Similarly for some other Ns: if something is a door of wood, it is rigid; but one can also go through the door. A book weighs a kilo and is a compelling story.

When we use sentences with concepts (semantic features), we show that we are conceptually sensitive to the features that their words have: even if we do not articulate the differences, they appear to configure our assumptions, presuppositions, beliefs, and expectations. For example, many words are (misleadingly) called "container words" (+AFFECTED ON THE OUTSIDE words?). To be told that someone has painted a house is to assume – unless there is indication to the contrary – that its outside has been painted. To be close to the outside wall of a house is to be near the house, while to be close to an inside wall of a house is not to be near a house. If in a cave and looking at its side, one is looking at a side of the cave, not a side of the mountain it is in. To look outside the cave at a mirror that reflects the outer surface of the mountain is, however, to look at the mountain's side. Notice in these and other cases that human interests, tasks, and intentions are somehow reflected in the FG-features that distinguish lexical items. This is particularly obvious with words for artifacts – *refrigerator*, *computer*, *table* – reflecting distinct human uses, serving human interests. The distinctions can be subtle. To go to a couple's house is not necessarily to go to their home (this distinction is not always "lexicalized" in other languages). Human concerns and intentions play an important role in our views of the identities of things. To burn a house is to destroy it. To dismantle a house, take the pieces somewhere else, and rebuild is to rebuild that house. To replace parts of a house (bricks, boards, beams) one-by-one and take the replaced parts elsewhere and build a house is not to rebuild the original house. Words for natural objects respect human intentions and actions too. To put a teabag in water makes the water into tea. If one's water supply is filtered at the water works through a filter made of tea, what comes out of the tap is water, not tea. There are innumerable examples of these and other sorts. So virtually any natural language lexical item (*not* scientific term) is a rich source of fine-grained distinctions that can be used by a person *because* they are a part of that person's linguistic *knowledge*, represented in lexical features. And these distinctions are provided at SEM to "other cognitive systems" – perhaps vision, perhaps something more "central." Ultimately, they appear as differences in naturally constituted cognitive tools that people can use to – among other uses – describe the world creatively.

The richness and detail of specific lexical items is greatly enhanced and refined when several are put together to compose a phrase or sentence. In sentences, but not lexical items, themes (doers of deeds, recipients of goods, etc.) are assigned, tenses specified, scope and specificity indicated, "agreements" fixed, etc. Ambiguities can arise: *They are flying planes.* Detail and focus of many possible sorts become possible: the dog that bit the cat that ate the rat that . . . Co-reference comes to be specified (or not): Harriet washed *herself*; Harriet washed *her*. Mood (interrogative, declarative, etc.) is specified. Intensification, diminution, and the like, become possible: very, very, very tedious speech. There is something like coordination of features: long trip, long walk, long conversation, long paper, long drink, long speech. More room is provided for imagination and speculation: the amiable person, amiable trip, amiable dog, amiable grouch, amiable table(?!). A potential for metaphor and other figures of speech arises: Tom the wolf, pussycat, suit, etc. (Unless used and "applied metaphorically," note, these are not metaphors, just complex meanings.) Phrases and sentential expressions provide at SEM *extremely* rich and detailed "perspectives" (Chomsky 1995b, 2000a), composed and focused in ways that through multiple features in multiple configurations support any number of uses. These are extraordinary cognitive tools. They do what meanings should.

Again, linguists are nowhere near providing a full list of the set of distinguishing features, nor are they certain about the kinds of configurations into which these features can go. They are not even sure whether they may have to postulate as many feature-terms as there are lexical roots. Will a relatively small set of FG-features and their possible configurations be sufficient to distinguish all lexical items from each other, or will the lexicologist have to provide hundreds of thousands, perhaps millions, of lexical root terms to capture the finest distinctions between not just all active lexical items in all people's mental dictionaries, but all the possible ones? Are the different roots for the noun and verb *wash* and the noun and verb *rinse* to be thought of as unique and indecomposable (RINSE and WASH), or decomposable instead (RINSE $= F_1 \ldots F_n$)? This raises the acquisition issue mentioned before: making sense of hundreds of thousands of latent concepts looks more difficult than dealing with a smaller set of features that can be put in arrays. There is also a modularity issue: DOG, for example, has both visual and linguistic features. Where does the linguist's responsibility end, and the visual scientist's begin? Do visual features enter a linguistic derivation? Do they come to be coupled with linguistic features "after" a derivation? A full theory of UG would speak to this issue too, if only by saying what language's contribution is. In spite of the unanswered questions, though, there seem to be FG features, and they seem to capture part of the conceptual "content" the language faculty contributes to cognition. In this respect, they can be thought to capture the linguistic part of what we think of as "understanding." That qualifies them, surely, as capturing linguistic meanings or linguistic "contents."

Perhaps by now FG-features – specifically, their detail and capacity to serve biological (interface) and human interests too – make SEMs (which as meaning interfaces are already cut out to play a conceptual role) look more conceptual and less syntactic. They can be made to appear even more conceptual by emphasizing that SEMs are mental events that can be seen as *constitutive of* human experience and understanding. Emphasizing that SEM contributes to other systems might suggest that, but a lot more can be said about language and its place in mind. Some details appear below. (For more, see Chomsky 1966: 65f/2002a: 98f; 1975, 1980, 1995b, 2000a; McGilvray 1998, 1999: chs. 2 and 6, 2002a, b).

Meaning in syntax and its use

Syntax broadly conceived is essentially an internalist discipline and, when a form of scientific theory, it is a naturalistic discipline. Natural language syntax is the study of the *intrinsic, internal* features and operations of a language. FG-features are syntactic; in essence, they are the "semantic" features that Chomsky suggests are carried along in the derivation of an expression and that make a difference at SEM. They – *and* phonological and formal features – are internal and intrinsic features, defined within a naturalistic theory – that is, intensionally defined.[12] This broad view of linguistic syntax includes the subject matters of morphology, phonology, lexicology, and – of course – syntax as usually conceived, which deals with categorial features (N, V, etc.), "functional" features such as T(ense) and AGR(eement), and issues such as how lexical items thought of as sets of features come to be put together (Merge), how and why some features move (Attract/Move), and how some come to be deleted (Erase). Syntax as usually conceived – the study of Merge, Attract/Move, etc. – can be called "narrow syntax." Chomsky's theory of meaning, like his theory of sound (phonology/phonetics) is syntactic, but broadly syntactic.

Syntax need not be linguistic. The internalist study of other mental systems, and of relations between the language faculty and those systems, constitute an even broader notion of syntax. Syntax so conceived is the internalist study of all internal operations of the mind – any conducive to theory. Internal operations might include relations between language and vision; they certainly include relations between core language faculty operations (C_{HL}) and performance systems such as those involved in perception and articulation. This very broad syntax also includes important parts of what has traditionally been thought of as formal semantics. Chomsky remarks this in 1999 when he speaks of syntax as including

the study of [internal, mental] symbolic systems, including whatever computational/ representational system we take to be internal to the mind/brain. That includes formal relations among the elements of these systems (e.g. rhyme and entailment, insofar as these are formal relations among internal symbolic objects), model-theoretic semantics (insofar as the models are considered to be internal objects, i.e. "mental models" – as in practice they are, in my opinion, contrary to what is often asserted), formal semantics based on a relation R (sometimes called "reference") holding between symbolic objects (e.g. between "London" and its "semantic value," not an entity in the world, or even the world as we conceive it to be, but of some internal system of thought that is [perhaps] itself related to the world), etc. (Transcript of speech)

Thus, relations between SEMs and a "commitment box" might also be placed in this very broad form of syntax, as – for example – the formal semantics that Pietroski and Crain appeal to in order to express (the guidance of) meanings. Whether there is a syntactic *science* of these internal objects and relations is an open question that depends – among many other things – on whether one can find the relevant objects and relations and construct a naturalistic science of them. There is reason to think there might be one. Perhaps what philosophers call "analytic truths" are crude descriptions of such relations. As Pietroski and Crain suggest, if Joan uses *Harriet persuaded Harold to walk the dog* and holds the claim to be true, she is also committed to holding that Harold intended to walk the dog. Plausibly, that commitment is due, in part, to the fact that this form of PERSUADE has built into it the feature CAUSE that structures the speaker's perspective so that – for this case – Harriet is construed as causing a state of Harold, specifically, his intending to walk the dog. So far, this is all internal to the perspective and the language faculty itself. But if it is seen as constraining a speaker's commitments, it has consequences for what happens beyond the core, combinatorial operations of the language faculty and its semantic interfaces. Perhaps these constraints can be thought of as "instructions" (Chomsky 1995c) that a SEM gives to "other systems" – in this case, a person's "commitment box." Perhaps they "say," "If you hold that *p* is true, you are also committed to *q*." But as the tentative terminology suggests, it is not clear what the systems on the other side of SEM are, nor how they are "instructed."

The success or failure of efforts to construct sciences of relations to systems on the other side of the linguistic interfaces is independent of the issue of whether there can be a broad syntactic *core* science of the interfaces – meaning and sound – themselves. There already are such theories; there is, then, a syntactic, albeit incomplete, "theory of meaning" – an internalist account of understanding by means of language. This theory is in no way a theory of language use. But it does say what linguistic conceptual resources are available for people to use, and – given the nature of the language faculty that is revealed by Chomsky's theory of language – it assures us that what is provided to other systems is usable ("interpretable," "legible") by them. Chomsky (2000a) speaks of meanings as "guiding" their use. Descartes might have spoken of a will's freedom to judge being constrained by some "ideas" of the "understanding," particularly if these ideas are "clear and distinct." Perhaps the discussion above of PERSUADE indicates what guidance and constraint consist in and it is possible to construct a science of constraint along the suggested lines. But it would still be a syntactic, internalist theory.

Perhaps – as Chomsky sometimes tongue-in-cheek suggests – a Martian or some other unworldly creature with a different form of mind and understanding than ours will be able to construct a science of language use. Perhaps our Martian friend will tell us about it – in a Transgalacticese idiom we can translate into Humanese or Humanscientificese. Until then, we had better settle for an effort to construct a complete theory of linguistic meaning on internalist and nativist grounds. That – and forays into other internal systems – should keep us busy for a very long time.

Linguistic tools that enable creativity

There are interesting connections between Chomsky's views and Ludwig Wittgenstein's. Wittgenstein told us to think of the words of languages as tools. He also suggested thinking of the meanings of these tools as the functions they have in "language games" (ways we use language). Chomsky agrees with Wittgenstein that if meanings are uses/functions or applications of words (their role in truth-telling, to mention one popular option), there is no *theory* of meaning but only commonsense *descriptions* of use. Putting this in a Chomskyan–Cartesian way, words' functions are the uses to which they are put by free agents, uses that might be "incited and inclined" by circumstance (Chomsky 1996a, b) but are certainly not determined by them, whether internally or externally. Chomsky differs from Wittgenstein in other respects, however. Where Chomsky thinks that words – or at least, the sounds and meanings of words – are natural mental entities that enable us to deal with problems in a flexible way, not artifacts, Wittgenstein seems to have thought that people *manufacture* words and language to meet their needs. Furthermore – and most important – Chomsky (1966, 2002a) thinks that the fact that words are not the products of human effort is precisely what makes it possible for humans to be the creative creatures they are even at a very early age. Other rationalists made this point, as did Humboldt. Language – or the "ideas" or concepts of language – have to be innate and part of our nature if we are to manage to so quickly and in such a sophisticated manner deal with the world, play social roles, understand others' motivations, and create paintings and poems.

Chomsky's biological rationalist picture of the mind illuminates this. One key is recognizing that language's meanings are "legible" to other systems in the head – that language, a modular system, offers its conceptual resources to the rest of the mind. In recent linguistic work, this is expressed by saying that language meets "interface conditions" set by the systems with which it communicates. These conditions state, in effect, that a derivation of an expression is successful if it yields at SEM a legible or interpretable concept – one that can be "useful." If this is on the right track, one can think of the language faculty and its products (SEMs) as virtually designed to be useful to other systems. Of course, we can *actually* use only those our systems can cope with: extremely long expressions, for example, would overpower them. But this is still an extremely large number. By one of Steven Pinker's (following George Miller's) very rough estimates based on the assumption that English speakers can readily understand twenty-word sentences, it would take 100 billion centuries for a person just to hear them all (Pinker 1993). Although we are finite, we will not run out of internally constituted and defined linguistic cognitive tools. And when we add the contributions of other systems, and the opportunity that a flexible form of cognitive organization affords, the possibilities seem endless.

We can speculate about what the systems with which language communicates might be. Plausibly, they are any of the systems that help us carry out the various projects that we humans engage in – the tasks in which language and its distinctive "perspectives" so often play a role. A minimal list would consist of the other known faculties of the mind – core vision and the systems with which it is intimately connected, such as facial configuration; object configuration (Marr's 3-D representations); perhaps systems that are tuned to body configuration in both self and others, such as those in which Rizzolatti's "mirror neurons" (Rizzolatti et al. 1996) participate; plus – in the case of sign language users – systems that "shape" visual scenes with linguistic contours (some of the same systems that deal with linguistic sounds, Petitto et al. 2000). To this must be added audition and the systems to which it is intimately related – music (systems for harmony and dissonance along with associated perceptual systems), phonetic and babbling-recognizing systems, and the like. We can add proprioception – which no doubt involves several subsystems – plus touch, taste, and the like. There seem to be systems sensitive to social/community hierarchy, others tuned to social "balance" – something like a "fairness" or "justice" system, evident even in small children's social interactions. There are undoubtedly many others. Language relates to all of these, we can assume, in complex ways.[13] We use linguistic concepts, and those of our other systems, from time to time, singly (rarely) and in concert, to understand and perhaps solve a massive set of problems that the confluence of our projects with the world and with other people and their projects pose for us. Chomsky calls the overall result of these cooperative efforts by systems to solve problems "common sense understanding" (1975, 1995b, 2000a) – a capacity that children develop early and, thus, a capacity that obviously depends heavily on native endowment. But it is also a capacity that is extraordinarily flexible and readily turned not only to crude practical problem solving, but to art and politics. Unless one is doing science, where commonsense concepts almost inevitably mislead rather than help, we rely on common sense for everything from coming to understand the motives of others and thinking about what we want to do next year to discerning the messages of works of art.

Combining recognition of the fact that language produces an in-principle indefinite number of highly specific, distinct perspectives, that vision is configurable to an indefinite degree (although we seem natively equipped to recognize and analyze only in certain specific ways), and that language and other systems relate to each other in a flexible manner, the conclusion is inescapable. The human mind is virtually designed to be flexible – almost as if it were a general-purpose cognitive device, although it clearly is not. When, furthermore, we add to this that language can be spontaneously internally stimulated – it does not depend heavily on "input," as vision typically does – and that other faculties can too, at least to an extent (as imagination reveals), we find that the human cognitive system is not only flexible, but can detach itself from circumstance and range widely. We can speculate, engage in wonder, and cultivate what Kant called a "free play between the imagination and the understanding." The human mind – especially because it is given the particular and unique contribution of language – is virtually designed to create, and does so, even at a very early age: children quickly engage in fantasy and play. To summarize: that we have innate concepts that do not have to be learned, that these concepts can be combined in endless fashion in sentential meanings, that they can be readily produced, and that they relate to other systems in flexible ways, makes possible creativity and that form of freedom that gives us a distinctively human form of satisfaction. We have these systems and their arrangement and enjoy using them.[14]

Science and scientific concepts are a different story. They come late, are manufactured in creating theories (are artifacts), and the project of science (and higher mathematics) seems to require maintaining a degree of regimentation in the use of scientific and mathematical symbols. Gottlob Frege's semantics for mathematics depended on this regimentation in use; since his time, "semantic theorists" have tried to apply Frege's semantics for mathematics to everyday language use. Wittgenstein warned against this. Chomsky heeds the warning – and honors the fact of creativity.

Creativity in the use of language

We are not all poets or innovative scientists, but we all have what might be called "ordinary creativity" (Chomsky 1966, 2002a). Descartes and some of the early Cartesians discussed the facts of this sort of creativity and their implications for the sciences of language and mind. The facts have not changed, and neither – Chomsky thinks – have their implications. First noted in print by Descartes in 1637[15] and worked out in more detail by Descartes's follower Cordemoy, later rationalists respected the creativity observations and the Romantics (only a few of whom – A. W. Schlegel, Wilhelm von Humboldt, and Coleridge – were also nativists) developed them into a major theme. Chomsky summarizes the various aspects of these observations in many writings. Language use "is typically innovative, guided but not determined by internal state and external conditions, appropriate to circumstances but uncaused, eliciting thoughts that the hearer might have expressed the same way" (1996a, b: 2). "Innovative" is sometimes glossed instead as unbounded, "uncaused" as stimulus free; appropriate is sometimes paired with "coherent." The phenomena these terms describe are readily apparent to anyone willing to spend a few minutes observing their and others' use of language. First, ordinary language use is not *caused* by "input" (it does not correlate with external or internal circumstance and so seems *stimulus free*); anyone might say anything, anytime, without regard to circumstances. Second, use is typically innovative, novel, or *unbounded*: a few formulae ("Hello, how are you?") aside, repeated sentences are the exception, not the rule. There does not seem to be any upper bound on what people can produce. Nevertheless, third, language use is *appropriate* and coherent to circumstances, whether those of the speaker's present perceptual environment or circumstances elsewhere and elsewhen, including those of fictive worlds (circumstances in some world speculated about, conjectured, constructed in fiction, imagined, hypothesized, etc.). *Unbounded*, *stimulus free*, and *appropriate* are all aspects of what Chomsky has in mind by pointing out that ordinary language use is "guided but not determined by internal state and external conditions."

Imagine Gertrude at a party. Her boyfriend is discussing with equally enthusiastic friends the comparative speeds of execution of the latest computer chips. Gertrude says, "I'm going to join the Canadian bobsled team." Her environment does not cause this sentence. She need not say anything at all, and could have said any number of other things. But the sentence (and an unbounded number of others) is "appropriate to circumstances." Perhaps she is letting her companions know that she is bored and wants to talk about something else, or reminding them that their meals are getting cold. Perhaps she really wants to join a bobsled team. So while circumstances do not cause her sentence, it is appropriate to them: she has a reason – perhaps several – to say what she does. Her companions might be surprised. But they, and we, have no difficulty explaining (in terms of reasons) why she says this, nor in adjusting with extraordinary sensitivity to subtly different circumstances, or any number of other sentences.

There is no prospect that the phenomena of creativity can be the subject matter of a science of language use, or a science of mind. The science of mind does, however, say *something* about the phenomena of creativity. Chomsky remarks (1972a: 13) that while no science can "explain intelligent behavior," it might explain how intelligent behavior is *possible*. The creative aspect of language-use observations focus on paradigm cases of intelligent behavior – appropriate but uncaused judgments. A good science of the mind should show how this form of intelligent behavior is possible. The picture of the mind drawn above shows how. I summarize to conclude.

Making creativity possible

Think of a scientifically based picture of the mind as presenting the machinery of the mind (as understood by the best relevant sciences) as having certain intrinsic features and standing in relationships to each other in ways that *make sense of* each module's contribution to human cognition and action. For language, the features to be made sense of are the unboundedness, stimulus freedom, and appropriateness of linguistic action. Unboundedness is made sense of by a language faculty that can in principle produce unlimited numbers of expressions. As for stimulus freedom, it is connected to a cluster of phenomena connected with modularity – to the fact that language in particular does not require external stimulation, to a degree of autonomy in the operations of specific faculties, and to flexible interrelationships between modules. Appropriateness is the most interesting. Plausibly, linguistic appropriateness can arise in minds that have language, plus a flexible form of overall organization, and a need/urge to "solve problems" of all sorts – practical, intellectual, artistic, etc. To have a concept is to have something like a focus that people can use to array, categorize, evaluate, etc. In performing a cognitive task, seeking a solution to a cognitive problem, interpreting others, constructing and understanding metaphors, etc., we routinely distinguish relevant applications of concepts from irrelevant – appropriate from inappropriate. The endless conceptual resources and built-in flexibility of the human mind make sense of how this is possible. They also make sense of why there will never be a specific class of expressions that is appropriate to a specific circumstance. As our pervasive use of metaphor, irony, and other figures of speech suggest, our minds are not only tolerant of innovative ways of understanding, but we find novel yet apt (fitting, plausible, interesting, intriguing, etc.) ways of understanding a situation satisfying.

It is remarkable that everyone routinely uses language creatively, and gets satisfaction from doing so. It is remarkable because unless one is willing to appeal to something like Descartes's second substance, or to theological "explanations" that hold that humans are products of a special creation that gives us this gift, the fact of creativity must somehow be lodged in our natures as biological creatures. A Chomskyan picture of a human mind that has flexibility biologically built into it in the form of endless (although biologically constrained) conceptual resources and minimal constraints on cooperative use of multiple faculties is a mind with free will. That mind can be turned to the performance of endless numbers of tasks. It can also be freed from current practical concerns to speculate and imagine.

So humans have the opportunity for linguistic creativity – and for all that this gives us, given the way language contributes to overall functioning – built into their biological natures. That helps explain why Chomsky seems to think that one of our fundamental needs as humans is to exercise this opportunity. Fulfilling our natures gives us satisfaction. If so, it is not surprising that Chomsky assumes that an ideal form of social organization must provide ample opportunity for people to do so.

Part III

Chomsky on values and politics

11   Market values and libertarian socialist values

Milan Rai

Many observers have been fascinated by the puzzle of tracing connections between Noam Chomsky's extraordinary contributions to two quite distinct domains of modern culture. Ronald Lunsford points out that some of these parallels would exist whatever area of inquiry Chomsky had chosen for his life's work – parallels that "arise from Chomsky's way of thinking, rather than from the disciplines themselves" (Haley & Lunsford 1994: 172). One critical element in his "way of thinking" manifest in both his professional and non-professional work is his commitment to rationality (a commitment summed up in the observation, "There are no arguments that I know of for irrationality" [Chomsky 1987a:22]). On a more abstract level, one finds in both his political and his non-political work a quality that Chomsky has sometimes referred to as "psychic distance." In linguistics, "if we can establish a kind of psychic distance from the object and try to see how similar normal common characteristics really are, against the background of a possible variety that can be imagined," we discover that "language structures really are uniform" (1988a: 151f). In politics, once we have extricated ourselves from conventional thought, we discover underlying similarities between apparent polarities – an underlying commitment to US power shared by, for example, Joseph Alsop (a Vietnam War "hawk"), and Arthur Schlesinger (a Kennedy liberal and a "dove").[1] The ability to achieve "psychic distance" is actually an essential element of the ability to inquire, and to achieve scientific progress.

Chomsky himself has noted some substantive (though tenuous) connections between his work in linguistics and his political writings, centred on his controversial conception of human nature. He notes that for the last few centuries of Western scientific thought it has been assumed that "physical structures are genetically inherited and intellectual structures are learned" (1988a: 399). In his view, on the other hand, a view that he traces back to Enlightenment thinkers, the mind is composed of many numbers of genetically-inherited systems, "each intricate and highly specialized, with interactions of a kind that are largely fixed by our biological endowment" (1988a: 500). Some of these mental "modules" or "organs" are concerned with language, the organization of perceptual space, a theory of number, and so on. In a different region, con-cerned with social relations, there may be a mental "module" devoted to the recognition of personality structure, "which undoubtedly is also a complex and creative intellectual achievement" (1988a: 240). Chomsky suggests that "among the biological characteristics that determine the nature of the human organism" there are "some that relate to intellectual development, some that relate to moral development, some that relate to development as a member of human society, some that relate to aesthetic development." Chomsky expects to find that to a large extent, these characteristics are "immutable": "That is to say, they are just part of being human the same way as having legs and arms is part of being human" (1988a: 147).

To be clear: just as it is the capacity to develop, or "grow," a human language that is innate, and not any particular language itself, so it is the capacity to develop a human moral system that is innate, not any particular morality. (Sim-ilarly for the capacities to relate to other humans in society, and to appreciate and create aesthetic experiences such as myth and ritual.) The moral "faculty" is not a universal moral code hidden in our DNA, but a mechanism for building human codes of morality. Chomsky notes that we do develop "implicit systems of moral evaluation" which are more or less uniform from person to person, with only very limited exposure to the moral standards of a particular society. While there are certainly moral differences, "over quite a substantial range we tend to make comparable judgements, and we do it, it would appear, in quite intricate and delicate ways involving new cases and agreement often about new cases, and so on, and we do this on the basis of very limited environmental context available to us."[2] The standard "poverty-of-stimulus" argument applies. There is, Chomsky argues, something in human nature that is common across different moral systems. Even at the outer limits, we still find Nazi leaders proclaiming that their actions were in pursuit of the common good. Chomsky notes that it is a rare person who will straightforwardly admit entirely selfish and ignoble motivations. "Even Himmler didn't say that" (Chomsky 1993c: 65). (In pass-ing, we may note Chomsky's suggestion that part of the human "moral faculty" is the genetically inherited need to protect our own self-image – this can give rise to racism, a belief formation needed by oppressors to maintain a positive self-image [1993c: 72f].)

The notion that there are structures of "unconscious knowledge" within the mind, "principles which form the sinews and connections of thought, but which may not be conscious principles, which we know must be functioning although we may not be able to introspect into them," is an insight of the seventeenth century expressed in modern language.[3] Chomsky has reasserted the place of linguistics within a modernized form of this rationalist conception of the human mind. This modernized rationalism can be seen as the intellectual hinge between Chomsky's work in linguistics and his political thought. Being careful to distinguish between rationalism in this sense, and a commitment to rationality,[4] we are in a position to unfold some of Chomsky's thoughts on moral values.

The social consequences of human nature

Chomsky argues that notions of human nature are fundamental to political thought and action. He suggests that every kind of political intervention is actually based on a conception of human nature, a speculation or belief concerning what is the essence of "being human." This is so, Chomsky argues, whether one is proposing social reform, the status quo, reversion to a previous era, or social revolution – "any vision that one has as to the nature of a better or utopian society, a society towards which we ought to strive, or (to be more incremental about it) any point of view that one takes towards the next small change in social evolution" (1988a: 245). Chomsky suggests that "if there is any moral character to what we advocate, it is because we believe or are hoping that this change we are proposing is better for humans because of the way humans are." For the change to be justifiable, there must be "something about the way humans fundamentally are, about their fundamental nature, which requires that this change we are advocating takes place" (1988a: 597). "Thus, if we are opposed to slavery, it is because we think that in some sense these institutions are an infringement on essential human nature" (1988a: 385), "because we think that slavery is inconsistent with fundamental human rights, which are rooted in the nature of humans, which demand that they be free and not owned by others," because it is part of "essential human nature, an essential human right to be free and under one's own control" (1988a: 597). The same connection to deeper intuitions can be found in the case of, say, a change in tax laws, unless the proposal is made purely for opportunistic reasons. If we believe that there is some moral content to what we are proposing, "if we trace that position to its origins, it will have to do with some assumption about human nature, about the central human nature": "Otherwise, there is no basis for taking a political position or a stand on issues," Chomsky suggests (1988a: 598). In his view, while these connections are "almost never" opened to inspection, it is "crucially important" to make these assumptions explicit, "and to see whether in fact we can find any evidence bearing on them" (1988a: 597, 245). Chomsky concedes that it is extremely difficult to make these kinds of assumptions explicit, "and so little is understood that the structures of the argument and belief that we develop are very loose" – so loose that "they are largely structures of hope and conviction rather than arguments with evidence." ("But nevertheless those are the structures that must be there for there to be any moral content to our advocacy and action" [1988a: 598]).

Within modern Western society, a conventional picture of human nature has grown up, with obvious consequences for social form – the human being as a self-seeking consumption-oriented social atom, "economic man" or "economic woman." Chomsky observes that human beings do not really live as maximizers of consumption. It is not true, for example, that in a typical family each member exerts herself or himself to secure as much food as possible, at the expense of other members of the family. "The official values of society are very remote, I think, from most of our actual life with other people," Chomsky suggests (1988a: 172). He argues that this concept of the "economic human" is "a psychological absurdity" which leads to "untold suffering" for those who try to mould themselves to this pattern, "as well as for their victims": " 'Look out for number one' is a prescription for demoralization, corruption, and ultimately general catastrophe, whatever value it may have had in the early stages of industrialization" (1981c: 226). Chomsky suggests that it would be "very liberating" for the wealthy as well as for the poor, for the privileged as well as for the underprivileged, to be able to live in a society where the human essence is not defined in terms of maximizing production, and producing "on demand" (1988a: 172).

He asks, "What reason is there to believe the crucial assumption that people will work only for gain in (transmittable) wealth and power, so that society cannot be organized in accordance with the socialist dictum?" (That dictum being, of course, "From each according to their ability, to each according to their need.") This would be true only if we assume that "applying one's talents in interesting and socially useful work is not rewarding in itself, that there is no intrinsic satisfaction in creative and productive work, suited to one's abilities, or in helping others (say, one's family, friends, associates, or simply fellow members of society)" (1971a: 137). This conventional belief, that without material reward human beings would simply vegetate, Chomsky describes as a "degrading and brutal assumption," and a "strange and demeaning doctrine" (1971a: 139, 143).

Separate from, but related to, this notion of *homo economicus*, is a picture of the human essence associated with Adam Smith. Chomsky observes that if we take the view "characteristic of Adam Smith," that essential to human nature is the "need to truck and barter," then we will develop a certain image of a just and proper society – "an early capitalist society of small traders," perhaps (1988a: 245). A clear example of the kind of connection between social advocacy and presumed human nature described above. Interestingly, despite the veneration granted to Smith in Western societies, few, if any, of his supporters advocate this form of society. Furthermore, Chomsky notes, few realize that Smith argued that under the right conditions, the rich "are led by an invisible hand to make nearly the same distribution of the necessaries of life, which would have been made, had the earth been divided into equal portions among all its inhabitants,"[5] equality of condition, not merely of opportunity. Smith's ideas have been comprehensively distorted, Chomsky suggests. When we turn to the real Adam Smith, we find a stinging critique of European colonialism (Chomsky 1993d: 4–16, passim), a denunciation of the human consequences of the division of labor (for making laborers "as stupid and ignorant as it is possible for a human creature to be") (1993d: 18), a passionate attack on the "malversion," "plunder," "knavery," "extravagance," "injustice," and general "indifference to anything but their own interests" of corporations (joint-stock companies)[6] and "the mean rapacity" and "monopolizing spirit" of business elites ("merchants and manufacturers").[7] Chomsky remarks that Smith's admiration for individual enterprise was tempered by his contempt for what Smith called "the vile maxim of the masters of mankind": "All for ourselves, and nothing for other people" (1993d: 19).

Really existing free market theory

In contemporary society, we find, on the one hand, rhetorical devotion to the "free market," and, on the other hand, an equally forceful commitment to violating traditional "free market" theory as developed by Adam Smith and others. Chomsky suggests that, "Neither at home nor abroad does the real world resemble the dreamy fantasies now fashionable about history converging to an ideal of free markets and democracy, 'a future for which America is both the gatekeeper and the model.' " A more accurate description of the "New World Order" would be that "the world is to be run by the rich and for the rich":

The world system is nothing like a classical market; the term "corporate mercantilism" is a closer fit. Governance is increasingly in the hands of huge private institutions and their representatives . . . With the rapid growth of TNCs [transnational corporations] to a level at which their foreign sales already exceed all of world trade, these systems of private governance gain undreamed-of power. They have naturally used it to create the "de facto world government" described in the business press, with its own institutions, also insulated from public inspection or influence. (Chomsky 1994:185).

It is widely suggested that the present form of "globalization," and its human consequences, are the result of what "the free market has decided, in its infinite but mysterious wisdom," or "the implacable sweep of 'the market revolution,' " or "Reaganesque rugged individualism" (Chomsky 1996a,b: 92f). The reality, Chomsky suggests, is revealed by the fact that the rugged individualists of the Reagan administration virtually doubled import restrictions to 23 percent, "more than all postwar administrations combined," while then-Secretary of the Treasury James Baker "proudly proclaimed that Mr Ronald Reagan had 'granted more import relief to US industry than any of his predecessors in more than half a century,' " and David Henderson of the OECD found that during the 1980s the United States had the worst record for devising new non-tariff barriers to trade (Chomsky 1994: 107). This is merely one aspect of the reality of the "market revolution." A 1992 OECD study concludes that "Oligopolistic competition and strategic interaction between firms and governments rather than the invisible hand of market forces condition today's competitive advantage and international division of labor in high-technology industries" (Chomsky 1996a,b: 129). The same is true of agriculture, pharmaceuticals, services, and major areas of economic activity generally, Chomsky observes. Just as, when discussing Adam Smith, one must distinguish between Smith's ideas and the ways in which those ideas have been used for particular purposes, so we must distinguish between "free market" theory (much of it based on Smith), and what Chomsky calls "really existing free market theory." The latter has two elements: restricting government intervention to protect the interests of the general public in the name of economic efficiency, while at the same time securing considerable government intervention to protect the interests of "merchants and manufacturers" – also in the name of economic efficiency: "If you look through the whole history of modern economic development, you find that – virtually without exception – advocates of "free markets" want them applied to the poor and the middle-class, but not to themselves" (Chomsky & Barsamian 1998: 17). Corporations seek government subsidies to help cover their costs and government "insurance" to protect them from market risks, while keeping profits. "Public subsidy and private profit" is the continuing pattern of the "market revolution," Chomsky argues.

We should note that Adam Smith's critique of government intervention was not motivated by his desire to see corporations allowed free rein, but by his concern that the governmental system had become an instrument of the "masters." "For 'the contrivers of this whole mercantile system,' the results of government intervention were beneficial, while for the general public there were considerable costs; 'our merchants and manufacturers have been by far the principal architects', and their interests have been 'most peculiarly attended to', Smith observed" (cited in Chomsky 1993d:16). Chomsky observes that in any society containing concentrations of private power, one would expect such institutions to gain power and influence over governmental structures (and indeed over cultural institutions, a matter we return to). In the case of the United States, "as elsewhere, foreign policy is designed and implemented by narrow groups who derive their power from domestic sources – in our form of state capitalism, from their control over the domestic economy, including the militarized state sector." Chomsky notes that studies of top advisory and decision-making positions relating to international affairs in the US government confirm the obvious: such positions are "heavily concentrated in the hands of representatives of major corporations, banks, investment firms, the few law firms that cater to corporate interests," and those technocratic intellectuals who serve the same interests (Chomsky 1982: 91). It was only natural, then, that when the US government began planning for the postwar era during World War II, the State Department collaborated with the business-based Council on Foreign Relations, to determine the "requirement[s] of the United States in a world in which it proposes to hold unquestioned power" (cited in Chomsky 1982: 96). The same objective was put clearly by the influential George Kennan while he was head of the State Department Policy Planning Staff immediately after the war:

We have about 50 per cent of the world's wealth, but only 6.3 per cent of its population . . . In this situation, we cannot fail to be the object of envy and resentment. Our real task in the coming period is to devise a pattern of relationships which will permit us to maintain this position of disparity . . . We need not deceive ourselves that we can afford today the luxury of altruism and world-benefaction . . . The day is not far off when we are going to have to deal in straight power concepts. The less we are then hampered by idealistic slogans, the better.[8]

This is, of course, a Top Secret document. In public, US leaders and opinion-formers were, and remain, much concerned with "idealistic slogans." To clarify Kennan's remarks, we must add Smith's class analysis: while the interests of business leaders are no doubt to be "peculiarly attended to" by such a mercantilist foreign policy, it is misleading to pretend that the interests of the rest of the 6.3 percent of the world's population are really a priority.

There are, then, two quite separate sets of "market values" in operation today: anti-welfare state, "free market" values imposed on the weak and powerless, both at home and abroad; and the protectionist, mercantilist values held by the powerful and their associates, committed to preserving their "position of disparity" through state intervention. Both kinds of "market values" must be distinguished from Adam Smith's ideas of "natural liberty," which belong to an earlier, pre-capitalist, period. Smith was part of the Scottish Enlightenment, with a genuine concern for the mass of the population. We may contrast his belief that one of the "two distinct objects" of "political economy" should be "to provide a plentiful revenue or subsistence to the people, or more properly to enable them to provide such a revenue for themselves," with Malthus's declaration that anyone lacking independent wealth "has no claim of right to the smallest portion of food, and, in fact, has no business to be where he [or she] is," apart from what his or her offer of labor will bring in the market.[9]

Enlightenment values

The Enlightenment was a broad, scattered, phenomenon, but there were certain commonalities to the thought of the period. Chomsky suggests that the ideals of the Enlightenment were the ideas that "people had natural rights, that they were fundamentally equal, that it was an infringement of essential human rights if systems of authority subordinated some to others, the insistence that there were real bonds of unity and solidarity among people across cultures," and so on (Chomsky 1988a: 764.) Perhaps the central concern of the Enlightenment, however, was its concern with rationality. The French thinker Condorcet predicted that, "The time will come when the sun will shine on free men [and women] who have no master but their reason," while Kant declared, "*Sapere aude*, have the courage to know; this is the motto of the Enlightenment" (cited in Outram 1995: 1, 2). Chomsky identifies with such sentiments: "I am a child of the Enlightenment. I think irrational belief is a dangerous phenomenon, and I try consciously to avoid irrational belief" (1988a: 773). Chomsky observes that, according to a tradition extending from Hume to Bertrand Russell,

Reason is concerned with the choice of the right means to an end that you wish to achieve, taking emotional and moral factors into consideration. Unfortunately, too many modern technocrats, who often pose as scientists and scholars, are really divorcing themselves from traditional science and scholarship, and excluding themselves from the company of reasonable persons in the name of a kind of reason that is perverted beyond recognition. (Chomsky 1975:219)

Chomsky is also a "child of the Enlightenment" in his adoption of the other values already described. At this point, it may be useful to distinguish between two elements of Enlightenment thought which Chomsky finds attractive. One might be called a "weak" set of commitments – to rationality, to equality, to the unity of humankind, and to honesty and elementary decency. This set of Enlightenment values are all that is needed to subject US foreign policy, or the "market revolution," or the mass media, to a searching critique. Then there is a core of ideas in classical liberalism which we might term "strong" Enlightenment values, concerning freedom and the essence of being human, which flower into a much wider, libertarian socialist, critique of Western society.

Wilhelm von Humboldt, an eighteenth-century libertarian with an interest in both language and freedom, held that

The true end of man, or that which is prescribed by the eternal and immutable dictates of reason, and not suggested by vague and transient desires, is the highest and most harmonious development of his powers to a complete and consistent whole. Freedom is the first and indispensable condition which the possibility of such a development presupposes; but there is besides another essential – intimately connected with freedom, it is true – a variety of situations. (cited in Chomsky 1973b: 177)

The "leading principle" of Humboldt's thought was "the fullest, richest and most harmonious development of the potentialities of the individual, the community or the human race." For Humboldt, "to inquire and to create – these are the centres around which all human pursuits more or less directly revolve" (Chomsky 1973b:177, 178). He argues that, "freedom is undoubtedly the indispensable condition without which even the pursuits most congenial to individual human nature can never succeed in producing such salutary influences": "Whatever does not spring from a man's free choice, or is only the result of instruction and guidance, does not enter into his very being, but remains alien to his true nature; he does not perform it with truly human energies, but merely with mechanical exactness." Chomsky summarizes, adding a final phrase from Humboldt: "If a man acts in a purely mechanical way, reacting to external demands or instruction rather than in ways determined by his own interests and energies and power, "we may admire what he does, but we despise what he is' " (1973b: 179). Chomsky remarks that this is a fundamental critique of the wage system, which is in its very nature a system of coercion, whereby persons may "choose" to rent themselves to a firm, under the duress of otherwise "choosing" to suffer deprivation and poverty. The classical liberal principle enunciated by Humboldt – that free, creative, work is the essence of being human – is therefore an indictment of what has been referred to as "wage slavery," and classical liberalism may therefore without distortion be developed into a critique of capitalism.

For Humboldt, the principal danger to freedom came from the state as "the influence of a private person is liable to diminution and decay, from competition, dissipation of fortune, even death" (Chomsky 1973b: 180). While he correctly pointed out that these "contingencies" could not be applied to the state, Humboldt failed to see that the joint-stock company might one day be legally recognized as a corporate "private person," with precisely the kind of potent immortality that he and other Enlightenment thinkers feared.

Chomsky detects a "line of development" in traditional rationalism, running from Descartes, through the more libertarian Rousseau, through Kantians such as Humboldt, into the nineteenth century, which holds that "essential features of human nature involve a kind of creative urge, a need to control one's productive, creative labor, to be free from authoritarian intrusions, a kind of instinct for liberty and creativity, a real human need to be able to work productively under conditions of one's own choosing and determination in voluntary association with others" (1988a: 594). In the nineteenth century, this notion of essential human nature was developed into a rejection of capitalism, and the power it concentrated in the hands of those who owned the productive resources of society, coupled with a rejection of authoritarian state socialism. Liberal ideas evolved in new circumstances into forms of libertarian socialism. Classical liberalism opposed state intervention in social life "as a consequence of deeper assumptions about the human need for liberty, diversity and free association." "On the same assumptions," Chomsky argues, "capitalist relations of production, wage labor, competitiveness, the ideology of 'possessive individualism' – all must be regarded as fundamentally anti-human": "Libertarian socialism is properly to be understood as the inheritor of the liberal ideals of the Enlightenment" (1973b: 157).

Humboldt's central concern was "the fullest, richest and most harmonious development of the potentialities of the individual, the community or the human race." Echoing Humboldt, anarchosyndicalist Rudolf Rocker observed that, "For the anarchist, freedom is not an abstract philosophical concept, but the vital concrete possibility for every human being to bring to full development all the powers, capacities and talents with which nature has endowed him [or her], and turn them to social account" (1973b: 151). "In a socialist society, as envisioned by the authentic left," Chomsky argues, "a central purpose will be that the necessary requirements of every member of society be satisfied":

Individuals will differ in their aspirations, their abilities, and their personal goals. For some person, the opportunity to play the piano ten hours a day may be an overwhelming personal need; for another, not. As material circumstances permit, these differential needs should be satisfied in a decent society, as in healthy family life. In functioning socialist societies such as the Israeli kibbutzim, questions of this sort constantly arise. (1987a: 192)

In a decent society, "socially necessary and unpleasant work would be divided on some egalitarian basis, and beyond that people would have, as an inalienable right, the widest possible opportunity to do work that interests them." People might be motivated by "self-respect," if they do their work to the best of their ability, "or if their work benefits those to whom they are related by bonds of friendship and sympathy and solidarity." Chomsky notes that such notions are "commonly an object of ridicule – as it was common, in an earlier period, to scoff at the absurd idea that a peasant has the same inalienable rights as a noble-man." He observes that there have always been, and will always be, those who cannot imagine a social order different from that which exists. "Perhaps they are right, but, again, one awaits a rational argument" (1973b: 142f). Chomsky's own "hopes and intuitions" are that "self-fulfilling and creative work" is "a fundamental human need," and that "the pleasures of a challenge met, a work well done, the exercise of skill and craftsmanship," are "real and significant," and are "an essential part of a full and meaningful life." He suggests that "The same is true of the opportunity to understand and enjoy the achievements of others, which often go beyond what we ourselves can do, and to work constructively in cooperation with others" (1988a: 394). "Compassion, solidarity, friendship are also human needs," Chomsky points out – "driving needs, no less than the desire to increase one's share of commodities or to improve working conditions" (1981c: 224). "Predatory capitalism . . . is incapable of meeting human needs that can be expressed only in collective terms, and its concept of competitive man who seeks only to maximize wealth and power, who subjects himself to market relationships, to exploitation and external authority, is anti-human and intolerable in the deepest sense" (1973b: 184).

No one who gives a moment's thought to the problems of contemporary society can fail to be aware of the social costs of consumption and production, the progressive destruction of the environment, the utter irrationality of the utilization of contemporary technology, the inability of a system based on profit or growth-maximization to deal with needs that can only be expressed collectively, and the enormous bias this system imposes towards maximization of commodities for personal use in place of the general improvement of the quality of life. (1981c: 223)

In modern capitalist democracies, there is a fundamental democratic "deficit" in that the entire world of commerce, industry and finance is excluded from democratic control. And within the capitalist firm, Chomsky suggests, there are hierarchical structures of authority "of a kind that we would call fascist in the political domain" (1987a: 32). There is an inescapable tension between capitalism and democracy, a contradiction which can be resolved either by eliminating democracy, or by extending it to the economy. The economy could not be democratized along classical liberal principles through state ownership and management, but through new democratic economic institutions. Summarizing the classical anarchist consensus, Chomsky observes, "one can imagine a network of workers' councils, and at a higher level, representation across the factories, or across branches of industry, or across crafts, and on to general assemblies of workers' councils that can be regional and national and international in character" (1981c: 249). Another system might organize along geographical lines, with local, regional and international assemblies. Both systems would control themselves directly, without a coercive apparatus above them. (Chomsky professes himself agnostic as to how the two systems might interact, or whether both are necessary.)

Such a prospect is a rather distant one. Chomsky has warned that any serious movement of the left should distinguish clearly between "its long-range revolutionary aims," and "certain more immediate effects it can hope to achieve" (1981c: 222). He has made a point of concentrating on the latter almost to the exclusion of the former. The immediate problems are to help people who are oppressed and under attack, to try to prevent environmental disaster, and to build a mass movement of reform. The latter should be "a movement for social change with a positive programme that has a broad-based appeal, that encourages free and open discussion and offers a wide range of possibilities for work and action" (1981c: 221f).

Chomsky hopes that a movement of reform can nurture more revolutionary tendencies committed to challenging the wage system and other aspects of economic authoritarianism. This more radical movement of the left "has no chance of success, and deserves none, unless it develops an understanding of contemporary society and a vision of a future social order that is persuasive to a large majority of the population." In the advanced industrial societies, the mass of the population have far more to lose than their chains – "On the contrary, they have a considerable stake in preserving the existing social order." The cultural and intellectual level of any serious radical movement, therefore, "will have to be far higher than in the past": "It will not be able to satisfy itself with a litany of forms of oppression and injustice. It will have to provide compelling answers to the question of how these evils can be overcome by revolution or large-scale reform." The left will have to "achieve and maintain a position of honesty and commitment to libertarian values," and avoid the temptation to adopt messianic illusions concerning the "vanguard party" (1981c: 222f).

Manufacturing consent

Standing in the way of all these developments, however, is the central problem of freedom of thought. In the case of the United States (and other modern capitalist democracies) there is considerable internal freedom in principle, but very little real freedom of thought, Chomsky charges. The dominant picture of the mass media is, of course, very different (as is the self-image of the media). Judge Gurfein, deciding in favor of press freedom in the Pentagon Papers case (when the US government attempted to suppress the publication of the leaked documents), declared that the United States had "a cantankerous press, an obstinate press, a ubiquitous press," which "must be suffered by those in authority in order to preserve the even greater values of freedom of expression and the right of the people to know." Supreme Court Judge Powell, in another case, argued that as "no individual can obtain for himself [or herself] the information needed for the intelligent discharge of his [or her] political responsibilities. The press performs a crucial function in effecting the societal purpose of the First Amendment," by enabling the public to exert control over the political process (Lewis 1987, cited in Chomsky 1989: 2). For Chomsky and his co-author Edward Herman, the "Free Press" serves a rather different "societal purpose": "It is the societal purpose served by state education as conceived by James Mill in the early days of the establishment of this system: to 'train the minds of the people to a virtuous attachment to their government,' and to the arrangements of the social, economic, and political order more generally." It is the societal purpose of "protecting privilege from the threat of public understanding and participation" (Chomsky 1989: 13, 14). This is achieved, according to Chomsky and Herman, through what they describe as "brainwashing under freedom." No central authority determines "the party line" and dictates to the organs of public expression what can and cannot be said. Intellectual conformity is not achieved through violence or the threat of violence, as in the Stalinist system of propaganda. The Chomsky/Herman "Propaganda Model" of the US mass media is a "guided free market" model, in which thought is controlled by market forces operating in a highly unequal society. Media institutions are themselves large profit-seeking corporations, "which are closely interlocked, and have important common interests, with other major corporations, banks and government" (Chomsky & Herman 1988: 14). They are also dependent on advertising revenue from other businesses, who gain a "de facto licensing authority" (Curran & Seaton 1985: 31) over the mass media. Complementing these and other institutional factors at the "macro" level is the process of education, selection, and cooption, by which individual reporters become attuned to the dominant ideology. Recruitment to a mass media organization is predicated on the candidate possessing the "right" attitudes. For those few who, once recruited, display an unacceptable independence of mind, pressures are soon brought to bear to help them develop a politically correct set of "news values." Much the same is true in academia, Chomsky observes:

To put it in the simplest terms, a talented young journalist or a student aiming for a scholarly career can choose to play the game by the rules, with the prospect of advancement to a position of prestige and privilege and sometimes even a degree of power; or to choose an independent path, with the likelihood of a minor post as a police reporter or in a community college, exclusion from major journals, vilification and abuse, or driving a taxi cab.

Given such choices, "the end result is not very surprising" (Chomsky 1982: 14). Another, "supportive," factor is "elemental patriotism" – "the overwhelming wish to think well of ourselves, our institutions and our leaders," another extension of the "moral faculty" discussed earlier (Chomsky & Herman 1988: 305).

Chomsky argues that thought control in free societies is most effectively achieved when, rather than setting down a single party line to be followed, the institutions of indoctrination set down the boundaries of acceptable opinion, and allow debate to flourish within these confines: "in a properly functioning system of propaganda," debate should not be stilled, "because it has a system-reinforcing character if constrained within proper bounds." What is essential is to set the bounds firmly. "Controversy may rage as long as it adheres to the presuppositions that define the consensus of elites, and it should furthermore be encouraged within these bounds, thus helping to establish these doctrines as the very condition of thinkable thought while reinforcing the belief that freedom reigns" (Chomsky 1989: 48).

Vietnam

Thus, in the case of the Vietnam War, the official version was that US intervention was needed to defend the Republic of South Vietnam against its aggressive, Communist, northern neighbor. When a secret US government history of the Vietnam War (the "Pentagon Papers") was leaked in 1972, those US citizens

who cared to know learned that when Washington determined on its major escalation of the war in February 1965, US intelligence knew of no regular North
Vietnamese units in South Vietnam; and five months later, while implementing
the plan to deploy 85,000 troops, there was only concern about the "increasing
probability" of such units in South Vietnam or Laos (Chomsky 1972b: 195).
"In the light of these facts," Chomsky observes, "the discussion of whether the
US was defending South Vietnam from an "armed attack" from the North – the
official US government position – is ludicrous" (1972b: 1960. Nevertheless, this
"ludicrous" assertion, converted into an unquestioned assumption, continues to
govern discussion of the Vietnam War in the United States and elsewhere in
the West. Mainstream debate turns on whether it was wise to attempt to defend
South Vietnam. The notion that the United States did not defend the people of
South Vietnam, but rather attacked them, does not figure even as a theoretical
possibility.

A Pentagon analyst, writing in the Pentagon Papers, noted that South Vietnam
was "essentially the creation of the United States" (cited in Chomsky 1982:
376n.27). This "creation" of the United States was the "legitimate local authority" which invited US military intervention. Chomsky cites the observation
of the London *Economist* in connection with Afghanistan, "an invader is an
invader unless invited in by a government with a claim to legitimacy." He comments, "outside the world of Newspeak, the client regime established by the
United States had no more legitimacy than the Afghan regime established by
the USSR" (1987a: 225).

Orwell's Problem

The power of the US propaganda system is demonstrated by the extraordinary
uniformity of articulate US opinion with regard to Vietnam. This is another
example of what Chomsky has termed "Orwell's Problem." "Plato's Problem"
is how, given so little evidence, we know so much. "Orwell's Problem" is "the
problem of explaining how we can know so little, given that we have so much
evidence." Orwell was concerned with the power of totalitarian systems to
instill beliefs that were firmly held and widely accepted despite being without
foundation, "and often plainly at variance with obvious facts about the world
around us." Chomsky sums up many years of work, with collaborators and
associates, by suggesting that "thousands of pages of detailed documentation"
have demonstrated "beyond any reasonable doubt" that in democratic societies
too, "the doctrines of the state religion are firmly implanted and widely believed,
in utter defiance of plain fact, particularly by the intelligentsia who construct
and propagate these doctrines" (1986: xxv, xxvi).

Throughout his career, Chomsky has insisted that "the level of culture that
can be achieved in the United States is a life-and-death matter for large masses

of suffering humanity" (1971a: 249). The level of honesty and decency in US society – the commitment of the general public to the weak form of Enlightenment values – can restrain US interventionism. The more that the general public pierces the fog of propaganda and comes to understand the realities of US foreign policy, the more vocal and widespread is the dissent, and the more constrained US policy-makers become, sometimes with enormous benefits for potential victims in far-off lands. Furthermore, unless and until the general public is able to break free from "brainwashing under freedom," hopes for a revitalized left-wing movement able to replace present institutions with more humane alternatives must be rather dim. Therefore, Chomsky urges, "For those who stubbornly seek freedom, there can be no more urgent task than to come to understand the mechanisms and practices of indoctrination" (1987a: 136). Luckily, all that is required for "intellectual self-defence" is "ordinary common sense," and "a willingness to look at the facts with an open mind, to put simple assumptions to the test, and to pursue an argument to its conclusion" (1977b: 5). Chomsky observes that "dispelling the illusions is just part of organizing and acting," "not something you do in a seminar or in your living room."[10]

Moving towards the fulfilment of Humboldt's classical liberal ideals in libertarian socialist forms, we must strengthen the hold of some rather weaker Enlightenment values (rationality, honesty, decency, and so on) in Western society, exposing and rejecting the use and misuse of "free market" values as ideological weapons. It is unclear whether there will ever be any unification of Chomsky's two sets of contributions to modern culture in a "science" of essential human nature, but what is clear is that there is a consistency and integrity to Chomsky's work in these different fields. There is an underlying and unifying respect, as Humboldt puts it, "a sense of the deepest respect for the inherent dignity of human nature, and for freedom, which alone befits that dignity" (Chomsky 1973b: 177).

12   The individual, the state, and the corporation

James Wilson

> Structures of governance tend to coalesce around domestic power, in the last
> few centuries, economic power.
>
> (Chomsky 1996d: 178)

Introduction

This chapter explores Chomsky's political morality by focusing on his ideas
about the individual, the corporation, and the state. This presentation is no
substitute for reading Chomsky himself. His propositions become far more
convincing upon studying the historical record he has assembled, a dismaying
collection which reveals how the actions and rationalizations of the ruling class
are remarkably predictable (at least by the standards of any social science).

I will follow Chomsky's approach of focusing on the United States to understand the interlocking relationships between state and private power. For more
than three decades, he has relentlessly pursued the task of documenting the
American political system's effects on its own citizenry and other nations. He
provides so many facts to support his claims and verify his predictions that
even the reader who ultimately rejects his analysis is likely to emerge less than
enthralled with most American foreign and domestic policies and more skeptical of how government officials and the media present these decisions to the
public. For instance, the idea of an idealistic, naïve United States easily manipulated by ruthless, clever foreigners is a sentimental myth. Far closer to the
truth is the fear Simon Bolivar expressed in 1822: "There is at the head of this
great continent a very powerful country, very rich, very warlike, and capable of
anything" (cited in Chomsky 1993d: 142; see also Wilson 2002).

Like most social critics, Chomsky has found it easier to criticize than to fully
develop persuasive alternatives. For many of us, his vision of anarchosyndicalism or libertarian socialism seems excessively optimistic. But for those of us
who believe that the human race can – indeed must – radically improve its social
practices, if only to survive, the structure of Chomsky's critique provides some
of the means necessary to develop a humane alternative to the existing order.
Imbedded in Chomsky's political writings are not just numerous expressions of

outrage at the injustices of Western societies, but also indications of the values and institutions necessary to create a more decent world.

The ideal and the individual

It is a commonplace that we know very little about ourselves. Chomsky puts a particular gloss on this when he notes that the science of human nature is little advanced:

> We don't know anything about human nature. If we're rational we know that it exists and undoubtedly there are very powerful biological constraints on the way we think, what we do, what we conceptualize, what we imagine and our fears and hopes, etc. But about what they are, you can learn more from a novel than from the sciences. You operate on the basis of your hopes. (Chomsky & Barsamian 1992: 354)

So while we can assume that our biology defines our nature, and while (contrary to the quotation) we do as scientists know a *little* about that nature – we have sciences of language and human vision, for example – there is clearly much more for scientists to learn about that nature and the *constraints* or *limitations* it puts on what we can think and do. The emphasis is on "constraints" and "limitations" because a science of human nature can speak to what "enters into" the choices we make and the thoughts we have (it can tell us about our conceptual tools), but it does *not* causally explain our particular choices or our behavior. It doesn't tell us how to "operate." The science of human nature is thus no science of human action; it certainly is not a "behavioral science." It is limited to determining the processes every person uses to make decisions.

As Chomsky suggests in his discussion of the creative aspect of language use (1966, 1988b, 1996a,b, 2002a), science does not have and likely cannot construct the tools (concepts) to deal with human choice and creativity. That is why crucial aspects of what it is to be a person – an individual's free will and the specific history of actions that such freedom engenders – are opaque to scientific investigation, now and probably forever. This has a bearing on what it means to be an individual. Chomsky, like Descartes, thinks of the person as an intellect associated with a will that freely chooses its course of action: humans are "free agents" who probably have a corresponding "instinct for freedom." In other words, any political/moral conception of "human nature" cannot be reduced to mathematical or biological models that can accurately predict future actions.

Another element is reflected in his respect for "the common man" and his related defense of full democracy – a democracy wherein all individuals are empowered to participate actively in *all* matters of concern to them, including economic and market choices. Chomsky's political views are compatible with the science of human nature which – even in its present, immature, state – clearly indicates that humans have readily available to them at an early age the conceptual materials they need to understand political, economic, and social issues and then make political choices. What we know about human beings (as we have seen in Chomsky's solution to the problem of explaining how children acquire languages so quickly and easily) indicates that everyone – every human, without regard to culture, history, training, background, wealth, etc. – has, or can easily acquire, the conceptual tools needed to understand the motivations and projects of others (whether acting as individuals or groups), assess the value and effects of those projects on their own interests, and make choices. Everyone has "Cartesian common sense" (1977c). Using this form of understanding, we chat, speculate, describe, soliloquize, wonder, conjecture . . . In gossip and thought, planning and advising, we complain about others, assess the chances of favorite sport teams, and criticize the policies of government and corporation. The shift from this scientific description of a mental power in all individuals to Chomsky's commitment to democratic principles should be obvious, even if it is a transition from an objective understanding to a normative conclusion. Cartesian common sense provides us all with the tools to deal with any political issue and, Chomsky holds, everyone ought to be given the opportunity to make decisions about the full range of human affairs.

Still another element in Chomsky's view of the individual – related to both of the factors mentioned above – is the postulate that the use of authority of any sort to control another or reduce their autonomy needs justification. The scientific fact of commonsense conceptual equality supports the normative requirement that the powerful must provide good reasons for imposing their views on others. Thus, the exercise of the authority of parents over children, instructors over students, generals over soldiers, priests over parishioners, corporations over workers, and states over populations all require justification. Sometimes authority satisfies that burden of proof. Chomsky points out that it is not difficult to defend a grandparent's restraining a grandchild from running into a busy street (Burchill & Chomsky 1998: 13). But in many cases – and especially when dealing with adults where their economic and political interests are involved – it may be very difficult. The principle that authority needs justification is one of the roots of Chomsky's anarchism or libertarianism.

A final element in Chomsky's conception of the individual is his (surely uncontroversial) assumption that individuals survive and thrive best when they live and cooperate with others in communities. Individuals need communities not only for support at early stages of development and for fulfilling cooperative projects (such as working together to make diesel engines), but also for all the data that are crucial to cognitive development, including the development of language. And the tools needed for cooperation and life in a community are by virtue of their biology built into everyone. We have the built-in cognitive equipment that facilitates love, friendship, sympathy, and support. People have something like what Hume called a "moral sense," a capacity not only to

understand the motivations, thoughts, and feelings of others, but also to sympathize with and put oneself in another's place. This is another premise underlying
Chomsky's syndicalism or socialism.

Returning to the quotation, some readers might be puzzled by Chomsky's
assertion that when it comes to comprehending the "very powerful biological
constraints on the way we think, what we do, what we conceptualize, what we
imagine and our fears and hopes," we can "learn more [about what they are
and how they affect our actions] from a novel than from the sciences." Better
than any other art form, the novel mimics the chatter of human consciousness
through the author's voice as well as the characters' thoughts. Because all of
us have "Cartesian common sense," we can understand the actions of ourselves
and others by putting ourselves in others' places. We "get inside" the characters'
minds, observing that they feel and react in familiar ways. Novels allow us to
do this in a focused, relatively uninvolved way. We appreciate and assess the
motivations, decisions, and choices that the novelist's characters make. This
focused exercise of the full range of our native cognitive capacities without
direct involvement provides a more fruitful study of "the way we think, what
we do, what we conceptualize, what we imagine and our fears and hopes" than
that offered by the findings of linguistics and the theory of vision or the simplistic
and skewed models of choice and rationality that permeate contemporary social
sciences. Particularly odious and misleading is the current obsession with a
simple and materialistic conception of "rationality" that assumes we always
choose to maximize benefits in the form of goods and profits for ourselves.
Quite simply, no simple model or theory of choice and motivation illuminates
as much as a good novel.

We must recognize the truth of the Aristotelian insight that in practical affairs
people ultimately rely on a rich form of "practical reason"; they intuitively
choose between competing sets of arguments that support (but never logically
"prove") different courses of action (Aristotle 1984: 1805). Almost by definition, this conception of intuition is elusive, involving contributions from each
person's unique character, predispositions, experiences, perceptions, beliefs,
understanding of circumstances, combined with and processed by – somehow –
an underlying human nature. Practical decision-making includes all political
thought and activity and it is fundamentally different than scientific and mathematical reasoning. Most of us would agree that humans should treat each other
decently, but such a statement is nothing like the assertion of a mathematical
principle. And when we try to decide about how to be fair in a specific case –
how to distribute goods among a group of people, for example – we are unlikely
ever to find the sort of consensus that mathematicians achieve when they offer
proofs of theorems.

All the above supports Chomsky's belief that every person has "an instinct
for freedom" (1992b: 335)[1] combined with a Humean "moral sense" (Rai 1995:
108). By positing such moral premises, Chomsky is proposing his own theory

of human operations, even if he is uncertain of their scientific validity. Thus the libertarian belief in the free and creative agent combines with the recognition of a moral assumption to create a principle resembling Kant's universalist humanitarianism: each of us should treat our fellow humans, who by all available evidence have the same amazing levels of perception, feeling, and understanding as ourselves, as equal moral agents – as ends, not as "mere instruments" for personal gain and pleasure (Chomsky 1993d: 288n.4).

So how do these premises and distinctions influence particular social practices? Unsurprisingly, Chomsky admires the libertarian-romantic Wilhelm von Humboldt (Chomsky 1993d: 19), who observed "It is the prosecution of some single object, and in striving to reach it by the combined application of his moral and physical energies, that the true happiness of man, in his full vigor and development, consists" (Humboldt 1993: 3–4). This kind of fulfillment can only arise when an individual has the opportunity to choose a particular goal and when the path to that goal offers a variety of situations: "Even the most free and self-reliant of men is hindered in his development, when set in a monotonous situation" (Humboldt 1993: 10). Workplace monotony and lack of autonomy are far too often the rule and not the exception. Personal productivity – potentially the most important area in which a person can express his or her autonomy while finding the satisfactions of life in a community – is usually under autocratic control. Echoing Adam Smith in the *Wealth of Nations*, Chomsky warns of the human costs accompanying the economic benefits of division of labor and "wage slavery" in autocratic structures that minimize or remove worker choice and participation. Only governmental control and action can eliminate such autocratic institutions to guarantee the worker's full participation in the workplace (Smith 1076: 303).

Reflecting human beings' need to exercise choice and to associate, Chomsky's ideal form of social organization is based on his view of the individual as a creature that needs to be creative and to freely associate with others for the fulfillment of common aims. Thus, for Chomsky, the ideal form of social organization is one that minimizes external authority (anarchism) and allows for free association of individuals (syndicalism). The result, which he calls "libertarian socialism" or "anarchosyndicalism," maximizes the opportunity to exercise autonomy, freedom, and creativity on the one hand, while finding friendship, solidarity, and love, on the other.

It seems unlikely that anything like Chomsky's anarchosyndicalist form of political organization can be fully realized. This criticism differs from that which might be offered by a neoliberal who makes (apparently) flawed assumptions about human nature. Neoliberals generally posit that humans seek to accumulate as many goods as they can and to dominate others (Chomsky 1996b). These features aptly characterize the aims of corporations, but not moral agents, unless they are pathological. The first claim – that people have an intrinsic need to accumulate as much as possible – is patently false. The second – that all people need to dominate others – is dubious, at best. Evidence that people seek to dominate, such as that reputedly offered by anthropological study of males in the Yanamamo tribe in Central America, or by studies of Igorot tribespeople, does not prove the case: among other things, it focuses on males, and males during specific phases of growth, not all people at all times. In favor of Chomsky's universalist position, on the other hand, there is a mass of historical, anthropological, and acquisition data. For example, there is good evidence that even very young children have an innate conception of fairness and that they find self-justification necessary whenever they act unfairly (Burchill & Chomsky 1998: 9). As noted above, Chomsky does not think we know enough about human nature to be confident of either polar position. But surely we know enough to recognize that neoliberalism's narrow assumptions about our fundamental needs are not just wrong, but pathological.

The case for some degree of hierarchy and institutionalized authority is based on five observations. One is that conflicts perpetually arise between humans concerning ownership, exchange, assault, affront, distribution of goods, and the like. Experience shows that resolution of these kinds of conflicts is usually most effective when it is performed by neutral third parties backed up with the authority to enforce their solution. People have a hard time reaching fair outcomes when they are personally involved in a dispute. Third-party dispute resolution requires at least some kind of state-vested hierarchy and, for enforcement, a form of authority and power assigned to individuals playing institutional roles that are constitutionally fixed and vested in a government. Second, management of complex institutions, including workplaces and industries, requires special talents and developed skills that take education, experience, and effort to develop. If so, some form of decision-making authority must be accorded to specific individuals. For better and for worse, lawyers and judges justify their authority in part upon their expertise gained through deep immersion in the legal system, a process that enables them to "think like a lawyer." Because both conflict resolution and specialization of management require vesting authority in specific individuals playing specific roles, it is not clear, at least to me, that something like Chomsky's bottom-up anarchosyndicalist form of social organization could be instituted. Third, there is the matter of efficiency: a form of organization in which individuals are randomly rotated through positions is likely to be inefficient. Individuals would have to learn to play their roles and would likely find that they have become good at it just about the time a new person takes over. Next, Chomsky's approach seems internally inconsistent; there needs to be some external authority (which violates any vision of pure anarchy) to check potential abuses by any anarchosyndicalist institutions. Finally, it is hard to refute neoliberal assumptions completely; history has shown again and again that many people are prone to aggression and greed, just as history contains innumerable instances of compassion. Such a mixed view of human nature prevents me from embracing pure forms of either neoliberalism or anarchism.

However, I have far fewer worries if one treats Chomsky's anarchosyndicalism as what he has called a "vision." As an ideal, even if not realizable, it serves as a measure to judge whether our current society meets the fundamental human needs of freedom and solidarity that Chomsky's Enlightenment view of human beings endorses. It can also help us decide what we should do to make our society approach the ideal.

Chomsky on the corporation and the state: an overview

Humans are, as Aristotle said, "political animals." Individual human beings are not self-sufficient, nor are their natures fully satisfied, unless they find recognition, love, solidarity, and friendship from others. In early life they need some sort of family structure to provide nurture, offer a wide range of experience, and – in certain respects – training during a lengthy, vulnerable childhood. Later, they increasingly require recognition of their creative activities from others, along with the material, social, and individual benefits of organized forms of labor that allow individuals to develop their specific talents and skills in the production of goods and services. The forms of organization labor takes can, and over history have, changed. In current, industrialized societies, autocratic corporations are the predominant form used to supervise labor. Unsuprisingly, Chomsky's historically informed critique of the corporation commingles with his view of the state.

States have mutated over history. Aristotle's small city-states, which required citizens to directly participate in legal, defense, welfare, and administrative matters, no longer exist. In current states, there is little except sentiment and propaganda left of the notion that citizens should fully participate in the government's legal, social, and administrative operations. Private corporations play a central, ever-increasing, role – indirectly through the control of transient capital and directly in the United States through campaign contributions to the two major political parties. As a result, a small group of people exercise most meaningful political authority. Voting procedures, largely indistinguishable political parties, massive campaign funding, corporations given the legal right to influence campaigns, and corporate-run media provide little voice to any but the rich. Corporate lobbying plays an extraordinarily important role in influencing legislation. Transnational corporations and business-influenced transnational organizations such as the World Trade Organization (WTO), the International Monetary Fund (IMF) and the World Bank largely control all but the most powerful nations. Chomsky the anarchist would prefer to replace all these top-down authoritarian structures with democratic institutions based on fully participatory worker organizations (his syndicalism). In circumstances such as those found in largely corporate-dominated democracies such as the United States and England, however, he knows that the sole form of control of authority that most people can exercise consists of voting for representatives in local, municipal, regional, and national forms of government. Thus, in current circumstances, Chomsky the anarchist paradoxically supports efforts to *increase* the power of the state, at least where it can serve to regulate and check otherwise largely unconstrained and otherwise unaccountable corporate authority.

Chomsky's view that in current society we must build up the regulatory powers of government demonstrates how his ideal of anarchosyndicalism simultaneously criticizes the status quo and provides alternatives. State authority is justified when it prevents autocratic authority that is not responsible to the populace and subsequently overwhelms the populace's autonomy and capacity to freely and fully associate with one another. Some defensive forms of military action can also be justified, although Chomsky maintains there is no evidence whatsoever to warrant the United States's military interventions in such places as Iraq, the Kosovo conflict, Vietnam, or Afghanistan. Generally speaking, state power or authority – particularly state military action – must be checked by requiring it to satisfy a heavy burden of justification. Institutions and practices cannot be defended solely by dogma; they can be determined to be illegitimate based on their inability to meet the needs of individuals. He also requires that every powerful institution be regulated internally by meaningful democracy, which consists of popular association, action, and control of all aspects of the institution, including management. These few, basic procedural and substantive requirements demand that we continually evaluate a government and other forms of institutional authority by asking such empirical questions as: how decently does the institution treat each individual member (including those "aliens" unofficially affiliated with but nevertheless profoundly affected by that society)? How are wealth and power distributed? How much choice do all people have in pursuing their chosen goals? How monotonous is their work? Which of those individuals subject to the institution have meaningful, adequate rights that protect them from violence and from private and/or state tyranny?

Chomsky (1996b) distinguishes between his long-term anarchistic "vision" and shorter term "goals." The latter range from exposing continuing oppression, eliminating the use of replacement workers (Chomsky & Barsamian 1998: 62), extending health benefits to all people (Chomsky & Barsamian 1994: 271–308), to enforcing basic human rights everywhere on the planet (Chomsky 1999f). He rejects the view that people must suffer now in order to become receptive to revolution later, a ruthless Leninist argument that raises the specter of a replacement ruling class's basing its legitimacy upon an alleged desire to help the people after they have accepted their place as subordinates. On the immediate level, Chomsky advocates political reforms that are as incremental as those sought by the remnants of the left wing of the US Democratic Party – slowly improving society through non-violent (Chomsky & Barsamian 1998: 139), democratic action.

The corporation

One of Chomsky's intermediate goals is to eliminate or at least reduce the private power of the wealthy few, a perpetual threat to stable and healthy societies. (He is particularly fond of quoting Adam Smith's "vile maxim" of "the masters of mankind": "All for ourselves, and nothing for other people" (1996a,b: 77)). He finds the current system of state corporate capitalism "illegitimate" (1999c: 146) and motivated by "inherent malice." Corporations are instituted to maximize profit and increase the power of the wealthy, not to serve the welfare of all individuals. In this system, corporations are immortal "legal persons" that have almost all the rights guaranteed to humans – short-lived moral persons. These rights are exercised to maximize profit. It is clear that the average citizen has far less power than the corporate executive who can demand a meeting with politicians and then exercise influence by threatening to withdraw future campaign donations. To Chomsky, the status of corporations as persons is an illegitimate legal fiction: "it's hardly clear why such institutions should have any rights at all" (1999c: 148).

Chomsky believes contemporary capitalism rests upon a dangerous ideology, a secular religion supported by a mythology for which there is little or no evidence. Consider, for example, corporate America's commitment to "free enterprise." Over two hundred years ago, Adam Smith warned that the corporate form of economic organization allows particular interests to combine forces to regulate prices. Chomsky concluded: "The pretence that corporations are necessary for the better government of trade, is without any foundation" (1999c: 148). Under this system, "efficient" means obtaining enough power within a particular market through financial profits to become immune from direct competition and to demand substantial governmental subsidies. To a significant degree, the economic concept of "economies of scale" now denotes "immunities from market forces" and "intimidation and control of employees." The 1998 merger of Mobil and Exxon demonstrates there is no limit to corporate efforts to concentrate wealth and power. Such concentration of power helps coordinate the global market; it is hard for the titans of industry to convene if there are too many titans. This process places the fate of the planet in fewer and fewer hands, hands completely unaccountable to the average person except through a person's very limited capacity to "vote with dollars."

A little over a century ago, the American diplomat John Hay described the United States as "of the corporations, by the corporations, and for the corporations" (quoted in LaFeber 1967: 17). John Dewey, in turn, lamented the shadow that big business cast over American culture (Chomsky 1999c: 146). Except for the Depression and its aftermath, the state has increasingly become capitalism's best tool, particularly in the US. Chomsky has argued for years that the Pentagon has little to do with national security, but everything to do with profit (1993d: 93). By pouring money into "defense," American taxpayers have financed advanced research into emerging technologies that are presented as having some relationship to military needs. Once those products have been refined to the level that they can be profitable, whether as arms sales (in which the US leads the world) or commercial transactions like the development of the Internet, they are shifted over to well-connected parts of the private sector. The profits are not returned to the taxpayer whose funds made them possible, but are funneled to the corporate sector. There are many examples of taxpayer aid that enriches the corporation. The National Institute of Health, like the Pentagon, directs subsidies for research to pharmaceutical companies that profit from this public largesse. When the US gives foreign aid, it places conditions on its disbursement, requiring the recipient government to purchase American goods. Corporations receive "corporate welfare" in the form of tax breaks, exceptions to regulatory principles, and lax enforcement of law.

Governmental discretion in its use of domestic force also benefits the wealthy. For instance, the Internal Revenue Service spends a great deal of its budget chasing after the working class's underreporting to gain an "earned income tax credit" while steadily reducing its oversight of wealthy taxpayers' returns. A large part of the domestic expenditure of the "war on drugs" budget consists not of efforts to improve conditions among the impoverished but increased police and prison expenditures. The targets of these expenditures are drug users and petty thieves – particularly those who are black – even though a large proportion of drug users are white, middle- and upper-class individuals. In contrast, there is little scrutiny of corporate theft, such as consumer fraud, corporate accounting shenanigans, and antitrust violations, and little is done about corporate violence in various forms – unsafe working conditions, dangerous products, and environmental contamination. When Congress makes a few minor reforms in response to the Enron/Worldcom scandals, the inadequately funded Securities and Exchange Commission subsequently diluted those efforts by watered-down regulations and lax enforcement. In recent years in the US, companies have been given increased access to low-wage prison labor, providing a pool of cheap tax-subsidized labor that requires no benefits. Industry profits from increased prison populations in another way too, of course: increased populations necessitate the private construction and even maintenance of high-cost prisons.

The wealthy control the state in various ways, both directly and through their corporate institutions. Lobbying and campaign financing are obvious examples. Both are difficult to control. The increasing clamor in the US for campaign reform, would, even if instituted, not eliminate the power of the rich. When

George Bush I was President, his son obtained many business "opportunities." After the first President Bush retired, he quickly obtained profitable employment in the private sector. It is important to remember that the wealthy have had inordinate influence over American politics since the country's inception. Equally difficult to regulate is the ruling class's primary instrument of control, the well-entrenched corporate-run media. Whether it be drumming up hatred for international villains (often servants of the American Empire who have forgotten their places, such as Saddam Hussein), inundating the populace with propaganda to reinforce the idea that the purpose of the corporate enterprise is to serve, and even redeem, the individual through consumption, or refusing to present different viewpoints, private media have become the primary "doctrinal institution" (Chomsky 1996d: 162) for control of the populace. Note that for this purpose it is not necessary to persuade the electorate to vote for a particular candidate or even to vote at all. It is enough if people become convinced that there is little that average individuals can do. Judging by voter opinion polls and diminishing voter turnout in the US, at least, corporate America has been very successful.

Corporate control of the state also yields international benefits. State-aided corporate control of international markets is often masked under the shibboleth of "free trade," but close examination of any free-trade agreement reveals that every country attempts to maintain protective legislation for its more vulnerable, yet internally powerful, private interests. In actuality, "free trade" is power trade, in which the powerful seek state protection and powerful nation-states attempt to keep more "undeveloped" countries in their subordinate position. Chomsky provides numerous examples of neoliberalism's hypocrisy – Western nations maintain their own protective barriers while they demand that poorer nations open their borders to free trade, which allows the invasion of corporate power at the expense of the average citizen and the environment (Chomsky 1993d: 33–64). For example, Mexican farmers are being wiped out by a combination of the North American Free Trade Agreement (NAFTA) and government subsidies to United States agribusiness. Industry then benefits from cheap labor, minimal unionization, and virtually no regulatory control.

The local gentry also benefits: some of the investment capital goes to them in the form of government "aid," generous loans, and bribes. Local governments funnel cash and industry inducements towards speculation, reinvestment in the First World, and military and other expenditures to maintain control. When the local markets crash, as they invariably have under this system, it is not the wealthy elite and local government leaders who received the benefits who must then pay, but the average person who is taxed to satisfy huge international debts that "justify" even more severe economic "cures." The resulting Third World "debt" is a political construct: the wealthy countries' banks, who provide the investment capital, demand that the poor country's general population assume legal responsibility for a rapacious local leadership's poor investment decisions.

Those in the workforce suffer the greatest damage from the increasing power of corporations. Often threatened with job loss should they protest or unionize, workers perform grueling work for which they are paid less and less in terms of absolute dollars and benefits. Over a period of decades, the steady reduction in their disposable incomes, compounded by ever-increasing desires for goods (drilled into them by corporate advertising/propaganda departments), has precluded them from having sufficient time and energy to adequately raise families, participate in their communities, and become involved in the political culture through unions and community organizations. One of the elite's great advantages is the amount of time they have to organize and distribute information, whether through endless meetings, conferences, or golf outings. Meanwhile, producers are kept out of the decision-making process, reduced to the narrow roles of worker and consumer. Their political participation is limited to periodic opportunities to select a few members of the ruling class through elections, members already culled by a process of campaign fund-raising that allows the rich extraordinary access and control (Wilson 1996: 439). This electoral formality is a far cry from Tocqueville's "Democracy in America." Neither fully human under Aristotle's conception of the human as a political animal, nor happy under Humboldt's definition of satisfying work, exhausted workers can drift easily into political apathy reinforced by the bland compensations of mass culture. Immersed in television and other forms of market-oriented "mass culture" and subjected to a mediocre education (increasingly subject to corporate intrusion), many citizens become disinterested in such "boring things" as law, politics, economics, and cultural management. Soon they are either not voting or voting against their own interests, thus confirming the ruling class's belief that the average person's incapacities warrant strong leadership.

Many people find it surprising that Chomsky places little importance on the personalities of individual leaders. He argues that there are more similarities than differences among those who run powerful public and private institutions, because the leaders feel both internal pressures and external market forces that reduce their discretion to accumulating more power for their institution pursuant to its enduring agenda. Such ruthlessness tends to require and attract ruthless individuals. Chomsky thinks that instead of creating a list of villains and heroes, it is better to study the system's underlying purposes. Its dehumanizing constraints are particularly noticeable in the corporate arena, affecting everyone – managers, investors, and workers. If a CEO actually wants to dramatically improve the conditions of the company's workforce, a goal that invariably costs money, the shareholders would probably see that he or she is fired. At the least, a more ruthless rival would probably purchase the relatively progressive corporation to eliminate its alleged "inefficiencies." The market is interested only in profit: Wall Street downgrades any company that does not have – or is seen to have excellent prospects of having – a competitive return on equity. Thus allegedly impersonal, apolitical, and rational "market forces" preclude major improvements in the workplace. Mutual funds must show a profit, so they buy stock only in those companies that return handsome profits. And the individual, cut out of the insider trading where much of the real wealth is distributed, must contend with a system that steadily reduces public services through "privatization" (as, for example, in education and government pensions[2]). The individual is thereby also driven to seek out the investments that are most likely to maximize return.

Chomsky has characterized corporations as "private tyrannies" or "totalitarian" institutions (Chomsky & Barsamian 1996: 153). These shocking terms accurately describe the constitutional structure of private corporations: power moves from the top to the bottom. Those who work at the lower levels of the corporation have no representation at the highest levels. Legally, they have no more access to these institutions' decision-making than the local community, the state, or the populace in general. Only the shareholders, generally consisting of a mixture of small individual investors and large corporate entities whose structures and ideologies are similar to those of the corporations they own, can demand some accountability – although their power in this regard is determined solely by wealth because it is based on the number of shares they own. In the absence of protests by shareholders or the Board of Directors, the CEO effectively holds legislative, executive, and adjudicatory powers, a concentration of power that James Madison once called "the very definition of tyranny" (Madison: *Federalist* no. 47). The typical CEO determines company policy, executes that policy, and decides which underlings have not adequately complied with that policy. On a daily level, the corporate culture can approach totalitarianism. Admittedly, some corporations are more tolerant and casual than others, but that tolerance can be retracted at any moment. Furthermore, an easy-going atmosphere can further advance corporate aims: many high-tech companies don't care how people dress as long as they work over sixty hours per week.

Many individual leaders of particular corporations will make such serious mistakes that they will destroy their previously potent companies, but most will use their power well enough to keep the overall system working. Collectively, private corporations are very good at maximizing profit. Those profits constitute an ever-growing source of capital, which enables the corporations to purchase more goods and services from both the private and public sectors. One of the major problems faced by the worker-owned factories that Chomsky advocates is their likely inability to compete effectively against single-minded corporate entities. Humane institutions of production face the same dilemma as anarchistic political societies contending with more aggressive rivals. Progressive systems may provide better long-term solutions for most of the populace, but they are vulnerable to predators. An anarchosyndicalist factory that cares about its workers will not be as financially strong in a "market"-driven society as its authoritarian rivals focused on the short term. The powerful drive out the decent, forcing a person either to try to get rid of all the power at once (a very unlikely and risky enterprise with unforeseeable effects) or to accept the status quo. Capitalist market norms also pressure successful worker-run organizations into either selling out or exploiting outside workers to maintain profit margins.

Dismantling corporate power and reducing concentrated wealth are just steps toward Chomsky's greater vision of a humane mix of anarchy, socialism, libertarianism, and democracy. One need not accept his longer-term anarchistic vision of eliminating the state to learn from him. Some believe that some sort of elite hierarchy is both inevitable (based upon differences in individual skills, fortunes, and motivations) and even desirable (to produce everything from stimulating art to good health care). As a reluctant defender of the need for some degree of elite power, I think that the more realistic solution is to constrain "the few" so that they cannot abuse their supplemental amount of power by plundering the majority. For those who worry that worker-owned factories might be far less productive institutions than those under management who aim towards profit, a less dramatic alternative is to limit capitalism through social democratic principles, hoping to obtain capitalism's flexible, wealth-generating capacities without suffering from its more pernicious traits.

A more humane political culture would offer state subsidies to allow worker-run institutions the time necessary to demonstrate that they can produce desired goods without degrading the environment or becoming as oppressive as the traditional private corporation (even if they never become as "efficient" or "profitable"). Such experimentation should not be dismissed as an unprecedented interference with the "free market" or as "socialism" – there is not much of a free market, particularly at the corporate level. Corporations are major recipients of public largesse. In particular, the accounting methods behind "profitability" need to be revisited. "Profit" currently is limited to the amount of wealth a corporation has managed to accumulate within corporate-internal accounts. Other interests' social expenses are excluded. For instance, a corporation might increase its profits by ten million dollars if it moves a factory from one city to another while simultaneously inflicting fifty million dollars of damage on a local community. But if the workers own the factory, it would not be moved and there would be less overall social cost. Moreover, corporations usually relocate because the new community is offering tax incentives, greater freedom from environmental constraints, and the like – resulting in avoidable short- and long-term damage to the population that "benefits" from the move. Very often, the total received benefit to the community in the form of wages and tax revenues does not equal, let alone exceed, the amount of corporate welfare provided to entice the corporation to relocate.[3] Including the costs of such "externalities" in private corporations accounts would reveal that they are by no means as efficient as they claim to be.

Capital mobility is the major corporate weapon used to reduce wages and extort state subsidies. Reducing capital mobility would weaken private power, increase public power at the local and national levels, and support alternatives based upon more cooperative, community-benefiting norms. As Chomsky and others have pointed out, this is not a radical proposal. Until recently, it was an accepted economic principle. The economist John Maynard Keynes recognized that free-flowing capital undermines civilized welfare states. Keynes successfully advocated imposing major constraints on the flow of international capital by creating the Bretton-Woods system. These constraints had a major effect on the global market until President Nixon opted for "open markets." It is not coincidental that the average American worker's income improved dramatically from the end of World War II until the early 1970s. Since then, there has been virtually no real increase.

The state

The Marxist vision has been partially validated: a ruling elite has relied upon a materialistic, pseudo-scientific ideology with worldwide ambitions to wither the state. The only problem is that the state is being replaced by a paradise for investors and managers, not workers. Acting both individually and collectively as members of an international capital market, corporations are creating a rival sovereign within each nation-state and an even more imposing worldwide system above each nation-state. In 1983, Harry Gray, the CEO of United Technologies described corporate utopia as "a worldwide business environment that's unfettered by government interference," such as "packaging and labeling requirements" and "inspection procedures" to protect consumers (cited in Chomsky 1996d: 163). According to him, government should be reduced to two roles: providing corporate subsidies and protecting the wealthy from domestic and foreign threats. As long as the US government fulfills its role in the partnership, it can count on the privately owned media to support it through biased news reporting that carefully documents every transgression by official opponents but scarcely discusses the atrocities of Israeli politicians (Chomsky 1983: 31) or South American dictators (Chomsky & Herman 1988: 37–86) who support the United States' leadership.

Within every country, but especially the United States, big business is furthering its agenda of redirecting public power so that its only obligation is to support big business (Chomsky & Herman 1988: 120–1). To provide further profits for excess capital, necessary social services – such as schools, basic medical care, prisons, and sanitation – are turned into opportunities for corporations through the allegedly efficient process of privatization. Even though the vast majority of US citizens do not know the actual figures on how much less a single-payer national health system – like that in Canada – costs to operate, they have long wanted single-payer health care because they believe every American should receive basic health care (Chomsky & Barsamian 1994: 226; Navarro 1994). But government listens to corporations much more than to people. The Clintons' "progressive" health care proposal included massive subsidies to large insurance companies to continue the inefficient, but lucrative, practice of bogging doctors and patients down in paperwork. The Democrats appear to be somewhat humane only because their rivals, the Republicans, make little pretense of caring for the average person. The Republicans obtain their twenty-plus percentage of the electorate (which is all it takes to win with so few people interested in voting) by pandering to religious and racist extremists. To avoid actual control by these groups, which often have agendas opposed to increasing the wealth of corporations, country club Republicans donate millions to their favorites, or even to Democrats, who now resemble the conservative wing of the 1950s Republican party. The resulting two-party system offers no room for genuine reform.

For decades, the rich and powerful have argued that the government, which they largely control, is inefficient, socialist, or worse. The media they control strips politics of its significance by reducing it to personalities and scandal. As Chomsky notes, all this might seem surprising until one recognizes that it is in the interests of the rich to denigrate public power. First, the government remains the most powerful potential threat to the corporations, just as the federal government was once the greatest threat to Southern slavery. Second, the wealthy do not completely control the government, especially in formal political democracies like the US (Chomsky 1987b: 114) where, although insufficient, the electoral process permits people some access to power if they are willing to organize and participate. In addition, formal state democracies have relatively little coercive power over their citizens; persuasion must be the primary tool of social control (Chomsky 1997b: 114).[4] Private power must use its doctrinal institutions to convince the populace that there is no hope in politics and that self-validation is available only through consumption. Private power's flagrant abuse of its control of the government works to its advantage; disgusted by the pervasive corruption, many people retire to their private life of family and friends. The field is left open to those who are ambitious and greedy, willing to serve in the government as go-betweens between private power and a surly public.

There are, of course, limits to corporate consensus. Chomsky observes that corporate America often disagrees over particular issues: one segment sees the utility of some governmental regulation, if only to preserve their own interests

(Chomsky & Barsamian 1996: 149–51). And there has long been a portion of the ruling class willing to share some of the wealth to guarantee political stability. The problem with relying on this kind of noblesse oblige, however, is that it can always disappear. Aristotle (*Politics* 2010) warned of the elite's insatiable greed and lust for power: "The fact is, that the greatest crimes are caused by excess, not by necessity." For example, many members of the American plutocracy wants to reduce Internal Revenue Service audits of taxpayers in high income brackets, turning the United States into a Russian-type system where only wage earners pay their legal share of taxes.[5]

The wealthy have not been satisfied with using corporate proxies, market muscle, and campaign donations to seize effective control of the United States government. They have joined with their colleagues throughout the world to form a "de facto world government"[6] to ensure the perpetual triumph of capitalism (Chomsky 1993d: 51). The list of institutions promoting this goal grows steadily: the United Nations (Chomsky & Barsamian 1998: 114–17), the World Bank, the International Monetary Fund (IMF), the North American Free Trade Agreement (NAFTA), the General Agreement on Tariffs and Trade (GATT), and the World Trade Organization (WTO). Chomsky helped spread the news about the proposed Multilateral Agreement of Investment, which would have made capital flow immune from governmental regulation for many years (Chomsky 1999c: 135). If it had been instituted, no one could have restrained capital from entering countries with egregious human rights violations (1999c: 149). Investors and corporations could have sued countries for creating environmental regulations that restrain the investors' "enjoyment" of their "foreseeable" profits (1999c: 141). The WTO would have had legislative, executive, and adjudicatory functions, staffed by private parties, with the power to trump the laws of sovereign states. Nor is there any reason to think that the rich would have stopped with these "reforms."

Faced with such overwhelming power, both private and public, it is understandable that so many citizens prefer apathy to despair. After all, there is more to life than politics. But as long as there is hope and the possibility of alternative institutions, dissent offers great satisfactions. Chomsky argues that labor unions and labor-based political parties must be part of this process. Until unions organize the lowly paid, develop formidable political action groups, and provide money and political organization to offset the disproportionate advantages of the rich, it is hard to envision significant change. But the goal is not just to revive union power, which could easily be coopted again. To achieve the sort of society that will allow the full development of individual potential, the populace must demand governmental support of alternative modes of production that are not measured solely by profit.

Chomsky has provided a concrete example of an alternative that is a major step in the right direction: the Spanish worker-owned enterprise called the

"Mondragon Cooperative Corporation." In 1998, it had over five billion dollars in sales and seven billion dollars in assets within its subsidiary banking system (Chomsky & Barsamian 1994: 290–1). The management is accountable to a cooperative congress and a standing committee. The cooperative congress consists of representatives elected from among workers in all the cooperatives in the system, with larger cooperatives receiving more representatives. The congress elects seventeen of its members to the standing committee, which appoints the CEO, approves the CEO's major appointments, and is the equivalent of a board of directors. Daily management is similar to that in conventional firms, but the workers retain significant influence and control through their representative system. The bank provides significant amounts of venture capital as well as traditional consumer and business loans (Freundlich 2000). Originally protected from foreign competition by Spanish laws, Mondragon now faces serious challenges as it competes against multinational corporations more willing to sacrifice the well-being of their workers.

Chomsky does not oppose state intervention in the economy. He notes that those countries with "state-guided development," such as Japan and Korea, which have not completely subordinated their citizen's interests to the wealthy or to the global market, have done much better than those nations that have totally capitulated to corporate Washington's demand for "free trade" (Chomsky 1996d: 155). During a radio interview, a listener asked: "One of the things I've always thought, and I know this is probably not democratic, is why there is not a limitation on the amount of profit anyone can make, any corporation, any business?" Chomsky replied: "I think that [such a limit] is highly democratic, in fact. There's nothing in the principle of democracy that says that power and wealth should be highly concentrated so that democracy becomes a sham" (Chomsky & Barsamian 1994: 195). This argument, like so many others, can be traced back to Aristotle (*Politics* 2008), who feared that large disparities in income would cause political chaos by creating large numbers of poor individuals, for "poverty is the parent of revolution and crime." Aristotle recommended limits both to the amount of wealth a person would have and to the lust for more goods: "[T]he legislator ought not only to aim at the equalization of properties, but at moderation in their amounts" (*Politics* 2010).

If the world shifted from private, profit-hungry corporations to syndicates owned and managed by workers, would the state be eliminated? Chomsky points out that even if we assume that a worker-owned factory would treat most of its employees better than a private corporation would, we cannot be confident that it would act fairly toward all its employees. A majority of workers might exclude people of a certain race or ethnic origin or assign people of a certain gender to low-paying jobs. They might be indifferent to such externalities as environmental damage. Also, to produce their goods, they have to trade with other syndicates, which requires some sort of externally enforceable system of property and contracts. If Hobbes's reading of history is at all reliable, one can assume ambitious leaders will seize control of some of these syndicates by claiming, perhaps accurately, that everyone in the organization will benefit if it becomes more aggressive. Some external agency is required to stop such predatory behavior, just as antitrust provisions should be currently used to stop the incredible consolidation of capital and power within a few private corporations.

Human institutions and the environment

Chomsky tends to ground his political analysis in human needs and interests. Consider one of his criticisms of GATT and NAFTA in 1994, a charge that is equally applicable to the newer WTO: "[P] roperty and investor rights are protected in exquisite detail . . . while workers' rights are ignored, along with the rights of future generations (environmental issues)" (1996d: 164–5). Although there is little doubt that the best way to persuade humans to change their behavior is to appeal to their own interests, including the interests of their progeny, it may be necessary to acknowledge that the rest of the ecological system has worth independent of human rights. Although Chomsky recommends institutions based on the humanistic philosophies of the ancient Greeks and the Enlightenment, we also must create alternative institutions and norms that transcend the humanist tradition, which is focused on our species alone. Perhaps Chomsky is heading in this direction: his commitment to "sustainable growth" implies an economic system that can sustain both the species and the planet. In 1999, he expressed sympathy for the norms underlying vegetarianism (although continuing to eat meat). Perhaps it is bourgeois sentimentalism to try to see the world through the eyes of other animals, but it is essential to move beyond the existing pillage of both humanity and nature to a world where people treat each other decently without denuding the planet in the process. Admittedly, most of us will identify far more with the spotted owl, the harp seal, and the salmon than with the cockroach and the AIDS microbe, but there is great fulfillment in identifying with life processes beyond one's species, just as there are enduring rewards in caring for humans other than oneself.

So what does Chomsky think an individual should do? First, turn off the television for as long as possible, at least until you have read enough to determine how the elite are managing the planet. Distrust political assertions unsupported by facts and clear argument. Look at the issues from many perspectives. He suspects you will emerge from this process profoundly disturbed by the extent of systemic injustice. The next step is to liberate yourself (assuming you have an income that meets your basic needs) from the circle of consumption to permit more time for family and friends. After that, talk to others and commit yourself to some form of public action, whether union organizing, demonstrating, writing letters on behalf of political victims, or teaching someone how to read. Relearn the pleasures of working with others to make this planet a better place for the average person. Become part of an alternative world vision not based purely upon accumulation and domination. As Chomsky put it: "Pick your cause and go volunteer for a group that is working on it" (Chomsky & Barsamian 1998: 152). Above all, never give up hope – for yourself, your country, your remarkable species, your planet.

13　Noam Chomsky: the struggle continues

Irene Gendzier

Introduction

". . . no great power – not even one so selfless and beneficent as the United States – has the authority or the competence to determine by force the social and political structure of Vietnam or any other country, no right to serve as international judge and executioner" (Chomsky 1971b: 86). Noam Chomsky's position was articulated with a characteristic blend of irony and blunt eloquence in his 1971 lecture in honor of Bertrand Russell. It was accompanied by his affirmation that "the radical reconstruction of society must search for ways to liberate the creative impulse, not to establish new forms of authority."

To these guiding principles of Chomsky's political thought, a third may be added, a commitment "to penetrate the clouds of deceit and distortion and learn the truth about the world, then to organize and act to change it" (1996a,b: 131). It is both a statement of purpose and a strategy for action. It defines Chomsky's political work – his ongoing critique of US foreign policy, and his relentless exposé of "the clouds of deceit and distortion" designed to mask it. The result is a record of historical retrieval that has fundamentally altered what we know of US foreign policy. The Chomsky files testify to the power embedded in such retrieval. To engage in retrieval is to question who we are and what we know. It is to explain why we have accepted a distortion of history that is akin to its theft. And it is to face the responsibility of change.

As Chomsky's work has demonstrated, the key to understanding this distortion lies in uncovering what is concealed by privileged elites who protect their interests by deflecting public scrutiny and masking their policies by creating the "necessary illusions" that are needed in a democracy. Edward Said, in his preface to *The Fateful Triangle*, described the contrast between true accounts of policy and their counterfeit as a "protracted war between fact and a series of myths" (Chomsky 1999b: vii). It is a war for the legitimation of policy that is fought in a democracy without resort to arms, coercion or formal censorship. The elites' weapons of choice are those of ideological control operating through the collaboration of the media and compliant intellectuals who uncritically – though not unwittingly – serve the interests of the state.

The theme dominates Chomsky's work. It explains his emphasis on exposing the legitimation of policy and its roots in what Edward Bernays approvingly described as "the engineering of consent" (Chomsky 1982: 66). The manipulation of opinion is an integral part of the public policy of democratic states allied to corporate power. Those responsible, the courtiers of state and corporate power, represent a "caste of propagandists who labor to disguise the obvious, to conceal the actual workings of power, and to spin a web of mythical goals and purposes, utterly benign, that allegedly guide national policy" (1982: 86).

The consequences of their actions are far-reaching. They shape the parameters of public debate, marginalize opposition and trivialize dissent in accord with the interests of those with power and influence in government and the private sector. The implications for the domestic legitimation of US foreign policy are difficult to exaggerate. "It would have been impossible to wage a brutal war against South Vietnam and the rest of Indochina," Chomsky and Herman observed in 1988, "if the media had not rallied to the cause, portraying murderous aggression as a defense of freedom, and only opening the doors to tactical disagreement when the costs to the interests they represent became too high" (Chomsky & Herman 1988: xv). *Manufacturing Consent* offered comparable evidence for the cover-up of US policy in Central America in the 1980s. Earlier, Chomsky had pursued the question in his unmasking of US policy in the Middle East after 1967. Furthermore, the end of the Cold War, as he frequently observed, in no way altered the practice, as the examples of the coverage of the Gulf War and that concerning US policy in Kosovo indicated, and as Chomsky showed in his exposé of the self-congratulatory rhetoric of the advocates of a new "military humanism" (1999e: 8).

The betrayal of intellectuals who have a responsibility to speak the truth remains a persistent current in Chomsky's work. It reflects his view of intellectuals as a separate and privileged category, including that of "ideological managers" (1987b: 53). It is a role that is all the more revealing in states – such as the United States – where intellectuals are free to act "without undue fear of state terror, to bring about crucial changes in policy and even more fundamental institutional changes" (1985: 1). As he wrote in 1980, "if we do not like what we find when we look at the facts – and few will fail to be appalled if they take an honest look – we can work to bring about changes in the practices and structure of institutions that cause terrible suffering and slaughter" (1982: 337). Hence, the culpability of those who echo deceptive formulas "used to justify the next defense of freedom" is all the more flagrant, in Chomsky's view (1969c: 359).

It was in the midst of the Vietnam War that Chomsky argued that the time had perhaps come to conceive of such an alternative, a society "in which freely constituted social bonds replace the fetters of autocratic institutions" (1987a: 153). The humanist vision of that society reflected the origins of Chomsky's political thought in anarchism, Enlightenment philosophy, and classical liberalism, all of which helped shape his views of the state and of "predatory capitalism" – and resistance to it represented in struggles for equality and social justice.

Chomsky's critique of US policy assumed a vision in which the "sight of 'ordinary people, fighting for their liberty and independence with courage and integrity,' " might one day be realized in practice (1988a: 773). This image was taken from Rousseau, but Chomsky's view of an alternative form of society also borrowed from Bertrand Russell and John Dewey, among others. Such a society would rest, he reflected, on the ideas of equality and democracy, not those of "accumulation and domination, but independence of mind and action, free association on terms of equality, and cooperation to achieve common goals," he wrote. The impact of such ideas would be revolutionary, he maintained, because people "would share Adam Smith's contempt for the 'mean' and 'sordid pursuits' of 'the masters of mankind' and their 'vile maxim': 'All for ourselves, and nothing for other people,' the guiding principles we are taught to admire and revere, as traditional values are eroded under unremitting attack" (1996a,b: 77). The Adam Smith of conventional accounts was not the one that Chomsky cited in such interpretations. It was, on the contrary, Smith's "rather nuanced advocacy of markets," to which Chomsky referred, an advocacy based "in part on the belief that under conditions of 'perfect liberty' there would be a natural tendency towards equality, an obvious desideratum on elementary moral grounds."

The struggle against the world of "sordid pursuits" was heavily compromised, in Chomsky's view, by the postwar alliance of corporate capitalism and the state. That alliance represented the conjuncture of economic, political, and ideological systems increasingly "taken over by vast institutions of private tyranny that are about as close to the totalitarian ideal as any that humans have so far constructed" he argued (1996a,b: 71). Exposing and resisting such forces led him to adopt short-term goals obviously at odds with anarchist ideals. But Chomsky maintained that strengthening "elements of state authority" was essential to preserving the considerable achievements of classical liberalism, namely, the extension of democracy as well as civil and political liberties (1996a,b: 73). Those achievements were threatened by the resurgent neoliberalism of the post-Cold War period, with its heady endorsement of privatization and globalization.

What then is to be done? Criticized for his pervasive pessimism, Chomsky in fact has not wavered in his insistence on the possibility of social and political change through collective action, albeit action that requires clarity with respect to values as well as a supportive institutional structure. The voluntarism implicit in his outlook is reflected in the position that "socioeconomic orders are human creations, and to that extent they are subject to change," he reminded listeners in New Mexico in the winter of 2000.[1] The same conviction was articulated earlier in his belief that the "drive towards intervention, militarization, increased authoritarianism, submissiveness to the doctrinal system, and possibly eventual nuclear destruction is the result of human decisions taken within human institutions that do not derive from natural law and can be changed by people who devote themselves to the search for justice and freedom" (1982: 215). That search assumed a clear understanding of the roots of American power that was a prerequisite to making sense of the world – and to changing it. But change, in the direction of "meaningful democracy," had other prerequisites, namely, "an organizational structure that permits isolated individuals to enter the domain of decision-making by pooling their limited resources, educating themselves and others, and formulating ideas and programs that they can place on the political agenda and work to realize" (1987b: 123).

Understanding the world

From his earliest writing on the Vietnam War Chomsky sought to map American power and to identify the official "reasons of state" and their implications for US policy in Southeast Asia and, by extension, much of the Third World (1973b). The results persuaded him of the importance of identifying the postwar foundations and recurring principles and patterns of US policy. He located the evidence in theory and practice, in US internal documents and the evidence of US policy. The conformity between the two was not in doubt. What the evidence of internal sources disclosed, however, was the gap between inside talk and that designed for the public, a gap reinforced by academic apologies and media echoes of government policy. The real story, for those seeking to understand US policy, as Chomsky's work made clear, was in part to be found in official sources, records of policy planning, such as the Pentagon Papers, and the reports of think tanks dominated by US political and business elites, such as the Council on Foreign Relations with their insights into postwar policy. These sources confirmed the connections between private and public sectors, between "representatives of major corporations, banks, investment firms, the few law firms that cater to corporate interests, and the technocratic and policy-oriented intellectuals who do the bidding of those who own and manage the basic institutions of the domestic society" (1982: 91).

The influence of such sectors marked the nature of postwar US policy with its complex of economic, political, and military corollaries. At one level it involved what Chomsky termed the "first principle," the commitment to "maintain an international order in which U.S.-based business can prosper, a world of 'open societies,' meaning societies that are open to profitable investment, to expansion of export markets and transfer of capital, and to exploitation of material and human resources on the part of U.S. corporations and their local affiliates" (1987b: 6). At another, it involved the political and military ramifications of such policies in the form of the containment of radical options deemed hazardous to US interests. The results were reflected in the identification of key zones of industrial and political reconstruction that functioned as pivots of American influence and in the accompanying restoration of traditional political forces designed to assure the containment of radical change. They were illustrated in such landmark policies of the postwar decade as the Marshall Plan, the Truman Doctrine, National Security Council Memorandum 68 with its militarized vision of unrestricted rollback policies, and the less frequently cited (1947) merger of US oil multinationals in ARAMCO, with its obvious importance to global US policy, especially for the Mediterranean and Middle East.

On this and the more general question of postwar US policy and the Cold War, Chomsky broke with dominant interpretations long before the collapse of the USSR and the communist regimes of Eastern Europe. He regarded the standard explanatory use of the Cold War as entirely inadequate (see 1996d: ch.1, §4). He charged both major powers with exploiting Cold War doctrine to justify their respective policies. For the former Soviet Union, Chomsky maintained, "the Cold War has been primarily a war against its satellites" (1991: 28), a war "illustrated by tanks in East Berlin, Budapest and Prague, and other coercive measures in the regions liberated by the Red Army from the Nazis, then held in thrall to the Kremlin; and the invasion of Afghanistan, the one case of Soviet military intervention well outside the historic invasion route from the West" (1991: 20). On the domestic level in the USSR, the Cold War "served to entrench the power of the military-bureaucratic elite whose rule derives from the Bolshevik coup of October 1917." In the case of the US, on the other hand, Chomsky argued that the Cold War represented a "war against the Third World" (1991: 28). It was a war that entailed a "history of worldwide subversion, aggression and state terrorism," accompanied at the domestic level with "the entrenchment of Eisenhower's 'military-industrial complex,' " which signified a "a welfare state for the rich with a national security ideology for population control (to borrow some counterinsurgency jargon), following the prescriptions of NSC 68" (1991: 21). Grand Area foreign policy (the US using military and economic power to control markets in as large an area as possible) would be wedded to a military-industrial complex at home. Market ideology would, in effect, drive US foreign and domestic policies.

In Chomsky's analysis, the Cold War was subordinated to another, that between North and South. In his scenario, the East–West conflict did not disappear, it was redefined to underscore the Western fear of the appeal to Third World nations of the Soviet Revolution of 1917 – fear that citizens of developing nations might take their economic affairs into their own hands. The Cold War was thus integrated into the Other War, that between an industrialized North and the global South, with its "resources, cheap labor, markets, opportunities for investment" (1993d: 33). The major themes in the battle of North against South are "imperialism, neocolonialism, the North–South conflict, core versus periphery, G-7 (the leading state capitalist industrial societies) and their satellites versus the rest" (1993d: 3). Considered in broad historical perspective, the Cold War represented "an interlude in the North–South conflict of the Columbian era, unique in scale but similar to other episodes in significant respects" (1993d: 65). From this vantage point, the collapse of the USSR did not signify the end of the Cold War redefined as a war against autonomous, democratic development. The policies of the industrial powers, Chomsky pointed out in a symposium on the question, "are adapted to changing circumstances, of which the end of the Cold war is only one aspect" (1992a: 85).

Chomsky's reconceptualization of the Cold War effectively established the primacy of the struggle for resources and markets as the principal postwar objective of US policy, an objective whose implementation necessarily involved a broad array of policies with a global reach. In this context, the future of decolonization struggles aroused obvious concern, and not only in Washington. US policy-makers – as well as their British and French counterparts – viewed the emergence of nationalist movements in the Third World as a development to be managed and redirected to serve their respective interests. The results were apparent in French, British, and US policies in Asia, Africa and the Middle East, and Latin America. They were apparent in the overt and covert interventions designed to roll back efforts of nationalist, populist, and radical regimes to regain control over their own political as well as economic resources. States and societies that sought an independent course were severely punished, lest their example inspire others, as Chomsky and Herman demonstrated in *The Political Economy of Human Rights* (Chomsky & Herman 1979a,b), and as Chomsky illustrated in countless works on postwar US policy in Europe, Asia, Latin America, and the Middle East.

The evidence of US policy Chomsky compiled confirmed the recurring patterns and underlying principles of US policy at work in such dissimilar environments. It was a record completely at odds with official endorsement of self-determination and claims to promote modernization and democracy. Instead, as Chomsky's files revealed, the record of US policy involved the subversion of democracy, the undermining of independent development and the legitimation of force in the Third World, in the name of democracy, development and the rule of law in the First.

Records of intervention

Vietnam

It was the US war in Indochina, the ferocity of the US destruction of South Vietnam, the "secret war" against Laos and the infernal destruction of Cambodia, the raining of death in the absence of war, that propelled Chomsky into the role of indefatigable critic of US policy (1969b: 60–1). His writings on Vietnam have been described as "among the most valuable ever written precisely because they show[ed] so much of the war's reality at the time, far more than most of the current outpouring of books reassessing the war's meaning today" (1987a: xv).

That reality concerned the US invasion of South Vietnam in the name of anti-communism and the infliction of mass suffering through campaigns of forced relocation and resettlement justified in the name of modernization. "The American war in Indochina," Chomsky wrote in 1969, "has been based on two principles: physical destruction in areas that are beyond the reach of American troops, and the use of what are euphemistically called 'population control measures' in areas that can be occupied by American forces or the forces that they train, supply, advise, and provide with air and artillery support" (1969b: 52–3). What this meant in practice was "massacre and forced evacuation of the peasantry, combined with rigorous control over those forced under American rule." That, Chomsky argued, "is the essence of American strategy in Vietnam."

Washington moved first to support and then to replace the French when they withdrew from Indochina in 1954, the year in which Washington undermined the Geneva Accords with their promise of elections and the prospects of reunification, and moved to take control of the Ngo Dinh Diem regime which it primed in pursuit of its rollback efforts. By that time the US was already "providing about 80 percent of the costs of the war" in Indochina and was close to deploying nuclear weapons (1987a: 323). Years earlier the State Department had recognized "that Ho Chi Minh was the sole significant leader of Vietnamese nationalism, but that if Vietnamese nationalism was successful, it could be a threat to the Grand Area, and therefore something had to be done about it" (1987a: 322). Vietnam's principal threat, in short, was the feared "domino effect" of its policies. It was met in 1962 by the "bombing and defoliation in Vietnam" by the US Air Force,

part of the effort to drive several million peasants into concentration camps where they could be 'protected' from the guerrillas who, the government conceded, they were willingly supporting, after tens of thousands had been slaughtered and the United States had effectively blocked any political settlement, including the offer of the NLF (the 'Vietcong' in terms of US propaganda) to neutralize South Vietnam, Cambodia, and Laos. (1987a: 52–3)

The bombing of South Vietnam assumed a new ferocity between 1965–9. Pentagon sources revealed the deployment of "nine times the tonnage of bombing in the entire Pacific theater in World War II, including Hiroshima and Nagasaki – 'over 70 tons of bombs for every square mile of Vietnam, North and South . . . about 500 pounds of bombs for every man, woman and child in Vietnam'" (1969b: 291). The figures were incomplete insofar as their account of military action or the toll of intimidation, repression, and torture by the US-backed South Vietnamese regime, as well as the US massacres of which My Lai was but a single example of a far more widespread phenomenon.

Chomsky's response was unequivocal. "With no further information than this," he wrote referring to the above, "a person who has not lost his senses must realize that the war is an overwhelming atrocity" (1969b: 291). The position was not widely shared in the US. In fact, it was widely denounced by critics of the war, let alone its supporters. Mainstream critics of the Vietnam War remained well within the acceptable bounds of criticism, formulating their regrets in terms of the inevitable limits of American benevolence or the cost-benefit analyses of an increasingly expensive war. In such circles, as Chomsky pointed out, those who refused to accept the "fundamental axiom, namely, that the United States has the right to extend its power and control without limit, insofar as is possible," were regarded as "hysterical critics" whose irrational views were beyond debate (1969c: 333). Viewed as deviants, their real crime, as Chomsky understood, was to defy apathy and to resist and oppose US policies. The "civic culture" defended by the "secular priesthood" could not tolerate such behavior or the threat of its extension to liberation movements across the Third World, including those emerging in the Middle East and Latin America. They were tarred with the label of the "Vietnam Syndrome," reserved for those who exhibit the aversion to "massacre, aggression, and torture," that reflects a "solidarity with the victims," as Chomsky explained (1987a: 337).

Chomsky's opposition to the Vietnam War extended to his denunciation of the distortion and deceit perpetrated by government officials and their academic acolytes, supported by the media. It was in this context that he called on intellectuals "to speak the truth and to expose lies," with the knowledge that they were in a position to disclose "the lies of governments, to analyze actions according to their causes and motives and often hidden intentions" (1969c: 324). He called on universities to provide refuge to students and to assist them in defending themselves from "massive government propaganda apparatus, from the natural bias of the mass media, and . . . from the equally natural tendency of significant segments of the American intellectual community to offer their allegiance" to power (1969c: 313–14). And he urged those willing to resist to publicize "the daily evidences of barbarism, and the still more severe duty of challenging the powers – state or private – that are responsible for violence and oppression, looking forward to the day when an international movement for freedom and social justice will end their rule" (1969b: 313).

Chomsky and Herman publicized the record of barbarism beyond Vietnam and their account of US actions in Laos and Cambodia showed how firmly the US adhered to Grand Area policy. It exposed the systematic deception that accompanied US policy; its veiled and distorted images rendered its victims "unworthy," in accord with the policy of the victors (Chomsky &

Herman 1979b). It is difficult to exaggerate the importance of their analysis and documentation of this phase of US policy, or the continuing controversy it has generated. The level and consequences of US bombings of Cambodia, the human, political, and physical devastation they caused, were ignored in the US and Western media. Cambodia became a proper subject of media coverage only in the period of Khmer Rouge "murderous rule" and "atrocities," the authors noted. The legitimacy proffered was self-serving. It stopped short of confronting the impact of US bombings and its obliteration of the prospects of "social and economic progress," ignoring "the brutality of the eventual victors" (Chomsky & Herman 1979b: 219). That outcome, as Chomsky and Herman's work demonstrated, was exploited in "a retrospective justification for earlier French and American crimes in Indochina, and [facilitated] the reconstruction of Western ideology after the Vietnam trauma . . ." (Chomsky & Herman 1988: 296).

Chomsky returned to US policy in Vietnam and Indochina throughout his later works as the US wars in Asia were reshaped "to preserve the image of U.S. benevolence, always a crucial element in imperial ideology," as Chomsky and Herman wrote in their 1979 account of the postwar condition of Indochina and "the reconstruction of imperial ideology" (1979b: 10).

Latin America

Geographically distant, US intervention in Vietnam and Central America had much in common. Chomsky said as much when he questioned whether US action in Vietnam was

simply a single outburst of criminal insanity, of no general or long range significance except to the miserable inhabitants of that tortured land. It is difficult, however, to put much credence in this possibility. In half a dozen Latin American countries there are guerrilla movements that are approaching the early stages of the second Vietnamese war, and the American reaction is, apparently, comparable. (1969c: 311)

The prognosis was accurate. The Vietnam interventionist policy was, in effect, reproduced in different form and context in Central America, save that the public reaction to the Vietnam War in the US precluded support for direct US intervention in Central America, a matter of overwhelming importance, as Chomsky insisted. Instead, there were to be proxy wars, doctrinally disguised in terms of the Nixon Doctrine, the Reagan Doctrine, and other intervening doctrines that assured that the US provided military and intelligence assistance, trained local forces in counterinsurgency, manipulated and funded politicians in accord with its vision of how to stem radical change at any cost.

What marked Chomsky's accounts of US policy in Latin America was not only his documentation of the punitive history of US relations with Latin

America, as in the record of US intervention in Cuba, Panama, Mexico, Haiti, the Dominican Republic, Guatemala, Nicaragua and El Salvador, Costa Rica, Chile, Brazil, and Colombia, among other cases. It was, first, the extensive evidence of the extent to which US officials, fully cognizant of existing conditions, deliberately elected to support repressive regimes to avert those of a reformist or radical cast. And, second, it was the extent to which the media legitimized such policies by their distortions or blanket omissions of their consequences, thus effectively purging them and their victims from the record.

US policies, Chomsky argued, illustrated Washington's profound antagonism to struggles for democracy, to efforts to address issues of poverty and injustice. The lesson of US policy was that those committed to

the needs of the poor majority, or who seek to construct a political system that will not be controlled by business-based groups and a military system not linked to and dominated by the United States, are 'Castros' who must be driven to reliance on the Soviet Union by unremitting attack, subjected to terrorist violence and other pressures, and crucially, prevented from perpetrating the crime of successful development in the interest of the poor majority. (1987b: 89– 90)

US policy – under a succession of Democrat and Republican administrations – was driven, in practice, by the double commitment to assure favorable conditions of trade and investment, guarantee access to raw materials, and promote export-oriented economies, while supporting compatible political regimes – irrespective of their repressive domestic policies, whose justification in the US was invariably in anti-communist terms. The practice led to a pattern of political, military, and intelligence support, organized on a region-wide basis, with the "standardization of Latin American military organization, training, doctrine and equipment along U.S. lines" (1987b: 20). In short, US policy conformed to the dominance of the "first principle," the "Fifth Freedom," and the feared domino effect of independent and radical regimes.

The examples are too numerous to fully recite. The response of the US to the Cuban revolution (1959) is perhaps the best known. The Kennedy administration's Bay of Pigs invasion was followed by policies that made Cuba "the prime victim of international terrorism for the next 20 years, probably surpassing the rest of the world combined," Chomsky adds, "if we exclude from the category of terrorism cases that might more properly be called outright aggression, such as Israel's bombing of Lebanon with US support from the early 1970s" (1987b: 74). But there were other cases with regimes of a different cast, such as that of Dominican President Juan Bosch, ousted from power by the military with US support and then reinstated, only to be blocked once again with the support of a military coup backed by the US dispatch of marines in 1965. Bosch was "a liberal democrat, committed to reformist capitalist democracy, meaningful democracy with programs designed to serve domestic needs" (1987b: 65).

Nearly a decade earlier there was the case of US intervention in Guatemala. In 1954, one year after the Anglo-American coup that ended the political career of the Iranian Prime Minister who had dared to nationalize the Anglo-Iranian Oil Company, Eisenhower intervened in Guatemala to assure the collapse of the Arbenz regime, punished for its successful land reform policies. In Guatemala US policies leading up to 1954 resulted in the collapse of the Arbenz regime and its reformist policies, decades of impoverishment for the indigenous population through support of terror and repression at the hands of US-trained military and intelligence agents, and an estimated 200,000 deaths. Chomsky and Herman described the years that followed as those in which Guatemala "gradually became a terrorist state rarely matched in the scale of systematic murder of civilians, but its terrorist proclivities have increased markedly at strategic moments of escalated U.S. intervention" (Chomsky & Herman 1988: 72). Human rights groups during the Reagan administration documented the same phenomenon, with "the indiscriminate killing of peasants (including vast numbers of women and children), the forcible relocation of hundreds of thousands of farmers and villagers into virtual concentration camps, and the enlistment of many hundreds of thousands in compulsory civil patrols" (Chomsky & Herman 1988: 73). An estimated 100,000 civilians (1978–85) were murdered (Chomsky & Herman 1988: 75), as the Guatemalan regime crushed indigenous human rights organizations, including those committed to discovering the "disappeared," such as the Mutual Support Group (GAM) (Chomsky & Herman 1988: 80).

Between the early 1960s and 1980 El Salvador witnessed the emergence of a proliferation of grassroots organizations as well as guerrilla groups committed to turning the tide against the progressive deterioration of living conditions in a country ruled through the alliance of the landed elite and the military. The US response – accelerated by the Sandinista revolution in Nicaragua – endorsed a "preventive" military coup. It was quickly followed by a succession of intra-military struggles into which the US intervened, this time with military backing for its candidate, José Napoleon Duarte, who presided over a slaughter of some 40,000 victims when in power (1987b: 82). US military advisors followed with training and support for the air war and the establishment of intelligence networks, backed from Honduras and Panama. Their targets were the advocates of domestic reform. Signs of increased popular participation in widely supported protest movements designed to address the urgent needs of the impoverished majority, inspired alarm in Washington, where "church-based self-help groups, peasant associations, teachers unions," among other opponents of the regime, were viewed as constituting an increasingly high risk to stability. The stability was measured in terms of the interest of ruling elites; the risks were those of "meaningful democracy in which the population at large may be able to participate in shaping public policy" (1987b: 80).

As the military and security forces in El Salvador escalated the pattern of retribution and violence, opposition intensified. Its victims included Jesuit priests, such as Father Rutilio Grande, the Archbishop of El Salvador, American churchwomen and countless others rounded up in the "state of siege" that reigned in 1980. Archbishop Romero, who had personally requested of President Carter that the US cease its support of right-wing terror, was murdered in the spring of the same year. The trail of atrocities against peasants, journalists, universities, libraries, and other signs of opposition accelerated. The response of the US media, as Chomsky and Herman reported, was a "virtual blackout" (Chomsky & Herman 1988: 47). Father Rutilio Grande's murder was registered in the media with regrets, as it perpetuated the myth initiated by the US government, that El Salvador's "moderate government" was "plagued by the terrorism of the extremists of the left and right," which it was unable to control (Chomsky & Herman 1988: 59). Yet, as Chomsky and Herman argued, US officials as well as journalists knew that those in control were the "U.S.-backed security forces," as well as "the paramilitary network they created to terrorize the population." Under the circumstances, they concluded, "these were crimes for which we bear considerable responsibility, since they were perpetrated by clients who depend on our support, so that exposure and pressure could have a significant effect in safeguarding human rights" (Chomsky & Herman 1988: 83).

In the case of Nicaragua, US clients were the counterrevolutionary exiles mobilized and supported by the US, the contras, whose purpose was to disable the regime and abort the revolution. With the fall of the Somoza regime in 1979, a major US ally, the Carter administration moved to assure its continuing influence over the US-trained Nicaraguan National Guard. Further, it focused on strengthening the private sector with international financial support. The objective, as Chomsky pointed out, was to assure the failure of the regime. It was, he indicated in citing US former CIA analysts, to provoke repressive measures that would confirm the regime's "allegedly inherent totalitarian nature and thus increase domestic dissent within the country" (1987b: 83). Its achievements in the areas of land reform, health, education, and popular participation, were internationally recognized, save in the US where Reagan sought to cut off aid and to pressure US allies in Latin America and Europe to follow suit. In short, the Sandinista case illustrated US fears of the "demonstration effect" of successful development in terms that might be meaningful to suffering people elsewhere, "endangering the Fifth Freedom," as Chomsky explained (1987b: 84).

As a consequence, the Reagan administration intensified its efforts to assure the political and economic destabilization of the regime. In 1983, Reagan authorized the mining of Nicaraguan harbors, while in 1984, the CIA attacked oil tanks, communication and military centers to disrupt Nicaraguan trade. Chomsky reported on the international reaction in *Necessary Illusions*, and in other works, including his discussion of *Rogue States*, whose operations were illustrated by the US response to the decision of the International Court. In June 1986 the International Court of Justice

condemned the United States for its support for the contras and illegal economic warfare and ordered it to desist from the violations of international law and valid treaties and to pay reparations. The decision was reported, but dismissed as a minor annoyance. Its contents were suppressed or falsified, the World Court – not the United States – was portrayed as the criminal, and the rule of law was held inapplicable to the United States.

As Chomsky pointed out, the response of the major representatives of the US media was to discredit the ruling, as "the US then vetoed a UN Security Council resolution calling on all states to observe international law, and voted in virtual isolation against similar General Assembly resolutions" (2000e: 4).

The Middle East

Chomsky moved to speak out on the Middle East in the midst of the Vietnam War. He faced the combined hostility of the US establishment, its liberal allies, and an anti-war movement that split on the question of Israel and Palestine. The Israeli–Arab war of 1967 had transformed the region. It underscored Israel's military superiority over its Arab neighbors, led to Israel's military occupation of the West Bank, the degradation of Palestinian life, the reorganization of the Palestinian resistance movement, and the radicalization of Middle East politics. Washington's response was a function of its primary interests in the region, uninterrupted access to the oil produced and transported by US multinationals, and the protection of conservative regimes on which US influence relied. Israel, enhanced by unconditional US political and military assistance, was an integral part of the US regional system designed to contain Arab radicalism in tandem with US regional allies. Israel's overt as well as covert Arab policies – including its anti-Palestinian policies – conformed to US objectives as well as to those of its conservative Arab allies, formally opposed to Israel but, in practice, beneficiaries of its anti-Palestinian and anti-radical policies.

Chomsky addressed these issues in an American context intolerant to criticism of Israel, one in which the dehumanization of Arabs and Palestinians, in particular, promoted the distortion of Middle East politics and the legitimation of US and Israeli policies. As he observed with respect to the 1967 period, "topics that were widely discussed and debated in Europe or in Israel itself were effectively removed from the agenda here, and a picture was established of Israel, its enemies and victims, and the U.S. role in the region, that bore only a limited resemblance to reality" (1999b: 29). Israel, it seemed, benefited from "a unique immunity from criticism in mainstream journalism and scholarship, consistent with its unique role as a beneficiary of other forms of American support" (1999b: 31). As Chomsky wrote in 1983, "when the intellectual history of this period is someday written, it will scarcely be believable" (1999b: 1(n)).

The long-term impact of such privileged distortion is difficult to exaggerate. It accounts for Israel's image as benevolent occupier, for the view of Palestinians as congenitally untrustworthy terrorists in waiting. It explains the prevailing ignorance of Arab states and societies, their image as primitive backwaters of resource-rich regions devoid of legitimate social and political movements, with the exception of those few friendly "moderate" regimes whose main characteristic is their pro-American outlook. Struggles for democracy and social justice in the Arab world have no part in this vision, since to include them would expose both Israeli and US policies in actively seeking to undermine them.

Chomsky's first full-length book on the subject, *Peace in the Middle East* (1974b) set out his views of the conflict and the conditions of its possible resolution. It warned against Israeli expansion, military occupation, creation of settlements, exploitation of Palestinian labor, and the continued rejection of Palestinian national demands (1999b: 20). And it exposed US support for Israel's occupation and its retreat from the internationally accepted interpretation of UN resolution 242, a resolution that offered no recognition of Palestinian national rights but that called for Israeli withdrawal from occupied territories. The shift in the US position, a matter of enormous consequence, as Chomsky demonstrated, was the product of a power struggle in Washington that resulted in the replacement of President Nixon's Secretary of State – William Rogers – with Henry Kissinger. In terms of Middle East diplomacy, the abandonment of the Rogers Plan (1969) was a prelude to military confrontation as opposed to diplomacy. Had this not been the case, Chomsky cites Israeli sources as conceding "that Israel could have had a peace settlement in terms of the prevailing international consensus, offering nothing to the Palestinians, by 1971" (1996d: 209). The foundations of Israeli rejectionism, as Chomsky consistently underscored citing Israeli sources, was not security but territory and resources that additionally explained the pattern of West Bank settlements. "The primary strategic motivation for Israeli rejectionism, whether of the Likud or Labor variety, is control over the territories and their resources," a factor whose importance was no less evident in the troubled course of negotiations between Palestinians and Israelis after 1991 (1996d: 211).

Writing in the post-1967 period, Chomsky argued that Israelis and Palestinians were bent on "self-destructive and possibly suicidal policies, and that, contrary to generally held assumptions, there were – and remain – alternatives that ought to be considered and that might well contribute to a more satisfactory outcome" (1974b: 10). Such alternatives included a "socialist binationalism," Chomsky maintained, as the "best long-range hope for a just peace in the region" (1974b: 210). It offered the most likely prospect of "reconciling the just and compelling demands of the two parties to the local conflict in the former Palestine," he suggested, recognizing that it was unlikely to be translated into practice immediately, he urged the importance of keeping "that hope alive until such time as popular movements within Israeli and Palestinian society, supported by an international socialist movement that does not now exist, will undertake to make such a hope a reality" (1974b: 38).

Chomsky's position on the core issues in the Israel–Palestinian conflict remained steadfast. He continued to uphold "the valid claims of those who regard the former Palestine as their home" (1999b: 39), clearly reiterating

the principle that Israeli Jews and Palestinian Arabs are human beings with human rights, equal rights; more specifically, they have essentially equal rights within the territory of the former Palestine. Each group has a valid right to national self-determination in this territory. Furthermore, I will assume that the State of Israel within its pre-June 1967 borders had, and retains, whatever one regards as the valid rights of any state within the existing international system.

The statement appeared in 1983, in the aftermath of the Lebanon War, widely anticipated by US, Arab, and Israeli critics of the Camp David Agreements (1979) between Israel and Egypt that effectively freed Israel to pursue its anti-Palestinian policies in Lebanon, where it simultaneously struck out against the Lebanese opposition to assure the restoration of a pro-Israeli Maronite leadership. Israel's Lebanon policy backfired with disastrous consequences for Lebanese and Palestinians.

The immediate cause for Israel's invasion of Lebanon, Chomsky observed, was not in doubt in Israel. It was the increasing international legitimacy of the PLO, a factor effectively "rated 'X' in the United States" (1996d: 214). The long-term cause of the invasion was no less in evidence, as Chomsky demonstrated by discussing its history and aftermath in his *The Fateful Triangle, the United States, Israel and the Palestinians* (1983, 1999b). The Israeli attack on Lebanon was designed to crush the Lebanese base of the PLO, thereby fatally undermining its influence in the West Bank. The US endorsed the plan in a much-discussed interpretation of the "green light" that Washington offered Tel Aviv. In practice, President Reagan supported Prime Minister Begin's policy with its demolition of the Lebanese opposition and the crushing of the PLO. The disastrous results of the invasion, with its destruction of Beirut, culminated in the Israeli supervised massacre of Palestinians in the Sabra and Shattila refugee camp, carried out by Israel's Lebanese Phalangist allies.

Chomsky approached the Palestinian massacre and the question of Israeli as well as US responsibility with an account of another massacre, that of the Jews in Kishinev in 1903. The memory of the earlier massacre framed the question of responsibility in the later one, and in so doing drew a wordless analogy that defied the dehumanization of its victims while exposing the crimes of its victimizers (1996d: 332). The international reaction to Sabra and Shattila was outrage. The Kahan Commission Inquiry in Israel investigated the responsibility of the Israel Defense Forces, leaving no doubts as to its implicit conclusions, as Israeli critics conceded (1996d: 408). US officials disclosed that the Israeli military had done "nothing to stop the carnage," as Chomsky indicated (1996d: 365). US intelligence was implicated as well, since US intelligence, according to Israeli press reports cited by Chomsky, had provided "hard intelligence information . . . confirming that Israeli military officers in Beirut were well aware of the brutal killings many hours before the Israeli Defense Forces actually went into the camps. . . ." For the then ex-deputy mayor of Jerusalem, Meron Benvenisti, "everything that has happened in Israel until now [Oct 4, 1982] has carried the stamp of American approval, or at least, it was tolerated by your government" (1996d: 391). That approval, Chomsky argued, was a function of " 'ideological support' for Israel in the United States, with its systematic falsification of the historical record and its practice of defaming the Palestinians and ignoring their torment," he argued (1996d: 393).

There is much that could have been done to present a fair and honest picture of what was and had been happening, and to change the U.S. policies that have predictably led to the rise of a Greater Israel that is a threat to its own citizens, to those subject to its military power, and to many others as well, and that lie behind the specific events of 1982. To the extent that we do not do what can be done, we have only ourselves to blame for the consequences.

The result of the Lebanon war and continued Israeli repression in the West Bank was revolt, the Palestinian Intifadah of 1987. Its impact extended to the Palestinian political class that would later challenge the authoritarian leadership of Yasser Arafat. In the interval, the Intifadah led to Israeli military reprisals, violence and savagery that escalated to what an Israeli Foreign Ministry official claimed was "becoming 'a real war,' " one dutifully kept off American screens and more pointedly, "from the eyes of the American taxpayer who funds it, a further contribution to state terror," as Chomsky wrote (Chomsky 1989: 214; Macedo 2000: 75).

The end of the Cold War, while appearing to herald a new age in the ongoing conflict, reified the consequences of earlier policies in altered international conditions that further undermined Palestinian prospects. The collapse of the former Soviet Union, followed within two years by the US-led invasion of Iraq to punish it for its aggression against Kuwait, reversed the former US support for the Iraqi dictator (Chomsky 2000c: 53). Within a year, the weakened leadership of the PLO agreed to the steps that led from Madrid to Oslo, Cairo, Wye, and other intervening stops in the "peace of the victors."

For Palestinians under continued Israeli military occupation, the offers of cantonization separated by a growing string of Israeli settlements, held out little promise. Peace under conditions of military rule in which human rights, let alone civil and political rights were violated, while access to water, electricity and food were threatened, was a form of pacification that assured continued conflict. The "peace process," Chomsky wrote, is about "whatever the United States happens to be doing, often blocking peace initiatives," as the case may be (1999b: 238). For those willing to confront the facts, however, it should "be understood as an impressive vindication of the rule of force in international affairs, at both policy and doctrinal levels: the former, by virtue of its operative significance, the latter, in the light of the broad acceptance of the rejectionist stance that Washington had maintained in virtual isolation for many years" (1997: 160–1). The results can only be ominous, he warned, with "much pain and suffering" ahead.[2]

After the Cold War

With the collapse of the Soviet Union and communist regimes of Eastern Europe, the Cold War came to an end. What changed in terms of US foreign policy that had, for decades, been justified in the name of anti-communism? Heralded as the dawn of a new era, US officials promised an era of profit and progress for all in the form of privatization and democratization. But, in practice, US policy endorsed the accelerated expansion of corporate power and profit in the name of support for free trade and the dismantling of statist regimes. The neoliberal orthodoxy of privatization and globalization led to deregulation of capital flow and systematic efforts to undermine labor and environmental protection. These had little to do with free trade and even less with democracy, as Chomsky's work demonstrated. They represented instead an acceleration of US monetary and trade policies redefined in the 1970s in an effort to stem the competitive advantage of US major industrial allies, Japan and Germany. Thirty years later, in the absence of the Cold War, the new international order involves an unheralded, if internationally contested, US military expansion that is designed to protect the gains of the new world order, the latest phase of that persistent other war, the one between the global North and South.

Chomsky's work exposed the pervasive mantras of the post-Cold War era, including the claims of free trade that masked the pursuit of protectionist measures critical to the American economy such as the "huge state component of the economy, which undergirded all of high technology industry during the 'golden age of free market capitalism.'" He unmasked the "ideology of the double-edged 'free market' state protection and public subsidy for the rich, market discipline for the poor." And in *Rogue States*, he confirmed that the indispensable accompaniment of this international order was the rule of force, as demonstrated by post-Cold War US policies in Panama, Colombia, Iraq, Israel and Palestine, and those of the US and its Western allies in East Timor and Kosovo. In *A New Generation Draws the Line, Kosovo, East Timor and the*

Standards of the West (2000d), Chomsky returned to a theme that dominated his earliest writings on US policy in Vietnam, namely, the need to understand the nature of policy as a prerequisite to changing it. Unless one confronts the myths at the center of foreign-policy justification, he argued, their implicit norms of conduct "are likely to prevail if self-serving doctrine remains immune to critical reflection, and moral truisms are kept at the margins of consciousness" (2000d: 21). The warning not only serves as an apt summary of fundamental aspects of Chomsky's political views, it represents the other side of globalization, with its widespread resistance and continued commitment to struggles for social justice and democracy.

The urgency of recovering the historical record was reinforced by the unprecedented nature of the events of September 11, 2001. No commentary on Chomsky's analysis of US foreign policy can ignore the depth of the ensuing crisis or the integrity of his response.

The attack on the World Trade Center in New York and the Pentagon in Washington left more than 3,000 dead (Talbot 2001: 16). But it was not the toll alone that rendered the event without precedent so much as what was perceived as the nature of the target. For the first time since the War of 1812, properties and civilians within United States territory became the subjects of direct attack (Chomsky 2001b: 11).

In the US, a palpable sense of solidarity temporarily erased political and social boundaries in the face of what was perceived as a national emergency. The fear of further attacks and the risks of bio-terrorism intensified the generalized apprehension. Washington called for an international coalition against terrorism. That, in practice, became a near-unilateral US and British war on Afghanistan, ostensibly in search of Usama bin Laden, the Saudi Muslim militant whose broad network of supporters were believed to be responsible for the September 11 attacks.

The vulnerability of the undisputed superpower shocked Americans, as it did much of the world. Sympathy for Americans abroad was widespread. It did not, however, preclude increasing criticism of Washington's preference for unilateral military action taken outside of existing international frameworks with calamitous consequences for Afghan refugees and civilian casualties of US bombings.

Chomsky voiced these and a range of other pointed criticisms against the US war in Afghanistan and the studied indifference to the toll of US policies in the Middle East, the taboo subject forcibly opened by the terrible events of September 11. Against the increasing conformism of the mainstream US media he counseled resistance to intimidation and warned against those who "demand silent obedience" (2001b: 118).

In characteristic fashion, Chomsky insisted that Americans confront the terrorist attacks as legacy of their government's policies. In the case of Afghanistan, that meant coming to grips with past US support for the Taliban, no less than with the dark legacy of Washington's new-found allies in that country, the forces of the Northern Alliance. He rejected claims that the US was under attack, insisting on the definition of the term in international law that undermined its applicability, while questioning Washington's declaration of a "war against terrorism" in the light of its own indictment of international terrorism. Washington's declaration was "a term of propaganda," Chomsky argued. "There cannot be a war on terrorism led by the one state in the world that has been condemned for international terrorism and supported by major terrorist states like Russia and China" (Chomsky & Hansen 2001: 7). Chomsky did not deny that the events of September 11 constituted terrorism, but "private terrorism" as opposed to "state terrorism" carried out by some of the above. And there was no mistaking Chomsky's view of what should be done in the wake of the "criminal atrocities" of September 11. Chomsky, like many other individuals in the US and abroad, argued in favor of "careful police work; a criminal investigation carried out by international authorities; the use of internationally sanctioned means, which could include force to apprehend the criminals; bring the criminals to justice; ensure that they have fair trials and international tribunals" (2001b: 91). It was also evident that the US had no intention of going before an international body, including the UN Security Council, to request authorization for its actions. The reasons were not difficult to imagine. Chomsky reflected, "my speculation is that the U.S. does not want to establish the principle that it has to defer to some higher authority before carrying out the use of violence," citing support for such a position by Clinton and his Secretary of State (2001b: 4).

Within days of the events of September 11, Chomsky gave a succession of live and written interviews in the US and abroad. He appeared in India and Pakistan in late November, where he was described by Ejaz Haider of *The Friday Times* of Pakistan as "the conscience that troubles everyone" (Haider: 2001). His was a conscience that troubled those unprepared to question the meaning of US justification of the "war on terrorism," or the risks of mass starvation facing some 7.5 million Afghan refugees, as international agencies repeatedly warned, or the scale of civilian casualties, however "unintended" as US officials claimed. More troubling to many – including leftwing intellectuals in the US – was Chomsky's reminder that the scale of the September 11 atrocity was not uncommon elsewhere in the world, including as a result of US policies such as the 1998 US attack on the pharmaceutical plant in the Sudan and the catastrophic toll of the US-backed Contra war against Nicaragua, among others (2001b: 45–54, 56, 85–6). Not to confront such policies, Chomsky has long argued and repeats anew, is to risk the escalation of violence "leading to still further atrocities such as the one that is inciting the call for revenge," he maintained in interviews given within two weeks of September 11 (2001b: 26).

The extensive interview Chomsky gave to the online journal, *Salon,* not only provided these and innumerable other insights into Chomsky's views, it offered an abridged guide to the moral foundations of his political beliefs. To the interviewer who questioned what difference confrontation with past US policies would make, he replied in favor of truth-telling as an "elementary step." Thus, "if we were more honest about some of the things that we've done," he claimed, "if we were honest, then we could at least evaluate what we do sanely. If we're dishonest, we know that whatever we do, only by the merest accident will it be justified. The first elementary step is honesty. After that you can go on and consider complicated issues on their merits" (Chomsky & Hansen 2001: 7). On the use of force, Chomsky conceded that he was no pacifist. "I think the use of force is sometimes legitimate" – but those who advocated it and particularly the use of "extreme violence" have a heavy burden of proof to meet. "That," he claimed, was "a moral truism" (Chomsky and Hansen 2001: 9). Elsewhere in the course of the same interview, he argued that "if there is a principle that we apply to others, we must insist that the principle apply to us," which translated into the world of September 11 meant that as it was right to cry out against the "horrible atrocity" that had occurred in the US, it was no less so to denounce "a crime when we commit it against others." As to what the US ought to do, Chomsky replied unhesitatingly that it ought to "stop participating in atrocities," citing examples from East Timor to Kosovo to the Kurds in Turkey, among others.

The challenge was magnified by the US-led invasion of Iraq, a war that was justified by the G. W. Bush administration as the response to Iraq's possession of weapons of mass destruction that allegedly constituted an imminent threat to the United States. In practice, the US-led war constituted a war of aggression whose justification was exposed as a form of mass deception. In fact, it was a war that intensified international terrorism and promoted the risks of weapons proliferation at an incalculable cost in human suffering.

Against the intellectual apologists of deception, Chomsky repeatedly addressed the responsibility of intellectuals to denounce the crime of silence and to address the veritable nature and consequences of policies carried out by the US and its allies in Iraq. He recognized the unprecedented international outcry against the war. And, as did Bertrand Russell at the International War Crimes Tribunal of 1967, Chomsky sought to – in Russell's words – "arouse consciousness in order to create mass resistance" (Chomsky 1971c: 1) to policies deceptively cloaked in the name of liberation.

Chomsky's voice was raised in support of free and rational inquiry that aimed at speaking truth and resisting power. It was a call, by "one of the truly great men of the twentieth century," as he had earlier described Russell, that was heard around the world by those with a common longing for survival and against hegemony.

14   The responsibility of the intellectual

Jean Bricmont

The tone and unyielding criticism long ago landed him [Chomsky] in the Siberia of American discourse. It's an undeserved fate. What Chomsky has to say is legitimate. If there is anything new about our age, it is that Chomsky's questions will eventually have to be answered. Agree with him or not, we lose out by not listening.

Business Week[1]

Introduction

When the South African freedom fighter Steve Biko said that "the most powerful tool in the hands of the oppressor is the mind of the oppressed," he was expressing an idea very similar to that of David Hume who observed: "'Tis therefore, on opinion only that government is founded; and this maxim extends to the most despotic and the most military governments, as well as to the most free and the most popular" (quoted in Chomsky 1991: 352). From the fall of the Shah of Iran to the changes in Eastern Europe or South Africa, examples abound that illustrate this thesis: a powerful group may have at its disposal all the military might that it wants, if the soldiers and officers, or even the vast majority of the population, are not willing to follow orders, it is effectively powerless. Hence, the importance of the battle of ideas and the necessity for any ruling class who wants to maintain its privileges in the long run of "regimenting the public mind every bit as much as an army regiments the bodies of its soldiers."[2]

The importance of thought control of the general population suggests precisely that the role of the critical intellectual is crucial for any movement aiming at liberating social change. I shall argue that the writings of Noam Chomsky offer an outstanding example of what a critical intellectual can do. Political activities of (leftist) intellectuals often oscillate between two extremes: either they absorb themselves entirely into militant work (usually when they are young) and do not really use their specific abilities as intellectuals; or they retreat from that kind of involvement, but then limit themselves to expressing moral indignation disconnected from genuine political analyses. Moral indignation is necessary, but it should be based on a rational analysis, rather than on emotional reactions, because our emotions are all too easily manipulated by the power and the media.

I cannot possibly do justice to the thousands of pages that Chomsky has written exposing the lies of Western governments and the deceptions of apologetic intellectuals and journalists. I can only hope to induce readers to look at the evidence themselves and make their own judgments. I shall first explain some general principles contrasting what intellectuals should do (next section) with what they actually do in Western societies as well as explaining the basic ideological mechanisms through which world affairs are usually presented (third section). Once these are understood, it "only" takes hard work to show how they function in various concrete situations, some of which[3] will be discussed in the fourth section. Unlike many intellectuals who write about "ideology," Chomsky puts facts and evidence before "theory." However, there are some general attitudes, as well as pitfalls to avoid, that can be gathered from his writings. The final section will be devoted to them.

What are intellectuals responsible for?

For Chomsky, the responsibility of the intellectual is to "tell the truth *as best one can*, about things *that matter*, to *the right audience*" (1996a, b: 55). However simple this statement may seem, every part of it requires some comment; first of all, the idea of "telling the truth" has become, for certain sectors of the Western intelligentsia that can loosely be described as "postmodernists," highly problematic: truth is viewed as an illusion or as merely a tool of power. Chomsky has neither sympathy nor patience for such ideas.[4] When asked about the antagonistic relation between science and anarchism, he replies: "Within the anarchist tradition, there has been a certain feeling that there's something regimented or oppressive about science itself . . . I'm totally out of sympathy with that attitude. There are no arguments that I know of for irrationality" (1987a: 22).

Chomsky views truth and rationality as weapons of the oppressed, not against them. *Claims* to truth, expertise, etc. are a different matter, of course, and are regularly used as a weapon by the strong against the weak; but Chomsky is opposed to what one might call the easy or lazy position, which is unfortunately quite widespread in the intellectual left nowadays, namely to reject all claims to truth on spurious philosophical grounds (relativism, postmodernism). On the contrary, the task of leftist intellectuals is to dig out the facts and correct abusive reasoning, but that of course presupposes that there is such a thing as a fact, that arguments do matter, and that not all stories are equal. When Chomsky hears that one of the postmodernist's complaints against "Reason" is that it tries to separate the "real" and the "not real," he replies:

At least, I know that I try to make this distinction, whether studying questions that are hard, like the origins of human knowledge, or relatively easy, like the source and character of U.S. foreign policy. In the latter case, for example, I would try, and urge others to try, to separate the real operative factors from the various tales that are spun in the interests of power and privilege. If that is a fault, I plead guilty, and will compound my guilt by urging others to err in the same way.[5]

A second qualification concerns "things that matter." Here, moral issues enter. One could write about the actions of Genghis Khan; that can be intellectually interesting, no doubt, but since nothing can be done for his victims, the moral relevance of such writings is nil. Turning to contemporary events, more delicate questions arise; since nobody can deal with every possible issue, one should ask which crimes to denounce and which lies to expose, at least primarily; in particular, should one concentrate on those committed by one's own country or by our enemies? The answer to that question, in the West, is straightforward, at least when it concerns intellectuals in enemy states, say the Soviet Union in the past. Their duty is to denounce, if they can, the crimes of their own state; what they say about other states does not matter much. In fact, if a Soviet intellectual did denounce *only* Western crimes (committed e.g. by the United States or Israel) he was regarded with contempt, because such denunciations, even if they were accurate, could only, within the context in which they took place, have the effect of strengthening the resolve and hence the violence of his own state. But when it comes to Western intellectuals, things change radically: our duty is supposedly to denounce the crimes of our enemies, not primarily those of our own governments.[6] But Chomsky refuses this double standard; for him "the crimes that matter" are those for which we are more directly responsible and about which we can do something, namely, primarily, the actions of our own governments.

Finally, there is the question of the audience. Chomsky strongly disagrees with the Quaker slogan "speak truth to power" (1996a, b: 60–1), because the constraints put by coercive institutions prevent people holding power in those institutions to act humanely. If the director of a major corporation suddenly became a human being concerned for the fate of the environment or for the wellbeing of his workers, the shareholders would immediately fire him, or his company would go bankrupt. If the President of the United States suddenly tried to dismantle the CIA or the Pentagon, he would be impeached. That does not mean that people holding positions of power cannot become moral agents, but then they will dissociate themselves from those positions. Chomsky simply does not write for people holding positions of power; his writings are meant primarily to be a service to activists. They can also be regarded as tools of intellectual self-defense against the dominant discourse, the media etc.

How does ideology work?

Whole libraries of books have been written on the notion of ideology, from the point of view of Marxism, psychoanalysis, critical theory, etc. Compared to those, Chomsky's approach may seem terribly down-to-earth (but that may turn out, upon reflection, to be an advantage rather than a defect). Anyway, ideology here will simply mean a mystification used by a social group in order to maintain its power.

As a paradigmatic example of a self-serving mystification, although it is not one that Chomsky often uses, consider priesthoods in traditional societies. By making people believe that they are the proper intermediaries between humans and some deities, and by convincing people that the current social arrangements result from the will of those deities, priests secure for themselves a privileged position under the benevolent umbrella of the ruler. In modern societies, priests no longer have such an important ideological role as in the past, and their role is played by what one might call the "secular priesthood," namely, academics, intellectuals, journalists. The function of those experts, a function which is often well rewarded, is to hide the way that private or state power actually works and to provide justifications, in terms of the pursuit of lofty ideals, for that power and for the awful violence that its exercise often leads to.

The basic functioning of the dominant ideological discourse in the Western societies is very easy to explain; when historians analyze a society in the distant past, say the Roman empire or Genghis Khan, they will try to relate the actions of the kings and rulers to their perceived economic and strategic interests. And, when they analyze the behavior of other actors, with less power, such as priests or military men, they will do so in terms of the institutional constraints imposed on them by the society under study. Such an attitude is taken for granted without question; in particular, nobody feels that one has to explain those behaviors on the assumption that the proclaimed intentions of the rulers are their true motivations. Quite the contrary, it is the "hidden" structure (political objectives, or institutional constraints) discovered by the historian that will be used to analyze the official discourse of the rulers and explain them as some kind of ideological justification.

In fact, such an attitude extends to everyday life: nobody wants to buy a used car from an unknown seller who says first that the car is in excellent condition and second that the price is so low because he/she is your friend. And of course, this attitude also extends to the analysis of contemporary societies, such as the Soviet Union (before its collapse) or China. It would be hard to find a Western analyst who would try to understand the Soviet "intervention" in Czechoslovakia or Afghanistan mainly as an attempt to "defend socialism." Rather, he/she will focus attention on the structure and rivalries within Soviet power. There is, however, one exception to this general methodological attitude: namely, present Western societies. The attitude then becomes spontaneously the exact opposite: it is axiomatic that the motivations of our governments are pure and are basically identical to those presented in official discourse (defense of human rights or democracy, etc). One is of course free to challenge the attainability of these objectives or the wisdom of those who try to implement them; but to question the purity of the motivations or their legitimacy is to put oneself outside the bounds of respectable discourse.[7]

A standard argument offered to support the dominant view, at least implicitly, is that present Western societies are "really different," both from past societies (including our own past) and from our barbaric enemies (such as Russia, China, the Arab world, etc.). That is because "we" (meaning our governments) are genuinely concerned by democracy, human rights etc. Defenders of that thesis will readily concede that we "erred in the past"; sure, colonialism was bad, slavery was abominable and during the Cold War, we supported far too many dictatorships. But now things have changed and we can at last all work together to build a better world.

Note that this thesis is often presented as an obvious truth because indeed democratic forms as well as human rights, which we are supposed to defend everywhere, are generally better respected in Western countries than elsewhere. But that true observation implies nothing concerning the nature of the foreign policy of the West. It is perfectly possible, for example, that within a society where some democratic forms are respected, an economic oligarchy forms itself and obtains enough control over the government and the media to direct the foreign policy towards goals that are far from noble. But, even without adhering to that idea, one should agree that this "obvious truth" should be evaluated empirically, if possible. The way to test it, as is often the case when one wants to test someone's sincerity, is to consider pairs of situations, one where it would be easy to attain the proclaimed noble goals (defending human rights for example) and one where it is hard. If one observes that, in the first case, nothing is done (or, worse, that many things are done that actually hurt the proclaimed goals, e.g. supplying military aid to brutal regimes) while, in the latter case, a great deal is done, for example sustaining major wars, but with little or no result, then the charge of hypocrisy cannot be avoided. A good deal of Chomsky's work is devoted precisely to the analysis of many pairs of examples that support this charge, both concerning the actions of Western governments and the way the mainstream media present them.[8]

A second structural feature of the way ideology works in the West is to have as strong a debate as possible within limited bounds. The typical form that such a debate takes is to concentrate on the means to achieve some – by assumption noble – goal and to avoid carefully any question regarding the sincerity of the enterprise. Thus, the debate will typically be centered on questions such as: do we have enough power, resolve, etc. to achieve our goals? Are our leaders sufficiently clever, determined, and strong? The more vociferous the debates, the more the implicit assumptions concerning the nobility of the intentions come to be reinforced. The Vietnam War is a good example: the hawks maintain to this day that with more determination, the United States could have "saved Vietnam" and that it was "lost," because the war effort was stabbed in the back by the peace movement. To that, the doves reply that the effort was doomed to fail, that it was too costly to the United States and maybe even killed too many people. At the end of the war, the *New York Times* gave a good summary of the terms of that debate: "There are those Americans who believe that the war to preserve a non-Communist, independent South Vietnam could have been waged differently. There are other Americans who believe that a viable, non-Communist South Vietnam was always a myth . . . A decade of fierce polemics has failed to resolve this ongoing quarrel."

To this Chomsky, together with Ed Herman, replied in an (of course, unpublished) letter, that "there was a third position: That apart from its prospects for success, the United States has neither the authority nor the competence to intervene in the internal affairs of Vietnam. This was the position of much of the authentic peace movement, that is, those who opposed the war because it was wrong, not merely because it was unsuccessful" (1977c: 37). The Vietnam War will be discussed in the next section, but just to see how odd the summary of the *New York Times* is, compare it with the following statement: "There are those Soviets who believe that the war to preserve a non-fundamentalist, independent Afghanistan could have been waged differently. There are other Soviets who believe that a viable, non-fundamentalist Afghanistan was always a myth . . . A decade of fierce polemics has failed to resolve this ongoing quarrel." In that situation, nobody has any difficulty seeing that there is a third position, the one that Chomsky and Herman adopt for the Vietnam War; but, here, the third position is hidden by the raging debate between the two "admissible" ones. Let us now turn to concrete examples of how all these ideological mechanisms work.

Examples

The Indochina Wars

Chomsky always considered the Vietnam War to be part of a larger framework, which one might call the one of the "rotten apple."[9] At the end of World War II, the leaders of the United States saw that their country could become the sole superpower and worked to obtain and maintain that position, which led to overt and covert interventions in Greece, Guatemala, the Dominican Republic, Brazil, Chile, Lebanon among others.[10] The idea of the rotten apple is that any country, no matter how small, that can escape from United States global dominion and develop itself independently or, even worse, set as one of its priorities the wellbeing of its own population, is a danger, because it might provide the wrong model for others (hence, spreading the "rot"). In fact, the smaller and the poorer the country (Cuba, Vietnam, or Grenada), the greater the threat, because the more impressive such an example would be.

The movement of national liberation in Vietnam did pose such a threat of "independence" after 1945. This led the United States not only to finance the French war in Indochina, but to undermine the Geneva 1954 peace agreements that ended that part of the war; it then supported a terrorist war by the Saigon regime against its own population, sent the US air force to bomb the countryside as early as 1962 (long before any North Vietnamese soldiers appeared in the South), and drove millions of people into camps called "strategic hamlets," in order to cut the South Vietnamese guerillas from their popular base. This escalated into a full-scale intervention with hundreds of thousands of ground troops and massive bombing of North Vietnam (and even more of South Vietnam) in 1965. Eventually, the war proved too costly for the US elites and they started to "oppose the war," but on grounds of effectiveness, not on any basis of principle. Chomsky is quite sarcastic with respect to that kind of opposition, which he does not view as morally superior to the possible opposition of German generals to their own war after Stalingrad.

Chomsky's criticism of "the new mandarins"[11] was directed primarily at intellectuals who supported United States power, notably in its aggressive wars against recalcitrant small countries such as Vietnam and, later, Nicaragua. However, his criticisms of various forms of misguided or excessively soft opposition to the war more clearly sets him apart from the left-liberal mainstream. Indeed, it is precisely by analyzing the discourse of opponents to the war and some of their delusions that one can appreciate how much even opponents can be indoctrinated by the dominant ideology.

Chomsky illustrates the power of our propaganda system compared with that of the Soviets by citing the story of Danchev, a courageous newscaster in Moscow who denounced the Russian invasion of Afghanistan (Chomsky 1987a: 223–6). Danchev actually called upon the rebels to resist. He was sent to a psychiatric hospital by the Soviets (but returned later to his position). His actions were praised in the West.

Notice that Danchev saw what anyone outside the Soviet Union could see, that the Soviets had *invaded* Afghanistan. This was contrary to official Soviet doctrine, which maintained that the Soviet Union was *defending* Afghanistan against CIA-supported rebels based in Pakistan and that they were invited in by the Afghan government. That defense was dismissed in the West on the grounds that the government was illegitimate, a mere Soviet puppet. Chomsky points out, however, that the same Westerners who saw the Soviet action as an invasion and praised Danchev for not only seeing it but denouncing it should, if they had been consistent in their moral evaluations and their praise, have been doing exactly what Danchev did, only directing their denunciations against the US government. For, if anything, it was even clearer that the United States had invaded Vietnam – that the US wanted to establish hegemony in Southeast Asia and that the South Vietnam government that "invited" them was a puppet. And the responsibility of the Western intellectual was greater, too, for Danchev acted in spite of the threat of prison or a psychiatric hospital, where the Westerner was subject to no such threat. Nevertheless, the expression "US invasion of South Vietnam" was virtually never heard, even in the peace movement. And only a very few marginalized critics recognized this invasion for what it was.

In the Soviet system, it was not thought itself that was controlled (even if that was the goal), but *expressions* of thought. Our system of "brainwashing under freedom," which does not control expressions of thought directly, and in fact encourages debates, as long as the purity of the intentions of our leaders remains unchallenged, is in fact a much more effective system of thought control than the Soviet one.

As another example of the kind of illusions that are widespread within the left, Chomsky criticizes misplaced notions of scientific and moral expertise. During the Vietnam War, in 1965, a conference was organized that tried to articulate the insights of social scientists and other individuals from "various theological, philosophical and humanist traditions" in order to "find solutions that are more consistent with fundamental human values than current American policy in Vietnam has turned out to be." Chomsky's reaction was biting:

The only debatable issue, it seems to me, is whether it is more ridiculous to turn to experts in social theory for general well-confirmed propositions, or to specialists in the great religions and philosophical systems for insights into fundamental human values . . . if there is a body of theory, well tested and verified, that applies to the conduct of foreign affairs or the resolution of domestic or international conflicts, its existence has been kept a well-guarded secret. (1987a: 71–2)

Of course, Chomsky does not deny that one should seek from the social sciences whatever information can be obtained. But he is violently opposed to the cult of the expert, "both self-serving and fraudulent." Many intellectuals love to play the role of "advisors to the Prince" and to claim to be technical experts who will, using some deep principles of social theory that are inaccessible to ordinary people, propose solutions to current problems. But if those problems, like the Vietnam War and its conduct, are basically due to relationships of power and domination, as Chomsky claims, then the people who present them as merely technical problems only help those who hold a position of power to hide their actions behind a discourse based on socially neutral categories.[12]

Finally, another illusion that Chomsky often denounces is the idea that the United States lost the Vietnam War.[13] This is only partly true: the United States had a maximal objective, which was to impose there their favorite regime, and that failed. But the minimal goal, which was to prevent the rot from spreading, by destroying any hope of autonomous development in Indochina, was completely successful. First of all, a heavily bombarded Vietnam was not exactly an attractive option for its neighbors but, also, the isolation imposed on a devastated Indochina after the war eventually led to its reintegration into the dominant world system. Moreover, the United States was able, during the Vietnam War, to consolidate its position in neighboring countries such as Thailand and Indonesia (through murderous coups, such as the one of Suharto in Indonesia in 1965, where, as former CIA agent Raph McGehee puts it, the agency created "conditions that led to the massacre of at least half a million Indonesians" [Chomsky 1987a: 305]).

The reconstruction of the imperial ideology

Nevertheless, the image of the United States was tarnished and its population had become massively opposed to direct foreign interventions. It was therefore necessary for the US elite to continue the war at the ideological level, and to try to construct new justifications for future interventions that were to take place in the 1980s and the 1990s. Notable examples include Central America and Iraq, leading to the deaths of hundreds of thousands through civil wars, counterinsurgency campaigns, and embargoes. It is interesting to note Chomsky's reactions, and to contrast them with the evolution of the majority of the intellectuals who have been opposed to the war, and who ended up basically accepting the mainstream discourse.

The atrocities committed by the Khmer Rouge as well as the exodus of the "boat people" fleeing Vietnam were to the mainstream media and the liberal intelligentsia heaven-sent gifts. The atrocities and the exodus could be used to shame the anti-war movement ("see, we told you what would happen") and to lay the ground for future interventions. Some people who opposed the war felt, for example, that they had a "special responsibility" to denounce human rights violations in Vietnam; some even came to reconsider their opposition to the war.[14] But, for Chomsky, this was an instance where people fell victim of the assumptions of the ideological system. To understand why, consider Soviet dissidents who would have opposed the invasion of Afghanistan. The fact that the fundamentalist Islamic leader Hekmatyar committed atrocious crimes after the Soviet withdrawal in no way implies that those dissidents have a "special responsibility" to denounce them. Those dissidents may very well say that the

Soviet intervention led to a disaster, that, by opposing that intervention, they did all they could to prevent it and that the further consequences of that disaster should be faulted on those who carried on and supported the intervention, not on those who opposed it. But the Western analogue of this straightforward argument is almost never heard.

In fact, already in 1970, Chomsky anticipated what was going to happen and, after quoting Kant's remarks on the French Revolution: "one must be free to learn how to make use of one's powers freely and usefully. The first attempts will surely be brutal and will lead to a state of affairs more painful and dangerous than the former condition under the dominance but also the protection of an external authority," he adds:

no rational person will approve of violence and terror. In particular, the terror of the postrevolutionary state, fallen into the hands of a grim autocracy, has more than once reached indescribable levels of savagery. Yet no person of understanding or humanity will too quickly condemn the violence that often occurs when long-subdued masses take their first steps toward liberty and social reconstruction.[15]

Moreover, the criticism by American war resisters of human rights violations or other indefensible acts committed by the victims of American violence again raises the question of the right audience. Given that any criticism of the victims of the US assault, made in the US press, would very likely be used to further "bleed Vietnam," through embargoes and other sanctions,[16] its only likely result would be to contribute to increased human suffering. However, unlike some leftists, Chomsky does not rule out such criticisms – in fact, he is himself often very critical of revolutionary societies such as Cuba or Nicaragua[17] – but he insists that those criticisms should be put into proper perspective and that we should not ignore the actual human impact of our declarations. This attitude is quite distinct from the moral posturing with which all too many intellectuals seek to display their ideological purity.[18]

A related issue that aroused considerable fury among Chomsky's opponents was his alleged "defense of Pol Pot." Of course, no such defense ever occurred.[19] The main theme of Chomsky & Herman (1979a, b, 1988) was a comparison between the responses of the media to the Khmer Rouge massacres in Cambodia and to the Indonesian massacres in East Timor at the same time and similar in scale (relative to the population). In the first case, where the massacres could be blamed on an official enemy, virtuous indignation and gross exaggerations were the rule; in the case of a massacre committed by a friendly state (Indonesia), almost total silence. The issue for Chomsky and Herman was not the nature of the Khmer Rouge regime, which was certainly bad enough, but the propagandist attitude toward an official enemy, where the only rule is "anything goes." A mechanism much like religious bigotry is set in motion: everybody feels the need to show that he is more virtuous than his neighbor in denouncing the crimes of the enemy; facts need not be checked and the grossest lies are considered to prove only the sanctity of their authors. Similar mechanisms are at work nowadays concerning Iran or North Korea. Whoever objects, even on perfectly demonstrable factual grounds, is regarded as a heretic and treated as such. Inasmuch as it was quite clear to everybody that there was nothing that could be done in Cambodia at that time, the discourse about the Khmer Rouge was purely ideological. Indeed, the United States could hardly have intervened in a country from which they had just withdrawn, nor did anyone else offer to intervene. Moreover, when the Vietnamese eventually did intervene and terminated the Pol Pot regime, the utter hypocrisy of the Western powers became obvious, since they strongly opposed that intervention, continuing to recognize the Pol Pot regime at the United Nations and supporting it militarily in indirect ways (Pilger 1998).

By way of comparison, consider the story of the Belgian babies killed by the Germans during World War I, a classic story of disinformation. While there is no doubt that horrible atrocities were committed by the German troops when they invaded Belgium in 1914, there is also no doubt that those atrocities were grossly exaggerated by the French and British propaganda machines, especially in order to draw the United States into the war. Therefore, pacifists, like Bertrand Russell, had to put those atrocities into proper perspective, to get the facts straight and in general to do everything they could to prevent the militarists from using *real or imagined* atrocities to stir up emotions, thereby encouraging the general population to accept, through the continuation of the war, further killings, and on a far greater scale (killings that, of course, did happen; but this does not mean that the efforts of the pacifists were misguided).[20]

Human rights: rhetoric and reality

The universality of the 1948 Universal Declaration of Human Rights is another object lesson in the hypocrisy of Western governments and mainstream intellectuals. The standard view about it in the West is that there are some "bad guys" (mostly African or Asian leaders and relativist intellectuals at home) who invoke cultural differences in order to deny the universal value of that declaration. Chomsky takes the declaration and its universality very seriously. But he does not agree with the standard view about who are the real "relativists."[21] Consider first the Civil and Political Rights, e.g. article 14 that grants the right to seek abroad asylum from persecution. Its implementation is extraordinarily politicized by the United States: of the more that 24,000 Haitians intercepted by US forces from 1981 through 1990, 11 were granted asylum, in comparison with 75,000 out of 75,000 Cubans. Or consider article 13, granting "the right to leave any country, including his own." This was constantly invoked with great passion against the refusal by the Soviet Union to allow Jews to leave. But the end of that article, which says "and to return to his country" is ignored. To understand why, note that a day after the Universal Declaration was ratified, the United Nations passed Resolution 194, which affirms the right of Palestinians to return to their homes (or to receive compensations); note also that this right, although regularly affirmed since 1948, is not even taken into account by the so-called Oslo peace process between Israel and the Palestinians.

The declaration also contains Economic, Social and Cultural Rights, including a right to health care, social security and adequate standard of living (article 25). Whatever one thinks of those rights, they are part of the declaration and are as binding on the signatories as any other part of the Universal Declaration. Nevertheless, the United States ambassador to the United Nations, Jeane Kirkpatrick, could call them a "letter to Santa Claus" without provoking much reaction. The notion of an adequate standard of living may be somewhat vague, but the fact that millions of people suffer from hunger in such an incredibly rich country as the United States is a clear violation of article 25. A similar remark applies to the three-fold *increase* in child poverty in Thatcher's Britain.

In the West, the Civil Rights part of the Universal Declaration is held to have absolute priority over the Economic and Social parts. (This is in itself an interesting example of "relativism" – just think of the reactions in the West if some Third World leader called the first part a "letter to Santa Claus"). In case this strikes you as obvious, imagine yourself being one of those two or three billion people (about half of mankind) that have to survive on more or less two dollars a day. What would be your view of the economic and social policies of the Cuban government, assuming that all relevant facts were available to you (of course, they are not available to the wretched of the earth, and for obvious reasons)? How would you weigh Cuban efforts to maintain public health, education and availability of basic necessities for the poor versus the limitations imposed on civil liberties? Consider that these efforts continued long after Cuba had stopped being "subsidized" by the Soviet Union[22] – and while it suffers from a very severe embargo as well as from numerous acts of sabotage caused by the single superpower, which forces them to divert resources to defense, counter-spying etc. Although Chomsky would certainly not use socio-economic rights to justify the abandonment of civil liberties, the contrast between the unequal emphases put on the two sorts of rights shows that the issue of "relativism" is not quite as simple as it is portrayed in the dominant Western discourse.

A critical attitude with respect to the dominant discourse of human rights often provokes indignant hysteria among Western intellectuals. The only plausible explanation is that these intellectuals feel threatened – not because of any use of power against them, but because they are being shown to be self-righteous hypocrites in the willing service of power, not genuine seekers of truth. They enjoy the privilege of free expression, and do not exercise it. Their form of hypocrisy, regrettably, only paves the way towards more atrocities and killings in US client states, where critical intellectuals really are threatened. The following comments, taken from the Jesuit Salvadorian journal *Processo*, illustrate this clearly:

If Lech Walesa had been doing his organizing work in El Salvador, he would have already entered into the ranks of the disappeared – at the hand of "heavily armed men dressed in civilian clothes"; or have been blown to pieces in a dynamite attack on his union headquarters. If Alexander Dubcek were a politician in our country, he would have been assassinated like Héctor Oquelí [the social democratic leader assassinated in Guatemala, by Salvadorian death squads, according to the Guatemalan government]. If Andrei Sakharov had worked here in favour of human rights, he would have met the same fate as Herbert Anaya [one of the many murdered leaders of the independent Salvadorian Human Rights Commission CDHES]. If Ota-Sik or Václav Havel had been carrying out their intellectual work in El Salvador, they would have woken up one sinister morning, lying on the patio of a university campus with their heads destroyed by the bullets of an elite army battalion. (Chomsky 1991: 354–5)

To summarize, the aspirations embodied in the Universal Declaration could be a powerful tool to challenge the powers that be. However, thanks to a very selective reading of the declaration and to a careful choice of targets of indignation, mainstream Western intellectuals have managed to make this declaration almost entirely harmless for Western governments and, in fact, have allowed them to use it cynically for their own purposes.

Hopes and challenges for the future

What is to be done? Unlike many other intellectuals, Chomsky is quite careful when he tries to answer that question. First, consistent with his libertarian ideals, he feels that each individual has to make his own choices. Besides, he is opposed to the attitude, rather widespread among intellectuals, that consists in offering (theoretical) solutions to complicated situations, like the Balkans, in which they are not directly implicated. Finally, since he regards a well-tested science that would give answers to difficult social problems as a "well-kept secret," he is very critical of various ideologies that masquerade as sciences and that claim to give all-encompassing solutions to human problems. For him, progress in the building of a humane society has to be based on experimentation and struggle and there is no point in treating either Marxism, or the free market or even anarchism as a religious dogma.

In politics, Chomsky teaches by means of example, and is often at his best in adverse situations. There is little doubt that, during and after the collapse of the Soviet system, the world has gone through one of the most reactionary periods of its history, similar to the restoration of monarchic order throughout

Europe after Waterloo, but now taking place on a world scale. This generalized "rollback" of the gains of workers in the rich countries as well as of the advances made by developing nations, was made possible, in part, by the discouragement that affected a good part of the left. It is interesting to see how Chomsky reacted to that situation.

First, the following excerpt, where Chomsky quotes excerpts from the work of Bakunin, clearly shows the differences between him and the dominant trends within Marxism:

"The organization and the rule of society by socialist savants," [Bakunin] wrote, "is the worst of all despotic governments." The leaders of the Communist party will proceed "to liberate [the people] in their own way," concentrating "all administrative power in their own strong hands, because the ignorant people are in need of a strong guardianship . . . [the mass of the people will be] under the direct command of the state engineers, who will constitute the new privileged political-scientific class." For the proletariat, the new regime "will, in reality, be nothing but a barracks" under the control of a Red bureaucracy. But surely it is "heresy against common sense and historical experience" to believe that "a group of individuals, even the most intelligent and best-intentioned, would be capable of becoming the mind, the soul, the directing and unifying will of the revolutionary movement and the economic organization of the proletariat of all lands." In fact, the "learned minority, which presumes to express the will of the people," will rule in "a pseudo-representative government" that will "serve to conceal the domination of the masses by a handful of privileged elite."[23]

For Chomsky, the Soviet Union was an example of rapid industrialization of an underdeveloped country, but was very far from anything that one might call "socialism." And so, having had no illusions to lose about the nature of Soviet "socialism," Chomsky does not join the chorus of those who celebrate (or lament) the "failure of socialism." He also notes that some people, who always claimed to be anti-Leninist leftists but felt "discouraged" after 1991, "were more deeply committed to Leninism than they believed" (1996c).

But Chomsky is not discouraged. Among reasons for hope, one should stress that during the second half of the twentieth century, remarkable developments along the path of human liberation have taken place: the liberation of the Third World from the most oppressive forms of Western domination, the women's liberation movement, enormous progress in the struggle against racism, changes in education both in the family and at school, sexual liberation; despite impressions to the contrary, the years between 1945 and 1980 may have been among the most emancipating in human history (1980 being roughly the beginning of the "rollback" period). Moreover, as Chomsky often stresses, the part of the anti-Vietnam War movement that was based on a principled opposition to the war represented a major breakthrough in the intellectual and moral level of the American youth (probably one of the reasons why so much effort is devoted to misrepresenting and slandering that period of history). The current worldwide opposition to corporate controlled "globalization," also waged in large part by the youth, shows an even greater degree of social awareness.[24]

However, if there is a sobering thought that one may have about the progress of civilization, it is that, at the same time as our proclaimed values have become more truly universal, there has been a considerable rise in hypocrisy. A leader who bases his rule mostly on, say, a racist ideology does not need to be too hypocritical. But if a violent power such as the United States constantly invokes Christian charity, international law or human rights, it needs the help of an intellectual class who will distort the facts and spread illusions in order to maintain its rule. It is unfortunate that so many intellectuals are quite willing to play that role; but people like Chomsky also remind us that this choice is not inevitable and that intellectuals can, if they want, play an important role in the construction of a truly humane society. Indeed, the struggle to expose the hypocrisy of the rulers may very well be an important element in the next emancipatory stage of mankind, during which, amidst and against the present horrors of capitalism, a radical post-Marxist left will arise, one that will reclaim the values of the Enlightenment and hopefully make them realize their full potential.

Notes

1. Some thinkers, usually classified as Romantics, can be included on the list because – unlike most other Romantics – they recognize that innate (native) conceptual resources are needed to exercise the kind of freedom and creativity that is characteristic of romanticism. Relevant individuals include Wilhelm von Humboldt, A. W. Schlegel, and Samuel Taylor Coleridge (Chomsky 1966, 2002a).
2. Traditional empiricists were not much concerned with reference, perhaps because they, like the traditional rationalists, were more sensitive to skeptical arguments about mind–world relationships than today's "realist"-inclined group.
3. For Putnam (1975), a linguistic meaning is a vector that includes a word's supposed scientific object as a part of its meaning. For Fodor (1998), who in some respects is a rationalist but in his externalism is not, a word's meaning is solely its (external, he insists) denotational target. As Fodor's presence in the externalist camp suggests, it is unclear how this form of concept/meaning externalism relates to empiricist learning views. Putnam is a learning empiricist (Putnam 1967), but his defense of meaning externalism does not speak explicitly to learning. Kripke and Burge do not commit themselves, although their Wittgensteinian views of language suggest sympathy for the training picture.
4. Columnist Jonathan Kay (2004), writing in Canada's *National Post* magazine *Business*, follows Milton Freedman in arguing that it is fine for corporations to perform socially responsible acts (selling a limited-supply drug at a price below what it could fetch from the well off, for example) that improve their public image and thus accord them more profit in the long run. But their agents (boards of directors) should ensure that their actions are "amoral": they must not see their task as serving the public interest unless appearing to do so increases profit. In influencing public officials to serve corporate needs (profit), then, corporations are only doing what serves their interests, not human interests. It is misleading, of course, to think of corporations – or any institutions – as natural objects, or of their "rights" as natural (cp. Burchill & Chomsky 1998: 19). Corporations are artefacts; they are made to serve the interests of the rich. Their "rights," unlike those of humans, are not natural.

1 CHOMSKY'S SCIENCE OF LANGUAGE

I am grateful to Annabel Cormack and Jim McGilvray for comments on an earlier version of this chapter.

1. Hence, requiring that linguistic rules be accessible to consciousness, for instance (Quine 1972: 442), is unmotivated.
2. Chomsky (2000a). Chomsky's insights into the human condition in the political domain are akin to Dostoevsky's, in the linguistic domain to Darwin's.
3. This locution is used regularly by Chomsky (1995c: 2, 2000a: 1) to refer to what is "in our minds, ultimately in our brains" (1980: 5). He repeatedly dismisses the so-called "mind-body problem" as unformulable in the absence of a coherent notion of body (1988b, 1995a).
4. Note that "generative" is used with systematic ambiguity in the literature. First, it appears as a near synonym of "explicit," on which reading almost all current grammars and theories are "generative"; second, it is used to refer specifically to work in (transformational) generative grammar associated over the years with Chomsky and his followers.
5. Chomsky (e.g. 2000a: 6) often attributes this insight to Wilhelm von Humboldt (1767–1835).
6. For introductory discussion, see Fromkin (1996); for Chomsky's view, see his (1999a).
7. Transformations change one structure into another structure, relating (for instance) statements to questions. They were central to Chomsky's work in the 1950s (see especially 1955, 1957a), and gave their name to the theory. They have been less visible in more recent incarnations of the theory, but remain the locus of research (and disagreement) by Chomsky and those influenced by him.
8. For Merge and Move, see Chomsky (1995c).
9. As determined by Binding Theory (Chomsky 1995c: 92ff).
10. For selection, see Chomsky (1986).
11. See Wiggins (1997) for a contrary view.
12. In fact, perfection in the sense of providing an optimal solution to particular problems is pervasive in biology: e.g. the existence of universal scaling laws (West et al. 2000).
13. For discussion of the differences between Chomsky's and Fodor's notions of modularity, see Smith (2003).
14. This claim is, of course, contested – e.g. Tomasello (2000).
15. The question was formulated as Plato's Problem in Chomsky (1986); Principles and Parameters theory is first set out explicitly in Chomsky (1981a,b).

2 PLATO'S PROBLEM, UG, AND THE LANGUAGE ORGAN

This paper incorporates material from Lightfoot (1999) and from Anderson & Lightfoot (2000), and I remain indebted to the people thanked there. Now I thank Brigitte Bedos-Rezak for discussing an earlier draft from the viewpoint of a non-linguist.

1. This represents a different analysis from the ones given in Lightfoot (1999) and Anderson & Lightfoot (2000). The silent, understood element following the second *is* might be some form of the adjective *happy* or, following the analysis of Chomsky (1977c), the trace of a WH element.
2. The technical notion of "c-command" is relevant here. In (5b), the NP *Jay's brother* c-commands *him*, but the NP that consists of *Jay*, contained within the larger NP, does not c-command *him* and therefore is unavailable for indexing.

3. This reflects the critical period hypothesis, that there is a genetically determined window of opportunity for language acquisition. If a child fails to develop language during this period, for whatever reason, then she will never attain a normal grammar and native-like competence. For good discussion, see Smith (1999: 120ff.).

4. SLI represents a genetically determined condition in which the language capacity is impaired in precise ways, while other mental domains seem to be normal. The problems relate to plurals, tense, gender, and aspect, but not temporal adverbs; the impairment seems to affect specifically those parts of grammar where abstract morphological features are implicated. There is some controversy about whether the cases grouped together under this diagnosis should in fact be taken together, but the distribution of SLI in some well-studied populations has been shown (in both epidemiological and genetic studies [Tomblin 1997] to be that of a simple Mendelian trait (Gopnik 1990; Gopnik & Crago 1991), perhaps even with a specific, identifiable chromosomal location.

3 GRAMMAR, LEVELS, AND BIOLOGY

I would like to acknowledge the very helpful discussion and/or suggestions of Cedric Boeckx, Noam Chomsky, and, especially, Jim McGilvray. Much of this chapter was written while I was a Fellow at the Center for Advanced Study in the Behavioral Sciences. I am grateful for the support provided by the John D. and Catherine T. MacArthur Foundation, grant no. 95-32005-0.

1. Although Chomsky's use of the term "generative" has remained constant throughout his writings, in the field at large the term has sometimes come to be associated with what Chomsky calls the creative aspect of language use – the ability of speakers to produce brand new sentences appropriate to situations, but in no sense directly triggered by them (in the stimulus-response) sense.

2. Chomsky and Halle (1968) argue for a considerably more abstract representation, but that difference need not concern us at the moment.

3. Words that are not subject to the alternation (such as *fife*, with plural *fifes*) simply have the element *f* at the morphophonemic level instead of *F*.

4. To allow for the generation of these examples, we must add to the phrase structure grammar in (13) either the possibility of rewriting NP as N with no determiner (NP → N) or the possibility of a silent Det. The choice between these two possibilities raises interesting questions, but is not relevant to the issue being discussed here.

5. Note that in this model, for a complex sentence there is no one initial P-marker that could provide the basis for semantic interpretation, since each clause has its own separate P-marker. Further, the final derived P-marker also does not provide sufficient basis for semantic interpretation, since quite often items occur displaced from the positions where they are interpreted, as in passive sentences like *Mary was selected*, where *Mary* is the understood (and underlying) object of the verb yet occurs in surface subject position. Thus, the T-marker is crucial to semantic interpretation.

6. Here, as in much work in the first couple of decades of generative syntax, research in phonology had led the way. In phonology, the concept of cyclic application of rules goes back at least to Chomsky et al. (1956).

7. Below, we will see that Chomsky, in developing his recent minimalist program, puts forward an argument rather reminiscent of this one.

8. One of the standard arguments for traces (though not one discussed by Chomsky [1973a]) comes from a contraction process in colloquial English by which *want* and *to* become *wanna* when they are immediately adjacent:

   (i)   a. You want to solve this problem
           b. You wanna solve this problem

   That this process demands adjacency between *want* and *to* is shown by the impossibility of (iib), based on (iia).

   (ii)   a. You want someone to solve this problem
           b. *You wanna someone solve this problem

   The relevant (and surprising) property of *wanna* contraction is that even if *someone* in (ii) is replaced by the corresponding interrogative *who*, which is then displaced by movement, contraction is still blocked:

   (iii)   a. Who do you want to solve this problem?
           b. *Who do you wanna solve this problem?

   Superficially, there does not seem to be anything intervening between *want* and *to* in (iiia), hence, nothing to prevent contraction. But if we assume that movement leaves a trace, then there is, in fact, something intervening – the trace of *Who*.

9. Government and Binding are two important technical terms of the theory. Chomsky came to feel that "Government–Binding theory" was a misleading appellation, since there were many other equally important technical terms in the theory, so that these two should not be singled out. Chomsky's preferred term was "Principles and Parameters theory," a name highlighting the fact that at the center of the framework were linguistic universals (principles) and simple limited ways that languages can differ (parameters).

10. Chomsky felt that the term "deep structure" conveyed the false impression that that level was what was important or profound about language, as opposed to the superficial or trivial surface structure. In reality, the levels played equally important technical roles in the theory, and "surface" properties, e.g. all of phonology, are surely as significant and rich in structure as any others.

11. (45) is a version of the third ("Condition C") of three conditions on anaphora proposed in Chomsky (1981a).

12. Chomsky puts it this way: "there are no levels of linguistic structure apart from the two interface levels PF and LF; specifically no levels of D-Structure or S-Structure" (1995c: 219). The apparent qualification is important, because none of Chomsky's minimalist writings addresses the early arguments for the levels discussed above directly relevant to phonology, such as morphophonemics and phonemics. Those levels evidently remain.

13. "Pied-piping" is the felicitous term introduced by Ross (1967) for situations where an item is compelled to move, but additional material follows along with it.

14. See also Jackendoff (1972), Lasnik (1972, 1976).

15. See Chomsky (1999a, 2000b), the latter of which was actually written earlier.

4 HOW THE BRAIN BEGETS LANGUAGE

I am sincerely grateful to the deaf and hearing parents and their children who gave me and my students and assistants their time, trust, and good humor. I also thank Kevin Dunbar, and my students and research assistants who helped in aspects of the analyses presented in this chapter, including Siobhan Holowka, Ioulia Kovelman, Gissella Santayana, Ulana Harasymowycz, Kristine Gauna and Elizabeth Norton. All research was funded by the following grants to L. A. Petitto: Social Sciences and Humanities Research Council of Canada, Natural Sciences and Engineering Research Council of Canada, the Spencer Foundation, USA, and a Dartmouth College research grant. I also thank the Guggenheim Foundation for a generous fellowship. Address all correspondence to Laura Ann Petitto, Department of Psychological & Brain Sciences and Department of Education, Dartmouth College, Hanover, New Hampshire, 03755, USA. For more information see Petitto Research Web Site: http://www.dartmouth.edu/~lpetitto or Petitto Laboratory Web site: http://www.dartmouth.edu/~lpetitto/lab. Email: Laura-Ann.Petitto@Dartmouth.edu.

1. For videotape examples of Optotrak babies producing linguistic versus non-linguistic hand activity see http://www.dartmouth.edu/~lpetitto and click on "Nature Supplement Petitto et al. 2001" (top upper right).
2. For videotape examples of baby linguistic versus non-linguistic, as well as smiling–mouth asymmetries, see http://www.dartmouth.edu/~lpetitto and click on "Science 2002 supplement."
3. For videotape examples of lexical and phonetic-syllabic hand stimuli in ASL see http://www.dartmouth.edu/~lpetitto and click on "PNAS supplement, Petitto et al. 2000."

5 CHOMSKY AND HALLE'S REVOLUTION IN PHONOLOGY

I would like to thank Morris Halle for discussing some of these issues with me, and Jim McGilvray for his detailed comments on an earlier version of this chapter. All errors of fact or interpretation are mine. I am grateful for the support of grants 410–99–1309 and 410–2003–0913 from the Social Sciences and Humanities Research Council of Canada.

1. For a detailed historical account of the context of twentieth-century phonological theory see Anderson (1985).
2. A rule of the form A → B/C _____ D is to be read, "A becomes B in the context C _____ D." Parentheses indicate optional material. Thus, rule (1) indicates that a vowel becomes [+long] before a glide followed by a voiced consonant or directly before a voiced consonant.
3. More precisely, Flapping may not precede the other two rules. In this case, the correct results would obtain if all three rules applied simultaneously to the underlying form. There are many cases, however, in which simultaneous application does not succeed.
4. I abstract away from details and refinements such as the cycle.
5. After a class of sounds called sibilants the plural has a third pronunciation, [əz], as in *busses, churches, bushes,* and *lounges.*
6. The relatively small number of features is a legacy of the work of Jakobson and Halle in the 1950s, who sought to arrive at the smallest possible number of features

required to distinguish contrastive sounds. For a more recent survey of the phonetic parameters that can be used distinctively in the languages of the world see Ladefoged and Maddieson (1996). Though the range of variation seen across the spectrum of the world's languages may be greater than was known in the 1950s, there still appear to be significant restrictions on how many of the possible contrasts may actually be employed in a single language. See Rice (2002) for a discussion of vowel systems.

7. In one of the earliest works in generative grammar, Chomsky, Halle, and Lukoff (1956) show that an elegant analysis of English stress can be achieved by rules that are sensitive to aspects of the syntax, in sharp contrast to previous treatments in the American structuralist tradition. This work constitutes an early argument against the notion that phonological analyses must be constructed without reference to other aspects of grammar.

8. Hockett (1951) argues that the generalization concerning the distribution of voiceless and voiced consonants can be regained at the morphophonemic level, where word boundaries and other morphological relations come into play. Thus, in his system the underlying morphophonemic representation of (9b) would be / / #patat#ak# / /. A morphophonemic rule of word-medial voicing would derive the (taxonomic) phonemic form / padatak /. The effect of this reshuffling of levels is to turn the taxonomic phonemic level into a surrogate phonetic level, with the morphophonemic level doing much of the work formerly (and subsequently) assigned to the phonemic level. Once a systematic phonetic level is added to the model of grammar, there is no need for another level (the taxonomic phoneme) to play a similar role.

9. Of course, there could have been: we might have found, for example, that *sip* derives from /ssip/ and *zip* derives from /sip/, and that the phonemic difference is between /s/ and /ss/, not /s/ and /z/. The analysis of a phonetic string is thus not possible in isolation, but must take into account other parts of the grammar.

10. Another well-known example is Swadesh and Voegelin's analysis of the morphophonemics of Tübatulabal (Swadesh & Voegelin 1939). This work, done under the influence of Edward Sapir (1884–1939), is a testament to a more liberal period, before the neo-Bloomfieldian framework had considerably narrowed the range of what was an acceptable analysis.

11. This interpretation of the status of morphophonemics was evidently not accepted by Swadesh and Voegelin (1939): "If it has been possible . . . to reduce the apparent irregularity of Tübatulabal phonology to system, this very fact guarantees the truth of our theory."

   The question of what sort of reality was to be attributed even to phonemic analysis did not receive a clear answer in American linguistic thought. Sapir argued unambiguously that phonological analyses were "psychologically real" (Sapir 1933), but this "mentalistic" interpretation was rejected by most American linguists (cf. Twaddell 1935). Psychological realism was replaced by a recurring debate in American structuralist linguistics as to whether an analysis should be thought of as "God's truth" or as "hocus-pocus" (see Joos 1957: 80). Chomsky (1957b) found these discussions to be "quite empty and sterile."

12. See the contribution by Lasnik in this volume for further discussion of this argument and the notion of levels in grammar. The notion has nevertheless persisted within generative phonology that there may be some fundamental difference between rules that deal only in contrastive feature values and rules that deal in redundant values.

One expression of this is the theory of Lexical Phonology and Morphology (Kiparsky 1982a, 1985), which divides the phonology into lexical phonology (roughly, the old morphophonemic rules) and the postlexical phonology (mainly allophonic rules), The dividing line between lexical and postlexical phonology thus occupies a place somewhat like that of the taxonomic phoneme, without, however, having to observe the old constraints on this level. A further difference is that proposals for a lexical–postlexical distinction in the phonological component are supported by empirical evidence, by showing, for example, that the components have different properties.

13. Discovery procedures are not to be confused with the generative quest for *explanatory adequacy*. The latter aims to account for how first language learners arrive at the grammar of their language, given that the available evidence appears to greatly underdetermine the choice of grammar. Chomsky has proposed that learners are endowed with a rich theory of Universal Grammar that guides and limits their acquisition of grammar. A theory of Universal Grammar differs from discovery procedures in that the latter are primarily intended to guide the *linguist*. Generative grammar posits no procedures to guide the linguist in the construction of a theory of Universal Grammar, nor are any conditions placed on how a theory of Universal Grammar can be related to the facts of language. Of course, an important criterion in choosing between different linguistic theories is how well they fare in explaining how language can be acquired.

14. This form of behaviorism is thus quite different from the classical empiricism of Hume and Locke. Though he believed in the priority of sense impressions over innate ideas in the sense of Descartes, Hume saw his task as discovering the principles of the mind, including innate properties such as the imagination.

15. Chomsky (1959) demonstrated this in his famous review of B. F. Skinner's *Verbal Behavior* (Skinner 1957). Chomsky showed that concepts that had concrete meanings in Skinner's (1938) *Behavior of Organisms*, where they were applied to classical but limited problems involving the relationship between stimuli and responses in rats and pigeons, became either trivial or false when applied to human verbal behavior.

16. Morris Halle continued, of course, to be at or near the center of developments in phonological theory for many years. In this essay, however, I focus only on his early work with Chomsky. See Halle (2002) for a collection of representative papers from 1954 to 2002.

17. For recent introductions to contemporary phonology, see Gussenhoven and Jacobs (1998) and Roca and Johnson (1999). For more detailed treatments of phonological theory up to the mid-1990s, see Kenstowicz (1994) and Goldsmith (1995).

18. The debate on abstractness was initiated by Kiparsky (1968). For a sampling of the extensive literature on the abstractness controversy from various points of view, see Dresher (1981a), Gussmann (1980), and Kenstowicz and Kisseberth (1977, ch. 1) on one side, and Hooper (1976), Linell (1979), and Tranel (1981) on the other.

19. In assessing learnability, it is relevant to ask what the learner already knows about the grammar. Kaye (1974) comments that derivations that are opaque in Kiparsky's sense may nevertheless aid a listener (and a learner) in recovering underlying forms, and hence the lexical identity of a morpheme. For example, the short raised diphthong in [rʌjɾər] (*writer*) in the dialects under discussion makes the Raising rule opaque, but signals to a listener who already knows the rule that the flap derives

from a /t/. In a dialect where the rules apply in a different order so that *writer* sounds the same as *rider*, the rules are less opaque, but the identity of the lexical items is more difficult to recover.

20. For further discussion of this case see Dresher (1996).

21. The *SPE* markedness theory was developed further by Kean (1980), but was otherwise not much pursued in the years immediately after *SPE*. Some version of markedness is found in most current approaches to phonology, albeit in different forms. Calabrese (1995) presents a version that is much in the spirit of Kean and *SPE*. The theory of Government Phonology (Kaye, Lowenstamm & Vergnaud 1985) builds markedness into phonological representations. The same is true of Modified Contrastive Specification (Avery & Rice 1989; Dresher, Piggott & Rice 1994).

6 UNIVERSAL ASPECTS OF WORD LEARNING

1. "Worth its salt" loosely translates as "an appropriate dissertation topic in linguistics." In the end, of course, distributional analysis will distinguish even among these, e.g. "The one animal other than an elephant who trumpets is a ——" or "the largest extant land animal is the ——".

2. This stipulation sounds innocent enough for the *dog* case, but is in fact not uncontroversial. For example, in positions related to that first popularized by Benjamin Whorf, the causal chain for word learning is argued to run at least partly in the other direction, the learning of words being the generator or at least molder of the concepts. For discussion pro and con see Gentner and Goldin-Meadow (2003), Papafragou, Massey, and Gleitman (2003), *inter alia*.

3. The availability of *grounding information* is particularly important if "bootstrapping" approaches are not to be circular in the sense whimsically suggested by the very term (one can't lift oneself by one's bootstraps if one is standing in the boots). Thus we must demonstrate that initial learning of the concrete nominal vocabulary need not invoke any syntactic or word-distributional knowledge (Gleitman & Gleitman 1997).

4. We should point out that the systematic relationship between core participant roles in a conceptual/semantic structure and noun phrases in a sentence is not easy to see in every sentence. Mature speakers of most languages systematically leave out noun phrases when their referents are recoverable in the discourse context (e.g. *Hanging too low*). Immature speakers leave out noun phrases even when their referents cannot be recovered, requiring us to look systematically at a large sample of their sentences to uncover what they know about their own verbs (Bloom 1970). Likewise, the sentences of young home signers tend to be short, about two signs long. Across utterances, however, a particular child can be observed to sign all of the participant roles required by the logic of each verb – just not all at once (Feldman et al. 1978; Goldin-Meadow 2003).

7 EMPIRICISM AND RATIONALISM AS RESEARCH STRATEGIES

I would like to thank Harry Bracken and Paul Pietroski for helpful comments on earlier drafts. I would especially like to thank Jim McGilvray for the detailed comments without which this chapter could not have been written.

1. Chomsky has been very active in identifying his precursors. These include many less well known thinkers including the Cambridge Platonists (e.g. Cudworth) and von Humboldt among others. See Chomsky (1966, 2002a) and McGilvray (1999) for discussion.
2. Knowledge is often analyzed as being justified true belief. In what follows I abstract away from the issue of justification and concentrate on how true beliefs can arise.
3. The text should not be taken to suggest that any of this is unproblematic. How abstraction is intended to function, how metrics of similarity are developed and where they come from is one of the problems for an empiricist theory of mind. We briefly return to this issue below in our discussion of Chomsky's views.
4. Similarity is a central empiricist notion. It was continually subjected to critical analysis and revision. This is precisely as it should be as this is what allows empiricist epistemology to get off the ground. Of course, to the degree that the similarity notion fails, empiricism will as well.
5. For a more elaborate discussion of what is only lightly glossed here, see Lightfoot (this volume).
6. For a discussion, of this point, see Hornstein and Lightfoot (1981). For a more recent discussion, see Crain and Pietroski (2001).
7. Modern empiricist learning theories have attacked this problem, but it is questionable whether they have entirely succeeded. The most recent sophisticated empiricist learning theories are cast in a connectionist mold. See Marcus et al. (1999) and commentary by Pinker (1999) for arguments claiming that current connectionist architectures cannot adequately generalize to rules. If this is correct, then the problem noted under (b) is far from trivial for an empiricist learning theory.
8. The modern reader will likely replace God with Darwin and reach for evolutionary accounts to fill in the gap. There is no current reason for thinking that Darwinian approaches will get one much further than Descartes's, at least for interesting domains of knowledge such as linguistic or mathematical knowledge.

8 INNATE IDEAS

1. This is *not* the trivial claim that "humans can acquire the languages they can acquire," if only because of the substantive constraints on human languages that linguists have discovered. Empirical inquiry suggests that the human faculty for language has a distinctive character that is responsible for many features of human languages. But the mental state of "knowing Japanese" is not innate, any more than having a well-exercised heart is innate. What is innate, according to Chomsky, is the mental system that makes it possible for any learner to acquire any human language – the language faculty. Occasionally, innate resources may be damaged, through trauma or (independently specifiable) pathology. In this regard, the language faculty is no different than the liver.
2. The process of going through puberty is governed largely by innate mechanisms; though even here, as Chomsky notes, environmental conditions matter. Adolescents who are underfed won't go through puberty, at least not in the normal way.
3. See Lasnik and McGilvray, both in this volume; see also Fodor (1998) and his reevaluation of Fodor (1975).
4. Empiricism is, nonetheless, alive and well. See Pullum (1996), Bates and Elman (1996), Elman et al. (1996), Cowie (1999). For a recent Chomskyan reply, see Crain

and Pietroski (2001). It is often suggested that a proper understanding of induction will reveal language acquisition as a special case of induction. But not only is this a mere promissory note, until someone explains how induction works, Goodman (1983) provides a compelling argument that induction is itself a form of human knowledge acquisition to which poverty-of-simulus considerations apply. Oddly, this is not the conclusion Goodman drew from his argument; though it is certainly the conclusion that Chomsky drew. And Chomsky has argued, on empirical grounds, that the underdetermination of linguistic knowledge by experience is not a special case of the underdetermination of inductive knowledge by experience. See Chomsky (1969a, 1986); cf. Quine (1960).

5. We suspect that this is why Chomsky tends to emphasize his connection with Descartes, rather than Kant. For while much of Chomsky's nativism is surely in keeping with Kantian themes, Kant himself tends to view (i) and (ii) as cons- trained – at least at some levels of description – by claims about how thinkers must be related to the world they inhabit in order to have any knowledge at all.

6. Moreover, showing someone a cow does not guarantee that he'll see it *as* a cow. And a rationalist might hold that while experience with cows can trigger (what comes to be) a person's cow-concept, such experience does not (in any interesting sense) shape the resulting concept. But the rationalist's claim is especially plausible with regard to ideas of things we *can't* experience.

7. If a very limited experiential base suffices for "averaging" and discerning similarities "across" cases, the core empiricist notions cease to have any interesting meaning. Cf. Chomsky's (1959) criticisms of extending behaviorist notions like "stimulus" and "response" from paradigms of operant conditioning to descriptions of verbal behavior.

8. While it is unlikely that many subjects would be as quick as Meno, Plato illus- trates how quickly one can come to know a very abstract proposition; and this suggests that such knowledge can be acquired with very little experience, given the right alternative "prompting" from a clever questioner. And if repeated expe- rience is not the only possible trigger for the knowledge, this reinforces the ratio- nalist claim: typical cases of knowledge acquisition, which involve a little more experience but less Socratic dialog, involve leaps beyond anything the senses provide.

9. A figure with area 2 is just a special case, though an especially interesting one. For had the dialog continued a bit, Meno could have been led to the idea of an irrational number (by thinking about the sides of a square with area 2). And what, in experience, provides the basis for that idea? At the risk of belaboring ancient mathematics, we also note that knowledge of infinite domains is presumably not acquired by experience; yet following Euclid, one can quickly show that there are infinitely many primes. (If some number N were the largest prime, then N would be the largest prime factor of N! + 1; but since N! + 1 is not evenly divisible by any integer less than or equal to N, N isn't a factor of N! + 1). The broader point is that just as an adequate human epistemology must do justice to our knowledge of mathematics, so it must do justice to our knowledge of language.

10. But it would be a mistake to deny Plato's conclusion on the grounds that he didn't provide a plausible account of how we come to have the cognitive resources that make mathematical knowledge possible. Similarly, it would have been a mistake to deny that humans have livers until someone explained how we come to have livers.

One can have excellent evidence that a species has certain traits independently of experience without yet knowing how they come to have those traits.

11. Whether such propositions are necessarily *true* is a complex matter, given non-Euclidean geometries (and the character of the physical universe). But in any case, even before seeing the proof, one knows that the Pythagorean Proposition is somehow *necessarily* correct if correct at all. And this fact about human thinkers is independent of any particular claim about what it is for a proposition to *be* necessarily correct.

12. As a candle burns it seems to vanish. We know, by investigation, that the matter does not cease to exist; it simply changes form. But its form changes enough that our unaided senses can no longer track the matter we perceived as a candle.

13. Hume – arguably, the greatest empiricist to date – wrestled with this question (and the corresponding questions about our ideas of necessity). And at least on one reading of Hume, endorsed by Chomsky, he grants the rationalist's psychological point: we do indeed have ideas that take us beyond experience; but for just that reason, we should be skeptics (in the ancient sense of neither affirming nor denying) with regard to many judgments involving those ideas. But again, the question here is not what could justify judgments involving Cartesian ideas. We think Chomsky's (2000a) views on semantics – and in particular, the irrelevance and futility of associating linguistic expressions with mind-independent referents – are usefully viewed in this light; see McGilvray (1998, 1999, 2002a), Pietroski (2002, 2003) for discussion.

14. He has also speculated on the issue of moral knowledge. See, for example, Chomsky (1988b); see Dwyer (1999) for an attempt to develop the neo-Cartesian speculations in more detail. These examples preserve analogs of the felt necessity that attaches to mathematical propositions. But it is an open question whether all knowledge that stems from "the hand of nature" is associated with felt necessity.

15. One can make the point without appealing to English *words*. Let R be a set-theoretic relation such that s1 bears R to s2 if and only if the set of things *not* in s1 is a subset of the set of things *not* in s2. Any determiner Δ that labeled R would be a counterexample to (12). For Δ *cows are brown* would be true if and only if the set of things that aren't cows is a subset of the set of things that aren't brown; and Δ *cows are brown cows* would be true if and only if the set of things that aren't cows is a subset of the set of things that aren't brown cows. So the following claim would be false:

if [(Δ cows)(are brown cows)], then [(Δ cows)(are brown)].

For this would say that if [the set of things that aren't cows is a subset of the set of things that aren't brown cows], then [the set of things which aren't cows is a subset of the set of things that aren't brown]; i.e. if everything that isn't a cow isn't a brown cow, then everything that isn't a cow isn't brown. But this is wrong. Trivially, everything that isn't a cow isn't a brown cow; but it hardly follows that everything that isn't a cow isn't brown. There are many other non-conservative set-theoretic relations. This raises the question of why we evidently can't use determiners to name relations like R, which (from a theoretical perspective) seems simpler than many relations named by complex determiners like *more than seventeen but fewer than twenty-six*.

16. As this discussion makes clear, arguments for innateness exhibit a multi-pronged structure. Initially, linguists consider an array of phenomena and propose some analysis (in terms of linguistic categories and rules) as a partial explanation of

the phenomena. Such analysis is followed by cross-linguistic research, in search of potential universals – candidates for inclusion in Universal Grammar. Given a potential linguistic universal, call it U, one can ask whether children could have inferred that their language respects U on the basis of data available to them. If *every* child acquires a grammar that respects U, but it is very implausible that every child encountered (and noticed) expressions that would have let them infer that their local grammar respects U, this strongly suggests that U is a reflection of (innate) Universal Grammar. If three-year-olds manifest knowledge of the very linguistic principles that characterize adult grammars, that compresses the learning problem considerably. This same strategy of providing converging (nondemonstrative) arguments for innateness is followed in other domains, using similar criteria: early emergence, throughout the species, of traits that seem to be (dramatically) underdetermined by experience. See Crain and Pietroski (2001) for further discussion.

17. Disjunction also seems to be "exclusive," at least with regard to pragmatic implicature, in cases like *Some cow ate broccoli or asparagus*. While the sentence might be literally true if the only cow that ate broccoli or asparagus ate both, this is not the natural expectation. Chierchia (2000) argues a (scalar) implicature of "exclusivity" is computed when disjunction appears in a non-downward entailing linguistic context (such as in the second argument of *every*, and in both arguments of *some*), but not in downward entailing linguistic environments (such as the first argument of *every*, or in either argument of *no*). See, Chierchia et al. (2001), for a semantic account of such implicature.

9 MIND, LANGUAGE, AND THE LIMITS OF INQUIRY

1. The standard papers here are Putnam (1975) and Burge (1979), plus Kripke's classic (1972).
2. Fodor himself recognizes this Fregean problem and has wrestled very interestingly with it over almost two decades and in many works right from the time he first formulated his naturalism about reference. See the next note for a crucial philosophical point about Fodor's views. Chomsky uses the term "perspective" sometimes to simply raise the Fregean problem just raised by this first argument for denotational views of meaning. But he also goes on then to give a systematic, internalist sprucing up of the idea of "perspectives" which finds its place at an interface where use of language picks up from. This sanitized notion of perspectives, however, is therefore not intended to *determine* reference as traditional Fregean notions of sense are supposed to. In fact reference becomes irrelevant to the sanitized notion of perspectives since it drops out of scientific linguistic study altogether for Chomsky. Again, see the next note.
3. The second argument and its conclusion would also undercut any effort to solve the problem created by the first argument, by appealing not to conceptions of things, but to purely syntactically or computationally described items, i.e. it would undercut any effort to solve the problem by appealing to anything which, unlike conceptions of things, would not amount to a kind of content. And it is because conceptions of things undeniably amount to a kind of content, that Fodor, in his keenness to say that there is no content but denotational content, has often in his efforts to deal with the Frege puzzles made just such an appeal to purely syntactically and computationally described items. See for instance his (1987, 1998). Those are items which may account for a misinformed thinker's rationality, but do so by means

not available to the thinker, not self-known to him. Chomsky finds a place for his notion of "perspectives" in what he describes broadly as "syntax," but in doing so he, unlike Fodor, gives up on the idea that perspectives (senses) are ways of feeding into reference, or solving anything like the problem created by the first argument. Since he has no desire to make a naturalistic study of language bear on notions of reference or intentional content, he can afford to do this, i.e. he can afford to ignore the self-knowledge constraint imposed by the second argument, which Fodor, because of precisely those aspirations, cannot. If Fodor were to reject the self-knowledge constraint on which the second argument above depends, it's not clear, as the second argument points out, that he could fulfil the aspirations of being continuous with an ineliminable intentional psychology. It may be that because he has seen this point that Fodor himself in his most recent work on concepts seems to have taken to stressing not so much that there will be syntactical and computational solutions to Fregean problems and puzzles raised for denotational semantics and the naturalist intentional psychology it is supposed to yield, but rather stressing some sort of Leibnizian metaphysical conspiracy which ensures that Frege puzzles do not arise too often in our world, so they do not really pose a threat to such a conception of semantics and intentional psychology.

4. Kripke explicitly claims that senses will not solve Frege puzzles for just this reason. See his (1976).

5. We use the word "internal" here in a way that contrasts with external items such as planets and cities. It is not intended to rule out the publicness or the abstractness of internal objects such as senses which Frege insists on and which is what makes them objects of thought in just the sense that Chomsky is attacking. To make them abstract objects is to make them fall afoul of the insight Chomsky invokes Reid and du Marsais for, the insight provided in the self-knowledge constraint that the second argument imposes.

6. See notes 2 and 3 for how the notion of perspectives sheds its traditional Fregean association of sense (as determining reference) to an internalistically sanitized broadly syntactic notion that has nothing directly to do with reference.

7. The argument that follows is stated most fully in Chomsky (2000a: ch. 4).

8. Except that it exaggerates the distinction between philosophy and science, by projecting the distinction between academic disciplines in universities after Kant into the past, when there was not such a great distinction – but only the sort of natural philosophy which was, then, both philosophy and science.

10 MEANING AND CREATIVITY

I am grateful to Noam Chomsky, Paul Pietroski, and Robert Stainton for reading and commenting on this chapter.

1. Some authors (e.g. Steven Pinker) have assumed that its usefulness must be the product of Darwinian natural selection for communication – "history" of another sort. Chomsky does not agree; see this volume's introduction and Hauser, Chomsky & Fitch (2002).

2. This explains why people who acquire a language late in life often have difficulty sounding like a native speaker. There does not seem to be a parallel difficulty with concepts, although the case is not closed: perhaps different languages exploit different "semantic fields," allowing for different ways to "cut up" conceptual space. For some

data, see Stephen Ullmann's work – following Trier's – on a "field" view of concepts (Ullmann 1957: 152f). The notion of a semantic field is sometimes attributed to Humboldt. It appears in several forms, e.g. Foucault's conception of a *grille* – for him, attributable to social power relations. It is possible to imagine several ways in which the nativist could accommodate it – parameterization, among others – should there be empirical evidence that that is needed.

3. Landau and Gleitman (1985) show that blind children acquire color and sight vocabulary as easily as sighted. Blind children do not, of course, experience *visual* REDS.

4. They also require a different "theory of meaning" than Chomsky's, which deals only with natural languages.

5. By "root" concept I have in mind one that would – in English – constitute the core in common to (say) *trivial, trivially, triviality, untrivial, trivialize*. Adult speakers of English can be counted on to have acquired over 50,000 root concepts.
   An account of *linguistic* concept acquisition need not explain acquisition of concepts in other faculties, nor explain how what might be called "cooperative" concepts are produced. Our commonsense understanding of the world clearly depends on more than language. For instance, BUCKET draws shape and color features from vision – facts that Marr emphasized when he pointed out that humans with damaged language centers retain a robust capacity to visually recognize buckets, although they cannot say what they are for. Language contributes (perhaps) CONTAINER, ARTIFACT, and USED TO MOVE MASSES OF NON-RIGID MATERIALS – the function of buckets, but not the abstract "shapes" Marr and others hold vision contributes.

6. The basic points of "aitiational semantics" were Moravcsik's (1975).

7. Linguists have for decades focused on the broad architectural aspects of the language faculty – on the structures of phrases, for example. Recently distributed morphologists (Halle & Marantz 1993, 1994; Marantz 1997; Harley & Noyer 1999) have absorbed lexical categories such as N and V into syntax.

8. His recent work (2000b, 2001a) makes the point even more obvious, although it changes the conception of derivation adopted in 1995c.

9. This is an informal suggestion; it is neither minimal nor "optimal" in Chomsky's sense (1995c: 235). It does, though, meet two obvious constraints: that it pair "sound" (phonological) features with "meaning" ones (those that appear at SEM), and that it indicate (crudely) what will appear at SEM and the phonetic interface (PHON).

10. It can help to think of specific SEMs as events – as occasions where the language faculty yields a "perspective" that is employed by other systems in the head to "configure" experience. To conceive of them as events, think of them and their contribution to cognition "adverbially" – as ways to experience, conceive, imagine, suggest, state etc.

11. Both may be the usual case, Chomsky suggests (1995c: 236). If so, ±CONCRETE would be a principle of UG for all nouns and only exceptions would need marking in a lexical specification.

12. Putting it this way makes it clear why I-languages are so-called: they are Individually, Internally, Intensionally (Chomsky 1986) and – we might as well now add – Innately and Intrinsically specified languages.

13. It is not clear how to think of cooperation. For this chapter, think of it as joint constitution of concepts.

14. These are insights emphasized by A. W. Schlegel and particularly Humboldt (Chomsky 1996a,b, 2002a).
15. Chomsky notes (1966: n. 9) that it is possible that Descartes was familiar with the work of Juan Huarte, who in his *Examen de Ingenios* in 1575 mentioned three levels of creativity. He tied the (distinctively) human variety to having something like a generative system or systems in the mind that is (are) detached from circumstance.

11 MARKET VALUES AND LIBERTARIAN SOCIALIST VALUES

1. Schlesinger doubted Alsop's predictions of victory, but added, "We all pray that Mr Alsop will be right" (*The Bitter Heritage*, cited in Chomsky (1971a: 240). In other words, Schlesinger's opposition to the Vietnam War was based on his estimation of its prospects for success, not his judgment of its moral or legal character. Chomsky observed that the views of Schlesinger and Alsop "bound a substantial range of American opinion," and that therefore it was of great importance to recognize that "each presents what can fairly be described as an apologia for American imperialism" (letter, *Listener*, January 15, 1970, p. 88). Schlesinger responded to these charges (January 29), and Chomsky had the last word (19 February).
2. Chomsky, of course, recognizes that our moral judgments "are obviously heavily conditioned by various doctrinal systems with social and historical roots, and by perceived choices and available interpretations that are socially and historically conditioned" (1988a: 468).
3. Chomsky's (1988a: 111) summary of Leibniz's view.
4. Confusion between these quite separate commitments is a fundamental flaw of, for example, Wilkins (1997).
5. Adam Smith, from *The Theory of Moral Sentiments*. Cited in Viner (1991: 90f).
6. Cited in Dwyer (1998:65).
7. For a puzzled contemplation of Smith's bitter critique, see Oakley (1994: 105).
8. Policy Planning Study (PPS) 23 of February 1948, cited in Chomsky (1987b: 15f).
9. Smith (1990: 204); Malthus cited in Chomsky (1994: 186).
10. Tape, "At the Rowe Center," Rowe, MA, 15–16 April 1989, tape 4, side A.

12 THE INDIVIDUAL, THE STATE, AND THE CORPORATION

1. Chomsky notes (1995b: 354) that the anarchist Bakunin coined this phrase.
2. The Miringoffs (1999: 40) created an index of sixteen measurable social health factors, such as teenage suicides, unemployment, and wealth inequality, demonstrating that America's "social health" generally tracked the Gross National Product until the early 1970s. Since then, the GNP has continued to grow while overall social health has significantly deteriorated.
3. An example from the UK is the Welsh development agency's providing funding on the order of a hundred million pounds to Korea's LG Semicon for the purpose of building a semiconductor plant in Cardiff. The plant was abandoned after being built and it is not clear what happened to the funds granted.
4. Chomsky explains: "It's not the case, as the naïve might think, that indoctrination is inconsistent with democracy. Rather, as this whole line of thinkers [Reinhold Neibuhr, Walter Lippman] observes, it's the essence of democracy" (quoted in Achbar 1994: 43).

5. Aside from lax enforcement, tax havens permit the wealthy to preserve their disproportionate power (Strange 1998: 131–7).
6. Chomsky discovered the phrase "de facto world government" in an article by James Morgan in the *Financial Times, Weekend FT*, April 25/26, 1992.

13 NOAM CHOMSKY: THE STRUGGLE CONTINUES

1. Draft of lecture entitled, "Control of Our Lives," delivered in Albuquerque, New Mexico, Feb. 26, 2000.
2. See Chomsky (1996d, 1999b) for discussion of the peace of the "victors"; Znet, Fall 2000 for Chomsky's analysis of the Al Aqsa Intifadah.

14 THE RESPONSIBILITY OF THE INTELLECTUAL

I thank Edgard André, Xavier Bekaert, Jim McGilvray, and specially Diana Johnstone for helpful comments on an earlier draft of this chapter.
1. *Business Week*, April 17, 2000. Patrick Smith (former correspondent of the *International Herald Tribune* in Asia).
2. In the words of the "respected Roosevelt-Kennedy liberal Edward Bernays in his classic manual for the Public Relations industry, of which he was one of the founders and leading figures". Quoted in Chomsky (1999e); also available as "Market Democracy in a Neoliberal Order: Doctrines and Reality" (Davie Lecture, University of Cape Town, May 1997) in *Z Magazine*, Sept. 1997: http://www.zmag.org/chomsky/articles.cfm.
3. Many topics that I will not cover here are analyzed in Chomsky's works from this viewpoint, including Central America, Israel, the "war on drugs," terrorism, South Africa, the Cold War and the arms race, etc.
4. It is interesting to note that Chomsky expressed his views on such topics long before the word "postmodernism" was invented. In 1966, in one of his first political essays, he contrasted his view of truth with Martin Heidegger's who wrote in 1933 that "truth is the revelation of that which makes a people certain, clear and strong in its action and knowledge". He also contrasted Heidegger's view with the "more forthright" view of Arthur Schlesinger who, after having explained that he had lied about the Bay of Pigs invasion, complimented the *New York Times* for having suppressed information on that invasion "in the national interest" (1987a: 60). For other discussions of postmodernism by Chomsky, see his debate with Michel Foucault (1974a), the papers in http://www.zmag.org/ScienceWars/sciencechomreply.htm, and the exchange in Raskin & Bernstein (1987: 104–56).
5. Special issue on Science/Rationality from *Z Magazine*, available at: http://www.zmag.org/ScienceWars/sciencechomreply.htm
6. This is the first of a series of comparisons to be made in this chapter, between two similar situations, whose goal is to awaken the reader to the strangeness of some proposition or of some attitudes that are often implicitly taken for granted within the dominant discourse; this rhetorical device is frequently used by Chomsky.
7. This radical shift in methodology is a significant sign of an ideological and apologetic attitude.

8. Some of which will be discussed below. Concerning the functioning of the media, see *inter alia* Chomsky & Herman (1988) and Chomsky (1989). For the actions of the West during the post Cold War period, see Chomsky (1999e).

9. The expression comes from the following statement of the Secretary of State of President Truman, Dean Acheson, made at the beginning of the Cold War: "Like apples in a barrel infected by one rotten one, the corruption of Greece would infect Iran and all to the east. It would also carry infection to Africa through Asia Minor and Egypt, and to Europe through Italy and France, already threatened by the strongest domestic Communist parties in Western Europe." Quoted in Chomsky (1987a: 211). For a more detailed analysis of recent history developing the "rotten apple" theme, see (1987b).

10. See e.g. the comments by George Kennan, quoted in Milan Rai (this volume).

11. Starting with Chomsky (1969c). The expression "new mandarins" was borrowed by Chomsky from Ithiel Pool, a political scientist at MIT who used it to refer to himself and his colleagues.

12. See also Chomsky (1987a: 243) for criticism of Hannah Arendt's views on the Vietnam War being due to "neither power nor profit," but rather to irrational factors, such as "image making."

13. A similar remark can be made about all the criticisms of the form: "the U.S. policy with respect to, say, Iraq or Cuba is a failure because it does not lead to the establishment of democracy, of a lasting peace, etc." That kind of criticism is easy and therefore appealing to many but, by taking at face value the proclaimed goals of the rulers, it only strengthens the illusion that those goals are the real ones. If one considers what are presumably the real goals, e.g. preventing the rot to spread, controlling the oil reserves, etc., these policies are actually quite successful.

14. See Chomsky (1996a,b: 64), in particular, for criticism of the position taken by the American journal *Dissent*.

15. Chomsky (1987a: 144–5); on another occasion, Chomsky quoted Bertrand Russell's remarks on the Russian Revolution: "every failure of industry, every tyrannous regulation brought about by the desperate situation, is used by the Entente as a justification of its policy. If a man is deprived of food and drink, he will grow weak, lose his reason, and finally die. This is not usually considered a good reason for inflicting death by starvation. But where nations are concerned, the weakness and struggles are regarded as morally culpable and are held to justify further punishment . . . Is it surprising that professions of humanitarian feeling on the part of the English people are somewhat coldly received in Soviet Russia?" (Chomsky 1971b); the quote is from (Russell 1920). Similar remarks could be made about Iran or North Korea today.

16. See Chomsky (1987a: 326) for examples of remarkable cruelty: the United States tried to prevent India from sending one hundred buffalo to Vietnam and American Mennonites from sending pencils to Cambodia.

17. See e.g. "Chomsky on Cuba," answer to a question, posted on http://www.zmag.org/chomsky/index.cfm.

18. For a more extended discussion, see Chomsky (1988a: 204–8).

19. For a detailed refutation of those and similar charges: Herman (1993).

20. The following story illustrates the permanence of certain methods of psychological pressure against pacifists and anti-interventionists. When in 1916 Bertrand Russell

managed to send an appeal to United States President Woodrow Wilson urging him to work in favor of a negotiated peace in Europe, he received from his long-time friend and collaborator Alfred North Whitehead (who, unlike Russell, supported the war) a newspaper report about German misdeeds against the French and Belgians, which Whitehead blamed on the "damping down among neutrals – America in particular – of the first protests against earlier atrocities." Adding, "what are *you* going to do to help these people"; see Monk (1997: 487).

21. For more details and references to original sources concerning this section, see Chomsky (1998). Available from: http://www.zmag.org/chomsky/articles.cfm.

22. This notion of subsidy is itself an interesting ideological construct, since it assumes that the form of trade (including maybe the international debt and its trapping mechanisms) between the rich countries and the poor ones are somehow "just," while the price stability and the guaranteed purchases offered by the Soviet Union to Cuba were a form of "subsidy."

23. From "Intellectuals and the State" (1977), reprinted in Chomsky (1982).

24. Since here motivations such as fear of the draft do not play any role.

References

Achbar, Mark (1994). *Manufacturing Consent: Noam Chomsky and the Media.* Montreal: Black Rose.

Anderson, Stephen R. (1985). *Phonology in the Twentieth Century: Theories of Rules and Theories of Representations.* Chicago: University of Chicago Press.

Anderson, S. R. & D. W. Lightfoot (2000). "The Human Language Faculty as an Organ." *Annual Review of Physiology* 62.

Aristotle (1984). *Nicomachean Ethics.* Princeton: Princeton University Press.

—— (1990). *The Politics of Aristotle.* Trans. Jowett. New York: Colonial Press.

Avery, Peter & Keren Rice (1989). "Segment Structure and Coronal Underspecification." *Phonology* 6: 179–200.

Baker, M. (2001). *The Atoms of Language.* New York: Basic Books.

Baker, S. A., W. J. Isardi, R. M. Golinkoff & L. A. Petitto (in press). "The Discovery of Phonetic Forms." *Memory & Cognition.*

Baker, S. A., J. Sootsman, R. M. Golinkoff & L. A. Petitto (2003). "Hearing Four-month-olds' Perception of Handshapes in American Sign Language: No Experience Required." *Published Abstracts for the Society for Research in Child Development 2003 Biennial Meeting*, Tampa, FL.

Barsky, Robert (1997). *Noam Chomsky: A Life of Dissent.* Cambridge, MA: MIT Press.

Barwise, J. & R. Cooper (1981). "Generalized Quantifiers and Natural Language." *Linguistics and Philosophy* 4: 159–219.

Bates, E. & J. Elman (1996). "Learning Rediscovered." *Science* 274: 1849–50.

Bellugi, U., S. Marks, A. Bihrle & H. Sabo (1993). "Dissociation Between Language and Cognitive Functions in Williams Syndrome." In D. Bishop & K. Mogford, eds. *Language Development In Exceptional Circumstances.* Hillsdale, NJ: Lawrence Erlbaum Associates.

Bickerton, D. (1999). "How to Acquire Language without Positive Evidence: What Acquisitionists Can Learn from Creoles." In DeGraff (1999).

Bishop, D. V. M. (1997). *Uncommon Understanding: Development and Disorders of Language Comprehension in Children.* London: Psychology Press.

Bloch, Bernard (1941). "Phonemic Overlapping." *American Speech* 16: 278–84. Reprinted in Joos (1957), 93–6. Also in Makkai (1972), 66–70.

Bloom, L. (1970). *Language Development: Form and Function in Emerging Grammars.* Cambridge, MA: MIT Press.

Bloom, P. (2000). *How Children Learn the Meanings of Words.* Cambridge, MA: MIT Press.

Borer, H. (1984). *Parametric Syntax.* Dordrecht: Foris.

313

Bowerman, M. (1987). "The 'No Negative Evidence' Problem: How Do Children Avoid Constructing an Overly General Grammar." In J. Hawkins, ed. *Explaining Language Universals*. Oxford: Blackwell. 73–101.

Brent, M. R. (1994). "Surface Cues and Robust Inference as a Basis for the Early Acquisition of Subcategorization Frames." In L. R. Gleitman & B. Landau, eds. *The Acquisition of the Lexicon*. Cambridge, MA: MIT Press. 433–70.

Bresnan, Joan W. (1971). "Sentence Stress and Syntactic Transformations." *Language* 47: 257–81.

Burchill, Scott & Noam Chomsky (1998). "Human Nature, Freedom, and Political Community: An Interview with Noam Chomsky." *Citizenship Studies* 2 (1): 5–21.

Burge, Tyler (1979). "Individualism and the Mental." In P. French, T. Uehling & H. Wettstein, eds. *Midwest Studies in Philosophy 6*. Minneapolis: University of Minnesota Press.

Calabrese, Andrea (1995). "A Constraint-based Theory of Phonological Markedness and Simplification Procedures." *Linguistic Inquiry* 26: 373–463.

Callanan, M. A. (1985). "How Parents Label Objects for Young Children: The Role of Input in the Acquisition of Category Hierarchies." *Child Development* 56: 508–23.

Carey, S. (1978). "The Child as Word Learner." In M. Halle, J. Bresnan & G. A. Miller, eds. *Linguistic Theory and Psychological Reality*. Cambridge, MA: MIT Press. 264–93.

Charron, F. & L. A. Petitto (1991). "Les premiers signes acquis par des enfants sourds en Langue des Signes Québécoise (LSQ): Comparaison avec les premiers mots." *Revue Québécoise de Linguistique Théorique et Appliquée*. 10 (1): 71–122.

Chierchia, Gennaro (2000). "Scalar Implicatures and Polarity Items." Paper presented at WELS 31, Georgetown University, Washington DC.
  (2001). "Scalar Implicatures, Polarity Phenomena, and the Syntax/Pragmatics Interface." Ms, University of Milan, Bicocca.

Chierchia, Gennaro, Stephen Crain, Maria Teresa Guasti & Rosalind Thornton (1998). "'Some' and 'Or': A Study on the Emergence of Logical Form." In A. Greenhill, M. Hughes, H. Littlefield & H. Walsh, eds. *Proceedings of the Boston University Conference on Language Development* 11: 97–108. Sommerville, MA: Cascadilla Press.

Chierchia, G., S. Crain, M. T. Guasti, A. Gualmini & L. Meroni (2001). "The Acquisition of Disjunction: Evidence for a Grammatical View of Scalar Implicatures." *Proceedings of the 25th Annual Boston University conference on child language development*. Somerville, MA: Cascadilla Press.

Chierchia, G. & S. McConnell-Ginet (2000). *Meaning and Grammar*, 2nd edition. Cambridge, MA: MIT Press.

Choi, S. & Bowerman, M. (1991). "Learning to Express Motion Events in English and Korean: The Influence of Language-specific Lexicalization Patterns." *Cognition* 41: 83–121.

Chomsky, N. (1951). *Morphophonemics of Modern Hebrew*. Masters thesis, University of Pennsylvania, Philadelphia. [Published 1979 New York: Garland Press.]
  (1955). *The Logical Structure of Linguistic Theory*. Ms. Harvard University, Cambridge, MA and MIT, Cambridge, MA. [Published in part by New York: Plenum, 1975; Chicago: University of Chicago Press, 1985.]

(1957a). *Syntactic Structures*. The Hague: Mouton.

(1957b). Review of R. Jakobson and M. Halle, *Fundamentals of Language*, *International Journal of American Linguistics* 23: 234–41.

(1959). "A Review of B. F. Skinner, *Verbal Behavior.*" *Language* 35: 26–58. Reprinted in Fodor & Katz (1964), 547–78, and, with added preface, in Jakobovitz & Miron, eds. *Readings in the Psychology of Language*. Englewood Cliffs, NJ: Prentice-Hall. 142–72.

(1964). *Current Issues in Linguistic Theory*. The Hague: Mouton. Also in Fodor & Katz (1964), 50–118.

(1965). *Aspects of the Theory of Syntax*. Cambridge, MA: MIT Press.

(1966). *Cartesian Linguistics*. New York: Harper and Row. [2nd edition: 2002a].

(1969a). "Quine's Empirical Assumptions." In D. Davidson & J. Hintikka, eds. *Words and Objections: Essays on the Work of W. V. Quine*. Dordrecht: Reidel.

(1969b). *At War With Asia*. New York: Pantheon.

(1969c). *American Power and the New Mandarins*. Harmondsworth: Penguin.

(1970). "Deep Structure, Surface Structure, and Semantic Interpretation." In Roman Jakobson & Shigeo Kawamoto, eds. *Studies in General and Oriental Linguistics Presented to Shirô Hattori on the Occasion of his Sixtieth Birthday*. Tokyo: TEC Company, Ltd. 52–91.

(1971a). *American Power and the New Mandarins*. London: Penguin/Pelican.

(1971b). *Problems of Knowledge and Freedom. The Russell Lectures*. New York: Pantheon.

(1971c). "Foreword." *Prevent the Crime of Silence* (reports from the sessions of the International War Crimes Tribunal). Bertrand Russell Peace Foundation, Ltd. Available at: http://www.911review.org/Wget/www.homeusers.prestel.co.uk/littleton/vltribun.htm

(1972a). *Language and Mind*. New York: Harcourt, Brace, Jovanovitch (expanded version of 1968 edition).

(1972b). "The Pentagon Papers as Propaganda and as History." In Noam Chomsky & Howard Zinn, eds. *The Pentagon Papers: The Senator Gravel Edition*, vol. V: *Critical Essays*. Boston: Beacon Press.

(1973a). "Conditions on Transformations." In Stephen Anderson & Paul Kiparsky, eds. *A Festschrift for Morris Halle*. New York: Holt, Rinehart and Winston. 232–86.

(1973b). *For Reasons of State*. New York: Pantheon.

(1974a). "Human Nature: Justice versus Power." [A debate with Michel Foucault.] In Fons Elders, ed. *Reflexive Waters*. Toronto: J. M. Dent.

(1974b). *Peace in the Middle East?* New York: Pantheon.

(1975). *Reflections on Language*. New York: Pantheon.

(1977a). *Essays on Form and Interpretation*. New York: North-Holland.

(1977b). *Language and Responsibility: Conversations with Mitsou Ronat*. New York: Pantheon.

(1977c) "On Wh-Movement." In P. Culicover, T. Wasow & A. Akmajian, eds. *Formal Syntax*. New York: Academic Press.

(1980). *Rules and Representations*. Oxford: Blackwell.

(1981a). *Lectures on Government and Binding*. Dordrecht: Foris.

(1981b). "Principles and Parameters in Syntactic Theory." In Hornstein & Lightfoot (1981), 123–46.

(1981c). *Radical Priorities*, ed. Carlos Otero. Montreal: Black Rose.

(1982). *Towards a New Cold War: Essays on the Current Crisis and How We Got There*. New York: Pantheon.

(1983). *The Fateful Triangle: The United States, Israel & the Palestinians*. Boston: South End. [2nd edition: 1999b.]

(1984). *Modular Approaches to the Study of Mind*. San Diego: San Diego State University Press.

(1985). *Turning the Tide*. Boston: South End.

(1986). *Knowledge of Language: Its Nature, Origin, and Use*. New York: Praeger.

(1987a). *The Chomsky Reader*, ed. James Peck. New York: Pantheon.

(1987b). *On Power and Ideology: The Managua Lectures*. Boston: South End.

(1988a). *Language and Politics*, ed. Carlos Otero. Montreal: Black Rose.

(1988b). *Language and Problems of Knowledge*. Cambridge, MA: MIT Press.

(1989). *Necessary Illusions: Thought Control in Democratic Societies*. London: Pluto; Toronto: Anansi.

(1991). *Deterring Democracy*. London and New York: Verso.

(1992a). "A View From Below." *Diplomatic History* 16 (1).

(1992b) *Chronicles of Dissent: Interviews with David Barsamian*. Stirling: AK Press.

(1993a). "A Minimalist Program for Linguistic Theory." In Kenneth Hale & Samuel J. Keyser, eds. *The View from Building 20: Essays in Linguistics in Honor of Sylvain Bromberger*. Cambridge, MA: MIT Press.

(1993b). *Language and Thought*. Wakefield, RI: Moyer Bell.

(1993c). *The Prosperous Few and the Restless Many*. Berkeley: Odonian.

(1993d). *Year 501: The Conquest Continues*. Boston: South End.

(1994). *World Orders, Old and New*. London: Pluto. [US edition: 1996d.]

(1995a). "Categories and Transformations." In *The Minimalist Program*. Cambridge, MA: MIT Press. 219–394.

(1995b). "Language and Nature." *Mind* 104: 1–61.

(1995c). *The Minimalist Program*. Cambridge, MA: MIT Press.

(1996a). *Perspectives on Power*. Montreal: Black Rose.

(1996b). *Powers and Prospects*. Boston: South End. [US edition of 1996a.]

(1996c). "Anarchism, Marxism and Hope for the Future." *Red & Black Revolution*, no. 2. (Available at http://www.zmag.org/chomsky/index.cfm)

(1996d). *World Orders, Old and New*. New York: Columbia University Press. [US edition of 1994.]

(1997). "Serial Veto." *Index on Censorship* 6.

(1998). "The United States and the 'Challenge of Relativity.'" In Tony Evans, ed. *Human Rights Fifty Years On: A Reappraisal*. New York: St. Martins. (Available at http://www.zmag.org/chomsky/articles.cfm)

(1999a). "Derivation by Phase." In *MIT Occasional Papers in Linguistics* 18. Also in M. Kenstowicz, ed. *Ken Hale: A Life in Language*. Cambridge, MA: MIT Press, 2001.

(1999b). *The Fateful Triangle*. Cambridge, MA: South End. [2nd edition of 1983.]

(1999c). "Language and the Brain". Address at the European Conference on Cognitive Science, October 1999, Siena. [Reprinted in 2002b.]

(1999d). *The New Military Humanism*. Monroe, ME: Common Courage.

(1999e). *Profit Over People: Neoliberalism and Global Order.* New York: Seven Stories.

(1999f). "The Umbrella of U.S. Power: The Universal Declaration of Human Rights and the Contradictions of U.S. Policy." Ms.

(2000a). *New Horizons in the Study of Language and Mind*, ed. Neil Smith. Cambridge: Cambridge University Press.

(2000b). "Minimalist Inquiries: The Framework." In Roger Martin, David Michaels & Juan Uriagereka, eds. *Step by Step: Essays on Minimalist Syntax in Honor of Howard Lasnik.* Cambridge, MA: MIT Press. 89–155.

(2000c). "US Iraq Policy: Motives and Consequences." In A. Arnove, ed. *Iraq Under Siege.* Cambridge, MA: South End.

(2000d). *A New Generation Draws the Line: Kosovo, East Timor and the Standards of the West.* London and New York: Verso.

(2000e). *Rogue States.* Boston: South End.

(2001a). "Beyond Explanatory Adequacy." Ms., Department of Linguistics, MIT. To appear in A. Belletti, ed., *Structures and Beyond: Current Issues in the Theory of Language* (in prep.).

(2001b). *9–11.* New York: Seven Stories.

(2002a). *Cartesian Linguistics*, ed. with a new introduction by James McGilvray. Christchurch, NZ: Cybereditions. [2nd edition of 1966; includes new translations, index, and bibliography. Available at http://www.cybereditions.com]

(2002b). *On Nature and Language.* Cambridge: Cambridge University Press.

(2003). *Hegemony or Survival.* New York: Metropolitan Books.

Chomsky, N. & David Barsamian (1992). *Chronicles of Dissent: Interviews With David Barsamian.* Monroe, ME: Common Courage.

(1994). *Keeping the Rabble in Line: Interviews With David Barsamian.* Monroe, ME: Common Courage.

(1998). *The Common Good.* Monroe, ME: Common Courage.

(1996). *Class Warfare: Interviews With David Barsamian.* Monroe, ME: Common Courage.

Chomsky, N. & Morris Halle (1968). *The Sound Pattern of English.* New York: Harper & Row.

Chomsky, N., Morris Halle & Fred Lukoff (1956). "On Accent and Juncture in English." In Morris Halle et al., eds. *For Roman Jakobson: Essays on the Occasion of his Sixtieth Birthday.* The Hague: Mouton. 65–80.

Chomsky, N. & Suzy Hansen (2001). Interview in Salon.com: "Noam Chomsky: The Nation's Most Implacable Critic of U.S. Foreign Policy Argues that the War is Unjust, America is the Biggest Terrorist State and Intellectuals Always Support Official Violence." Jan 16. (http://monkeyfist.com/ChomskyArchive/interviews/salon.html).

Chomsky, N. & Edward S. Herman (1979a). *The Washington Connection and Third World Fascism*, vol. 1 of *The Political Economy of Human Rights.* Boston: South End.

(1979b). *After the Cataclysm: Postwar Indochina and the Reconstruction of Imperialist Ideology*, vol. 2 of *The Political Economy of Human Rights.* Boston: South End.

(1988). *Manufacturing Consent: The Political Economy of the Mass Media*. New York: Pantheon.

Clahsen, H., S. Bartke & S. Gollner (1997). "Formal Features in Impaired Grammars: A Comparison of English and German SLI Children." *Essex Research Reports in Linguistics* 14: 42–75.

Clark, E. V. (1990). "Speaker Perspective in Language Acquisition." *Linguistics* 28: 1201–20.

Cole, P. & G. Hermon (1981). "Subjecthood and Islandhood: Evidence from Quechua." *Linguistic Inquiry* 12:1–30.

Cormack, A. & N. V. Smith (2000). "Fronting: The Syntax and Pragmatics of 'Focus' and 'Topic.'" *UCL Working Papers in Linguistics* 12.

Cowie, F. (1999). *What's Within: Nativism Reconsidered*. New York: Oxford.

Crain, S. (1991). "Language Acquisition in the Absence of Experience." *Behavioral and Brain Sciences* 14: 597–612.

Crain, Stephen & Paul Pietroski (2001). "Nature, Nurture, and Universal Grammar." *Linguistics and Philosophy* 24: 139–86.

Crain, S. & R. Thornton (1998). *Investigations in Universal Grammar: A Guide to Experiments on the Acquisition of Syntax and Semantics*. Cambridge, MA: MIT Press.

Croft, W. (1990). *Typology and Universals*. Cambridge: Cambridge University Press.

Cudworth, Ralph (1995 [1737 (1688)]). *A Treatise Concerning Eternal and Immutable Morality*, ed. Hutton. Cambridge: Cambridge University Press.

Curran, J. & J. Seaton (1985). *Power Without Responsibility: The Press and Broadcasting in Britain*, 2nd edition. London: Methuen.

Davidson, Donald (1967). "Truth and Meaning." *Synthèse* 17.

Dawkins, R. (1976). *The Selfish Gene*. Oxford: Oxford University Press.

DeGraff, M. (ed.) (1999). *Language Creation and Change: Creolization, Diachrony and Development*. Cambridge, MA: MIT Press.

Descartes, René (1984). *Discourse*. In Cottingham, Stoothoff & Murdoch, trans. *The Philosophical Writings of Descartes*. Cambridge: Cambridge University Press.

Dobzhansky, T. (1970). *Genetics of the Evolutionary Process*. New York: Columbia University Press.

Dowty, D. (1991). "Thematic Proto-roles and Argument Selection." *Language* 67: 547–619.

Dresher, B. Elan (1981a). "Abstractness and Explanation in Phonology." In Hornstein & Lightfoot (1981), 76–115.

(1981b). "On the Learnability of Abstract Phonology." In C. L. Baker & John J. McCarthy, eds. *The Logical Problem of Language Acquisition*. Cambridge, MA: MIT Press. 188–210.

(1985). *Old English and the Theory of Phonology*. New York: Garland.

(1996). "Learnability and Phonological Theory." In Jacques Durand & Bernard Laks, eds. *Current Trends in Phonology: Models and Methods* 1: 245–66. Manchester: European Studies Research Institute; University of Salford Publications.

Dresher, B. Elan, Glyne L. Piggott & Keren Rice (1994). "Contrast in Phonology: Overview." *Toronto Working Papers in Linguistics* 13 (1): iii–xvii.

Dretske, Fred (1981). *Knowledge and the Flow of Information*. Cambridge, MA: MIT Press.

Dwyer, John (1998). *An Age of the Passions: An Interpretation of Adam Smith and Scottish Enlightenment Culture*. East Linton: Tuckwell Press.

Dwyer, Susan (1999). "Moral Competence." In K. Murasagi & R. Stainton, eds. *Philosophy and Linguistics*. Boulder, CO: Westview.

Edwards, S. & R. Bastiaanse (1998). "Diversity in the Lexical and Syntactic Abilities of Fluent Aphasic Speakers." *Aphasiology* 12 (2): 99–117.

Elman, J. L., E. Bates, M. H. Johnson, A. Karmiloff-Smith, D. Parisi & K. Plunkett (1996). *Rethinking Innateness: A Connectionist Perspective on Development*. Cambridge, MA: MIT Press.

Epstein, Samuel D. (1999). "Un-principled Syntax: The Derivation of Syntactic Relations." In Samuel D. Epstein & Norbert Hornstein, eds. *Working Minimalism*. Cambridge, MA: MIT Press. 317–45.

Feldman, H., S. Goldin-Meadow & L. R. Gleitman (1978). "Beyond Herodotus: The Creation of Language by Linguistically Deprived Deaf Children." In A. Lock, ed. *Action, Symbol, and Gesture: The Emergence of Language*. New York: Academic Press. 351–414.

Fernald, A. (2003). "How 2-year-olds Look as They Listen: The Search for the Object Begins at the Verb." Paper presented at the Biennial meeting of the Society for Research on Child Development, Tampa, FL.

Fillmore, C. J. (1968). "The Case for Case." In E. Bach & R. T. Harms, eds. *Universals in Linguistic Theory*. New York: Holt, Rinehart and Winston. 1–88.

Fisher, C. (1996). "Structural Limits on Verb Mapping: The Role of Analogy in Children's Interpretations of Sentences." *Cognitive Psychology* 31: 41–81.

(2000a). "From Form to Meaning: A Role for Structural Analogy in the Acquisition of Language." In H. W. Reese, ed. *Advances in Child Development and Behavior* 27: 1–53. New York: Academic.

(2000b). "Who's Blicking Whom? Word Order Influences Toddlers' Interpretations of Novel Verbs." Paper presented at the Biennial International Conference on Infant Studies, Brighton, England.

(2002). "Structural Limits on Verb Mapping: The Role of Abstract Structure in 2.5-year-olds' Interpretations of Novel Verbs." *Developmental Science* 5: 56–65.

Fisher, C. & L. R. Gleitman (2002). "Language Acquisition." In H. F. Pashler (series ed.) and C. R. Gallistel (volume ed.) *Stevens' Handbook of Experimental Psychology*, vol. 3: *Learning and Motivation*. New York: Wiley. 445–96.

Fisher, C., L. R. Gleitman & H. Gleitman (1991). "On the Semantic Content of Subcategorization Frames." *Cognitive Psychology* 23: 331–92.

Fisher, C. & J. Snedeker (2002). "Counting the Nouns: Simple Sentence-structure Cues Guide Verb Learning in 21-month-olds." Paper presented at the Boston University Conference on Language Development, Boston, MA.

Fodor, J. A. (1975). *Psychosemantics*. Cambridge, MA: MIT Press.

(1983). *The Modularity of Mind*. Cambridge, MA: MIT Press.

(1987). *Psychosemantics: The Problem of Meaning in the Philosophy of Mind*. Cambridge, MA: MIT Press.

(1990). "Substitution Arguments and the Individuation of Belief." In Fodor, *A Theory of Content and Other Essays*. Cambridge, MA: MIT Press.

(1998). *Concepts*. Cambridge, MA: MIT Press.

(2000). *The Mind Doesn't Work That Way: Scope and Limits of Computational Psychology*. Cambridge, MA: MIT Press.

Fodor, J. A. & J. J. Katz (eds.) (1964). *The Structure of Language*. Englewood Cliffs, NJ: Prentice-Hall.

Frege, Gottlob (1892). "Über Sinn und Bedeutung." *Zeitschrift für Philosophie und Philosophische Kritik* 100.

Freundlich, Fred (2000). *The Mondragon Cooperative Corporation (MCC): An Introduction*. Ownership Associates Resource Library (http://www.ownershipassociates.com).

Friedmann, N. & Y. Grodzinsky (1997). "Tense and Agreement Agrammatic Production: Pruning the Syntactic Tree." *Brain and Language* 56: 397–425.

Frith, U. (1991). *Autism and Asperger Syndrome*. Cambridge: Cambridge University Press.

Fromkin, V. (1973). *Speech Errors as Linguistic Evidence*. The Hague: Mouton.

(1996). "Some Thoughts About the Brain/Mind/Language Interface." *Lingua* 100: 3–27.

Froud, K. (2000). "Prepositions and the Lexical/Functional Divide: Aphasic Evidence." *Lingua*.

Garnsey, S. M., N. J. Pearlmutter, E. Myers & M. A. Lotocky (1997). "The Contributions of Verb Bias and Plausibility to the Comprehension of Temporarily Ambiguous Sentences." *Journal of Memory & Language* 37: 58–93.

Gentner, D. (1982). "Why Nouns Are Learned Before Verbs: Linguistic Relativity Versus Natural Partitioning." In K. Bean, ed. *Language, Thought, & Culture*. Hillsdale, NJ: Erlbaum. 301–34.

Gentner, D. & L. Boroditsky (2001). "Individuation, Relativity and Early Word Learning." In M. Bowerman & S. Levinson, eds. *Language Acquisition and Conceptual Development*. New York: Cambridge University Press. 215–56.

Gentner, D. & S. Goldin-Meadow (2003). *Language in Mind*. Cambridge, MA: MIT Press.

Gillette, J., H. Gleitman, L. R. Gleitman & A. Lederer (1999). "Human Simulations of Vocabulary Learning." *Cognition* 73: 135–76.

Gleitman, L. R. (1990). "The Structural Sources of Verb Meanings." *Language Acquisition* 1: 3–55.

Gleitman, L. & H. Gleitman (1997). "What Is a Language Made Out Of?" *Lingua* 100: 29–55.

Gleitman, L. R., H. Gleitman, B. Landau, & E. Wanner (1988). "Where Learning Begins: Initial Representations for Language Learning." In F. J. Newmeyer, ed. *Linguistics: The Cambridge Survey*, vol. III: *Language: Psychological and Biological Aspects*. New York: Cambridge University Press. 150–93.

Gleitman, L. R., H. Gleitman, C. Miller & R. Ostrin (1996). "Similar, and Similar Concepts." *Cognition* 58: 321–76.

Goldberg, A. E. (1995). *Constructions: A Construction Grammar Approach to Argument Structure*. Chicago: Chicago University Press.

Goldin-Meadow, S. (2003). *The Resilience of Language*. New York: Psychology Press.

Goldsmith, John A. (ed.) (1995). *The Handbook of Phonological Theory*. Oxford: Black-well.

Goodman, J. C., L. McDonough & N. B. Brown (1998). "The Role of Semantic Context and Memory in the Acquisition of Novel Nouns." *Child Development* 69: 1330–44.

Goodman, Nelson (1983). *Fact, Fiction, and Forecast*, 4th edition. Cambridge, MA: Harvard University Press.

Gopnik, M. (1990) "Feature Blindness: A Case Study." *Language Acquisition* 1 (2): 139–64.

(1997) "Language Deficits and Genetic Factors." *Trends in Cognitive Sciences* 1: 5–9.

Gopnik, M. & M. Crago (1991). "Familial Aggregation of a Developmental Language Disorder." *Cognition* 39: 1–50.

Gordon, P. & J. Chafetz (1990). "Verb-based versus Class-based Accounts of Actionality Effects in Children's Comprehension of Passives." *Cognition* 36: 227–54.

Gould, S. J. & R. Lewontin (1979). *Proceedings of the Royal Society of London* 205: 581–98.

Grimshaw, J. (1990). *Argument Structure*. Cambridge, MA: MIT Press.

Gussenhoven, Carlos & Haike Jacobs (1998). *Understanding Phonology*. London: Arnold.

Gussmann, Edmund (1980). *Studies in Abstract Phonology*. Cambridge, MA: MIT Press.

Haider, Ejaz (2001). "Why Are We Flocking to Hear Chomsky?" *The Friday Times*. Nov. 25 (http://www.thefridaytimes.com).

Haley, Michael C. and Ronald Lunsford (1994). *Noam Chomsky*. New York: Twayne Publishers.

Halle, Morris (1959). *The Sound Pattern of Russian: A Linguistic and Acoustical Inves-tigation*. [Revised version of 1955 Harvard University Ph.D. dissertation.] The Hague: Mouton, 2nd printing, 1971.

(2002). *From Memory to Speech and Back: Papers on Phonetics and Phonology 1954–2002*. Berlin: Mouton de Gruyter.

Halle, Morris & Alec Marantz (1993). "Distributed Morphology and the Pieces of Inflec-tion." In K. Hale & S. J. Keyser, eds. *The View from Building 20*. Cambridge, MA: MIT Press.

(1994). "Some Key Features of Distributed Morphology." MITWPL 21: *Papers on Phonology and Morphology*. Cambridge, MA: MITWPL.

Harley, Heidi & Rolf Noyer (1999). "Distributed Morphology." *Glot International* 4 (4): 3–9.

Harris, Zellig (1951). *Methods in Structural Linguistics*. Chicago: University of Chicago Press.

Hauser, M. D., N. Chomsky, & W. T. Fitch (2002). "The Faculty of Language: What Is It, Who Has It, and How Did It Evolve?" *Science* 298: 1569–79.

Herman, Edward S. (1993). "Pol Pot, Faurisson, and the Process of Derogation." In *Noam Chomsky: Critical Assessments*, ed. Carlos Otero. London: Routledge.

Hirsh-Pasek, K. & R. M. Golinkoff (1996). *The Origins of Grammar: Evidence From Early Language Comprehension*. Cambridge, MA: MIT Press.

Hockett, Charles F. (1951). Review of *Phonology as Functional Phonetics* by A. Martinet, *Language* 27: 333–42. Reprinted in Makkai (1972), 310–17.

Holowka, S. & L. A. Petitto (2002). "Left Hemisphere Cerebral Specialization for Babies While Babbling." *Science* 297: 1515.

Holowka, S., F. Brosseau-Lapré & L. A. Petitto (2002). "Semantic and Conceptual Knowledge Underlying Bilingual Babies' First Signs and Words." *Language Learning* 52 (2): 205–62.

Hooper [Bybee], Joan (1976). *An Introduction to Natural Generative Phonology*. New York: Academic Press.

Hornstein, N. & David Lightfoot (eds.) (1981). *Explanation in Linguistics: The Logical Problem of Language Acquisition*. London and New York: Longman.

Huang, C.-T. James (1981/82). "Move *wh* in a language without *wh*-movement." *The Linguistic Review* 1: 369–416.

(1982). "Logical Relations in Chinese and the Theory of Grammar." Doctoral dissertation, MIT, Cambridge, MA.

Hubel, D. (1978) "Vision and the Brain." *Bulletin of the American Academy of Arts and Sciences* 31 (7): 28.

Hubel, D. & T. Wiesel (1962). "Receptive Fields, Binocular Interaction and Functional Architecture in the Cat's Visual Cortex." *Journal of Physiology* 160: 106–54.

Humboldt, Wilhelm von (1993). *The Limits of State Action*. Indianapolis: University of Indiana Press.

(1999). *On Language: On the Diversity of Human Language Construction and its Influence on the Mental Development of the Human Species*, ed. Michael Losonsky, tr. Peter Heath. New York: Cambridge University Press.

Hume, D. (1978 (1739)). *A Treatise on Human Nature*. Oxford: Clarendon.

Ingham, R. (1998). "Tense Without Agreement in Early Clause Structure." *Language Acquisition* 7: 51–81.

Jackendoff, R. (1969). *Some Rules of Semantic Interpretation for English*. Doctoral dissertation, MIT, Cambridge, MA.

(1972). *Semantic Interpretation in Generative Grammar*. Cambridge, MA: MIT Press.

(1983). *Semantics and Cognition*. Cambridge, MA: MIT Press.

Jakobson, Roman & Morris Halle (1956). *Fundamentals of Language*. The Hague: Mouton.

Jakobson, Roman, C. Gunnar, M. Fant & M. Halle (1952). *Preliminaries to Speech Analysis*. MIT Acoustics Laboratory Technical Report No. 13. Reissued by MIT Press, Cambridge, MA. 11th printing, 1976.

Jenkins, L. (2000). *Biolinguistics: Exploring the Biology of Language*. Cambridge: Cambridge University Press.

Jerne, N. K. (1967). "Antibodies and Learning: Selection Versus Instruction." In G. C. Quarton, T. Melnechuk & F. O. Schmitt, eds. *The Neurosciences: A Study Program*. New York: Rockefeller University Press.

(1985). "The Generative Grammar of the Immune System" [Nobel lecture]. *Science* 229: 1057–9.

Joanisse, M. & M. Seidenberg (1998). "Specific Language Impairment: A Deficit in Grammar or Processing?" *Trends in Cognitive Sciences* 2: 240–7.

Joos, Martin (ed.) (1957). *Readings in Linguistics I*. Chicago: University of Chicago Press. [2nd edition New York: American Council of Learned Societies, 1958.]

Joshi, A. & B. Srinivas (1994). "Disambiguation of Super Parts-of-speech (or Supertags): Almost Parsing." *Proceedings of the 15th International Conference on Computational Linguistics (COLING '94)*. Kyoto, Japan. 154–60.

Jusczyk, P. W. (1999). "Narrowing the Distance to Language: One Step at a Time." *Journal of Communication Disorders* 32 (4): 207–22.

Kako, E. & L. R. Gleitman (in prep). "Information Sources for the Learning of Nouns."

Katz, Jerrold J. & Paul Postal (1964). *An Integrated Theory of Linguistic Descriptions.* Cambridge, MA: MIT Press.

Kay, Jonathan (2004). "Ethical Dilemmas." *Business* (March 2004). Magazine published by Canada's *National Post*.

Kaye, Jonathan D. (1974). "Opacity and Recoverability in Phonology." *Canadian Journal of Linguistics* 19: 134–49.

Kaye, Jonathan D., Jean Lowenstamm & Jean-Roger Vergnaud (1985). "The Internal Structure of Phonological Elements: A Theory of Charm and Government." *Phonology Yearbook* 2: 305–28.

Kean, Mary-Louise (1980). *The Theory of Markedness in Generative Grammar.* Ph.D. dissertation, MIT (1975). [Published Bloomington: Indiana University Linguistics Club.]

Keenan, E. L. (1976). "Towards a Universal Definition of Subject." In C. N. Li, ed. *Subject and Topic.* New York: Academic Press. 303–33.

Kenstowicz, Michael (1994). *Phonology in Generative Grammar.* Oxford: Blackwell.

Kenstowicz, Michael & Charles Kisseberth (1977). *Topics in Phonological Theory.* New York: Academic Press.

Kiparsky, Paul (1968). "How Abstract is Phonology?" Bloomington: Indiana University Linguistics Club. Reprinted in Kiparsky (1982b), 119–64.

(1973). "Abstractness, Opacity, and Global Rules." Bloomington: Indiana University Linguistics Club. Also in O. Fujimura, ed. *Three Dimensions of Linguistic Theory.* Tokyo: TEC. 57–86.

(1982a). "From Cyclic Phonology to Lexical Phonology." In Harry van der Hulst and Norval Smith, eds. *The Structure of Phonological Representations (Part I).* 131–76. Dordrecht: Foris.

(1982b). *Explanation in Phonology.* Dordrecht: Foris.

(1985). "Some Consequences of Lexical Phonology." *Phonology Yearbook* 2: 85–138.

Kosslyn, S. M., M. S. Gazzaniga, A. M. Galaburda & C. Rabin (1999). "Hemispheric Specialization." In M. J. Zigmond, F. E. Bloom, S. C. Landis, J. L. Roberts & L. R. Squire, eds. *Fundamental Neuroscience.* San Diego: Academic Press.

Kovelman, I. & L. A. Petitto (2002). "Bilingual Babies' Maturational and Linguistic Milestones as a Function of Their Age of First Exposure to Two Languages." *Published Abstracts of the 32nd Annual Meeting of the Society for Neuroscience.* Orlando, FL.

(2003). "Bilingual Exposure at Different Ages in Childhood: Do They Exhibit 'Stage-like' Language Acquisition Similar to Young Monolinguals?" *Published Abstracts of the International Symposium on Bilingualism.* Tempe, AZ.

Kripke, Saul (1972). "Naming and Necessity." In D. Davidson and G. Harman, eds. *Semantics for Natural Language.* Dordrecht: D. Reidel.

(1976). "A Puzzle About Belief." In Avishai Margalit, ed. *Meaning and Use.* Dordrecht: D. Reidel.

Ladefoged, Peter & Ian Maddieson (1996). *The Sounds of the World's Languages.* Oxford: Blackwell.

LaFeber, Walter (1967). *The New Empire.* Ithaca: Cornell University Press.

Landau, B. & L. R. Gleitman (1985). *Language and Experience: Evidence From the Blind Child*. Cambridge, MA: Harvard University Press.

Larson, Richard & Gabriel Segal (1995). *Knowledge of Meaning: An Introduction to Semantic Theory*. Cambridge, MA: MIT Press.

Lasnik, Howard (1972). "Analyses of Negation in English." Doctoral dissertation, MIT, Cambridge, MA.

(1976). "Remarks on Coreference." *Linguistic Analysis* 2: 1–22. [Reprinted in Lasnik, *Essays on Anaphora*. Dordrecht: Kluwer, 1989. 90–109.]

Lederer, A., H. Gleitman & L. R. Gleitman (1995). "Verbs of a Feather Flock Together: Semantic Information in the Structure of Maternal Speech." In M. Tomasello & W. E. Merriman, eds. *Beyond Names for Things: Young Children's Acquisition of Verbs*. Hillsdale, NJ: Lawrence Erlbaum. 277–97.

Lee, J. & L. R. Naigles (2002). "Syntactic Bootstrapping with Missing Arguments: Mandarin Chinese." Paper presented at the IXth International Congress for the Acquisition of Language, Madison, WI.

Lefebvre, C. (1998). *Creole Genesis and the Acquisition of Grammar*. Cambridge: Cambridge University Press.

Lely, H. K. J. van der (1996). "Specifically Language Impaired and Normally Developing Children: Verbal Passive *vs.* Adjectival Passive Sentence Interpretation." *Lingua* 98: 243–72.

Levy, Y. & G. Kavé (1999). "Language Breakdown and Linguistic Theory: A Tutorial Overview." *Lingua* 107: 95–143.

Lewis, Anthony (1987). "Freedom of the Press – Anthony Lewis Distinguishes Between Britain and America." *London Review of Books*, Nov. 26.

Lewontin, R. (1990). "The Evolution of Cognition." In D. N. Osherson and E. E. Smith, eds. *An Invitation to Cognitive Science*, vol. 3, *Thinking*. Cambridge, MA: MIT Press. 229–46.

Li, P. (1994). "Subcategorization as a Predictor of Verb Meaning: Cross-language Study in Mandarin." Unpublished manuscript, University of Pennsylvania.

Liberman, A. M. & I. G. Mattingly (1989). "A Specialization for Speech Perception." *Science* 243: 489–94.

Lidz, J., H. Gleitman & L. R. Gleitman (2003). "Understanding How Input Matters: Verb Learning and the Footprint of Universal Grammar." *Cognition* 87: 151–78.

Lieberman, P. (2000). *Human Language and Our Reptilian Brain: The Subcortical Bases of Speech, Syntax, and Thought*. Cambridge, MA: Harvard University Press.

Lightfoot, D. W. (1999). *The Development of Language: Acquisition, Change and Evolution*. Oxford: Blackwell.

Linell, Per (1979). *Psychological Reality in Phonology: A Theoretical Study*. Cambridge: Cambridge University Press.

Locke, J. (1690). *An Essay Concerning Human Understanding*, ed. A. D. Woozley. Cleveland: Meridian Books, 1964.

Locke, J. L. (2000). "Movement Patterns in Spoken Language." *Science* 288: 449–51.

Ludlow, Peter (2002) "LF and Natural Logic: The Syntax of Directional Entailing Environments." In G. Preyer and G. Peter, eds. *Logical Form and Language*. Oxford: Oxford University Press.

Macedo, Donaldo (ed.) (2000). *Chomsky on MisEducation*. New York: Rowman and Littlefield.

MacNeilage, P. F. & B. Davis (2000). "On the Origin of Internal Structure of Word Forms." *Science* 288: 527–31.

Madison, James (n.d.). *The Federalist Papers*. [Available: federalistpapers.com]

Makkai, Valerie Becker (ed.) (1972). *Phonological Theory: Evolution and Current Practice*. New York: Holt, Rinehart and Winston.

Manzini, M. R. & K. Wexler (1987). "Parameters, Binding Theory and Learnability." *Linguistic Inquiry* 18: 413–44.

Marantz, Alec (1997). "No Escape from Syntax: Don't Try Morphological Analysis in the Privacy of Your Own Lexicon." *Penn Working Papers in Linguistics* 4:2. Philadelphia: University of Pennsylvania.

Marcus, G. F., S. Vijayan, S. Bandi & P. M. Vishton (1999). "Rule Learning by Seven-month-old Infants." *Science* 283: 77–80.

Marlett, Stephen A. (1981). "The Abstract Consonant in Seri." In *Proceedings of the Berkeley Linguistics Society 7*. Berkeley: University of California at Berkeley. 154–65.

Marlett, Stephen A., & Joseph P. Stemberger (1983). "Empty Consonants in Seri." *Linguistic Inquiry* 14: 617–39.

May, Robert (1977). "The Grammar of Quantification." Doctoral dissertation, MIT, Cambridge, MA.

McCawley, James D. (1968). "The Role of Semantics in Grammar." In Emmon Bach & Robert T. Harms, eds. *Universals in Linguistic Theory*. New York: Holt, Rinehart and Winston. 124–69.

McGilvray, James (1998). "Meanings are Syntactically Individuated and Found in the Head." *Mind and Language* 13 (2): 225–80.

(1999). *Chomsky*. Cambridge: Polity.

(2002a). "MOPs: the Science of Concepts." In W. Hinzen and H. Rott, eds. *Belief and Meaning, Essays at the Interface*. Frankfurt am Main: Hansel-Hohenhausen.

(2002b). "Introduction for Cybereditions." In Chomsky, *Cartesian Linguistics*, 2nd edition. Christchurch, NZ: Cybereditions.

McGinn, Colin (1994a). "The Problem of Philosophy. *Philosophical Studies* 76: 133–56.

(1994b). "Reply to Carol Rovane." *Philosophical Studies* 76: 169–74.

Miringoff, Marc & Marque-Luisa Miringoff (1999). *The Social Health of the Nation*. New York: Oxford University Press.

Monk, Ray (1997). *Bertrand Russell. The Spirit of Solitude*. London: Vintage.

Monod, J. (1972). *Chance and Necessity*. London: Collins.

Moravcsik, Julius (1975). "Aitia as Generative Factor in Aristotle's Philosophy of Language." *Dialogue* 14: 622–36.

Naigles, L. (1990). "Children Use Syntax to Learn Verb Meanings." *Journal of Child Language* 17: 357–74.

Naigles, L. G. & E. T. Kako (1993). "First Contact in Verb Acquisition: Defining a Role for Syntax." *Child Development* 64: 1665–87.

Naigles, L. R. & P. Terrazas (1998). "Motion-verb Generalizations in English and Spanish: Influences of Language and Syntax." *Psychological Science* 9: 363–9.

Naigles, L., H. Gleitman & L. R. Gleitman (1992). "Children Acquire Word Meaning Components from Syntactic Evidence." In E. Dromi, ed. *Language and Cognition: A Developmental Perspective*. Norwood, NJ: Ablex. 104–44.

Navarro, Vincente (1994). *The Politics of Health Policy: The U.S. Reforms, 1980–1994*. Cambridge, MA: Blackwell.

Newport, E. L. (1990). "Maturational Constraints on Language Learning." *Cognitive Science* 14: 11–28.

(1999). "Reduced Input in the Acquisition of Signed Languages: Contributions to the Study of Creolization." In DeGraff (1999).

Norton, E. S., S. A. Baker & L. A. Petitto (2003). "Bilingual Infants' Perception of Handshapes in American Sign Language." Poster presented at the 6th Annual Summer Undergraduate Workshop, Institute for Research in Cognitive Science, University of Pennsylvania, Philadelphia, PA.

Oakley, Allan (1994). *Classical Economic Man: Human Agency and Methodology in the Political Economy of Adam Smith and J. S. Mill*. Vermont: Edward Elgar.

Outram, Dorinda (1995). *The Enlightenment*. Cambridge: Cambridge University Press.

Papafragou, A., C. Massey, & L. R. Gleitman (2002). "Shake, Rattle, 'n' Roll: The Representation of Motion in Language and Cognition." *Cognition* 84: 189–219.

Penhune, V. B., R. Cismaru, R. Dorsaint-Pierre, L. A. Petitto & R. J. Zatorre (2003). "The Morphometry of Auditory Cortex in the Congenitally Deaf Measured Using MRI." *NeuroImage* 20 (2): 1215–25.

Petitto, L. A. (2000). "On the Biological Foundations of Human Language." In K. Emmorey & H. Lane, eds. *The Signs of Language Revisited: An Anthology in Honor of Ursula Bellugi and Edward Klima*. Mahwah, NJ: Lawrence Erlbaum. 447–71.

Petitto, L. A. & S. Holowka (2002). "Does Early Simultaneous Bilingual Language Exposure Cause Children to be Language Delayed and Confused: Special Insights from Bilingual Babies and Young Children Acquiring a Signed and a Spoken Language." *Sign Language Studies* 3 (1): 4–33.

Petitto, L. A. & I. Kovelman (2003). "The Bilingual Paradox: How Signing-speaking Bilingual Children Help Us Resolve Bilingual Issues and Teach us About the Brain's Mechanisms Underlying All Language Acquisition." *Learning Languages* 8 (3): 5–18.

Petitto, L. A. & P. Marentette (1991). "Babbling in the Manual Mode: Evidence for the Ontogeny of Language." *Science* 251: 1493–6.

Petitto, L. A., R. J. Zatorre, K. Gauna, E. J. Nikelski, D. Dostie & A. C. Evans (2000). "Speech-like Cerebral Activity in Profoundly Deaf People While Processing Signed Languages: Implications for the Neural Basis of all Human Language." *Proceedings of the National Academy of Sciences* 97 (25): 13961–6.

Petitto, L. A., M. Katerelos, B. Levy, K. Gauna, K. Tétreault & V. Ferraro (2001). "Bilingual Signed and Spoken Language Acquisition From Birth: Implications for the Mechanisms Underlying Early Bilingual Language Acquisition." *Journal of Child Language* 28 (2): 1–44.

Petitto, L. A., S. Holowka, L. Sergio & D. Ostry (2002). "Language Rhythms in Babies' Hand Movements." *Nature* 413: 35–6.

Petitto, L. A., I. Kovelman & U. Harasymowycz (2003). "Bilingual Language Development: Does Learning the New Damage the Old?" *Published Abstracts of the Society for Research in Child Development Biennial Meeting*. Tampa, FL.

Petitto, L. A., S. Holowka, L. Sergio, D. Ostry & B. Levy (2004). "Baby Hands that Move to the Rhythm of Language: Hearing Babies Acquiring Sign Languages Babble Silently on the Hands." *Cognition* 93: 43–73.

Piaget, J. & B. Inhelder (1968) *The Psychology of the Child*. London: Routledge.

Piattelli-Palmarini, M. (ed.) (1980). *Language and Learning: The Debate Between Jean Piaget and Noam Chomsky*. London: Routledge and Kegan Paul.

(1986) "The Rise of Selective Theories: A Case Study and Some Lessons from Immunology." In W. Demopoulos & A. Marras, eds. *Language Learning and Concept Acquisition: Foundational Issues*. Norwood, NJ: Ablex.

(1989). "Evolution, Selection and Cognition: From Learning to Parameter Setting in Biology and in the Study of Language." *Cognition* 31: 1–44.

Pietroski, Paul (2002). "Meaning Before Truth." In G. Preyer and G. Peter, eds. *Contextualism in Philosophy*. Oxford: Oxford University Press.

(2003). "The Character of Natural Language Semantics." In A. Barber, ed. *Epistemology of Language*. Oxford: Oxford University Press.

(2005). *Events and Semantic Architecture*. Oxford: Oxford University Press.

Pilger, John (1998). *Hidden Agendas*. London: Vintage.

Pinker, S. (1984). *Language Learnability and Language Development*. Cambridge, MA: Harvard University Press.

(1989). *Learnability and Cognition*. Cambridge, MA: MIT Press.

(1993). "The Central Problem for the Psycholinguist." In G. Harman, ed. *Conceptions of the Human Mind: Papers in Honor of George Miller*. Hillsdale, NJ: Erlbaum.

(1994). *The Language Instinct*. New York: William Morrow.

(1999). "Out of the Minds of Babies." *Science* 283: 40–1.

(2002). *The Blank Slate*. New York: Penguin Putnam.

Pinker, S. & P. Bloom (1990). "Natural Language and Natural Selection." *Behavioral and Brain Sciences* 13 (4): 707–84.

Popper, K. (1963). *Conjectures and Refutations: The Growth of Scientific Knowledge*. London: Routledge and Kegan Paul.

Postal, Paul M. (1968). *Aspects of Phonological Theory*. New York: Harper & Row.

(1972). "The Best Theory." In P. S. Peters, ed. *Goals of Linguistic Theory*. Englewood Cliffs, NJ: Prentice-Hall. 131–70.

Premack, D. & G. Woodruff (1978). "Chimpanzee Problem-solving: A Test for Comprehension." *Science* 202: 532–35.

Premack, D. (1980). "Representational Capacity and Accessibility of Knowledge: The Case of Chimpanzees." In Piattelli-Palmarini (1980).

Premack, D. (1990). "Words: What Are They, and Do Animals Have Them?" *Cognition* 37 (3): 197–212.

Pullum, G. K. (1996). "Learnability, Hyperlearning, and the Poverty of the Stimulus." In J. Johnson, M. L. Juge & J. L. Moxley, eds. *Proceedings of the 22nd Annual Meeting: General Session and Parasession on the Role of Learnability in Grammatical Theory*. Berkeley: Berkeley Linguistics Society. 498–513.

Pustejovsky, James (1995). *The Generative Lexicon*. Cambridge, MA: MIT Press.

Putnam, Hilary (1967). "The Innateness Hypothesis and Explanatory Models in Linguistics." *Synthèse* 17: 12–22. Reprinted in Putnam, *Mind, Language and Reality*. Cambridge: Cambridge University Press, 1975.

(1975). "The Meaning of 'Meaning'." In K. Gunderson, ed. *Language, Mind and Knowledge: Minnesota Studies in the Philosophy of Science, 7*. Minneapolis: University of Minnesota Press.

Quine, W. (1960). *Word and Object*. New York: Wiley.

(1972). "Methodological Reflections on Current Linguistic Theory." In D. Davidson & G. Harman, eds. *Semantics of Natural Language*. Dordrecht: Reidel. 442–54.

Rai, Milan (1995). *Chomsky's Politics*. London: Verso.

Rappaport-Hovav, M. & B. Levin (1988). "What to Do With Theta-roles." In W. Wilkins, ed. *Syntax and Semantics*, vol. 21: *Thematic Relations*. New York: Academic. 7–36.

Raskin, Markus G. & Herbert J. Bernstein (eds.) (1987). *New Ways of Knowing: The Sciences, Society, and Reconstructive Knowledge*. Towota, NJ: Rowman and Littlefield.

Rice, Keren (2002). "Vowel Place Contrasts." In Mengistu Amberber & Peter Collins, eds. *Language Universals and Variation*. Westport, CT, London: Praeger. 239–70.

Rizzolatti, G., V. Gallese, L. Fadiga & L. Fogassi (1996). "Action Recognition in the Premotor Cortex." *Brain* 119: 592–609.

Roca, Iggy & Wyn Johnson (1999). *A Course in Phonology*. Oxford: Blackwell.

Ross, John Robert (1967). "*Constraints on Variables in Syntax*." Doctoral dissertation, MIT, Cambridge, MA. Published as *Infinite Syntax!* Norwood, NJ: Ablex, 1986.

Russell, Bertrand (1920). *The Practice and Theory of Bolshevism*. London: Allen and Unwin.

Sapir, Edward (1933). "La réalité psychologique des phonèmes." *Journal de Psychologie Normale et Pathologique* 30: 247–65. Reprinted as "The Psychological Reality of Phonemes." In D. Mandelbaum, ed. *Selected Writings of Edward Sapir in Language, Culture, and Personality*. Berkeley and Los Angeles: University of California Press (1949), 46–60. Also in Makkai (1972), 22–31.

Seidenberg, M. S. & L. A. Petitto (1979). "Signing Behavior in Apes: A Critical Review." *Cognition* 7: 177–215.

    (1987). "Communication, Symbolic Communication, and Language in Child and Chimpanzee: Comment on Savage-Rumbaugh, McDonald, Sevcik, Hopkins, and Rupert (1986)." *Journal of Experimental Psychology* 116 (3): 279–87.

Sellars, Wilfrid (1974). "Meaning as Functional Classification." *Synthese* 27: 417–37.

Shipley, E. F., I. F. Kuhn & E. C. Madden (1983). "Mothers' Use of Superordinate Category Terms." *Journal of Child Language* 10: 571–88.

Sieratzki, J. & B. Woll (2002). "Toddling into Language: Precocious Language Development in Motor-impaired Children with Spinal Muscular Atrophy." *Lingua* 112 (6): 423–33.

Skinner, B. F. (1938). *Behavior of Organisms*. New York: Appleton-Century-Crofts.

    (1957). *Verbal Behavior*. New York: Appleton-Century-Crofts.

Slobin, D. I. (1982). "Universal and Particular in the Acquisition of Language." In E. Wanner & L. R. Gleitman, eds. *Language Acquisition: The State of the Art*. New York: Cambridge University Press. 128–70.

Slobin, D. I. (2001). "Form-function Relations: How do Children Find Out What They Are?" In M. Bowerman & S. C. Levinson, eds. *Language Acquisition and Conceptual Development*. New York: Cambridge University Press. 406–49.

Smith, Adam (1759). *The Theory of Moral Sentiments*. Available at http://www.adamsmith.org/smith/tms/tms-index.htm

    (1990). *An Inquiry into the Wealth of Nations*. Chicago: Encyclopaedia Britannica.

Smith, N. (1998). "Jackdaws, Sex and Language Acquisition." *Glot International* 3 (7): 7.

    (1999). *Chomsky: Ideas and Ideals*. Cambridge: Cambridge University Press.

    (2000). "Foreword" to Chomsky (2000a). vi–xvi.

(2003) "Dissociation and Modularity: Reflections on Language and Mind." In M. Banich & M. Mack, eds. *Mind, Brain and Language*. Hillsdale, NJ: Lawrence Erlbaum. 87–111.

Smith, N. & I.-M. Tsimpli (1995). *The Mind of a Savant: Language-learning and Modularity*. Oxford: Blackwell.

Snedeker, J. & L. R. Gleitman (in press). "Why It Is Hard to Label Our Concepts." To appear in D. G. Hall & S. R. Waxman, eds. *Weaving a Lexicon*. Cambridge, MA: MIT Press.

Snedeker, J., K. Thorpe & J. Trueswell (2001). "On Choosing the Parse With the Scene: The Role of Visual Context and Verb Bias in Ambiguity Resolution." *Proceedings of the 22nd Annual Conference of the Cognitive Science Society*, Edinburgh, Scotland.

Sperry, R. (1968). "Plasticity of Neural Maturation." *Developmental Biology Supplement* 2: 306–27.

Strange, Susan (1998). *Mad Money: When Markets Outgrow Governments*. Ann Arbor: University of Michigan Press.

Supalla, S. (1990). "Segmentation of Manually Coded English: Problems in the Mapping of English in the Visual/gestural Mode." Ph.D. dissertation, University of Illinois.

Swadesh, Morris & Charles F. Voegelin (1939). "A Problem in Phonological Alternation." *Language* 15: 1–10. Reprinted in Joos (1957), 88–92.

Talbot, Margaret (2001). "The Lives They Lived." *The New York Times*. Final edition, Dec. 30, section 6.

Talmy, L. (1985). "Lexicalization Patterns: Semantic Structure in Lexical Forms." In T. Shopen, ed. *Language Typology and Syntactic Description*. New York: Cambridge University Press. 57–149.

Terrace, H. S., L. A. Petitto, R. J. Sanders & T. G. Bever (1979). "Can an Ape Create a Sentence?" *Science* 206: 891–902.

Tomasello, M. (2000). "Do Young Children Have Adult Syntactic Competence?" *Cognition* 74: 209–253.

Thompson, W. D'Arcy (1917). *On Growth and Form*. Cambridge: Cambridge University Press.

Tomblin, J. B. (1997). "Epidemiology of Specific Language Impairment." In M. Gopnik, ed. *The Inheritance and Innateness of Grammars*. New York: Oxford University Press.

Tranel, Bernard (1981). "Concreteness in Generative Phonology: Evidence from French." Berkeley, CA: University of California Press.

Trueswell, J. C. & A. E. Kim (1998). "How to Prune a Garden Path by Nipping It in the Bud: Fast Priming of Verb Argument Structure." *Journal of Memory & Language* 39: 102–23.

Turing, A. M. (1950). "Computing Machinery and Intelligence." *Mind* 59: 433–560.

(1952). "The Chemical Basis of Morphogenesis." *Philosophical Transactions of the Royal Society of London*. 37–72.

Twaddell, F. (1935). "On Defining the Phoneme." *Language Monograph*, no. 16. Reprinted in Joos (1957), 55–80.

Ullmann, Stephen (1957). *The Principles of Semantics*, 2nd edition. Oxford: Basil Blackwell.

Uriagereka, J. (1998). *Rhyme and Reason: An Introduction to Minimalist Syntax*. Cambridge, MA: MIT Press.

(1999). "Multiple Spell-out." In Samuel David Epstein & Norbert Hornstein, eds. *Working Minimalism*. Cambridge, MA: MIT Press. 251–82.

Viner, Jacob (1991). *Essays on the Intellectual History of Economics*, ed. Douglas Alwrin. Princeton: Princeton University Press.

Waxman, S. R. & D. B. Markow (1995). "Words as Invitations to Form Categories: Evidence From 12- to 13-month-old Infants." *Cognitive Psychology* 29: 257–302.

Wernicke, C. (1874). *Der aphasische Symptomencomplex*. Breslau: Kohn & Weigert.

West, G. B., J. H. Brown & B. J. Enquist (2000). "The Origin of Universal Scaling Laws in Biology". In J. H. Brown & G. B. West, eds. *Scaling in Biology*. Oxford: Oxford University Press. 87–112.

Wiggins, David (1997). "Languages as Social Objects". *Philosophy* 72: 499–524.

Wilkins, Peter (1997). *Noam Chomsky: On Power, Knowledge and Human Nature*. Basingstoke: Macmillan.

Wilson, James G. (1996). "Commentary: Noam Chomsky and Judicial Review." *Cleveland State Law Review* 439.

(2002). *The Imperial Republic: A Structural History of American Constitutionalism From the Colonial Era to the Beginning of the Twentieth Century*. Aldershot, UK: Ashgate Publishing.

Wittgenstein, Ludwig (1963). *Philosophical Investigations,* trans. G. E. M. Anscombe. Oxford: Basil Blackwell.

Woodward, A. L. & E. M. Markman (1998). "Early Word learning." In W. Damon (series ed.); D. Kuhn & R. S. Siegler (vol. eds.) *Handbook of Child Psychology*, vol. 2: *Cognition, Perception, and Language*, 5th edition. New York: Wiley. 371–420.

Zatorre, R. J. & J. R. Binder (2000). "Functional Imaging of the Chemical Senses." In A. Toga & J. C Mazziota, eds. *Brain Mapping: The Systems*. San Diego, CA: Academic Press. 124–50.

Index

.